SLOUCHING TOWARD FARGO

"Neal Karlen proves you don't have to be a baseball fan
to follow the St. Paul Saints. An hilarious treatise
on slouching."
—Michael Feldman, host of *Michael Feldman's Whad'ya Know?*
on NPR: National Public Radio

"A classic . . . *Bull Durham* meets *Meatballs* in this raucous
yet meaningful tale of a minor-league club with major-
league characters . . . an anti-establishment book that captures
the essence of America's true pastime."
—*Kirkus Reviews*

"Pure fun and mischief . . . a splendid read."
—*Toronto Sun*

"Easily the best book in the spring's baseball lineup . . . one
of those rare books that gets away from clichés and turns
the genre of baseball books on its head."
—*Newark Star Ledger*

"This is a grand way to start a new baseball season. You'll find
yourself scanning sports pages in search of a mention of the Sioux
Falls Canaries, the Thunderbay Whiskey Jacks, and the
Fargo-Morehead Red Hawks."
—*Arizona Daily Star*

"When you mix the hilarious stroytelling talents of Neal Karlen
and the antics of a farm team owned by a movie star, led
by a felon, and mascotted by a pig, you can't go wrong. Read
this book, but don't believe anything in chapter 11."
—Eleanor Mondale, CBS News Entertainment Correspondent
and Minnesota's Favorite Daughter

Also by Neal Karlen

TAKE MY LIFE, PLEASE:
THE AUTOBIOGRAPHY OF HENNY YOUNGMAN

BABES IN TOYLAND:
THE MAKING AND SELLING OF A ROCK AND ROLL BAND

SLOUCHING TOWARD FARGO

A Two-Year Saga of Sinners and St. Paul
Saints at the Bottom of the Bush Leagues
with Bill Murray, Darryl Strawberry,
Dakota Sadie and Me

NEAL KARLEN

Perennial

An Imprint of HarperCollinsPublishers

HarperCollins books may be purchased for educational, business, or sales promotional
use. For information please write: Special Markets Department, HarperCollins
Publishers Inc., 10 East 53rd Street, New York, NY 10022.

First Spike paperback edition published 2000.

Reprinted in Perennial 2003.

Designed by Rhea Braunstein

The Library of Congress has catalogued the hardcover edition as follows:

Karlen, Neal.
  Slouching toward Fargo: a two-year saga of sinners and St. Paul Saints at the bottom
of the bush leagues with Bill Murray, Darryl Strawberry, Dakota Sadie, and me / Neal
Karlen.
     p. cm.
   "An Avon book."
   Includes index.
     1. St. Paul Saints (Baseball team). 2. Murray, Bill 1950- . 3. Strawberry, Darryl.
I. Title.
GV875.S73K37 1999   99-11513
796.357'64'09776581—dc21   CIP

ISBN 0-380-79215-X (pbk.)

03 04 05 06 07 FOLIO/RRD 10 9 8 7 6 5 4 3 2

In memory of my late Aunt Helen Kaplan, who when I visited her at age seven in Chicago immediately ordered me to Wrigley Field to see the ivy growing on the outfield walls.

And for Mike Veeck, the hero of this story, who taught me the meaning of second chances and that scar tissue is indeed the most beautiful sight in life—and whose late father planted that ivy in Wrigley Field over two generations ago.

Contents

Cast of Characters

Bill Murray: Alienated movie star reborn as official "czar" and co-owner of the St. Paul Saints.

Darryl Strawberry: Right fielder, St. Paul Saints; most notorious felon in major league history; blackballed from organized baseball.

Mike Veeck: Co-owner and president, St. Paul Saints; black-

Mike Veeck and Midway Stadium
Courtesy of St. Paul Saints

	balled from major leagues since he threw "Disco Demolition Night" for the Chicago White Sox, 1979.
Bill Veeck:	The holy ghost; Mike's late father; former owner of the Cleveland Indians, the Chicago White Sox, and the St. Louis Browns; elected to Hall of Fame, 1991.
Monica Toppen:	The Most Beloved Woman of the Northern League; community relations and press director of the Madison BlackWolf.
Jack the Bastard Morris:	Pitcher, St. Paul Saints; won 253 major league games; pitched one of the best World Series games ever; renowned as "the biggest bastard in baseball"; quit the Cincinnati Reds, 1995.
Ila Borders:	Pitcher, St. Paul Saints; first woman to ever play for men's professional team; "the pitcher with the ponytail."
J. D. Drew:	1996 College Baseball Player of the Year and the best prospect in the land; kept warm during the 1997 and 1998 seasons with the St. Paul Saints as he held out for several million more dollars from the Philadelphia Phillies.
Steve Howe:	Pitcher, Sioux Falls Canaries; tested positive half a dozen times for abusing cocaine and alcohol.
Sister Rosalind Sister Roz Gefre:	Seventy-four-year-old Benedictine nun who provides massages for Saints fans down the third base line; almost released by convent in 1980s for her passion for her healing touch.
Wayne Twig Terwilliger:	Seventy-two-year-old first base coach, St. Paul Saints; and wise man of league; fired by the Minnesota Twins, 1993.

Ed   Singin   Ed
Nottle:

Manager, Sioux City Explorers; nightclub singer and wise man of league; groomed by the Oakland A's and the Boston Red Sox to be a manager, but he was fired when he wouldn't give up his crooning ways.

Don Wardlow:

Radio color announcer, St. Paul Saints; first blind announcer in baseball history, assisted by his play-by-play partner Jim Lucas.

Kenishi Kato:

Rookie pitcher, St. Paul Saints; from Chiba, Japan; a twenty-one-year-old who will lose much face back home if he doesn't make the Saints.

Daryl
Henderson:

Saint pitcher and former Chicago street kid released by the Texas Rangers for his penchant of punching his own teammates.

Dave Wright:

Walter Mitty-like play-by-play radio man for the St. Paul Saints, in 1996; dreams of being next Red Barber.

Gabe s:

Bar near the Saints' Midway Stadium where the groupies hang out; Jill Muellner's pulpit.

Charysse
Strawberry:

Role model for all ballplayers' girlfriends.

Marty Scott:

Manager, St. Paul Saints; called "Dad" by Darryl Strawberry; fired as director of the Texas Rangers farm system, 1994.

Doug Simunic:

Manager of the loathed Fargo-Moorehead RedHawks; despised in St. Paul.

Marty Neff:

Outfielder, St. Paul Saints, head case with his own fan club; released by the Pittsburgh Pirates, 1993.

J. T. Bruett:

Center fielder, St. Paul Saints; released by the Minnesota Twins, 1995.

Kevin Garner:

First baseman, St. Paul Saints; league home run king; number-one draft choice of the San Diego Padres, 1987; released from Organized Baseball, 1994.

Paul Roma Romanoli:

Leading reliever, St. Paul Saints; the team Romeo; released by the Florida Marlins, 1995.

Steve Solomon:

Left fielder, St. Paul Saints; nice young Jewish man; released by the Philadelphia Phillies, 1996.

Glenn Davis:

First baseman, St. Paul Saints; former slugger with the Houston Astros and the Baltimore Orioles; released by the Orioles after a fight outside what he calls "an adult entertainment center."

Hector Villanueva:

Catcher, St. Paul Saints; former St. Louis Cardinal and Chicago Cub; renowned for having largest ass in league.

Dan Thomson:

Pitcher, St. Paul Saints; young man with a grunge goatee and a Kurt Cobain attitude.

Hillory and Dakota Sadie :

The toast of Fargo; two young women who do a little dance out to the scoreboard before each game, climb a ladder, and hang signs up with scores and stats on the antique board.

Minnie Minoso:

Former major league star; crown prince of Midway Stadium.

Bill Fanning. Tom Whaley. and Annie Huidekoper:

General manager, director of operations, and director of community relations of the St. Paul Saints.

Eleanor Mondale:

CBS News reporter and crown princess of Minnesota.

Sammy Davis. Jr.:

Singer whose recording of "Theme from Shaft" is the Saints' official rally song.

Neal Karlen:	Me.
Jann Wenner:	The Big Cheese.
Besides Bill Veeck s. the ghosts of Otis Redding. Buddy Holly. and Roger Maris:	As themselves.

Things fall apart; the center cannot hold mere anarchy is loosed
   upon the world.
And what rough beast, its hour come round at last,
Slouches towards Bethlehem to be born?

—W. B. Yeats, "The Second Coming," 1921

That is one last thing to remember: *writers are always selling somebody out.*

—Joan Didion, *Slouching Towards Bethlehem*, 1968

Who's the cat who won't cop out/When there's danger all about?
Shaft! Right On!
He's treated with respect/His friends let him know when there is danger.
Shaft! Can you dig it?

—From "Shaft," the official late-inning rally song of the St. Paul
   Saints baseball team, as sung by Sammy Davis, Jr., most often
   heard when Darryl Strawberry was batting.

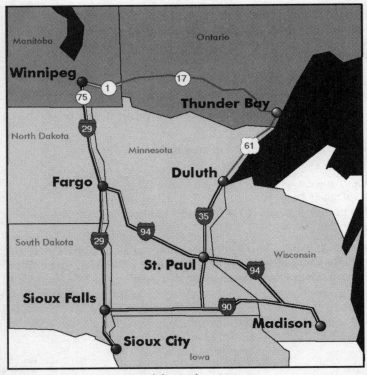

Map of the Northern League
Courtesy of Bill Tyler, Northern League Webmaster, www.nlfan.com

SLOUCHING TOWARD FARGO

P<small>ART</small> O<small>NE</small>

The Season of Last Chances

Introduction:
The Redemption of Cigarette Boy

*But he redeemed his vices with virtue. There was ever more in him
to be praised than to be pardoned.*
—Ben Jonson, *Timber; or, Discoveries Made upon Men and Matter*

July 3, 1996

Bill Murray, a cultural icon in flight from his own fame, paces in
the St. Paul Saints' dugout as Darryl Strawberry picks up his bat a
few feet down the bend. "Gimme a jack, meat!" Murray yells to
Strawberry, ordering his most infamously disgraced player to hit a
home run.

"Okaў, Meat!" Strawberry yells back, laughing as he heads to the
on-deck circle in St. Paul's bandbox Midway Stadium. "You sign my
paycheck, you the man."

Murray, the team's co-owner who has been variously listed as
their official "czar" and "team psychologist," claps his hands as
Strawberry is announced to the home crowd. The movie star then
turns to his own two young boys, who are sitting next to him on
the bench, and directs them to pay close attention to Darryl's
magic swing.

It's early July, and another Saints sellout of 6,329 responds to the
sight of Strawberry with one more standing ovation for the phoenix
who—for $1,250 a month—has spiritually risen here in the ash can
of the bush leagues. Over the summer in St. Paul, the most notorious
felon and drug abuser in major league history has become the patron
saint of lost causes and last chances.

It was a perfect fit between player and fans. For St. Paul, a de-

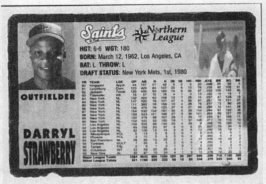

pressed industrial town on the Mississippi, had been in a psychic and economic spiral roughly since the day in 1958 when the Dodgers abandoned Brooklyn for Los Angeles and their owner, the satanic Walter O'Malley, discarded the original St. Paul Saints, one of their top farm clubs at the time.

Those Saints had also been a kind of social barometer. When the Dodgers signed the great catcher Roy Campanella from the Negro Leagues in 1948, they first sent him to St. Paul. Campy smashed a double with his first swing as a Saint and was so overjoyed that he stuck out his arm to shake the umpire's hand. The ump, instead, turned his back and walked away.

But the old Saints were as much about weirdness and taking chances as today's Saints. In 1937, the Saints' Bill Norman fainted in left field while chasing a fly ball (he swallowed his chewing tobacco). In 1954, the Saints' Jack Cassini tried to steal home four times in one game (he was thrown out on each attempt). But by 1960, those Saints were dead and the city, it seemed, was in decline.

"This town needs this team," Bill Murray says thirty-six years later, "and this team needs St. Paul."

Though Pauline Kael called him the master of "transcendent slapstick," Murray, like Strawberry, is largely reviled in the New York and Hollywood celebrity communities for turning away from the *Ghostbusters*-like roles that had made him the number-one box office star of the mid-1980s. But now, hanging with his team, Murray looks far happier than bicoastal gossip columnists, who have long painted him as a bitter and crabby ingrate, have indicated.

"The Saints can't do anything about all of Darryl's problems," Murray says as Strawberry sets up at the plate. "All we can do is give him a place to play again when no one else will have him. He's here for one last chance to make baseball fun again for himself, the way it was before he was DARRYL STRAWBERRY."

Murray grows suddenly silent. This baseball park is also one of the few spots where Bill Murray can be the way *he* was before he was BILL MURRAY.

"I come here to get away from the pressure," Murray says. "When I'm in the dugout, or selling beer in the bleachers, or coaching first base, there's nothing but the pressure of the game. That's real and honest pressure."

Strawberry takes two called strikes. And then, from behind home plate, comes the Foghorn Leghorn baritone of a drunken, obese redneck wearing the colors of the Saints' archenemies, the Fargo-Moorhead RedHawks. "Hey, Darryl!" the yahoo screeches, the entire ballpark within earshot. "Where can a white guy get some coke on a Saturday night in St. Paul?"

Strawberry slowly, sadly, shakes his head twice before lifting the next pitch 463 feet to the opposite field, over Sister Rosalind "Sister Roz" Gefre, the seventy-four-year-old Benedictine nun who gives massages in the grandstand, over Jack "the Bastard" Morris warming up in the Saints' bullpen, over the MOTHER'S STRAWBERRY SCHNAPPS billboard behind the warning track, over a train choogling past and blowing its horn on the railroad tracks that run just four feet beyond tiny Midway Stadium's outfield wall.

Saints flood out of the dugout to high-five the jubilant Strawberry, who looks for Murray in the scrum. "There's your jack, meat," he says. "I want a raise."

Murray got his jack during his first weekend that season with his Saints. I'd been monitoring his meandering progress to St. Paul all summer, not an easy task for that rare celebrity like Murray with no publicist or home base. I was quizzing him on assignment from *Rolling Stone*—with a far different attitude toward my subject than I have now.

Jann Wenner, the publisher and founding editor of *Rolling Stone,* my boss and tormentor for four years in the wild eighties, still had to approve every assignment and expense account along the way.

And later that July, Wenner made it clear to my beleaguered editor what he wanted done if I wanted back into *Rolling Stone* after a long stint as a prodigal: Bill Murray, a co-owner of the St. Paul Saints, and Darryl Strawberry, he of the notable rap sheet, had to be carved.

Wenner—word had it in the *Rolling Stone* hallways during the years I wrote for them—had never forgiven Murray for his starring role as Dr. Hunter S. Thompson in *Where the Buffalo Roam,* a 1980 cult classic wherein a thinly-veiled Jann Wenner, played with a padded butt by Bruno Kirby, was hilariously and accurately savaged and ridiculed by Murray as a cheap corporate bastard who wouldn't pay his writers their expense money. Earlier in the summer, Murray had further enraged *Rolling Stone* by refusing to set up an all-day studio shoot with a fancy New York photographer for the article I was writing.

In 1980, Wenner had refused to cooperate with the film, and he became "Marty Lewis," Dr. Thompson's editor and publisher at *Smash* magazine. He had struck back in the pages of *Rolling Stone* by having a reporter write a review accusing Murray of participating in "hacking out an embarrassing piece of hogwash utterly devoid of plot, form, movement, tension, humor, insight, logic, or purpose." Dr. Hunter S. Thompson, the greatest star Jann Wenner had ever produced, was slammed with: "Only a drug-crazed greedhead would sell his name to such a cheap piece of exploitation." It didn't help that in the movie Murray mocked Jann's notorious use of *Rolling Stone* to abet his social climbing with lines like "You don't want bogus journalism, do you Marty, not after your picture was in *Newsweek* playing horsie with Caroline Kennedy."

And Jann played favorites too. He gave his blessing to the universally panned 1998 movie version of Dr. Thompson's *Fear and Loathing in Las Vegas* by putting its star, Johnny Depp, on the cover of *Rolling Stone* and having his reporter call the film "delightfully crazy." Even though it was accepted wisdom that the picture was indulgent trash, the poor schmuck writer couldn't say that the film had neither Murray's panache in representing Thompson, nor Jann Wenner's sadism in torturing his workers.

Now *Rolling Stone* had received a new demand to hatchet Murray; vicious cartoons would accompany the story if I got the right dirt on this star, who was so big that he wouldn't pose for *Rolling Stone.* It wouldn't be hard. I already had enough quotes and scenes with Murray that could be twisted and taken out of context. In short, I could hang him by using special "tricks of the trade" that every celebrity journalist knows.

That was my job, and I'd already done several hatchetings on Jann's behalf during the time I'd worked for *Rolling Stone*. The fee for the Murray assassination would be $7,500 for a summer in the sun, all expenses paid. Seeing as how the previous week I'd vacuumed my couch for change for that month's rent, I thought I could *temporarily* unretire as a hatchet man. "*Nem di gelt.* [Get the money!],'' Henny Youngman once told me in Yiddish. "That's the first rule of show business."

"And the second rule?" I asked.

Said Henny, "The star is always right."

Well, not this time, I thought as I signed the contract to tar Murray. And hey—what could be better than being paid to spend a couple months traveling the back roads of America like Kerouac, Steinbeck, or Kuralt while gathering the evidence to disrespect in print an apparently hyperbitter movie star? Hopefully, as the summer progressed and the cast expanded, I'd also be lucky enough to witness Darryl Strawberry, that nationally known bad guy, fall off the wagon in a place like Thunder Bay, Ontario, then maybe he'd go apeshit like he used to when he was cranked up on coke and a $20 million contract. Now *that* would be the perfect color for my story.

At first, I figured I would spend only a few weeks, maybe a month at the most, scamming free merchandise and scribbling notes as I made it to Sioux City and Fargo via the Saints' team bus (Greyhound) and my own trusty, rusty beater. After the games, I would stealthily follow with my notebook as the players whored, drank, and gambled their way around the pathetic Northern League circuit, the lowest in the land.

But I would learn that, like Strawberry, I too was seeking a second chance I may not have deserved, a shot at redemption for all my accumulated sins as a journalist and failed soul. The hasty recent end of a Vegas marriage to the notorious Baddest Girl in Minneapolis had also laid me lower than Eddie Gaedel, the midget who pinch-hit for the 1951 St. Louis Browns. My ex-wife and I had courted over baseball, and I needed to learn to love again the game I now loathed. It was time to put my scorecard in order. As I followed the team, I would be searching for some clue to my own battered spirit.

I would also respectfully search out the Iowa ballroom where Buddy Holly played his last concert, the spot in Wisconsin's Lake

Monona where Otis Redding crashed, and the Roger Maris Museum, which was opened in a North Dakota shopping mall for Fargo's most famous, tortured, and misunderstood son. In Darwin, Minnesota, I saw the biggest ball of twine in the world. In Vermillion, South Dakota, I found the most exquisite collection of ancient, priceless violins. In New Ulm, I visited the Minnesota Music Hall of Fame, whose inductees include Bob Dylan, nee Bobby Zimmerman of Hibbing; Judy Garland, nee Frances Gumm of Grand Rapids, and Whoopie John Wilfahrt, nee John Wilfahrt, the Johnny Appleseed of polka, who so spread the beat that Minnesota now hosted a mass gathering called Polkapalooza.

I would spend two seasons with the team. Wenner, through an irony I doubt he could appreciate, for once played the role of Virgil, leading my sorry ass to Paradise. For during my time with the St. Paul Saints, I also came to realize that just as Strawberry, Murray, and St. Paul needed this team, so did I.

But in the beginning I was there as Jann Wenner's Nazgul, told to fly forth dutifully from Mordor to lay waste to Murray, Strawberry, the Saints, and any others who might cross my path as I chased the team from Thunder Bay to Sioux Falls and back home to St. Paul. It was a test that I, as a journalist, was for the moment comfortable with.

Months into my journey and already tardy with my story, I would phone *Rolling Stone* with my impressions of Murray and Strawberry. They seemed to be nice guys who wouldn't naturally provide the sexy scenes and weird personal habits I knew celebrity magazines demand in their profiles. Any hack writer can cough up such a story on demand if they have a little face time with a celebrity, pay a bit of attention, and have access to the Nexis computer system to track down shitty old news reports, true or not, about the intended victim.

My editor at the magazine was not happy to hear I wasn't finding Jann's kind of sexy story. "Sexy" in the magazine world implies much more, but sometimes it has little to do with actual fornication. In a celebrity puff piece, "sexy" means providing faux, intimate, and revealing cotton candy anecdotes; in a hatchet job, "sexy" means providing dirt dished as if at a banquet.

Dirt is what Jann Wenner was paying me $7,500 and expenses for this one story. Wenner's instructions after my midsummer report to my long-suffering editor were simple: if I wanted to get this story and myself back into *Rolling Stone,* I had to show him "Bill Murray driving the Saints' team bus while Darryl Strawberry is freebasing crack in the backseat."

I wanted back into *Rolling Stone,* and I knew that there was a good chance that Jann would stiff me on my fee and expenses if I didn't give him what he wanted. I knew how to hatchet, but I'd retired years ago, primarily because the practice made me feel dirty. A decade of Hebrew school and an aborted career as a rabbi had taught me the important difference between the *emes* (in Yiddish, "the ultimate Truth" and "the Big Lie.") But like most reporters, I instead worked that ethically ambiguous area in the middle, the land of spin, selective quotes, unnamed sources, and half-truths made certain only by ink upon paper, black upon white.

At *Newsweek,* where I got my first job as a fact checker, I learned in biannual libel classes just what reporters could get away with. A. J. Liebling's dictum was right: freedom of the press is reserved for those who own one or work for someone who does. Later, as a *Newsweek* writer, I took on in a series of articles the Bhagwan Shree Rajneesh, an Indian guru and charlatan who every morning drove one of his ninety gold Rolls-Royces around the Oregon commune where he lorded over the hundreds of devotees he'd fleeced.

Bhagwan paid me back by placing a curse on my soul, a curse that was delivered by one of his henchmen. Bhagwan, however, was soon dead, his devotees scattered; I, meantime, had moved on to *Rolling Stone,* where Jann Wenner, cofounder, publisher, editor-in-chief, and Grand Poobah, had lured me to the masthead shared by my journalistic hero, Dr. Hunter S. Thompson, by cutting my salary 300 percent, taking away my dental insurance, and promising me both an office and that I could write the word "fuck" as often as I wanted in my stories. (Of course, in the contract Wenner sent over for me to sign, he'd left out the part about my office and scrawled in "You can carve your name on a desk." I was in my twenties and it was the eighties, so the better parts more than made up for the rest.)

I wrote puff pieces when Jann demanded: my first cover story was on Jamie Lee Curtis, a good egg who was about to star in a phony piffle called *Perfect,* in which a *Rolling Stone* reporter impersonated in cardboard by John Travolta befriends Curtis, who plays an aerobics instructor. Travolta promises Curtis that he'll write a shiny happy story about her gym. Instead, he hatchets her and all her friends in

Rolling Stone, abetted by Jann himself, who starred in the film as his own favorite person.

The project resulted in unbelievable on-screen leakage of Hollywood chutzpah, media vanity, and Jann's bullshit. Even though the film was universally lampooned as a disaster, Jann put *Perfect,* on me, the new recruit. My job was to do the dirty work of typing that *here* was a terrific movie that fully deserved this *Rolling Stone* cover.

So I wasn't exactly innocent, and I soon learned that no one really cared what you wrote in celebrity journalism, for the medium was the message. "You're the reporter from *Rolling Stone?*" many celebrities asked when I showed up for an interview. "Am I supposed to smoke a joint with you?" I was twenty-six and, like Dr. Hook and the Medicine Show sang on the cover [sort of] of the *Rolling Stone.* I bought five copies for my mother.

The price? Jann, Dick Clark's evil twin in charting the eternal youthquake, was famous for wet-kissing his friends in print. One would think that Michael Douglas, Jann's longtime pal and social ladder to the stars, was the finest actor since Edwin Booth by the number of times he's been on the cover. And Jann was immune to hurting stars who he decided he didn't care about after all. Hence, I spent twenty excruciating Hollywood hours for a cover story in the Cleopatra-style tomb bedroom of Cher, tape-recording Her Nibs's memories. But Jann changed his mind by the time I got back to New York and decided not only was he not going to put Cher on the cover, he wasn't going to cover her at all. Cher was pissed, I heard, and I felt guilty; Jann didn't give a shit—he was off social climbing on a different mountain of celebrities.

But who was I to judge? Even a true journalistic hero like the late Joseph Mitchell, the king of the profile, was perplexed. At the end of his life, the *New Yorker* writer who invented the New Journalism when Tom Wolfe was still a teen admitted, "I have long since lost the ability to detect insanity. Sometimes it is necessary for me to go into a psychopathic ward on a story, and I never notice the difference."

Years later, my last *Rolling Stone* cover story was another interview with the Howard Hughes of rock & roll, the Artist Formerly Known as Prince, a five-foot-two-inch genius and pain in the ass who I came to refer fondly as simply "that little purple *meshuggener.*" For over a decade, I was the only reporter with whom Prince would talk. By the end, he was pulling such star shit as making me chase him across Europe on Wenner's iffy dime, then not letting me either tape-record or take notes of our interviews. Instead, I was forced to feign a urinary tract infection in Switzerland so I could run to the bathroom every ten minutes to scribble notes of our conversation on toilet paper and soap wrappers.

If I didn't get the story, I'd been warned the day before by *Rolling Stone's* music editor, Jann would not be happy with an expense report that looked like a Grand Tour of Europe. Out of fear, I stopped eating. But the next day Prince gave me enough fresh words that Wenner could put him on the cover with the headline PRINCE TALKS. I was in the boss's good graces one more time.

But at twenty-nine going on thirty, I was tired of the inanities of most celebrities, the synthetic hooey of *Rolling Stone*-style personality journalism that had overtaken most of the magazine industry, and the whims of a Grand Kleagle/publisher who fancied himself William Randolph Hearst, but more closely resembled the rich kid bully at camp who wouldn't share his foot locker full of candy unless you did his chores on the job wheel. I knew I had whored myself.

And I had learned how Dr. Thompson had fossilized into a piece of petrified shtick who treated women like dog dirt. Don't meet your heroes.

But who was I to judge Dr. Thompson's corruption, his turning into just the kind of pompous blowhard that he once so brilliantly mocked? In New York in my twenties in the eighties, didn't I proudly carry as a status symbol my *Rolling Stone* business cards and press pass, the latter featuring a picture of me looking properly stoned above Jann Wenner's signature? Yes.

But no more. All those years of Hebrew school kept nagging at me that something was wrong, that I was doing the devil's work in a lower ring of hell. I had to get out of New York. "If you don't go home after ten years," Janet Flanner wrote of her own hometown of Indianapolis, "then you're hooked." I had to be blasted out of town, temporarily losing just enough of my mind at the end of the decade to bring me home to Minneapolis broke and broken, yet oddly renewed.

I fell off the *Rolling Stone* masthead a year and a half after returning home, begging off when they offered me occasional assignments. I was now thirty and had always vowed not to be one of those pathetic geezer/scenesters hanging around a world of hip meant for teenagers.

"I ain't gonna work on Mr. Wenner's farm no more," I said for the next four years, even if he did let me write "fuck" when things like that mattered to me. In any case, no one new and hip ever passed through Minnesota, meaning I could try and reinvent myself as the real reporter I thought I once was. The rewards, while interesting and morally defensible, had at times been frighteningly unremunerative.

I was broke.

Jann Wenner's checks, if you could get him to okay them, always cleared. So I said yes in 1994 when Wenner Communications promised me $7,500 if I could be the first reporter to find and interview Courtney Love after her husband, Kurt Cobain, blew his head off. It was heinous work, exactly what I vowed never to do again. But I knew Courtney from other stories, she'd always been nice to me, felt at the time like a weird kind of *mishpochah*, and like I said, Jann's checks always cleared once he gave the order.

So coming out of rock writer retirement, I staked out all of Courtney's haunts in Los Angeles, fielded class from another of Jann's editors (who was worried about my expanding Sunset Marquis hotel bills), and waited by the phone, afraid Jann would make me pay for the $7.50 can of peanuts I was eating for dinner while I waited for Courtney to save my ass. She did, absentmindedly giving me her sunglasses as I squeezed out enough quotes to make Jann happy.

I gave the shades to Jann back in New York, like Dorothy handing the Wizard of Oz the Wicked Witch of the West's broom as proof of encounter and victory. Jann took the glasses, insulted my story, mocked my lead, told me I looked like shit, and asked me if I hadn't once been fat or had a genetic glandular disease. He also invited me back into his pages.

But until Bill Murray came along two years later, I said no thank you. Murray was different, an utter bully and prick, I'd heard. I'd first heard it some years before from some Hollywood film types I was interviewing, who said they were sure he was a jerk, even though they'd never actually met him. Still, they said, everyone in the "community" knew.

So I figured that at least I could rationalize this hatcheting as righteous. And what better place to take Murray apart than *Rolling Stone?* Mar Ralnick, one of my Torah teachers (who also taught Joel and Ethan Coen, decades before they gloriously ridiculed our home state in *Fargo*), had first planted this notion of journalistic duty by laying out history as a battle between bullies and victims. If you could draw blood from a bully, he lectured, recalling the Cossacks and our Martyrs, you were doing the Lord's work.

According to this ethos, Murray seemed ripe for the hatcheting, although it wouldn't be easy, I realized, as I researched him. Going through old clippings and books, I discovered that Bill Murray apparently hated the press and was known to be violent.

What made him cool to the cognoscenti was that Murray treated Hollywood showbiz executive types used to having their asses kissed with no more respect than he did journalists or glad-handing weasels. Ironically, some of his best characters defined smarm to a new degree of unctiousness.

On "Saturday Night Live," there was Jerry Aldini, a wormlike talent scout for Polysutra Records who was continually offering all who wanted a "tootski, tootski" of cocaine. In the movie *Scrooged*, Murray played a network executive so evil that he wanted to staple antlers on the ears of squirrels to make them look like reindeer for a Christmas special. Shitty lounge singers, corrupt low-life personal managers, an arrogant weatherman who would say anything to get a woman in bed—Bill Murray made them breathe.

He had no publicist and no permanent address. And because he owned a piece of the *Ghostbusters* megasmash, he could wander the world doing whatever he wanted to do, star in any bent independent comedy he wanted, or play golf in the middle of a professional tournament at Pebble Beach. He didn't need, or want, publicity.

His movie choices now seemed almost perverse and small. When he turned in great performances, as in *Groundhog Day, Kingpin,* or *Rushmore,* it almost seemed like an accident. He had said fuck you to the showbiz world and its executives in a way almost no stars can and still retain a career. Many of these insiders, used to being treated as sultans by the "talent," revenged Murray's disrespect by calling pals who wrote gossip columns and spreading the word that the movie star was a difficult dick.

Only a few of the intelligentsia had caught on to the wonder of his declaration of independence.

One was Ron Rosenbaum, who wrote a piece called "Bill Murray, Secret Zen Master" in 1996 in the New York *Observer*. "The point is not that he is, literally, the Supreme Being," wrote Rosenbaum, "but that there is some ineffable transcendent sublimity to his persona, a loving generosity that through the Impervious Cool shtick signals a spiritual agenda. (He loves us, man!)"

Much of his other press simply called him an asshole.

During the summer, I read, he would appear for several games of the St. Paul Saints. I later learned that he often would appear out of nowhere, like Kane in "Kung Fu," showing up at St. Paul's Midway Stadium ten minutes before the game was due to start and selling beer. Other times, I learned, rumors would hit the Saints' office twenty-four hours in advance that he was supposed to be coming; most of the time, those rumors were untrue. I would have to become buddy-buddy with the Saints' staff, I realized, for distant early warning signals.

But most of all, I learned from those moldering clips that Bill Murray was dangerous when he felt his privacy had been violated. He had never spoken of his hobby of owning minor league baseball teams, had never had his favorite haven violated.

Books about "Saturday Night Live" told me that even tough and macho John Belushi was always physically frightened by Murray, that Murray had once taken a swing at Chevy Chase minutes before the beginning of an episode of "Saturday Night Live," and that he'd carried the reputation as a true street brawler since his anonymous days learning how to be funny at the Second City improvisational troupe in Chicago. During a Second City show in Toronto, he once stopped a show, stepped offstage, and took a heckler out into the alley. The heckler returned, bloody and beaten up, to his seat, while Murray retook the stage for his next sketch.

Like his pal Mike Veeck, he'd spent some nights in jail. "There's some danger involved . . . something in Bill's eyes," Lorne Michaels, the executive producer of "Saturday Night Live," told *Rolling Stone* in Murray's first cover story while he was on the show. The magazine seemed out to get him even then: they'd reported, unlike any other stories I'd seen, that Murray had been "dealing suitcases full of dope in the early seventies," that he'd "been busted at the Chicago airport with eight and a half pounds of grass," and that the "bust made the front page of the *Chicago Tribune*."

What chance would I have of not getting punched while getting what Jann wanted? Fifty-fifty, I figured. It would make for a better story if he took a whack. After all, my hero, Willie Mays, once made me cry, kicked me out of his sportscar with "Say Hey" license plates—and I got my byline for that puff piece turned hatchet job turned into a cool anthology.

And what about Straw, who would enter the tale during spring training? You never knew with Straw, but for certain he was no less deserving a target, I thought.

Here was perhaps the most self-destructive man in baseball, who'd only a few years ago, under federal indictment, said, "The Feds can kiss my ass" when it was announced that he was a suspect in a tax fraud case. A man who, in 1995, while a San Francisco Giant, had gotten drunk, then done line after line of cocaine, even though he knew he'd be tested in days. No matter, he was planning on killing himself by driving off a road after the last line was done. But he didn't. Then he was tested and was soon booted out of baseball again.

For years, people had said he was a lazy ballplayer who'd blown his chance at Cooperstown out of pure sloth. "Even a dog will run after a ball," one of his old managers, Tommy Lasorda of the Dodgers, had said of him.

Even the government seemed to be coming down on him in ways beyond mere tax charges. When Strawberry had his brief swing with the Yankees in 1995, Lee Brown, President Clinton's chief drug administrator, told the world that George Steinbrenner was sending "the wrong message" to America's children by giving the miscreant one more chance.

Steinbrenner, a convicted supporter of Richard Nixon and a man who enjoyed playing the Great White savior, be it with Billy Martin, Dwight Gooden, or Darryl Strawberry, immediately began backing away from his latest reclamation project. Steinbrenner's ire against Darryl was spurred on by Bob Watson, the Yankees' general manager, who felt Darryl was a defensive liability, a pain in the ass, and a social risk the Yankees didn't need. The Yankees insisted that Strawberry and his entire family be required to take drug tests, kept him under virtual house arrest, and cut him after the season.

So fuck Bill Murray, I thought as I started out, and fuck Straw too, I thought later, before I'd met or talked to either of them. And let Wenner print it big.

Back in the dugout after his dramatic home run, Strawberry motions me to the locker room runway. "Got a cigarette, Cigarette Boy?" he asks.

Cigarettes were Strawberry's last remaining vice and the key to my setting him up for my hatchet job in *Rolling Stone*. Unable to carry smokes in his uniform because they would break if he had to slide, Strawberry had for weeks let me feed him Newport Menthols, his John Shaft-like brand of choice. I'd pick up the cigarettes each morning on the way to the ballpark as my bait. And for the time it took him to finish each one, he would talk to me without resorting to the born-again "Praise Jesus" bromides and jock-talk clichés with which he used to armor himself against the reporters, fans, and teammates who poked and pointed at him like he was a hungry bear chained to a stake.

He was still perceived as the baddest man in baseball, a ballplayer who only by the grace of the God he now praised so incessantly was spending his summer hitting jacks in St. Paul instead of guarding his arse in federal prison. And with the help of my ready pack of cigarettes, I had him.

"The Yankees don't want me. Bob Watson hates me," Strawberry said, depressed, the all-purpose say-hey smile that he showed the public limp with hurt. Taking a deep drag off the Newport, he mulled the refusal of Watson to even consider giving Darryl one last chance to redeem his once-glorious major league career.

I'd even started smoking again, just for the moments in the locker room or under the grandstand when Darryl Strawberry would call me "Cigarette Boy" and confide in me as a fellow smoker and exile from the city, one eighties burnout to another.

True, I felt like an utter and total shit. After spending weeks with the man, I genuinely *liked* him. If he was a con man, he was an *excellent* con man. Strawberry listened to the cheers of the St. Paul fans, who were still applauding his dinger, reverberating above. "I can't take this much longer," he said, sighing. "That last bus ride to Thunder Bay to play the Whiskey Jacks killed my legs."

I nodded sympathetically, taking notes. "One day at a time," I said, parroting the Twelve Steps talk of Alcoholics Anonymous that Darryl had learned in his visits over the years to seemingly every drug detox center between the Betty Ford Center in California and the Smithers Clinic. I'd already made contact with a woman who'd been in Strawberry's therapy group at Betty Ford. Because of her, I already knew many Strawberry secrets—the father who'd left him at the age of twelve, the partners and hangers-on who'd fled with all of his money, the years spent playing major league baseball wired or hung over from cocaine, alcohol, or amphetamines. "You're making your amends," I said.

I was a shit for accepting such clues, but I was grateful for the tip. Yet it continued to gnaw at me. How could I do this to the man?

Strawberry nodded at my Twelve Steps reference. I hadn't exactly lied to him that day in the Saints' locker room a few weeks before, when, desperate to get an angle on the ballplayer forever surrounded by cameras, I'd told Strawberry that I too was now in "recovery."

"I checked into Hazelden last year," I had told him, not exactly lying to him that first day of training camp, name-dropping the

world-famous Minnesota drug and alcohol clinic where the likes of
Eric Clapton, Liza Minnelli, Kitty Dukakis, Calvin Klein, and a whole
benefit concert worth of Seattle grunge musicians had gone for the
cure. "It's a cool place to get into recovery, and Minnesota is a
caring place to heal. This is where they invented the phrases 'chemi-
cally dependent' and 'codependent,' " I'd added.

Strawberry listened warily to me, hearing the same language he
was hearing at his thrice-weekly meetings of Alcoholics Anonymous.
What I didn't tell the ballplayer was that I'd actually checked into
the clinic not for a drug problem, but for a new one-week quit-
smoking program that Hazelden had developed using the same meth-
ods with which they weaned junkies and drunks from heroin and
booze.

"Care for a cigarette?" I'd asked soon enough, pulling out my
first pack in a year. "One day at a time," I told Darryl as I lit up.

Several weeks later, Bill Murray, my main prey, walked into the
locker room wearing a Saints uniform and a red mop wig. He stuffed
a towel inside the uniform for a mammoth gut, put on outlandish

Bill Murray raking the infield between innings
Courtesy of St. Paul Saints

outsize clown glasses, and told us he was going to coach first base next inning dressed as Marge Schott, the universally loathed owner of the Cincinnati Reds.

"Hey, can I bum a cigarette?" Murray asked me. "I mean, Marge Schott smokes, right?"

"Right," I said, extending my hand. Murray nodded thanks, then mounted a St. Bernard that represented Schottsie, Marge Schott's dog.

"Don't hose me, please," Murray says to me before heading out, watching my right hand scribbling notes while my left hand gives him a smoke. "I've been hosed a lot before and the Saints are my last oasis. Please don't ruin it for me."

"I promise," I said, crossing my fingers. Then I watched as Murray rode the dog out to take Wayne "Twig" Terwilliger's spot in the first base coach's box for three outs.

Could I do this to Bill Murray and still live with myself? For weeks I'd thought yes, there was no other choice, I was at the end of the line. I had rent. I enjoyed eating meals out now and again. I had credit card bills at 18 percent. But I was beginning to have my doubts about nailing the Saints and its leaders: the weeks I'd already spent with Strawberry and the team had evolved for me into a full-scale crisis of confidence. How could I write the typical magazine-type grandiose jive about these painfully human characters?

For starters, I'd grown genuinely fond of Darryl Strawberry, seen him go from silent curio to authentic prairie hero to symbol of St. Paul's civic rejuvenation in a matter of weeks. I'd seen his lips purse in momentary shame when the tap came indicating it was time for another urinalysis or meeting with his probation officer, heard him tell me between cigarette puffs that chants of "Dar-ryl! Dar-ryl!" still hurt as much in Sioux City as they did in Boston. I'd seen him sign autographs for hours after a game, not knowing any reporter was present, for hundreds of pie-eyed kids from dinky Midwestern towns who had never seen a real-live major leaguer before.

At home, I obsessively reread New Yorker writer Janet Malcolm's opening two sentences in The Journalist and the Murderer. There, Ms. Malcolm, who herself had famous trouble with a profile subject who'd felt unfairly fucked over, had simply written:

Every journalist who is not too stupid or too full of himself to notice what is going on knows that what he does is morally indefensible. He is a kind of confidence man, preying on people's vanity, ignorance, or loneliness, gaining their trust and betraying them without remorse.

Indeed.

I turned around to see the Saints' front office staff, who I would also be shortly taking to the hose factory. Standing silent and alone against a stadium gate was another Saints co-owner, Mike Veeck, who as a youth once planned the most infamous promotion in major league history, only to finally redeem himself with the lowly Saints fifteen years later.

Also buzzing about under the ballpark were the other dozen quixotic, admirable self-described misfits working for the Saints, who'd already shown me that summer the healing effects of watching a carnival from behind the curtain. Between puffs I waved to Annie Huidekoper, the beloved and beautiful director of community relations for the Saints, who doubled as the June Cleaver-type mom to the team's backstage dysfunctional family. I nodded my head to Tom

Courtesy of Bonnie Butler

Annie Huidekoper

Whaley, who looked like a carnival rat in his unkempt Fu Manchu mustache and wraparound shades, who played the baddest guitar in St. Paul in a band called Tarwater, but who also doubled as the Saints' lawyer.

I peeked at Bob St. Pierre, the Saints' sales intern who'd earlier refused my $100 bribe offer for the huge Alfred E. Neuman head he'd just paraded around in on the field on "*Mad* Magazine Night." I looked up to the pressbox, where I saw Dave Wright announcing the game with the hilarious now-hear-this voice and authority of Edward R. Murrow that he thought would eventually get him to the major leagues too. I looked up, and saw Steve Golden, one of the only two St. Paul off-duty, in-uniform policemen the Saints needed to hire to keep the peace among the team's delirious 6,329 fans. Officer Golden, a former regional boxing champion now known as "the toughest Jew in St. Paul," waved at me.

Officer Golden had also caught the Saints' fever; if the team were trailing in the late innings, he would turn his police cap backward on his head and patrol the stands as a "Rally Cop." His partner in Midway Stadium was Officer John Pyka, who not only participated as a "Rally Cop," but also helped me try and break into my car a couple times I'd locked in my keys.

Looking at them all, I thought "fuck Joan Didion": the biggest thing to remember *wasn't* that a writer was always selling somebody out. I couldn't, not here in Midway Stadium, where any ballplayer who hit a home run through the hole in the bagel on a left field billboard would win $100,000; where the rally song was Sammy Davis Jr.'s jaw-dropping rendition of "Shaft," featuring Isaac "Black Moses" Hayes on synthesizer; where out in the parking lot thousands would thrust a bratwurst and a beer and a folding chair for a stranger with a notepad who at first meant to do them all in.

Meantime, out on the field, Bill Murray continues to commemorate the recent suspension of Marge Schott, the Hitler-loving, vodka-swilling Cincinnati team owner. Murray, in his mop wig, padded gut, unlit cigarette, and hideous Carol Channing glasses, is standing in the first base coach's box, looking like the Wicked Witch of the Reds.

While the St. Paul crowd roars its approval, Murray sends hand signals quickly rotating around his prosthetically enhanced gut to the Saints' batters. It's delicious vaudeville, and at the end of the inning, the 6,329 fans shoehorn his sweltering Day-Glo bonkers as Murray leaves the field, once again straddling the St. Bernard, which now appears to be the size of a Chevy Cavalier.

"You look like a hundred bucks!" Murray tells an elderly woman asking for an autograph in the runway near the Saints' dugout, where he likes to watch the game.

"Are you Faith Daniels of CBS News?" he asks a six-year-old girl wearing a hat shaped like a pickle as he signs her ball. "I love your show."

"You know, I was reading the Gettysburg Address the other day," Murray tells another man as he signs, "and that guy was really onto something."

And then Murray saw me scribbling notes again and looked me square in the eye. "Please don't hose me," he repeated. "And please don't hose the Saints. And most of all, don't hose Mike Veeck," he said, pointing to the Saints' co-owner, who was still watching the game silently, by himself, through an iron gate a few feet away.

"He's the heart and soul of this team," Murray said, "and he's the one you should be writing about. I don't want to be in your magazine, unless it gets Mike some recognition."

"Doesn't matter, Bill," Mike Veeck says, overhearing. "After 'Disco Demolition Night,' I'm invulnerable. Pressure doesn't exist. No one can say anything meaner about me now than the Chicago press said seventeen years ago. *Rolling Stone* screwed me in the issue in 1979 right after 'Disco.' Why would they be any nicer now?"

"Do the right thing," Murray said to me, wagging a finger.

I couldn't do this to them, I decided right then. Murray, my hunch accurately told me, was a nice guy on vacation with his family and looking for a little peace. A star, yes, but Murray didn't even register on the celebrity asshole meter I'd seen over the years, even when he had a few beers in him. And I was once again a publicity cog whose apparent only skill was to dismember or puff up a personality, depending on the day of the week, the state of their career, or an editor's disposition.

But if I "got off the merry-go-round," as Jane Fonda said before willing her death in the film of Horace McCoy's *They Shoot Horses, Don't They?*, how would I make even a miserable living? I went back up to my seat in Midway next to my best friends in Minneapolis, Dick Mammen and Jim Nelson, inner-city community organizers with hearts, as they say in the Midwest, "as big as all outdoors."

"I'm going to have to kill myself," I kiddingly told Dick, truly the blackest white man I'd ever known.

"No, you're not," he said, laughing, ordering three beers for us as the Saints went down in order and two men in inflatable sumo suits took the field. "You've got more innings to pitch. You may have to develop a new pitch, but you're not canceling Christmas, motherfucker."

" 'Motherfucker' is right," added Jim, an ordained Baptist minister not afraid to quote either Tupac or Scripture: "God is with thee in all that thou doest." (Genesis 21:22)

I pondered my friends' words, my next check, my assignment.

"Fuck you, Jann," I said out loud as the Saints retired three straight Fargo batters and ran back to the dugout. I was conducting my own private requiem for a hatchet man.

For the first time in weeks, I felt clean, if not happy.

"Free at last, free at last, thank God Almighty, you're free at last," said Reverend Jim, a beer in his hand, a Saints batting helmet on his head, and Martin Luther King, Jr., on his lips.

"So what is this about, you and the Saints?" I asked Murray in the dugout. "What's the connection?"

"You have to find that out for yourself," he said. "I can't tell you."

1

Waiting for Bill Murray

Absolutely!
If you don't get a little,
A few butterflies,
No matter what you do,
On the first day of anything,
You're not human.
—Phil Rizzuto, "Field of Butterflies"
   (Opening Day, April 12, 1991,
   New York Yankees against the Kansas City Royals,
   first inning, no outs, bases empty, first batter)

March 28–29, 1996 (three months earlier)

I had learned how to disembowel an entire baseball team ten years earlier, when I still loved baseball. The story—for Jann, of course—was called "Bad Nose Bees" and dealt with a low-down minor league team in San Jose, California, populated almost entirely by head cases and drug addicts kicked out of the major leagues for crimes against humanity and the dugout.

For three weeks, I'd lived with and befriended the team, led by Steve Howe, a former Los Angeles Dodger who'd been banned from the big leagues for several dances too many with cocaine (although, like Strawberry, he would return to play for the Yankees). I bought everybody drinks and slept on a greasy mat alongside three of the Bees in a windowless room underneath the stadium, smoked dope with half the team, and took notes outside Fresno and Bakersfield motel rooms where the players whored away their meager paychecks.

Then I completely betrayed the team in print, savaging the Bees and Steve Howe with all the confidences I'd milked from them in the middle of the darkest nights of their souls. My guilt when *Rolling Stone* ran the story was overwhelming, but my treason proved to be a smash with my editors.

Over a decade later, my first task at hand in destroying the St. Paul Saints was to high-tail it down to Florida for the end of spring training. The Saints were a member of the woebegone Northern League, whose eight independent teams had no ties with any of the twenty-eight major league clubs (at that time) or the couple hundred minor league affiliates who make up what is officially known as "organized baseball."

As such, Northern League teams relied on the castoffs, rejects, and never-weres of organized baseball. Every year, on the couple days after all the major league organizations had made their final spring training cuts, the Northern League held its annual Florida tryouts for all the shell-shocked young athletes who'd just been told that their dreams of playing major league baseball were over.

The tryout, to be held at Tinker Field in Orlando, would make a perfect scene of doom and degradation to begin my piece about broken men insanely fighting to keep their one hope alive, that by playing this children's game, they would still be discovered and made heroes and stars. Unfortunately, I had gotten the time wrong for the Northern League tryout, and by the time Chuck Strouse, my traveling companion and old college roommate, and I pulled up, the little ballpark was deserted. Chuck, a hard-news reporter who'd won a Pulitzer Prize with *The Miami Herald,* didn't seem too concerned.

I, on the other hand, was fucked. I'd spent over a grand getting down there and hadn't even gotten the scene I'd constructed in my mind of pathetic, forlorn players desperately trying to impress the low-rent talent scouts of teams with names like the Thunder Bay Whiskey Jacks and the Sioux Falls Canaries.

"I hate baseball!" I screamed to Chuck, my yell ricocheting around the abandoned bandbox. "And I especially hate spring training!"

Mention baseball to me back in college, and I would have thought about long, languid evenings spent under a clear night sky, T-shirts and shorts, freshly shorn grass, hot dogs and cold beer. But in Minneapolis, nights didn't get languid until July, and my Minnesota Twins played indoors on a field that was painted, not mowed. So I never wanted to wait until the end of our five-month winter to see big league baseball. Instead, I, like many others, made a tradition of heading south in the spring for an early taste of the best of summer. For me, spring training was also the best of baseball.

While my Eurotrash classmates at Brown headed for St. Bart's sun and the regular folks headed toward Daytona's beach, I piled into a dented maroon Chevy Impala and set off for Orlando and the tamer pleasures of fly balls and infield practice.

My ultimate destination was this same Tinker Field, but the same only in the way that Liz Taylor in *Butterfield 8* is the same Liz Taylor in *The Flintstones*. Although it had been the spring training home to sixty years' worth of major league players, including the Twins, who'd trained there when I visited them in the early 1980s, it had long ago disappeared from the Florida tourist map. Perhaps the local cartographer ran out of room for the lovely, tiny ballpark after coloring in nearby Walt Disney World, the Epcot Center, and the Stars Hall of Fame Wax Museum. Perhaps he saw no point in noting a place now resting quietly in an unfashionable part of town, one you reached by passing decrepit houses with overgrown lawns and by parking your car on the street, leaving it to bake in the sun. Perhaps he'd just become an Orlando Magic fan.

Handfuls of the committed, however, still managed to find the little field built in 1914, guided by private visions of dollar beer, the holy water of baseball season, and most of all, the chance to bask in the laid-back good karma that spring training used to generate.

Spring training fans back then were largely a mismatched amalgam of baseball cranks, footloose hipsters, and on-sabbatical intellectuals. The low-rent carnival feel of the proceedings was a major part of the appeal.

Access to players was guaranteed in spring training. During a weeklong visit, fans could virtually count on a close encounter with one celebrated baseball personality or another passing through the Little League-sized surrounding. Some of the ancient stars were still in uniform; Tinker Field served as a ballpark for the Senior League, an unfortunate experiment in seeing if retired big leaguers could still hit and run. They couldn't.

At one spring training I attended, a charming, unknown Minnesota Twins rookie named Kirby Puckett asked me to hold his pool-cue case while he tied his shoe in the Tinker Field parking lot. Minutes later, the Twins' owner, Calvin Griffith, a notorious curmudgeon, nailed me in the shins when he opened the door to the little dented trailer used by the team for their spring training offices.

Mr. Griffith told me to get a haircut, then reached into his pocket for an autographed baseball as recompense for my bruise.

Tinker Field was abandoned by the bigs in 1991; it was sold for use by the bush league Orlando Cubs. The Twins fled to Fort Myers, Florida, seduced by a massive, modern, and colorless baseball facility. Such capacious spring training ballparks are still in style, their expanded dimensions serving to both insulate players from the fans and to seat the influx of new customers, mostly well-scrubbed families, swarming to Florida and Arizona each March.

Through 1994, organized charters and tours to the Grapefruit League in Florida or the Cactus League in Arizona had swelled attendance to the point that most exhibition games were 10,000-seat sellouts. As a further affront to those who'd discovered spring training before it was popular, mass market guidebooks featuring maps began appearing. One no longer needed a compass to find a spring training ballpark.

And then spring training and I got old, and baseball carried only bad memories. I hadn't gone back for the first breath of spring with some Florida baseball until now. To get some of the old pepper back, first we watched several major league teams play their final spring training games at the camps surrounding Miami. Everywhere we saw the same dispiriting sight of fans sitting listlessly like unplugged robots in big half-filled, sterile stadiums. Whatever I had once loved about the game, whatever had kept me going to the Leamington Hotel as a kid to get the autographs of visiting major leaguers, was truly gone.

At least the baseball labor dispute of the 1994 and 1995 seasons had nipped the flow of tourists who had been turning spring training into a mass happening; figures for the 1996 exhibition season showed a 24.5 percent drop in attendance from 1994's figures. It may have been the only good thing about the strike. We now had space to stretch out, and the sun was shining. But baseball, I told Chuck as we lolled in the stands watching the big leaguers play out their exhibition seasons, still definitely sucked.

Within days, the major league teams and their minor league organizations had made their final cuts and gone north to begin their seasons. Now it was time for the Northern League to bottom-feed like carp on their leavings, just as I would feed off the Northern League's sorry summer stories. Like the sad-sack ballplayers who'd tell me how they "coulda been a contender," I felt like I'd already missed the bus.

"C'mon," Chuck said, "let's at least go inside and see what the old girl looks like these days." We walked in and sat down behind Tinker Field's visiting team dugout. In front of us lay the detritus of that morning's Northern League tryout: gloves, buckets of dirty, scuffed balls, and bats watched as closely by their owners as if they were irreplaceable body parts.

"You're welcome to hang out here," yelled the only other person present, a groundskeeper who was raking the edges of Tinker Field's tired-looking basepaths. We thanked him for his un-big-league-like hospitality to two ordinary schmoes, and settled into the seats behind home plate to soak in the karma. In time, we wandered off to find something to eat. In the parking lot of a service station a block away, an elderly black man was grilling barbecue sandwiches in a metal contraption that looked like the Tin Man's suit.

Sitting back behind home plate back in the empty stadium, Chuck and I chowed down as if we were young again. As we ate, we watched the groundskeeper mount a tiny tractor and ride it around and around the infield.

This wasn't exactly the spectacle I'd meant to record of my pilgrimage back to Tinker Field to spy on the St. Paul Saints, but the groundskeeper still managed to put on a surprisingly good show. His circles were geometrically perfect.

"You know," the groundskeeper said after dismounting his tractor, "there's another day of tryouts tomorrow."

Thank you, God, I murmured silently as Chuck and I headed off to our Motel 6. As I'd learned at Hazelden during my quit-smoking class, one must always be grateful.

We returned to Tinker Field the next day. Most of the sixty assembled athletes were palpably desperate; official spring training had been over for forty-eight hours, but the young men had refused to go home, sure they'd been misjudged by the organizations that had just cut them. Instead, they'd hitched rides and buses to get to Tinker Field and the chance to try out for a spot at baseball's end of the line, with independent teams representing no major league organization. Warming up in the beatific spring green of Tinker's outfield, the ballplayers looked like court-martialed soldiers in their scavenged, mismatched uniforms, stripped of all insignia, that they'd gotten from some other team, some other time.

"This is the league of the last hurrah," explained Marty Scott, the

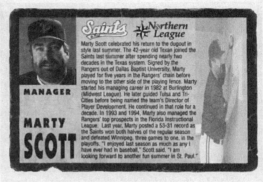

manager of the St. Paul Saints, as he looked over the iffy talent before him. For ten years, the stocky Scott, who looks remarkably like Raymond Burr, had been the highly respected director of minor league operations for the Texas Rangers. It had been a big league job for a big league mind.

"During that time," Scott said, "I had to personally release several hundred players, tell several hundred human beings that the dream they'd had since they were little was over, so go clean out your locker. Some of them cry when they get the news, some of them yell, some of them would sit numb in my office like they were in a coma. It's the hardest thing any baseball man has to do: release a player. But I'd always do it personally. You have to be a man about it."

But then, in 1994, Marty himself was cut, the victim of an executive shuffle in the Rangers' organization. He'd taken the Saints' field manager job as a way to tread water until another major league organization came knocking for his talent at appraising talent. Nobody had rung yet: maybe he didn't look major league enough anymore, with his untidy belly and tell-it-like-is tongue.

So here he was too, when he just *knew* he should be up north with a major league organization, dressed in Bermuda shorts and a Charlie Brown-like striped T-shirt pulled over his gut, looking at the unseemliest load of ballplayers he'd ever seen.

What he saw before him that day in Tinker Field was not tripping his trigger. "I know as a former minor league player myself that as long as there's that last little flicker inside you that says you can still play, you'll try," he said. "The worst thing that can happen to a former ballplayer is to be thinking ten years after he quit: 'what would have happened if I'd given it one last shot?' "

Well, this was the last shot, and as managers of the eight Northern League teams looked on, bearing clipboards and stopwatches, the players went through their frenetic paces. Many were so obviously inept, here on a lark or a prayer, that Chuck and I were tempted to hop the fence, borrow some bats, and try out ourselves.

Marty Scott knows how that feels. He still has the flicker of the third baseman who made it all the way up to AAA himself in the Texas Rangers' organization before accepting their offer to join management. "I was in the high minors and had my own model bat made by Louisville Slugger," Marty says proudly. "Not too many guys who made it to AAA, which is only one step from the majors, can say that. My only regret is that my father didn't live to see me play baseball professionally after I graduated from Texas Baptist."

Marty is very genial. He tells people bad news for a living, and everyone still likes Marty.

The assembled Northern League managers tried to keep a semblance of professionalism to the cattle call of scrubs. All nonpitchers were timed in the sixty-yard dash; outfielders then took their positions and made five throws apiece to second base, third base, and home plate. Infielders were judged on their range and hands, while catchers were clocked on their setup and release time in getting the ball down to second base.

"Most major league teams have a scouting system that grades player's tools on a two-through-eight system," Scott explained. "An eight is a superstar, a five is average for a major league player."

From the looks of things at Tinker Field, most of the players rated about a 0.7. Only one athlete had caught Scott's eye, an intense twenty-four-year-old fireplug from the South named Chris Evans who'd batted .302 for Corpus Christi in the Texas-Louisiana League last year, but had not been picked up by any major league organization.

A former pre-med student, he'd intrigued Scott with his almost frightening devotion to the drills. Calling the outfielder over, Scott began telling Evans of the special nature of the St. Paul Saints.

"What state is St. Paul in?" Evans interrupted.

Saint Paul Saints

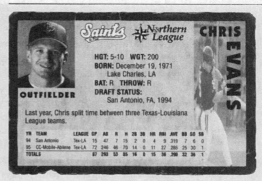

"Minnesota," Marty said, shaking his head. "You were pre-med, and you don't know where St. Paul is?"

Fifteen minutes after the tryout ended, ten players were told that they'd been drafted by Northern League teams. Each of the franchises would hold additional training and tryout camps up north in the coming weeks to fill out their rosters before the start of the season in late May.

Signing players like Chris Evans to a contract calling for $1,100 a month, said Scott, was what his team was all about: birth, rebirth, and the hope that comes anew each spring. "I know firsthand that the cliché is true: as long as you've got a uniform on and are playing somewhere for somebody, you've got a chance. All they want from us is that *last* chance."

Evans's place, Scott thought, might be as the Saints' starting right fielder. Unless, that is, the Saints were able to sign a particular somebody else who no one else in organized baseball wanted. "You ever heard of Darryl Strawberry?" Scott asked.

Oh God yes, I thought, let it be true! Please let the Saints sign Strawberry. If anybody deserved the kind of Old Testament retribution I had been contracted to dish out, it was him.

The 1983 Rookie of the Year with the New York Mets, Strawberry hit more home runs in his first five years in the majors than Mickey Mantle, had made eight National League All-Star teams, and had logged 297 career home runs.

Over the years, he'd also tested positive for cocaine use while playing with the Mets, the Los Angeles Dodgers, and the San Francisco Giants. He'd once pointed a loaded gun at the head of his first wife, Lisa, and stirred a bowl of ice cream with his genitals in the Mets' clubhouse. He'd signed a $20.25 million contract with the Dodgers in 1990; now broke, he'd been convicted of felony tax fraud in 1995 and couldn't afford to pay his alimony, child support, or to have Lisa's name, tattooed on his shoulder, inked over or removed.

I'd seen him in the mid-1980s at New York press parties, looking loaded, glassy-eyed, and talking mean and street. But the years had humbled Strawberry, perhaps, the way they'd humbled me. Better yet for my story if they hadn't—if he was still as fearsome as he was in the days in the eighties when the champion New York Mets would gobble amphetamines in the clubhouse as if they were M&Ms.

Released by the New York Yankees at the end of last year as a part of George Steinbrenner's refound morality program for players, it was a well-known fact that no team in organized baseball would come near Strawberry even with an Ebola protector suit and ten-foot calipers. Only teams with no affiliations to big league ball could bid on the disgraced ballplayer; could it really be the Saints?

"Maybe," said Marty Scott, "I know they've been talking. Now it's all up to Mike Veeck."

2

Veeck and Son and Disco Demolition Night

A man who is cautious never sleeps with a girl, quite. He's so timid he never savors anything completely. Even an after-dinner speaker should be a little drunk on a tightrope. It keeps everyone's attention.
—Chicago White Sox owner Bill Veeck, as quoted by
Thomas Boswell in *The Washington Post* on May 31, 1981
(Boswell overheard Veeck giving instruction to his manager,
Tony La Russa, on the importance of taking grand chances)

"Eddie, how would you like to be a big league ballplayer? Eddie, you'll be the only midget in the history of the game. You'll be appearing before thousands of people. Your name will go into the record books for all time. You'll be famous, Eddie. You'll be immortal."
—St. Louis Browns owner Bill Veeck, *Veeck as in Wreck*
(Veeck's account of midget Eddie Gaedel's 1951 at-bat in
his first autobiography)

"The hero of your story," Bill Murray told me several times during the summer, "is Mike Veeck." But it is also, in many ways, the story of Mike's father, baseball legend Bill Veeck.

The late Bill Veeck, peg-leg promoter (he lost his appendage at Bougainville in the South Pacific during World War II), is literally in the air at Midway Stadium. When patrons enter, they pass a large mural of the park that features the kindly visage of Bill Veeck on a cloud, looking down benificently. From the press box, a blown-up image of his last cover on *Sports Illustrated* hangs over the mantel, an icon from the seventies when Bill Veeck's face, aided by decades of bleacher sun and four packs of cigarettes a day, had taken on the well-hewn countours of the moon's Tranquility Base. His ashes rest in a Folgers coffee can near Mike's office phone.

With that in mind, then, it makes perfect sense that every day during baseball's summer, Mike, derided by his enemies as a madman, will take a walk through the outfield to have a talk with his father, who died in 1986. Today in late spring the subject is Strawberry, and Mike has agreed to let me walk with him for a while.

"My dad wore the jacket, took the blame for me, in 1979 after 'Disco Demolition Night' at Comiskey Park," Mike now says, recalling the defining moment of his life. "The White Sox had to forfeit the next game, which was one of the few times in the entire history of baseball that a game was forfeited. Big deal."

But it was. Since 1876 there, in fact, have been 20 forfeits—out of over 147,000 major league games played. " 'Disco Demolition Night' was the only spot on Dad's half-century of good vibes in baseball," says Mike. "If I hadn't planned 'Disco Night,' they probably would have put my dad in the Hall of Fame while he was still alive and could enjoy it, instead of waiting five years after he died."

Still, Bill Veeck did make baseball's Hall of Fame, enshrined in Cooperstown, New York, with a couple hundred of immortals among the over 13,000 or so who've darkened a major league field or boardroom over the last century. His plaque in the actual Hall might tell the story even better than his autobiographies, reading:

BILL VEECK
OWNER OF INDIANS, BROWNS, AND WHITE SOX
CREATED FAN INTEREST AT EVERY STOP WITH INGENIOUS
PROMOTIONAL SCHEMES LIKE FAN PARTICIPATION, EXPLODING
SCOREBOARD, OUTRAGEOUS DOOR PRIZES, NAMES ON UNIFORMS.
SET MAJOR LEAGUE ATTENDANCE RECORD WITH PENNANT WINNER
AT CLEVELAND IN 1948. WON AGAIN WITH "GO-GO" SOX IN 1959.
SIGNED AMERICAN LEAGUE'S FIRST BLACK PLAYER, LARRY DOBY, IN 1947
AND OLDEST ROOKIE, FORTY-TWO-YEAR-OLD SATCHEL PAIGE, IN 1948.
A CHAMPION OF THE LITTLE GUY.

"Dad *was* a champion of the little guy, and it's great that they put that on his plaque," his son says. Mike then stops walking in the outfield. "But 'Disco Night' *was* my fault. It was my idea, with the help of some others not working for the White Sox. I got Dad to approve it, but he had no idea what 'Disco Night' was. The second the riot started, I knew my life was over. But Dad loved me so much that he took the blame for me. No one believed him, of course—it was his fuckup kid's fault—and when Dad sold the White Sox not long after, no baseball team would touch me. They thought I was the nut son."

The irony of this all is that "The Disco Demolition Riot" of 1979 has come to be properly seen historically as a great defining end to a ridiculous and violent decade. Documentaries on the seventies routinely end with footage of Mike Veeck's "Disco Demolition Night" run amuck, and the Rock and Roll Hall of Fame in Cleveland shows film from the insurrection as the symbolic conclusion to the counter-culture's version of the "Me Decade."

"The 1970s created a whole army of middle class stoners who were leading dissolute 1960s lifestyles, but shorn of any political or social idealism," says Jonathan Alter, now a *Newsweek* columnist and Senior Editor, who, immediately after graduating college, spent much of that fateful summer of 1979 unemployed in Chicago. "Five years later in the 1980s, [that army was] making good money, wearing yellow ties and maybe in substance abuse recovery," Alter continues. "And if they were there that night [for Disco Demolition Night] they brag about it the way my grandfather bragged about seeing Babe Ruth's 'called shot' at Wrigley Field in the 1930s. I'm sure 500,000 Chicagoans say they were at Comiskey Park that night [in 1979]. Each year, as the legend grows, another 50,000 'were there.'"

But none of "Disco's" social import mattered to Mike because he had been ruined for baseball, blackballed by those who don't approve of men in their twenties getting major league games forfeited. He may have provided the pictures for the end of the decade, but no one who mattered would ever hire him again.

"People these days think I'm in baseball right now because my name is Veeck," Mike says. "But I'm actually in baseball *despite* the name Veeck. The fans loved my father, but organized baseball, the other owners, all hated Bill Veeck. He wrote two books—*Veeck as in Wreck* and *The Hustler's Handbook*—where he made fun by name of the people who controlled baseball, and they never forgave him his apostasy.

"My father died absolutely broke, and I think that's great," Mike continues. "Our last conversation in 1986 was about buying another team. When he realized baseball would never let him and his carnival of investors back one more time, that the game was over for him, he died. Still, even with no dough, he'd come up at the end of his life, he thought, with a way to buy a major league team."

But that was 1986. Today baseball may still be quaintly called "the American pastime," but basketball and football are the sports that more people watch and buy overpriced merchandise for. Lagging far behind, boring baseball has at last realized that they should have long ago listened to Bill Veeck's idea of sports as Showtime.

I walk away so Mike can have some time alone in the outfield of Midway Stadium with his father. It's really a monologue on Mike's progress and setbacks, his ups and downs, his concerns about the team, and his questions of Dad, about what *he* would do if he were in Mike's shoes.

"Should I sign Darryl Strawberry? Nobody, and I mean *nobody,* wants him. But we've heard some good reports, and the Saints would be his last chance. My gut says no, leave him alone, we don't need the bad press if it screws up. Would *you* have signed Darryl Strawberry?"

In his day, Bill Veeck had championed beauty—he is the one who as a young man planted ivy on Wrigley Stadium's outfield walls when his own father, Mike's grandfather William, was president of the Chicago Cubs. He also enjoyed dissonant cacophony—Bill Veeck was the man responsible for the late announcer Harry Caray belting out "Take Me Out to the Ball Game" over the Comiskey Park PA system during every seventh-inning stretch in Chicago.

But most of all, Bill Veeck had always liked taking last, desperate chances, especially with the despised and outcast. In 1944, three years before Jackie Robinson appeared in the major leagues, Bill Veeck, according to legend, almost bought the Philadelphia Phillies in order to stock them entirely with members of the Negro League. Later he signed Doby and Paige.

In 1951, he'd sent a three-foot-seven-inch man to bat for the St. Louis Browns. And he was forever on the lookout for a woman who could throw a major league fastball.

Nonetheless, Mike wanted to know, would even Bill Veeck have signed Darryl Strawberry?

No answer.

"I don't think anybody needs to get real concerned about my mental health until Dad starts talking back," Mike says later.

When he got back to his agonizingly neat cubicle under the Saints' ballpark, Veeck took a phone call from financier Marv Goldklang, an owner of a tiny slice of the New York Yankees as well as a

business partner of Mike, Bill Murray, and filmmaker Van Schley in
several minor league teams, with the Saints serving as their flagship.

Mike keeps his doubts about Strawberry to himself at the moment,
despite the fact that Goldklang, a New Yorker whose hobby is scouting players with the tenacity of Sam Spade, had solid information
that Strawberry had definitely cleaned up over the winter.

The previous season had been hell for Strawberry as a New York
Yankee. He'd only batted eighty-seven times, and though the team
held a $1.8 million option on his next year, there was no way he'd
be kept. Meantime, Bob Watson made George Steinbrenner believe
that Strawberry sucked in the field and had grown into an aged
liability at the plate.

In December of 1995, Watson told Strawberry he was gone, and
the Yankees bought out his contract for $160,000. Holed up in his
mansion in Rancho Mirage, California, Strawberry said he would
quit rather than go begging for a job. This, despite the fact that he
still owed the IRS $100,000 for previous tax felonies and his ex-wife
wanted $300,000 in child support and Straw's ass in jail.

He'd contemplated suicide a couple times before, but now he only
felt anger as major league team after team refused his offer for a
cheap Darryl Strawberry. The Boston Red Sox were briefly interested,
but a newspaper campaign ignited a fan revolt, so there would be
no "Dar-ryl! Dar-ryl!" in Fenway Park.

Then tragedy struck in the off-season, a series of events that
seemed sure to send Darryl into another tailspin of drugs, destruction, and depression. His beloved agent Bill Goodstein, the only
father figure in his life, died of a heart attack. Then, weeks later,
Ruby Strawberry, his mother for whom he'd give his own life, died of
breast cancer. Darryl drove ever inward. He kept going to Alcoholics
Anonymous, but he'd lost all interest in baseball.

Mexico, the home of outlaw baseball, was out—Strawberry's back
would never survive the long bus rides over the terrible roads, and
his own pride forbade the fall. And then Straw's new agent, Eric
Grossman, told him of the Northern League and made a few calls.
Interest was shown by the St. Paul Saints, in the form of Yankee
limited partner Marv Goldklang.

"Why should I play there?" Strawberry asked Bob Klapisch, an
East Coast reporter who'd called him about the idea of playing for
peanuts in St. Paul.

But Goldklang, through sources only he knew, had it that Darryl
was straight and, with a little prodding, could be ready to play. With

Marv's connection to the Yankees, it would then only be a few conversations with George Steinbrenner before Darryl was back in New York, back where he belonged. Or so Marv thought.

As spring training ended, there was no hint that the New York Yankees would ever want to come near Strawberry again. "Where am I supposed to play him?" Bob Watson asked. "Where does Darryl Strawberry fit on this team?"

As the last days wound down before the Yankees headed north from Florida, Watson was asked one last time if he'd been thinking about Strawberry at all. "Strawberry? Oh sure, I've thought of Strawberry. Had strawberry shortcake for dinner last night. It was good too."

Goldklang, however, had never stopped thinking about Straw. Still, Mike wasn't convinced. Didn't Marv understand the ramifications for the team if Strawberry messed up in St. Paul?

"Yes. Don't worry, Mike. It'll work."

Mike was still thinking no that afternoon when he was driving to Owatonna, Minnesota, to give a Saints sales speech, accompanied by his wife Libby and the voice of Marv Goldklang coming over the cellular phone. It was Libby, the mother of their three-year-old child Rebecca, who had stood by her man Mike when they couldn't afford to pay their bills, when Mike would write hundreds of unanswered letters over the years to baseball teams begging for a job, any job. And it had been the usually conservative and button-down Goldklang who was one of the people who'd officially offered Mike his long-hungered-for return gig to baseball in 1990 with the minor league Miami Miracle. Now he was telling Mike that Darryl Strawberry was worth all his carry-on baggage for an independent team like the Saints.

Goldklang had already spoken with Eric Grossman, Strawberry's agent, and determined that the ballplayer was also serious about starting over for an independent team like the St. Paul Saints. "It won't be a publicity stunt," Goldklang said. "It will be his last chance to prove to other teams that he can make it back to the major leagues."

"But what if something goes wrong?" Mike fretted aloud. It had taken baseball almost twenty years to forgive him for "Disco Demolition Night." Even "Disco Night," at the time, sounded like a much safer promotional event than giving Darryl Strawberry an arena in which to fuck up one last time.

Mike Veeck and Marv Goldklang
Courtesy of Neal Karlen

"No," he finally said to Marv. Mike did not want to be the only man on the planet willing to give Strawberry a second chance.

Goldklang hung up after offering parting thoughts that Strawberry was as close to being blackballed from professional baseball as any man could be.

"That word 'blackball' hit me right between the eyes," Mike recalled.

Mike turned to his wife and told her Goldklang's final words.

" 'Blackballed,' " repeated Mike's wife. "Aren't you doing to Strawberry exactly what was done to you?"

Her thought stopped Mike. "It wasn't like Saul getting knocked to the ground by God's words to him in the Old Testament," he

said, "but it was a pretty clear revelation. I realized that what I was
doing to Darryl was what everyone had done to me all those years
when I not only couldn't get a job, but couldn't get anybody in
baseball to even listen to my side of the story. Now, here I was,
turning around and doing just that to somebody else."

"Disco Demolition Night" had started innocently enough in
Mike's brain back in the late 1970s, when his father owned the
Chicago White Sox and Mike was the team's director of promotions.
He had paid some dues, but Mike was born to the baseball manor.
He'd literally grown up in an apartment located in the bowels of
Sportsman's Park when Bill Veeck owned the St. Louis Browns. Mike
had used the stadium's bullpen as his sandbox.

Still, Mike didn't much know his father before he himself was an
adult and went to work for the White Sox. When Mike was a child
and young adult, Bill Veeck was mostly away running his circuses.
But when Mike was twenty-five, Bill Veeck invited his son to work
for him on the last baseball team he would ever own. Mike would
begin at the bottom, his beloved father told him, where Bill Veeck's
own father had set him to work with the Chicago Cubs in the 1920s.

Until then Mike had spent the previous three years since college,
where he graduated last in his class from Loyola of Baltimore, traveling the country with a rock band. Mike remembers becoming an
expert gin drinker and developing a deep antipathy for disco music.

"My band would be playing something in a bar, then somebody
would put KC and the Sunshine Band on the jukebox and everybody
listening to us would go dance to that. I just hated disco."

But he was intrigued by the idea of going to work for his father.
A deal was consummated in Chicago after an all-day binge of drinking between father and son, a common way for Bill Veeck to do
business as he flicked cigarette ashes into the ashtray he'd built into
his peg leg.

"Dad and I went to lunch one day at eleven A.M., sauced all day,
and at eleven at night he finally asked me if I wanted to come work
with him in Chicago," Mike remembers. "I said okay. Neither of us
were drunk. Back in those days, the fact that you could drink all
day and not get loaded was the mark of a good drinker. I was
brought up that you didn't drink six beers and get goofy—you drank
six hundred beers and kept it together enough for cogent talk. Conversation—smart conversation—was always very important to my
father. He was amazingly literate. Every day when he was soaking

his leg stump for hours, he'd read history, literature, philosophy, everything."

They were wild drinking days in Chicago, and in time Mike hoisted many with a menagerie of talents, including Billy Murray, a then-anonymous actor with the Second City theater troupe located across the alley from many of the hippest joints in town.

Mike began selling White Sox ticket packages door to door. When he wasn't learning how to sell, he was cleaning Comiskey Park's bathrooms. When he wasn't sweeping, he was watching in awe as his father operated a major league baseball team. "Working for my father was a graduate school in fun, not sports marketing. That's why one of the Saints' slogans is 'Fun Is Good.' There is something intrinsically healing about fun."

The best ideas for promotions, Bill Veeck taught his son, "were things that intrigued ourselves. He wasn't looking to sucker people like P. T. Barnum—he hated when people compared him to Barnum. Instead, we acted as if we were our own customers. If we thought up a promotion that didn't make him laugh or me laugh, then we wouldn't try it."

Then, in 1976, Mike planted the seeds of "Disco Demolition Night." Drinking with Jeff Schwartz, a local record company executive and pal, they came up with an idea for a promotion at the ballpark that was purely for 100 percent rock & roll fans.

It wasn't until 1979, three years later, that the idea bore fruit. A local Chicago deejay and hipster agitator named Steve Dahl blew up a disco record on the air of WLUP, a tiny radio station with five thousand watts and probably far fewer listeners. "Afterward," Mike remembers, "Jeff Schwartz called me up and said, 'Hey, remember that night a few years ago when we talked about a night at the ballpark for fans of pure rock & roll? Well, why don't we have an antidisco night?' "

"That," remembers Mike, "sounded like great fun to me."

A group of collaborators under Mike's direction and Dahl's choreography came together in the coming weeks to plan for the big night of July 12, 1979. The general idea would be to collect disco records brought by fans, who would be granted 98 cent admission that night to the ballpark in exchange for their copy of the much-loathed music. "I thought to myself, 'It would be funny to blow up the albums on the field between games of a doubleheader,' " Mike adds.

Bill Veeck, meantime, had no idea what Mike's antidisco crusade meant. Bill was an old man then and wouldn't have understood the inner evil of KC and the Sunshine Band. "He didn't okay it, because he didn't know what disco was," says Mike. "I take full responsibility. One of the great ironies is that the week before the promotion, my dad did a radio ad for the White Sox station talking about the antidisco night, and when he got off the air, he asked me, 'Mike, what *is* this? What are you *doing?*'"

Mike reassured his father that it was nothing, just a little promotion that he guaranteed would draw 35,000 fans, an unheard-of number for a Thursday night twinight doubleheader against the Detroit Tigers. "That day there were thirty-five thousand people lined up outside the stadium by three o'clock in the afternoon," Mike remembers. "I felt like a genius. I was patting myself on the back for this great idea."

Over 60,000 fans went through the Comiskey Park turnstiles that night, with another 40,000 left outside. Traffic was jammed up all the way back to O'Hare Airport, and Mike felt like he had succeeded like no one short of his father. Still, he remembers a sense of foreboding.

"There was more dope smoke in that stadium before the game than at any other place in the city," he remembers. "The air was just heavy. You knew something was going to happen."

Indeed. What happened was the most spectacular promotional failure in major league baseball history, "Dime Beer Night" at Cleveland's Municipal Stadium notwithstanding. After a few innings, several hundred in the audience began whipping their albums like Frisbees, instead of holding on to them for the big disco bonfire and explosion. The game had to be stopped several times to clear records off the field, and the Detroit Tigers' Ron LeFlore had a golf ball thrown at him.

But this was only the warm-up. Between games, a buxom fire goddess dubbed Loreli ignited the records in a great explosion. Suddenly seven thousand fans were scaling walls and on the field, running wild, stoned, and amuck.

Bill Veeck himself, who hated to ever take the field, was so mortified by the scene that he hobbled down, wooden leg and all, and pleaded with the rioters over a microphone to go back in the stands. Announcer Harry Caray tried to calm the crowd, to no avail. At last, a squadron of Chicago police in full-helmeted riot gear cleared the field and arrested fifty of the worst offenders.

Dave Phillips, the umpire in charge, quickly decided that the field was too beat up to play the second game. Within twenty-four hours,

Lee MacPhail, the president of the American League, granted Detroit one of the few forfeits in baseball history.

Bill Veeck, who had always counted on the benificence of the ordinary fan, was shattered. "I'm shocked, amazed, and chagrined," Bill Veeck said sadly, taking the blame.

Up in the broadcast booth, however, White Sox announcer Jimmy Piersall was laying the blame directly on Veeck the Younger. The two had tangled before, after Piersall had called Mike's mother, Mary Frances, a "colossal bore," and the two had argued. Some say Mike challenged Piersall to a fight.

Piersall had gained fame in the book *Fear Strikes Out* as a talented Red Sox ballplayer who nursed a nervous breakdown in a mental hospital in 1952; a biopic with the same title was filmed in 1957 starring Anthony Perkins. Decades after he was institutionalized, Piersall still liked to say, "I'm crazy, and I've got the papers to prove it." Now, even before "Disco Night," Piersall went so far as to say young Mike came up from behind him and tried to sucker-punch him for insulting Mike's mother.

Whatever. Jimmy Piersall's verdict on "Disco Demolition Night" was the verdict of the people of Chicago. "I knew my life was over the second that first guy shimmied down the outfield wall," Mike says. Not since Frank Sinatra, Jr., had one fucked up so magnificently at his father's profession.

Bill Murray, up in Canada shooting *Meatballs,* looked at the DISCO DEMOLITION RIOT headlines in his paper and shook his head in amazement. "It was in every paper in the world, and I thought, 'Jeez, Mike, that was *big!*'"

Murray thinks back. "Back then, they weren't even playing rock & roll in baseball parks. I mean, people everywhere were saying, 'I can't dance to disco,' but to then go so far as to blow up records in a stadium as a way to say that disco should be despised? Whoa, Mike!"

When his father sold the team, Mike had the surest one-way ticket to Palookaville that baseball could offer. Screw up in the big leagues like Mike, no matter who your father is, and you're out. Bill Veeck would die five years before being elected to the Hall of Fame and seasons before the public redemption of his son.

It was impossible for me *not* to relate to Mike's fucking up. Ten years before, I'd been writing cover stories for fancy magazines in New York, perhaps not a wunderkind, but living in a fancy two-bedroom co-op on the Upper West Side of New York with my fiancée, an executive and beloved girlfriend of five years.

Then, one Saturday night in 1989, I was mugged while walking home alone from a swank New York party. Hearing footsteps, I turned and was met by two crackheads who proceeded to kick the living shit out of me, beating their fists against my face, breaking my glasses, then throwing me into the path of an armada of speeding taxis on Columbus Avenue.

Within days, I'd gone temporarily nuts. In any case, in those few short days after I was beaten, I crazily tossed away my future with my fiancée, my home, and much of the goodwill I'd built up as a nice guy in my decade in the sharky waters of New York's media community.

In shame, I moved back to Minneapolis. I wrote almost nothing in *Rolling Stone* for the year after I moved home to Minnesota, choosing to disappear into my hometown, a spot in nowheresville that almost nobody in New York or Los Angeles even cared existed. Bearing an Everest of high-living-in-Manhattan debt, I moved into a furnished residence hotel in Minneapolis with lime-green carpeting and wished myself invisible.

Mike Veeck, meantime lost his first marriage and custody of his son William, also known legally as "Night Train." He then drank his way to Florida, where he spent lost years hanging drywall, swilling booze, berating himself for "Disco Demolition Night."

The low moment, Mike says, was before he met Libby, when he was pulled over drunk by a policeman in some town in Florida. Mike was so obviously fried and broke "that the officer decided just to send me home and let me try and find fare for the cabbie. For the next half an hour, I was on my knees in my house, looking for the nickels and dimes to pay the guy off. That was my bottom."

The next day Mike looked up Alcoholics Anonymous in the phone book and began a regimen where he went to 263 meetings in ninety days. In the end, it wasn't for him. "I needed the temple of baseball to survive, not AA," Veeck says.

So he'd have a single beer now and then. But no hard liquor—ever. And he worked at pulling his life together, getting a job at a Florida advertising agency while he continued to write letters to every team in Organized Baseball.

"All he wanted was one more chance," says his wife, Libby, "but Mike had been blackballed. I think it broke his heart."

Tough, said the elders of baseball.

One day in 1989, California documentary filmmaker Van Schley and Roland Hemond happened to be on the same charter flight to scout ballplayers in Florida. Hemond, who, helping to run the 1998 expansion Arizona Diamondbacks, had for years been Bill Veeck's general manager and is still a major heavyweight in baseball circles. Hemond loved Bill Veeck; in *People* magazine in 1976 he said, "Veeck knows everything there is to know about running a baseball team. He can count a big stack of tickets just by riffing through them with his thumb. He can tell you what kind of grass you ought to have in the outfield. He can tell you what pitch a pitcher is having trouble with."

But Bill Veeck was dead, and Hemond was sitting next to Schley, whose avocation was scouting ballplayers and owning independent minor league teams with his partners, Marv Goldklang and Bill Murray. The group had just bought a real stinker: the Miami Miracle, an unaffiliated team that was drawing bupkes. The team needed someone new to actually run it. Did Roland Hemond, Van Schley asked, know of any baseball men who might be willing to take on a virtually impossible task?

Hemond thought. He'd stayed in contact with the Veeck family and had recently learned that Mike had at last cleaned up his act in a nine-to-five world. He also knew that Mike's mailbox remained empty, at least in terms of job offers from organized baseball.

"Mike Veeck," Roland Hemond said, one baseball man to a layperson trying to learn.

"Okay," Van said, "Mike Veeck."

When Marv Goldklang called Mike to offer him the job, for $20,000, of running one of the worst baseball teams in existence, Mike thought it was a practical joke and hung up. When Marv called again, Mike was back.

Before his speech in Owatonna, Veeck called Marv back on his cell phone. If Mike's own sources in baseball told him that Strawberry was sober and serious, he was willing to give the ballplayer his chance. Calling around, Mike placed a great deal of trust in the opinions of Tom Keegan, the *New York Post*'s national baseball beat writer renowned for his deep-throat locker room sources and honest appraisals of who was up and who was dying. He also called Peter Richmond, a writer for *GQ* who he'd befriended and whose insights he respected.

According to Keegan and Richmond and others, Strawberry was okay. The cure had seemed to work this time, and the born-again

stuff looked real, unlike in '91 when Darryl had first tried to pull
that "Praise Jesus" stuff.

Enough said.

"I want Darryl Strawberry to be a St. Paul Saint," Mike finally
said. "I want him to go back to the majors and hit a great home
run for everybody who ever needed a second chance in life."

However, there would be no spring training for the Northern
League's number one fan, a title St. Paul's Bill Tyler held not just
because he ran the unsanctioned Northern League online fan guide.
Being the number one fan was a gig with no vacations, for even
in the off-season, Tyler had to constantly update the frighteningly
comprehensive web page for the league's devoted.

Yet it was when the season began that Tyler would truly bloom. A
thirtiesh, bearded computer programmer, he smuggled into Midway
Stadium each game one man's band worth of airhorns, bells, and
triangles, a nice homage to the Brooklyn Dodgers Symphony of decades past. While making his cacophony, Tyler would simultaneously
keep written score of every pitched ball, listen to the game on the
radio over headphones, and engage in a nonstop patter of statistics
and anecdotes with the dozens who came for an audience with the
league's most fanatic follower.

Surprisingly, Tyler had a life. And a wife. Indeed, the only Saints
game he'd ever missed was for his wedding. His spouse Noreen was
an artist, so she was grateful to get him out of the house for those
hours and paint uninterrupted for blocks of time. "This is my
art," he said of his role as the league's number one fan, "that is
her art."

3

Strawberry the Elephant Man

Faith, You gotta have faith.
You know, they say time heals all wounds,
And I don't quite agree with that a hundred percent.
It gets you to cope with wounds.
You carry them for the rest of your life.
—Phil Rizzuto, "Prayer for the Captain"
  (Pregame show, August 3, 1979, New York Yankees against
  the Baltimore Orioles, after the death of Thurman Munson)

May 15, 1996

With a few words from his wife, Libby, Mike's gut instinct on
Darryl Strawberry had turned. "We're a baseball team based on the
idea that nothing heals like laughter, and that everybody deserves a
second chance, and that if the Saints can make Darryl enjoy baseball
again, he will succeed, as we all will."

But what was funny about Darryl Strawberry?

"My father always said that there is nothing so beautiful as scar
tissue," Mike said repeatedly in response to some of the various
things that Darryl Strawberry had been charged with and convicted
of in the past. "Scar tissue" was one thing that Darryl Strawberry
had in tremendous supply. But would Saints fans buy it? Veeck knew
that Straw would be a hard sell to a city that is still overwhelmingly
churchgoing and parochial, where not everybody in town has experienced a felon from the hardscrabble streets of the worst ghetto in
Los Angeles.

And yet they were a people used to healing and to laughter.

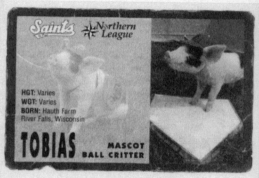

This was a city with a team where the rally song, played over the loudspeaker whenever the Saints were behind in the late innings, was Sammy Davis, Jr.'s, version of "Theme from Shaft." A trained pig named Tobias delivered fresh baseballs to the umpire, and patrons could get a haircut or massage while comfortably watching the game from the stands.

Mike's promotions since he helped found the team in 1993 have been constant and ridiculous. When Veeck realized that both Babe Ruth and Elvis Presley died on the same day in August, he marked the anniversary at a stadium event called "Two Dead Fat Guys Night."

Later he threw a promotion called "Say Hey Tommy Night," when a psychic at home plate attempted to contact Thomas Edison to thank him for his advances in electricity, which made night baseball possible.

And so, here on this bush league Elba, populated by players nobody wants, Mike had turned the St. Paul Saints into what *The New York Times* termed "the funkiest team in baseball." They have also been among the most successful, selling out Midway Stadium for every game, setting short-season minor league attendance records, and earning millions in profit for their owners.

So hip is the venue that the Twin Cities' most popular bands vied for the honor of playing "The Star-Spangled Banner" before games. Here the PA piped in punk rock from the Ramones and stadium announcer Mike Haiduck announced half the game in a boozy Harry Caray voice. ("Whiskey hands!" Mike/Harry would grumble if a fan dropped a foul ball.)

Still, there were major obstacles to the Saints' success beyond playing in a league for scrubeenies. The largest problem loomed right across the river in Minneapolis, where the major league Minnesota Twins played. But the Twins played inside the Hubert Horatio Humphrey Metrodome, which was not just your normally sterile dome stadium in the country—it was *oppressively* sterile. During the summer on Minnesota's rare golden days, going inside to watch baseball seemed depressing, sad, pathetic, and very expensive.

Thousands of fans in the Upper Northwest had boycotted baseball altogether since the Metrodome was built in 1981. There was much talk that the Twins might very well be leaving town when their lease ran up in 1999, but few seemed to care.

Enter the St. Paul Saints in 1993, playing baseball on real grass under the sun and stars at tiny Midway Stadium. To fill those 6,329 seats, Veeck realized, he had to make St. Paul proud enough to shell out $7 for his team's highest-priced ticket (bleachers are $3).

"St. Paul needed healing," he said. "It's always been the less glamorous, publicized, and populous of the Twin Cities. It's always had an inferiority complex toward Minneapolis because it's smaller and less noticed. St. Paul needed healing too, so it was the perfect spot for our team. Minneapolis doesn't respect us, but that's okay—we'll make our own fun if they are ridiculing us."

To put it mildly. In Minneapolis, people tended to look at St. Paul the way people from Manhattan look at those who live in New Jersey. You actually *go* there?

St. Paul was seen by its twin city as a mutt town, which only made more fitting and appealing the mongrel Saints' players, who, though only paid an average of $1,100 a month, seemed to hustle and play harder than the lethargic and distant major league millionaires playing a few miles across the Mississippi.

Thus had it always been. In 1961, shortly after the Twins moved from Washington, *Sports Illustrated* headlined an article about the Minneapolis/St. Paul rivalry as NO FEUD LIKE AN OLD FEUD. The subheadline read simply: "Caught in the traditional animosity between St. Paul and Minneapolis, the Twins are open to box office trouble."

Of course, one blown-out knee in St. Paul's own Northern League, one fraction of a second lost in bat speed, and the players were back selling Slushies at 7-Eleven. There literally was no tomorrow for these ballplayers, and if Minneapolis didn't care, who cared?

Even the venerated Bill Veeck had ridiculed St. Paul. Veeck's first team was Milwaukee in the minor league American Association, a league he shared with the original St. Paul Saints in the early 1940s. While Bill Veeck prospered, St. Paul floundered. Milwaukee's owner couldn't help but notice how little money he made as his visitor's share when his team played in St. Paul.

To put more fans in St. Paul's seats, Mike's dad decided to start a feud that he revealed in *The Hustler's Handbook*, his second autobiography:

Promotionally, St. Paul had only one asset I could see: the blood rivalry with Minneapolis. I went on the radio in Minneapolis and blasted the city of St. Paul. I blasted their fans and their park and their bridges and their hotels and I expressed grave misgivings about their sewer system. I was going to have my young players stay at the Nicollet Hotel in fine Minneapolis and take them in and out of St. Paul by streetcar, preferably under cover of darkness. I have no intention of forcing my players to stay in St. Paul for one minute longer than is absolutely necessary.

The ploy worked, Bill Veeck reported. On Milwaukee's next trip to St. Paul, the stands had filled with citizens eager to boo the owner who disrespected their city in favor of Minneapolis.

But these days in St. Paul, joy reigned. Somehow, inside the walls of Midway Stadium, the constant and ridiculous promotions didn't feel like a geek show, but an old-time carnival. Best of all, it also felt like baseball, the old-fashioned way. "There were the fans who had forgotten what it felt like to watch baseball outdoors," Mike said. "They also needed healing."

A couple times when both teams were in town, the Saints even outdrew the Twins in their 55,000-capacity stadium across the river. Somehow Mike with his litter of runts had understood the equation that his father expressed as follows:

Baseball's unique possession, the real source of our strength, is the fan's memory of the times his daddy took him to the game to see the great players of his youth. Whether he remembers it or not, the excitement of those hours, the step they represented in his own growth, and the part those afternoons—even one afternoon—played in his relationship with his father are bound up in his feeling toward the local ballclub and toward the game.

Mike had recaptured that feeling for people in St. Paul with laughter, and the major league Twins had not. And now the Minnesota Twins were dying.

The laughter had helped the Saints make the second chances they promised. Most notable of the Saints' early outcasts was Leon "Bull" Durham, a former slugging star with the Chicago Cubs who'd lost the tail end of his career to two cocaine-related charges. Durham, tested for cocaine twice a week during the Saints' season, thrived with the team, quickly became a crowd favorite, and went on to a successful career as a minor league coach. More recently, the Saints had nearly signed the newly drug-free Dwight Gooden, but then New York Yankee owner George Steinbrenner had decided that he would try and be Gooden's personal savior.

But Darryl Strawberry? Mike would have to gear up to sell him. He would have to talk like he'd never talked before, and Mike often didn't like to talk. In fact, the president of the St. Paul Saints could be as silent as a monk for long stretches of time. However, he would then start yelling. Mike lives on another planet and is proud of it.

"Of course I do," he says. "Everyone who works for our merry band of misfits doesn't fit in anywhere but the Saints."

"The first time you meet Mike Veeck, you get the idea there's something definitely not right with him," Bill Murray said later in the summer. "He goes from zero to a hundred decibels in one second. And then he's silent for five hours. When we drive away together to away games, we just throw tapes in the cassette deck and keep silent the entire ride."

Not once, Murray said, had Mike asked him how he planned to play his father in the upcoming movie of *Veeck as in Wreck*, a role Mike asked Murray to take. "He trusts me"—with a sarcastic wink—"which is his first mistake.

"The first time I'd seen him in the years since 'Disco Demolition Night,'" Murray went on, "was when he was hired to run this team we had in Pompano Beach, Florida. Mike had had a great gig with the White Sox and lost it, and I knew he'd been wracking himself over the coals ever since that night in 1979. Now all I knew was that he had been hanging drywall for years and trying to get back into baseball, like some guy trying to break into show business.

"So I didn't know what to expect when I dropped in on the club's office in Pompamo Beach for the first time. I walk in, sit down, and there's this complete airhead woman sitting there, not blinking, and laughing madly, 'Heh-heh-heh!'

" 'Say, does Mike Veeck come around?' I asked.

" 'Heh-heh-heh'—she laughed madly—'check the bleachers.' "

Murray pauses. "And I'm thinking, 'If this is who Mike has hired, what could he be like now?' So I walked onto the field, and there was Mike Veeck, sitting alone in the bleachers, kind of talking to himself, and outlining plans and plotting promotions on a piece of a paper. He looked either like a very strange man . . . or a genius."

Murray hung around that night with him for the Miracle ball game and was appalled at the shape of his team, the team that Mike had just been hired to run. "They had nothing," remembers Murray. "No players, no fans, no excitement. All they had was this dog, Jericho, that Mike had found that would race little kids around the basepaths between innings, always just losing by an inch. It was magic. It was golden. With that dog, we had something to work with, and Mike started his comeback. He had gold out of which to spin more gold."

Silence had always appealed to Mike. One of the few promotions of Mike's at Midway Stadium that didn't work was "Mime Night," when pantomimists from the local college of art and design did instant replays on the field. They were pelted with hot dogs. "I didn't know that Minnesotans hated mimes," Mike said at the time.

But now he would have to strategize on how to pitch Straw to St. Paul and Greater Minnesota. Mike, sometimes a quiet and reflective thinker, other times a gregarious and outspoken showman, would try and convince the local media and the good family folks of Lake Woebegone that he wasn't bringing Satan to town.

Meantime, Darryl was fretting about joining the Saints at his home in Rancho Mirage, California, a desert retreat heavy on celebrities that he bought when he had two dimes to rub together, where one of his neighbors was Stubby Kaye, the ancient round comic who sang "Sit Down, You're Rockin' the Boat" in *Guys and Dolls*. Darryl Strawberry continued to have his own doubts about joining the Saints. Eric Grossman tried to convince him it was his last place to showcase his perhaps age-eroded talents.

Grossman told of the camera crews that would surely follow him around as Strawberry blasted 500-foot home runs off pathetic Northern League pitching and reinforced the fact that there was no place else to go—not even Japan, where its rules of ballplayer decorum and past history would torch Darryl Strawberry. Finally Grossman called upon several sports reporters from New York who Strawberry knew to try and get him to go to St. Paul for one last shot.

"Okay," Strawberry finally said, "I'll go. Because if this is the end, I want to end it my way."

"Okay," Marv Goldklang said to Eric Grossman. And so, at a salary of $2,000 a month, Strawberry would have a place to play. True, he still owed several hundred thousand dollars in child and spousal support payments, but if he succeeded with the Saints, he conceivably might be soon making major league money again.

In the Northern League, he would be tested three times a week for drug use during the season, a process that would be supervised by his probation officer. If any team in Organized Baseball wanted to sign Strawberry while he played for the Saints, he would be free to leave, with the Saints receiving only $3,000 in recompensation.

With that, Darryl Strawberry found his way out of the desert. He was coming to St. Paul. "Darryl," said Mike, "stands for everybody who ever needed one last chance."

May 3, 1996

Patrick Reusse, the most powerful sportswriter in the Midwest, waddled into Darryl Strawberry's press conference with his trademark smirk atop a multi-chinned face, a surreal vision of the Michelin Man on a very bad day. Reusse had publicly despised Mike Veeck and the St. Paul Saints since the team had been reborn in 1993, and his presence at this event could only mean no good for the team.

In his sports column in the pages of the Minneapolis *Star Tribune*, Reusse often wrote of his ongoing recovery from alcoholism, an occupational hazard of late-middle-aged reporters who'd traveled with too many ball teams for too many seasons. Boozing was what reporters *did*, the only way to simultaneously pass the tedium of endless afternoons in hotels in Cleveland and push away the nightly pressure of banging out halfway accurate game gibberish for tomorrow morning's newspaper.

While a cub reporter, I'd seen Patrick Reusse at what I believed was his drunken, meanest, most vile worst. It was spring training,

1984, and I witnessed him cruelly mock for the amusement of a gaggle of other cackling beat sportswriters the tortured on-field contortions of a young Minnesota Twins outfielder named Jim Eisenreich. At the time, everyone in baseball thought Eisenreich was a head case comparable to Jimmy Piersall or a young man with the worst case of on-field stage fright that any sportswriter had ever seen.

In fact, Eisenreich's on-field spasms and hyperventilations weren't caused by nerves, it turned out later, but by an undiagnosed case of Tourette's syndrome. The ballplayer eventually recovered his career, but I'll never forget the look of unrestrained bully on Patrick Reusse's beet-red face as he mocked at Jim Eisenreich's torment.

Since then, Reusse had publicly gone dry. He'd also grown obese, immense, a circus fat man with a poison pen. His own problems had not made Patrick Reusse any more kind to those of others; his columns grew ever more vicious after he was sober.

No one was sure why Patrick hated Mike Veeck and the St. Paul Saints so much. He was what was called in the sobriety movement a "dry drunk"—someone who didn't drink, but still acted as cruelly as if he did. Rumors in the Saints' press box also had it that the old sportswriter had once been at odds with Bill Veeck and was now taking a feud with a father out on the son. Others simply surmised that Reusse enjoyed the lavish complimentary buffet offered reporters by the Twins (reporters covering the Saints might get a bag of peanuts, a Coke, and a slice of pizza if they were lucky).

In Reusse's columns, the president of the Saints was called "Smug Mike." One Christmas, he named Mike a close contender for Turkey of the Year in his annual award to the biggest idiot on the local sports scene. What the Saints played wasn't even baseball, Reusse declared, it was "budgetball"—a kind of indentured servitude in which used-up players were brought together for Arby's-style wages, mainly as an excuse to sell watery beer to drunken yahoos who thought they were watching actual baseball.

"Reusse doesn't bother me, because I was hatcheted by the best after 'Disco Demolition Night' in Chicago," Mike said. "How do you compare Reusse as a writer putting you down when the great Mike Royko is calling you the city's Anti-Christ?" But Reusse's slams did hurt Mike, and he kept his columns thumbtacked to his bulletin board.

There were other local slights, such as one from Andy MacPhail.

A third-generation baseball man, Andy MacPhail was a respected major league executive, the Twins' brains, and he would soon move on to run the Chicago Cubs, a job which many in the Veeck family felt was their family birthright dating back to grandfather William's tenure as team president in the 1920s. Meantime, according to Andy, Mike had only his "beer league."

Those words bothered Mike for years. When *The New York Times* would later ask him about a team and a league that would dare sign Darryl Strawberry, he replied, "It has pained me over the years to have the kind of baseball we play here criticized. I really don't think that it's fair to assume that a player of [Strawberry's] caliber would want to play in what people have called a 'beer league.' "

It gnawed at Mike that that kind of casual disrespect from the major leaguers in Minneapolis was the norm during the Saints' first couple of years in town. And Patrick Reusse, as the most powerful and entertaining poison pen in the grander of the Twin Cities, took up on the side of Andy MacPhail and the major league types in the cheerless Hubert Horatio Humphrey Metrodome across the Mississippi.

And so, over the years, Patrick Reusse kept hammering away at Mike Veeck, aka "Mr. Smug," who he also accused of being a pathological liar (he isn't). Because of Mr. Smug, he wrote, "budgetball came to St. Paul, and Twin Citians found another asphalt strip on which to overindulge. After proper lubrication, the fans advance inside and drink some more. With all this lubrication, they are loose enough to laugh at stale jokes."

"Stale jokes"? Mike? The man who threw "Two Dead Fat Guys Night"?

"I am in favor of cheap theatrics, yes," Mike said. "But that 'stale jokes' thing hurt."

So it was with no cheer that the Saints' brass saw Reusse at their press conference to introduce Darryl Strawberry.

Mike, seated in a room near Midway Stadium, introduced Strawberry to the gathered press with a few words. Careful not to sound like a Barnum trying to get 'em in the tent with a publicity stunt, Mike pointed to the seated Straw and spoke simply, quietly, and humbly of his own redemption.

"Having spent quite a number of days in an AA program myself, I admit that my opinion is very personal. I can simply say that we're here to have fun, and hopefully Darryl can have some fun on the way back to the major leagues. I would also like to apologize to Darryl for judging him before I knew him. I, of all people and with my history, should have known better."

Darryl, dressed in a black-and-white three-piece suit with pearl-buttoned collar, arose from his seat next to manager Marty Scott. "Gooood afternoon," Straw said humorously, but no one laughed.

After thanking Mike, he said simply, "Playing for the Saints is an opportunity for me to play baseball. Even if I don't get back to the major leagues, at least the end of my career would have been my decision."

A photograph of Darryl trying on a Saints baseball cap at the press conference ran deep inside in the next morning's *New York Times*, accompanied by the headline STRAWBERRY "BLACKBALLED." All he got was a blurb:

Darryl Strawberry said yesterday he is looking forward to starting in right field for the independent St. Paul Saints. At a news conference in St. Paul, the former Met, Dodger, Giant, and Yankee said: "I believe major league baseball has black-balled me. I'm not bitter about it. I didn't really know I was going to play baseball again."

Patrick Reusse's opinion in the Minneapolis *Star Tribune* was a tad more pointed:

Last summer, when George Steinbrenner added Strawberry to the Yankees' lineup, he again was derided nationally and in New York as an egomaniac with a pathological need to get his name in headlines. This was merely a suspicion in the case of Veeck until Friday, when he proved he is Steinbrenner's soul mate in the ego department. . . . Does Darryl really think it is going to be easier for an aging ballplayer to resist the temptations when he has $500 per week in salary to blow when he sees those bright lights of Sioux City?

Mike, meantime, launched a highly animated counteroffensive, going on virtually any local television or radio show to defend the Saints signing Strawberry. On Minnesota Public Radio, Mike made literary remarks about the meaning of redemption. On WCCO, the 50,000-watt station that broadcast the Minnesota Twins across the entire Midwest, he told jokes, talked of the healing power of fun, and said there was no reason the Saints couldn't coexist peacefully with the Twins.

Mike also took to the road, enduring untold pieces of rubber chicken on a sports banquet circuit through the hinterlands to explain like a politician pushing a hard-sell piece of legislation. "Who amongst you hasn't needed a second chance like Darryl Strawberry?" he thundered, not like a sermonizing Billy Sunday, but with the goodwill tidings of a Reverend Robert Schuller.

Darryl, meantime, moved slowly and mechanically, like a robot in Disneyland's Hall of Presidents, afraid to say anything for fear of offending anybody. "No, I didn't mean to say baseball was black-balling me at the press conference," he said afterward, self-correcting without being asked. "What I meant to say was that I had blackballed myself from baseball."

For the rest of the summer, he would try and resort to the jive-ass clichés that he'd refused to resort to when playing in New York. Speaking his mind had only helped him get to St. Paul, and now he had become a master of saying nothing behind a shower of typical jock verbiage.

Still in his suit, Strawberry went with manager Marty Scott to Midway Stadium to check out the dimensions of his new home. "See that second tree out there?" Scott asked, pointing out a tree about seventy-five feet beyond the left field wall. Darryl nodded, somnambulent.

"A guy named Kevin Garner for Sioux Falls hit one off that second tree last year," Scott said.

"Oh, did he?" Strawberry asked politely, still not quite looking like he believed he was really here in St. Paul, in Midway Stadium, with a team where the Show was only a rumor.

"Yeah," Marty Scott said, pointing one more time. "Second tree. Gives you something to shoot for."

Strawberry said nothing, looking way past that second tree at nothing in particular.

Rolling Stone, meantime, was quite pleased with the news that Darryl Strawberry, the baddest ass in all of baseball, was now playing for Bill Murray's wacky baseball team. "One mistake," I was told by Wenner via my editor, "and fry Darryl's ass. If he's doing drugs or fucking around, our readers want to see it."

This was the gospel according to Jann.

4

The Most Beloved Woman
of the Northern League

A legion of ballplayers have experienced serious withdrawal symptoms when they were forced to retire because of age. Included in this group are such great stars as Ty Cobb, Babe Ruth, Joe DiMaggio, Jimmie Foxx, and Willie Mays.
—Robert Obojski, *A History of Minor League Baseball*

May 16, 1996

The Saints' abbreviated spring training began shortly thereafter in St. Paul with the arrival of several dozen players who were aiming for a spot on the team. League rules were quite specific about who could stay and who must go—each team had to carry twenty-two players and were allowed four veterans with five or more years of professional baseball experience. To make sure no one brought in high-priced ringers—or that none of the players bit into the thin profit margins of most of the owners—a salary cap of $72,000 had been put on each team.

Darryl Strawberry got to the ballpark on time for the first day of practice and undressed silently in the Saints' pint-sized locker room, a dressing area befit for the high school baseball teams that Midway Stadium was originally built for. He said nothing and he revealed nothing, nothing but a vague sense of amazement that he'd been finally released as Stubby Kaye's neighbor in Rancho Mirage.

Strawberry pulled into the locker room almost invisibly, but all eyes were upon him as soon as he stopped at the locker of honor reserved for him, directly across from the locker occupied by Jack "the Bastard" Morris, the team's other former major league star, whose temperament had not changed in the two years since his original retirement from baseball.

STRAWBERRY had been magic-markered on surgical tape above the star's skinny little locker, and he rose his head only to nod to the anonymous ballplayers gathering around him as he tried on his number 17 uniform for the very first time. "Just blend in," manager Marty Scott told him, and Strawberry nodded silently, heading out the runway to stretch out on the ground, hidden by the swarms of unknown ballplayers that Scott had plucked from secret sources, personal research, leaking sources, and professional hunches.

Marty Scott knew his shit about player personnel: in the *New York Post*, which was covering the arrival of Strawberry in St. Paul, Tom Keegan described him as "Saints manager Marty Scott, farm director for the Texas Rangers for ten seasons until getting fired so somebody else could take credit for the Rangers residing in first place."

But how much control could Marty exert on his most famous charge? So far, things looked good on the Strawberry patrol. Any carnal or pharmacological cravings Strawberry might have in St. Paul are purely hypothetical. For accompanying him for his trip to the bottom of the minors are his second wife, Charysse, and their two small children. Charysse, a Gucci- and gold-bedecked young woman, is a fashionable replica of a Major League Wife. When she passes in the grandstand, the young women who work in St. Paul bars and sell tickets at theaters while their boyfriends play ball stare at her with a potent mix of envy and awe. Also along to protect him is Charysse's Uncle Rodney, a burly giant who serves as Strawberry's bodyguard and gatekeeper when he's not on the field. (When Straw was on the field, Uncle Rodney chased women in the ballpark with the abandon of a real ballplayer.)

For his last chance, Darryl would be watched by in-laws who would keep all potential scumbags away from the oft-troubled Darryl. And this time around, Strawberry said, he would not be doing any partying or even going out. "My family is like American Express," Strawberry said. "They don't leave home without me."

Already outside on the field is Jack Morris, who I'd last encountered in his salad days with the Detroit Tigers in 1984. It was the Tigers' great year when they won the championship and Morris pitched a no-hitter; I remembered clearly after an early season win how Morris, stretched out fully naked on the floor in the Tigers' locker room, refused to look any reporter in the eye as he opined

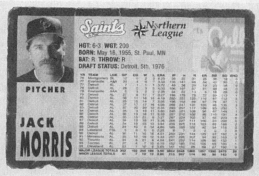

about the meaning of himself, and occasionally spit on the shoes of any journalists within hocking distance.

Still, at the time, Morris's grandiosity seemed earned, for he was indeed a great pitcher in his day. Bill Veeck himself had written about the importance of arrogance to a supreme pitcher:

> When you're out there in the big league pressure cooker, a pitcher's attitude—his utter confidence that he has an advantage of will and luck and guts over the hitter—is almost as important as his stuff.

Verging on forty-one, Morris was now a potential Hall of Famer who'd won 254 major league ballgames in eighteen seasons, including three world championships. As the ace of the Detroit Tigers, he'd won more games in the 1980s than anyone else and held the record for the most consecutive starts on Opening Day, having begun the season fourteen straight times for Detroit, Minnesota, and Toronto. Yet even Jack could not help being Jack.

Only a day after his greatest victory, his 1–0 ten-inning shutout in Game 7 of the 1991 World Series for the Twins, he filed for free agency, turning off the Minnesota fans who'd been listening to him spiel all year about how wonderful it was to finally play before his hometown crowd. By 1994, he was with the Cleveland Indians, who fired him in midseason after Jack demanded to show up only for games in which he pitched so he could spend more time on his 600-acre ranch in Montana. Attempting a comeback with Cincinnati in 1995, he quit the team in spring training, claiming emotional turmoil.

"For whatever reason, I haven't been best friends with the writers who decide who's in the Hall of Fame, but what's done is done," he says, spitting on my shoes. "This is not about getting back into the limelight with my head held high. It's pretty basic for me: I want to get on the mound. I love pitching and it's eating away at me. I want to go out pitching the way I want to go out pitching."

Hatchet-faced and still mean, a kind of Charles Starkweather of the mound, he lectured that first day of tryouts to some of the Saints' pitchers who dared speak to Morris about how to win. Morris would not be playing Mr. Chips to the Saints' pitchers; if they wanted to learn, he said, just watch him. But today he talked to the young pitchers. The answer, Jack said, was chin music, not letting the hitter dig in at the plate, frightening him with close pitches, coming so close with his deliveries that injury to the batter was not unthinkable. "You've got to pitch inside," Morris said. "I know a lot of guys in the majors and minors who don't want to do that, but if you want to win, you'll always pitch in."

None of the other players Marty Scott had dredged up looked familiar. He'd found many of these men, self-described as misunderstood, through contacts nurtured by decades in baseball. Many came from his old Texas Rangers organization; one of his prime reclamation projects was another Daryl, Daryl Henderson, a starting pitcher who'd been released by the Rangers in 1994 in order to be given psychiatric treatment. "If Daryl has benefited from the help," Marty said, "I think he still might have a major league arm.

"Daryl was a Chicago street kid who grew up fighting all his life," the manager said, "and he'd even fight with his teammates. He respects authority completely. When he's talking to me he's all 'yes sir, no sir.' He's just got the kind of focused, complex personality where he might just walk up to a couple of teammates and pop them for no reason. He pitched well for the Rangers' organization, but we had to suspend him to get him the psychological help to cope."

Henderson isn't so sure about his two-year banishment to get shrunk. "I was misunderstood. I still have it in me to win some games, I just know it. I've had things happen to me that Darryl Strawberry can probably relate to. We can help each other."

And so Henderson became Strawberry's shadow, asking him for autographs, carrying his equipment bag, standing next to him in the outfield when it was time to shag fly balls.

All around, as players did their stretches in the outfield, different tales of woe came out. Veteran Marty Neff, one of the most renowned head cases (by Northern League players) and beloved showboats (by the Northern League fans), was back with his pot belly and big swing for one more season of The Life.

The Pirates signed Neff, now twenty-six, as a sixth-round draft choice. As a child, his family had moved from Missouri to California so young Marty could play baseball all year round. In his final year of college ball at the University of Oklahoma, he made second-team All-American and hit .390. But as soon as he hit professional baseball, Neff somehow sensed that in some ways the baseball organizations were fixed.

"I was putting up numbers better than the number-one draft choice of the Pirates, but I was the one who got released for having a bad attitude. I'm not an ass kisser, but every day somebody was saying something bad about me. I got suspended, yelled at, and finally blackballed. It's all because I get mad at myself and don't know how to handle the fact that in baseball you're going to fail seven out of ten times, and you can't fly off the handle every time things don't go right. Maybe I picked the wrong sport."

Neff went on to explain how baseball was indeed about politics.

Saint Paul Saints

STEVE SOLOMON

OUTFIELDER

HGT: 6-0 WGT: 180
BORN: April 9, 1970
Los Angeles, CA
BAT: L THROW: L
DRAFT STATUS:
Philadelphia, 6th, 1992

YR	TEAM	LEAGUE	GP	AB	R	H	2B	3B	HR	RBI	AVE	BB	SO	SB
92	Batavia	NY-Penn	10	28	5	11	2	0	0	3	.393	0	7	4
93	Spartanb.	So. Atlantic	81	300	59	88	16	4	1	33	.285	39	49	14
94	Clearwater	Fla. State	131	497	88	150	29	5	9	62	.302	51	71	21
95	Reading	Eastern	119	355	50	81	19	6	3	42	.228	48	82	17
	CAREER TOTALS		341	1187	202	330	66	15	13	140	.278	138	209	56

Every team has "prospects" and "organization men," he explains. "The 'prospects' are the high draft choices who the major league teams have spent a lot of money on and are going to give every chance to make the majors. The 'organization man' fills out the minor league teams, gets cut in a second, and if he keeps his nose clean, might get some job with the organization at the end of his career."

Around and around the excuses went as Marty Scott surveyed his motley crew. The place might as well have been a prison yard. After climbing the minor league ladder, Steve Solomon, twenty-six, had just been released by the Philadelphia Phillies' organization after one poor year at their AA Reading, Pennsylvania, farm team and also had some opinions about it.

"There's a lot of politics in baseball," says Solomon, a graduate of Stanford. "In baseball you can get labeled. Whether it's right or wrong, that's what people think of you. If you get labeled in a negative way, it's bad—all you need is one person to say, 'He's lazy' or 'He's a head case' and it's all over. My older brother was drafted by the Seattle Mariners a few years ago, but they labeled him as 'slow' and let him go after his first year in the minors. He was *not* slow."

And his own banishment? "Last year I didn't click with my hitting coach at Reading," Solomon says. "He wanted me to change the batting style I'd used my entire life, and I was fighting with him. It

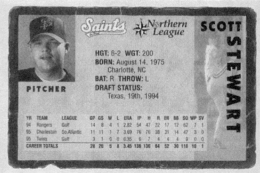

became this big head game that of course I was going to lose. And this spring I got released. No matter what I did, the decision had already been made. But I wouldn't be here if I didn't think I could get to the majors."

No one doubted that Solomon worked harder to make it to the bigs than anybody on the team. During the season, he videotaped each televised Saints game from a local cable company and stayed up until 2 A.M. analyzing his own swings from that night. Left unsaid was that at twenty-six, Solomon was nearing the outer bubble at which players make the big leagues.

He, like many of the Saints, was the forty-year-old guitarist who'd almost made it, the twenty-two-year-old gymnast who'd peaked a couple years before, the fifty-year-old office funny man who wanted to embark on a career as a professional comedian. Solomon might not be too old, but he was getting there.

The youngest player on the team and in the entire Northern League, twenty-year-old Scott Stewart, also had a tale of woe. Quickly nicknamed "Country" for the fact that the native North Carolinian talked like one of the pig-faced extras out of *Deliverance,* Stewart was evicted from the Texas Rangers' organization the previous year for actively, physically disagreeing with the pitching coach for his team in the South Atlantic League.

"I was pitching," Stewart said, "and I threw a fastball. The pitching coach then signaled me to throw a curveball that he'd shown

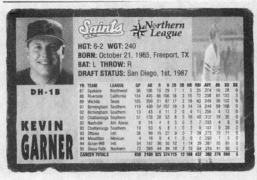

me before the game in the bullpen. But I didn't want to. So I threw another fastball. Then the pitching coach signaled one more time for a curve. I don't know why, but I threw the ball at him in the dugout and yelled, 'Take this fucking curveball and shove it up your ass!' I was released that day."

Still, there was hope. "Scott is so young," manager Marty said, "that if he matures and catches some breaks, he could make the majors."

Meantime, Stewart's two favorite off-field questions to his teammates in the coming days were: "Any of you bow hunt?" and "This ain't a homo bar, is it?"

All these goings-on and excuses were being listened to with an air of bemused indifference by Kevin Garner, the thirty-year-old designated hitter who'd led the league in home runs the previous year with Sioux Falls. Of all these never-weres, Garner above all should have made it. A 1987 first-round draft choice as a pitcher for the San Diego Padres after an All-American career at the University of Texas, he'd quickly hurt his shoulder in the pros and turned to hitting.

While most of the players drafted under him in the first round that year made the majors and are now multimillionaires, the damaged Garner, still considered a prospect, wasn't quite good enough, making it only as far as AAA, one step away from the bigs. Trained for nothing else, with no hope of going anywhere else, he now toiled for teams from north to south, from the Northern League to the Mexican League, in search of a paycheck.

"I once dated Mary Lou Retton," he volunteers *both* truthfully and sarcastically as the highlight of his career. Now, he falsely claims to be writing an autobiography about his failed attempt to reach the majors. *"In Pursuit of a Nightmare,* I'll call it. The subtitle will be *The Reason I Never Got There? I Took the Dirt Road."*

And then, stretching in the middle of the outfield, is a three-foot-two-inch Saints player with stumps for legs. He is Dave Stevens, thirty, who paid his own way here from his job as a producer at ESPN in order to practice with a real baseball team. "He wouldn't stop calling me," recalls Mike Veeck. "He kept saying that even though he was three-foot-two, he wasn't Eddie Gaedel, a promotion, but a real ballplayer. After about two hundred of these calls, I finally turned him over to Marty Scott and said, 'It's your call.' "

Stevens began his telephone assault on the Saints' manager, and it worked. "Dave touched my heart," says Marty Scott in explanation of why he invited the man with no legs to practice with the Saints during spring training.

"He really does wants to be seen as an athlete, not as one of Jerry's kids," says Scott. "He'll be gone by Opening Day, but he's a great presence on the field and in the clubhouse—especially for any players here who might be pitying themselves or their present situations."

One of the few players not bitching about how they got there is Kenishi Kato, age twenty-one, from Chiba, Japan. His parents had paid the orange-haired youngster's way for the trip to a Northern League tryout camp in California so he could pursue his dream of making it as a professional pitcher in America.

"Do you speak any English?" Marty Scott asks Kato as he stretches.

Kato nods, not understanding.

"How about Spanish? Do you speak Spanish?"

Kato nods again, not understanding. In the clubhouse he blasts punk rock through his Walkman and dresses like an American teenager; when he's not, he's quickly taught by other ballplayers how to say with no comprehension the words "Big Mac," "six-pack," and "blowjob."

The stakes for Kato were huge. "It will be a humiliating loss of face for him with his family if he doesn't make the team," says Marty Scott after watching Kato throw from the mound for several innings worth of pitches. Marty didn't like what he saw. "He throws strikes, but his fastball isn't fast enough and his curveball doesn't curve. He's a nice kid, but his fastball just isn't what I thought it would be."

With fourteen pitchers in camp and only ten he can keep, Marty motions Kato to join him in the manager's tiny office a few days later in training camp. He then dials up the Japanese agent in California who arranged for Kato to come to an American training camp. "He's sitting right next to me now," Scott tells the agent, "and please tell him in Japanese that I think he's a very nice gentleman to be around and that he works very hard. Tell him we're making cuts, and he's not going to be put on the final team. I've got his travel arrangements right here. Maybe you can talk to him and then give the phone back to me and I can say some more things to him to not make it hurt so bad."

Marty Scott hands the phone over to Kato, who is told that his dream is all over. Kato doesn't blink or make a sound. "It's still the worst part of this job: cutting someone," says Marty Scott. "I used to not be able to sleep the night before. About fifty percent of the people you cut just say 'Thank you' for the chance, twenty-five percent say, 'you've got to be kidding,' two percent yell at me, and the rest just sit there."

Kato just sat there. Tomorrow he would be going home to Japan without face. Though he doesn't understand a word of English, he has become in these few days a favorite of his teammates for his cheery disposition and teenage punk rock style. Now the orange-haired pitcher walks slowly around the locker room, unable to take off the last uniform he might ever wear. Finally he removes his Saints shirt; an hour later, he finally takes off his Saints cap, which is replaced with a backward-worn Nike model.

Word has spread among the players, who now count Kato as one of the dead. Long ago, each learned not to get too close to any other player, because their best friend on the team, if they had one, might be traded or released tomorrow.

A few minutes later, Kato puts back on his Saints hat and paces through the locker room as his former teammates watch ESPN's "SportsCenter." Kato watches too, *from the back,* comprehending nothing, then goes over to pretend to read the team's bulletin board.

He steps into the dugout, pacing back and forth, swinging a bat, talking to no one. Finally Kato steps into Marty Scott's office and bows. He comes out and stares at the backs of ten teammates who are still watching television. No one turns around for a final good-bye. His coffin is already closed.

Finally Kato is gone. Team trainer Tom Tisdale goes over to Kato's locker and rips the tape off bearing the player's name. He takes it over to the cinder block wall by his training table and affixes it under a GON' FISHIN' sign. On that wall is the roll call of who has lived and died this season on the team, and it will multiply several times over before the season is through.

Marty Scott, when angry at an athlete, isn't always as nice in releasing players as he was with Kato. Take the case of Joe Serna, a twenty-three-year-old pitcher cut by the Detroit Tigers' system last year. So far, his most noted achievement as a Saint was refusing to ever shower after a practice, no matter how hard his teammates begged him. Then Joe came to the unfortunate conclusion that he pitched better if he drank the night before at Gabe's, the bar down the road from the ballpark. He was wrong.

"Joe, can I see you?" Marty asked Serna, like a warden reading a writ of execution. "Joe," Marty said simply, "I'm releasing you. You're not doing the job."

Gon' fishin'.

For the first several days of practice, Strawberry spoke to virtually no one unless addressed first. When he did talk, he was quiet and polite, disappointing the camera crews who congregated around him, hoping for color from Darryl like in the old days in New York in the eighties, when he was so jacked on speed that anything might come out of his mouth.

In the first couple of days of spring training in St. Paul, he slowly began talking to the black guys on the team and, within days, to the whites. But the place he talked most was in the batting cage; all action in Midway Stadium stopped when the six-foot-six-inch natural looping swing would send eight or nine of the ten balls thrown to him over the stadium walls; half seemed to measure over 500 feet.

True, the man pitching batting practice was Wayne "Twig" Terwilliger, a seventy-year-old man in his forty-seventh season in a baseball uniform who had been released in a humiliating fashion by the despised Twins as their first base coach two years ago to make room for a younger strategist. Terwilliger, who'd played major league ball for the Cubs, the Dodgers, the Senators, the Giants, and the A's—and who'd coached the Twins to World Series victories in 1987 and 1991—was now the Saints' first base coach.

Twig was also universally acknowledged as a wise man of the game, a Yoda of the diamond without a bad word about anybody still living. No one in the history of the game, it was also figured, had hit more fungoes than Twig, who carried his two taped fungo bats like priceless Stradivari. "Can't get these kind anymore," he'd say, refusing to let anyone carry his wood.

"Straw's still got it," Twig said, reaching for another bucket of balls for Darryl to hit far way. "I think this fella is going to make it."

After practice, Strawberry would usually dress silently and head outside to be met by his wife, Charysse, and gatekeeper, Rodney, signing autographs with a smile and a nice benign word or two for any fan who wanted. But on the next day of practice, he finally began to come out of his shell. It happened the moment he walked into the hellhole of the Saints' locker room.

That day Straw found himself alone in the locker room with Dave Stevens, who was taking off his artificial legs and buttoning up his Saints uniform over his stumps. "Hey, little man, how you doing?" Strawberry asked, amazed, as Dave Stevens hopped off the bench, all dressed, and invited Strawberry onto the field of Midway Stadium with him.

Born without legs and then immediately given up for adoption by his birth mother, Stevens was a former college wrestler and football nose guard at Augsburg College in Minneapolis. True, he'd been invited to practice with the Saints during spring training at his own expense, mostly as an antidote for self-pitying Saints. But he really could play baseball, able to catch virtually any fly ball or grounder hit within twenty-five feet of him.

He had played catcher in high school in Wickenburg, Arizona, where at three-feet-two he broke the state record held by former Atlanta Braves star Bob Horner for most walks received in a season (forty-one).

"I'm here because I'm an athlete," said Stevens. "I now play outfield, second base, and catcher. You'd be surprised how much ground a man with no legs can cover. As I've said before, I'm not one of Jerry's fucking kids."

Darryl Strawberry hadn't been moping, but his polite silences distanced himself those first days from his new teammates. Stevens was the first, and for a few days seemingly the *only* Saints ballplayer who Strawberry would talk to. Darryl wasn't particularly standoffish, just vaguely suspicious of every man in uniform or not who approached him.

Dave Stevens, Darryl Strawberry and Daryl Henderson shagging flies
Courtesy of Bonnie Butler

Except for legless Dave Stevens. He and Strawberry talked that first day out of the locker room and onto the field and then talked during practice. They had much in common: both were recovering cocaine addicts, each had lost his mother to breast cancer that winter, and both spent much of their days having strangers point at them as if they were horrific freaks.

Shagging flies in the outfield with Stevens and Daryl Henderson during batting practice the next day, Strawberry erupts with the first genuine-sounding laughs he's issued all spring as Stevens, propped up on his stumps, waiting for the next fly ball, tells of the practical jokes a man with no legs can get away with.

In high school, Stevens tells Strawberry, a friend once ran out of the ocean, shrieking to a full beach of a shark attack. Moments later, in full view of a horrified audience, Dave Stevens, sans legs, hurried out of the surf and onto the beach, shrieking that he'd just been half-eaten.

"You're a stud, you know that?" Strawberry tells Stevens. "That's what I'm going to call you: 'Stud.'"

"You'd be surprised by the sex stories I could tell you about myself," Stevens said. "I'm not proud of them—the worst happened when I was deep into cocaine, a long time ago."

Strawberry says nothing. Stevens's tales of half-body shenanigans is interrupted by a fly ball to his left. He takes off with his hands and throws his torso in front of the ball.

"All right, Stud!" Darryl Strawberry yells across right field as Stevens makes a diving, rolling catch. Strawberry then pounds applause into his glove for the first time this spring with an enthusiasm belying his station as an exile.

"God blessed me with talent and then I made mistakes," Strawberry says in explanation one more time of why he is spending his summer shagging fly balls in the darkest basement of the minors. "But how can I feel sorry for myself when I see what Dave Stevens has accomplished after being born without legs?"

Stevens, running with his arms through the grass of St. Paul's Midway Stadium, returns to his usual perch next to Strawberry, their height differential greater than Stevens's height. "Good catch, Stud!" Strawberry says, low-fiving his turf-stained teammate's upstretched fingertips.

"Did you call me Stud or *Stub?*" Stevens shoots back.

Strawberry chortles. Together the two amble in from the outfield to take their batting practice swings. It was a scene from a Dali painting, the long-legged black giant loping in perfect lock-step with a white man half his size loping with his hands.

When they get to the batting cage, Dave separates from Strawberry and hops around in search of his bats. "Look at that little guy," Strawberry says, shaking his head as he watches the little man take some practice swings, then hop into the batting cage for some cuts.

"What amazed me after watching Dave play ball that first day of spring training was that he wasn't just some guy pretending to be a baseball player," says Strawberry. "He was a *real* baseball player. I mean, the man can really hit, catch, and throw. Dave reminded me of what baseball is supposed to be about. It's about *trying* when everybody says stop."

Uh-oh, I thought, readying myself for another of the sermons that Strawberry had been delivering to all the national reporters who were following him around. But those by-rote dodges didn't come when Darryl Strawberry was talking about Dave Stevens.

"Dave really gives me inspiration and hope," Strawberry said. "A lot of the times I think he's the only one here who really understands what I've been going through. Everyone looks at both of us like we're the Elephant Man."

For his first two weeks in Minnesota, Darryl and Stevens became inseparable friends on and off the field. Stevens picked Strawberry up each morning for practice, ferrying him back in a car that was specially equipped with hand controls. After practice, they usually went to dinner together at a local restaurant. Strawberry especially appreciated that Stevens took a lot of the national publicity heat off Darryl. When ESPN, the New York *Daily News,* and "This Week in Baseball" came to town, they ended up doing pieces on the inspiring white guy with no legs instead of the scary black guy with no chances.

It was a nice story, but it wasn't the story I needed. The national press corps had already come in search of Darryl on some sort of wild rampage and gone home with only the same earnest quotes and images of Strawberry that would be unusable for my mission of destruction.

"Many times over this past winter, I thought I should just quit," he'd say again . . . and again . . . and again. "But I realized I didn't want to end my career that way. I still believe I've a lot to give. And even if playing for the Saints doesn't get me back to the majors, at least I'll be able to play baseball again. I owe Mike Veeck for all he's done to get me here."

His talk was a curious patois of jock cliché, born-again blessings, and Twelve Steps speak. "My bottom was the day I realized I was sick and tired of being sick and tired," he said. "I'm living one day at a time."

To make matters worse for me, Darryl Strawberry was just so damn likeable. He wasn't doing drugs, he was saying all the right things to all the right people, and he stayed polite, smiling and staying for hours after every practice to sign autographs, even when he was sure all the spying reporters had gone home.

But I needed dirt, not bromides. Until Bill Murray showed up and I could really set to work with my hatchet, perhaps I could get incriminating quotes from Strawberry with the specter of women. Once, while he stood next to Dave Stevens in the outfield shagging batting practice fly balls, I stalked onto the field with Bonnie Butler, a local photographer who shot for *Rolling Stone,* who was also the foxiest photographer in the Twin Cities, a specialist in rock & roll bands.

"You're my blonde bait," I told her.

While she snapped pictures of Darryl shagging flies, I guarded her head and eavesdropped for trash talk. The sight of a beautiful blonde had reduced many a born-again ballplayer into a dog, and I needed to start getting results.

To Darryl's credit, I didn't get much. After ascertaining that my photographer/bait worked with rock bands, Darryl uttered to his legless pal, "Stud, I should have been a rock star."

"You are, Darryl, you are," Stevens replied.

"No, I mean rock stars have fifty groupies lined up around the block. [As a ballplayer] I couldn't just go into the clubhouse and get some."

Stevens ponders a response.

"And rock stars get all the beauties," Strawberry adds. "The six-foot-tall kind with legs up to there. I'm telling you, I should have been in a rock band."

"Me too," says Stevens.

"Hey, Stud, you like redheads?" Darryl asks. "I bet you like redheads."

"Yes, I do" comes the response from Stevens. "Yes, I do. I've made much mischief with redheads." With that, Straw let out a laugh that lit up the outfield.

I was disgusted with myself. Any groupie cravings Strawberry might have in St. Paul, I reminded myself, were held in check by Charysse in her Chanel suit and body armor of jewelry, two small children, and Rodney the overseer, all sitting a few hundred yards away.

Later that day, when Strawberry was in the locker room, I saw my break. Darryl, excusing himself from his teammates, headed for the showers, bummed a cigarette from a Saints functionary, and headed out to smoke.

After practice the next day, I desperately lit up a cigarette and offered one to Darryl as I opened my notebook. "I know you think I'm just saying this," Strawberry said, exhaling his own smoke. "But I forgot what it's like having fun playing baseball. Now I'm beginning to remember."

"One day at a time," I said, revealing to him my stay at Hazelden. "You can tell you've made a fearless moral inventory," I went on, quoting the steps of Alcoholics Anonymous. "You're making your amends."

Strawberry nodded and looked at me as if I'd just said, "Open sesame."

I told him that I too was an eighties New York burnout, that I

used to see him at the parties I used to have to cover as a nightlife
correspondent. "You were mean, man," I said laughing, "all glassy-
eyed and looking for trouble."

Strawberry looked me over and said nothing. "What are you?" he
said. "My 'Cigarette Boy' or something?" He paused again. "Back
then, by the end of a night, I might have ten beers, like it was no
big deal," he said. "I liked getting drunk. I was a happy drunk."

"Didn't look like it," I said, an emboldened Cigarette Boy.

"It was the amphetamines," he said. "Half the team was taking
them. Nobody told me in the minors that those amphetamines were
what you were supposed to do if you were hung over. I caught on."

"I see," I said, handing over another smoke. "So when did you
hit bottom?" I asked, using Twelve Steps parlance for the moment
when it most seemed as though the end was near.

"No, really," I insisted, needing more than the clichés. Maybe, he
said, it was the time in 1993 when the Dodgers tried to release him
on waivers, and nobody else in the majors would take him. "I kind
of wondered what it would be like if I wasn't around no more. Then
I guess people and the fans and the sportswriters wouldn't have
nothing to talk about, right?"

"Right," I said as Strawberry put out his butt and started dressing.
"Cigarette Boy," he said, chortling.

In the coming days of abbreviated spring training in St. Paul
and four exhibition games, Strawberry behaved like a deacon, linger-
ing for at least an hour after each game to cheerfully sign autographs.
He patiently sat through a myriad of interviews with small-town
newspaper reporters who stammered with nerves and ignored the
vulgar catcalls and derisive chants of "Dar-ryl! Dar-ryl!" that echoed
painfully around the intimate Midway Stadium.

On May 20, 1996, the first exhibition game at home featured
Jack Morris hurling against the Duluth-Superior Dukes. Jack looked
terrible, allowing the first five Duluth batters to score as he, in turn,
pitched wildly. In one inning he gave up five runs on two doubles,
two singles, a walk, a wild pitch, and his own throwing error. "I'm
sore everywhere," he said when he was mercifully taken out. "I'm
right on schedule. I still haven't built up the strength to throw my
forkball, but it will come." If Jack were to get back to the majors,
his forkball would be the reason.

Strawberry didn't do much better in the first exhibition game,
blooping a single to right in his first at-bat, then striking out swing-

ing and hitting into two more mediocre outs. The Saints lost 9–6, but nobody seemed worried. "It's just the beginning," Strawberry said.

What if it really *was* the beginning, I asked Strawberry after the game, handing over another smoke. He took a deep drag. "Imagine if I'd gotten sober ten years ago," he said. "Imagine. I just didn't know how to get my life back. It was drinking, the women were around, the drugs were around, and by the time I got to the stadium back then, I felt like I wanted to die."

When I went outside to the Saints' parking lot that day, I felt like I wanted to die a little too. I had parked my battered Toyota Corolla near the Saints' administrative offices, where I'd been directed, below the stadium's back rung, and a foul ball had crashed into the windshield, sending a crack all the way across the pane.

Shit. I didn't have the dough to fix it. And I wouldn't have the dough until I got paid in full for chopping up Bill Murray and Darryl Strawberry. Looking at the other Saints' employees cars in the lot under Midway, I noticed the same thing—unfixed, cracked windshields. The people who worked here in the Northern League were certainly not in it for the money.

On May 22, two days later at home, the Saints lost 1–0 in an exhibition match with the Fargo-Moorhead RedHawks. Morris pitched well this time, giving up only one run in four innings. Strawberry went one for two, walked a couple of times, and patiently waited to get into his groove.

As did manager Marty Scott. "Darryl's done everything we've asked," said Marty. "Once he proves his head is screwed on tight, he'll be in the major leagues in a snap."

It sounded like more manager claptrap, but Baptist-straight Scott had broken through to Strawberry like no manager in Strawberry's career. Strawberry's father had split when he was twelve, a wound his psychiatrists in the press said he'd never recovered from. A badass from that moment, he'd proceeded to alternately, con, confound, and amaze male authority figures ever since.

To New York Mets manager Davey Johnson, who often had to deal with the fact that Strawberry was so hung over he couldn't play, exasperation gave way to rage. In Los Angeles, Tommy Lasorda compared him unfavorably to a dog. But in St. Paul, Marty waited patiently and played the benevolent dad Strawberry never had.

"Yeah, there was some abuse in my family, in terms of my father drinking," Strawberry admitted as I fed him cigarettes. "And I admit that I used to slap my first wife around. But let me tell you—

domestic violence comes straight from drinking and using drugs. I made mistakes."

Now, on May 27, it was time for the Saints' first road game and last exhibition against the Madison, Wisconsin, BlackWolf, one of the league's two expansion teams that year. Dave Stevens was not scheduled to make the 250-mile bus trip, and to instead head home to Connecticut. But Strawberry prevailed upon his manager to let his legless pal come along for the team's bus ride. "He's a part of the team," Darryl said. "He should go with us."

After ascertaining that the five-hour bus ride wouldn't wreak havoc with Stevens's stumps, Scott agreed. It was a blessed event that Stevens came, even for those, like me, looking for dirt. There was only room for one more on the bus, though—either Stevens or me. "A player with no legs," said a coach with unbeatable logic, "beats a reporter from *Rolling Stone*."

As the team boarded the bus, rumor had it that Madison also had working for them "the Most Beautiful Woman in the Northern League," a woman who claimed that she was going to own her own minor league baseball club someday. According to league gossips, there were already about seventy-five men around the league in all capacities who thought they were three phone calls away from bedding this woman.

She didn't, however, date ballplayers, meaning she didn't fit into the two most common ballplayer categories for women: "wives or whores." "Maybe she's a lezzy," guessed Scott "Country" Stewart. "I ain't chasing no tail into no homo bar."

It was a relief to drive the 250 miles to Madison, to get away from the tedium, I then believed, of one-dimensional ballplayers. They were like children: if you interviewed one, you had to interview them all or they'd get pissed. If you talked to them about baseball, they'd get bored. If you asked them about their relationships with other players, they'd yawn. Ballplayers, no matter at what level, never get close to other ballplayers.

I drove alone, stopping along the way only at the Circus World Museum in Baraboo, Wisconsin, home of the original Ringling Bros., as well as the largest circus museum now open in the world. Once there, I searched through the library for references to Bill Veeck's first marriage in 1935 to Eleanor Raymond. In Gerald Eskenazi's estimable biography of Bill Veeck, he quoted the old man as saying

Eleanor was a bareback rider "who liked to ride through rings of fire sidesaddle."

And there Eleanor was, in the library clips of *Billboard* magazine, described as a bareback rider who'd been educated in "fashionable Eastern finishing schools." Bill Veeck hadn't been lying. "The divorce was my fault," he told Eskenazi. "I couldn't leave baseball alone."

They weren't officially divorced until 1948, when Veeck sold his beloved Cleveland Indians to pay for the breakup. The team was the American League champions, but Veeck recalled returning to his apartment alone the night the great season ended. "At that moment of triumph," Veeck said, "I had never been more lonely in my life."

Bill Veeck had eventually gotten a second chance at reclaiming his game. His soul mate and Mike's mom, Mary Frances, is a baseball fanatic who forever cured his loneliness, and knew his owning the St. Louis Browns and Chicago White Sox would mend his spirit. Still suffering from my own divorce, I didn't know yet that the Most Beloved Woman in the Northern League would start to mend mine. My heart remained as shattered as Miss Havisham's, but she'd make me love baseball again.

Finally, on the outskirts of Madison, my cracked car found Warner Park, a ramshackle facility built on a mosquito patch built in the beautiful city's worst part of town. It was, I would eventually learn, the most uncomfortable park in the league.

And then, between early innings, there she was on Madison's field, Monica Toppen, the Black Wolf's director of both community and press relations. She wasn't what I expected. The word around the league was that the expansion team was an organizational mess. Monica, except for player personnel decisions, was basically running the team. At the moment, while wearing a dressy pantsuit, she was conducting the "dizzy bat race" on the field, wherein two adults put their foreheads on a bat, spin around ten times, then dizzily try to race each other without falling down. It's a minor league classic that is considered too low-brow for the majors, as were the other stunts with fans Monica ran on-field between innings. When the inning began, Monica had to run up to the press box to keep the batter-by-batter score that she would fax into the league office after the game was over.

Tall, in her mid-twenties, with the tastefully big hair of a Texas beauty queen, Monica seemed like an apparition, not of romance, but of magic: black or white, I wasn't quite sure. I looked closer. Be

Monica Toppen, dressed up for the ballpark
Courtesy of Neal Karlen

careful, I warned myself. I never subscribed to the players' simplistic and degrading categories of women around baseball, but I did know that a special breed of women existed, women who knew their way around a baseball diamond and who were as much femme fatales as Veronica Lake or Mata Hari. Stay away, I told myself.

So I did, but I needn't have worried. For during the coming season, the Most Beloved Woman in the Northern League and I became pals and lovers of a different sort. Lanky with the high-coif of a 1960s astronaut's wife, Monica was meant to fall in love with an athlete, not a shrimpy writer a couple inches shorter than her. And I still looked at love as a sucker's bet. Instead, our "romance," as she put it, consisted simply of her season-long attempts to make me rediscover the beauty of baseball.

But that was still to come. For the moment, I just needed to meet this woman who had the whole league talking before the season even started. After the eighth inning, as Monica finished the water balloon toss, I interrupted her. She was striking, so beautiful, that even the ballplayers, known for their piggishness, treated her with brotherly respect and would kick the shit out of anybody who showed even the slightest sign of disrespect to her. In any case, as Scott Stewart had correctly learned, Monica didn't date ballplayers. She was straight, but not a masochist.

"Why are you so dressed up for a ball game?" I asked her.

"I don't wear jeans to the ballpark because this is my temple, and I wish to honor my temple," she said.

Christ, I thought.

Monica, who was raised by college academics in Los Angeles, had had a teenager's crush on a minor league player with the San Bernardino Indians. He'd broken her heart, and though she still follows his progress through the minors by reading the publication *Baseball America,* she made an important decision: she wanted to own a minor league baseball team.

"I'm embarrassed about this now, but the first time I wanted to own a team was when that ballplayer broke up with me. I wanted to buy his team, then release him," she says, blushing, stressing that he was the only ballplayer she ever went out with. "My motives about baseball became more altruistic, less personal, after that."

Monica tells people around the league that she is twenty-seven, but she is really twenty-two. After graduating from high school at sixteen, she moved to Montana with her father, who had received a provost job at the University of Montana, to attend college. Graduating in three years, she enrolled in law school, planning on a career in the public defender's office. But she dropped out of the University of Montana's law school the first year when a shitty job opened up with the Butte, Montana, Copper Kings.

"By day," she remembers, "I had an internship in the public defender's office, where I worked with this kid who'd chopped up his parents and put them in the fireplace. At night, just to get away, I started going to baseball games by myself."

Butte's team was, well, horrific. "It was the kind of place where they broadcast games from a card table," she said. "But Butte is where I fell in love with baseball and really decided that even though I was so young and a woman, I would someday find a way to own my own minor league team. When the games were over, no matter who won, it left me with an ache inside—it was like leaving the congregation and community."

She was quickly hired by the Great Falls, Montana, Dodgers, a low-rent team that was impressed by her wunderkind résumé. Everyone else in her family was shocked.

Hmm, potential danger, I thought. I could see why Monica Toppen was the Most Beloved Woman of the Northern League. She was beautiful, but so were many of the corn-fed honeys who congregated around the players and ballparks of the league. Unlike them, though, she also intrigued enough for me to worry she'd melt the wall of lead I'd built around my aorta and ventricles.

"I only have two interests: minor league baseball and baseball history," she told me. "Wait. Three interests. I want to build a little memorial for Otis Redding, who died in a plane crash in Madison on December 10, 1967. He crashed into Lake Monona with his backup band the Bar-Kays. His bandmates told him not to fly that night, but he said he didn't want to let down the people of Madison."

Four Bar-Kays died, one survived the crash, and one missed the plane. Redding died strapped to his seat. "Otis. . . ." Monica says, returning to practicality. "I'd like to erect a little plaque on the bench nearest the shore where you can see where the plane went down. I'm trying to raise money from other Northern League teams, but so far, no one's chipped in. I guess they don't like R&B."

Her favorite Otis Redding songs are "I've Been Loving You Too Long" and "(Sittin' on) The Dock of the Bay." She also loves "Tramp," which was a duet that Otis recorded with Carla Thomas. "To be honest," she says, "I'm more into Frank Sinatra. A man can make me cry by putting Frank on a jukebox, sweeping me into his arms in a bar, and dancing with me to 'Summer Wind.' "

Good. I'm safe. I hate Frank Sinatra.

But mostly, she says, her love is baseball. "I'd skip the rent to buy an old baseball book," she says. "I just bought John McGraw's autobiography," naming the cantankerously brilliant New York Giants manager who'd written his life story over half a century ago. "My favorite, though, of all time is Lawrence Ritter's *The Glory of Their Times*. I also have this tin sign advertising shoes with Shoeless Joe Jackson. I think Joe Jackson should be in the Hall of Fame, don't you?"

The half-inning was ending, and Monica had to retake the field to help a little kid race the team mascot, a teenager inside a cartoonish wolf outfit, around the bases. She continued when she got back, scoring the game as she talked. "The weird thing is is that I care more about how Christy Mathewson did in 1910 than what Ken Griffey, Jr., does tomorrow. I just finished this great biography of Mathewson. Why don't they make men like that anymore? I'm single, and he's who I'm waiting for: Christy. I have this 1920 book, *Pitching in a Pinch* by Christy Mathewson. It's about pitching . . . and life. Why aren't there men like that anymore?"

"Thank God," I thought about Monica's infatuation with a straight-arrow Hall of Fame pitcher who'd been dead for seventy-one years. Even if I were to be so unprofessional as to fall for her, I knew I more closely resembled Shecky Greene than Christy Mathewson.

"There never really were," I guessed.

"I bet even Mathewson had his warts. If there's one thing I've learned as a reporter it's that you never want to meet your heroes, even if you have to contact them with a Quija Board."

"Cynic," she said. "Until I find Christy, I'll just be waiting to get my own minor league team and run it the way it should be."

Darryl Strawberry finally had his bust-out game in that exhibition game, hitting two majestic home runs, driving in five Saints, and getting four hits in five at-bats. The Saints were leading by an ugly score of 16–12, and Strawberry marched to the batter's box in the ninth inning to take his last swings.

Nearing the plate, he turned around and walked back into the dugout. "I've had my swings," he told Marty Scott. "Let the little guy bat. I want him to be able to hear over the PA: 'Now batting for Darryl Strawberry, Dave Stevens.' "

"You sure?" Marty Scott said. Darryl nodded.

So that's exactly what Dave Stevens heard over the tinny public address system of the BlackWolf's stadium. Stevens grabbed a bat with one arm and slowly made his way out to the plate.

The pinch-hitting carried a remarkable piece of verisimilitude from Strawberry's early, still-innocent career as a cultural icon in the 1980s. "Darryl himself was in my favorite episode of 'The Simpsons' ever, " said Stevens. "In the episode, Darryl, who played himself, goes nine for nine in a game, and then is pinch-hit for by Homer Simpson. That's how it was in Madison, except this time *I* was Homer Simpson."

So the three-foot-two-batter placed himself in the batter's box and waited for a pitch to hit to a swell of applause from the opposing crowd. After fouling off three pitches, Stevens finally struck out. Two days later, the Saints' regular season would begin on the road with the Duluth-Superior Dukes, but Stevens was already back in Connecticut, working at ESPN, telling his nonbelieving coworkers that for one brief golden time he was, in fact, Darryl Strawberry's personal best friend and pinch hitter.

"Things are great here," Strawberry would say for the rest of his time with the Saints, "except that I miss the little guy."

The tape above Stevens's locker, meantime, was ripped off and put on the GON' FISHIN' sign next to trainer Tom Tisdale's rubdown table.

After the Madison game, the Saints board their bus and head immediately home to save a night's motel fare. Monica, meantime, faxed her score sheets to league headquarters and prepared to go home alone.

"I don't go out with ballplayers, because I don't want our fans ever seeing me that way, and I don't even go to bars anywhere near here," she said. "Sometimes when I'm sad, I'll go to some bar way out in the boonies where nobody knows me and I'll just play Frank Sinatra and Otis Redding on the jukebox, have a few drinks, and cry."

She walks me to my car and notices the cracked windshield. "Congratulations," she said. "You now have a Northern League car."

"What?"

"Everyone who works for the Northern League gets their windshield shattered by a foul ball, but is so broke that they can't fix it."

"Can I see you tomorrow?" I asked. "For my story? I'm not hitting on you."

"Yeah, that's what they all say," Monica said.

"I don't know who I am," I said, "but I'm definitely not Christy Mathewson."

"Maybe. Okay."

The next morning I first went to the library in Madison and looked up Christy Mathewson in *The Biographical History of Baseball.*

Christy Mathewson (Hall of Fame, 1936). Mathewson was the only one of the National League's great early-century pitchers who would have received the *Good Housekeeping* seal of approval. In studied contrast to his tobacco-chewing contemporaries, he was a Bucknell graduate who had headed two college literary societies, sung for the campus choir, and attracted attention for his championship play in everything from football to checkers. . . . He was publicized as such a model of clean living that he inspired fictional baseball heroes for children and was considered personally responsible for attracting women and entire families to the [New York Giants'] Polo Grounds.

Well, no wonder she was alone. "I'm good at being alone," she said later that day when we met near the bench where she wanted to put up the plaque to Otis Redding. "You have to be if you're going to make baseball your career."

To own a team, she said, she would first have to pay her dues by moving all over the country. "It's the general theory of people who make baseball their life. The first time you move to another team in another city you fly. The next time you put everything you own in a car. The next time you put a trailer behind your car. The fourth time you have your car towed behind a moving truck."

And the loneliness of knowing you'll soon be leaving wherever you are? "I'm very good about doing my boundaries," Monica said. "It's like when players are traded, it's as if they're dead," said the Most Beloved Woman of the Northern League. "We all have to have our protective shells."

"I gotta go," I finally said. "I've got a long drive back, and I'm riding the bus to Duluth with the team tomorrow," I told her.

"Be careful," she said.

No kidding, I thought.

5

In Which Ballplayers Fuck
on Opening Day in Duluth

Baseball Annie (noun): Generic name for unattached woman who favors the company of baseball players. The phrase was given prominence after the Phillies' Eddie Waitkus was shot without provocation on June 15, 1949. First printed use: "He sat up in bed and tolerantly described Ruth Steinhagen, a nineteen-year-old, as a 'Baseball Annie,' one of an army of hero-worshipping teenage girls who follow the players around." (Time magazine, June 17, 1949). The Waitkus incident is portrayed fictionally in the film The Natural. *Also known as: Baseball Sadie (noun): Woman whose weakness is ballplayers.*
—*The Dickson Baseball Dictionary*

Minneapolis, Summer 1971

I learned early that Baseball Annies, Sadies, or "flies," as some players called them, never referred to themselves as Annies, Sadies, or flies. I was eleven, waiting with the usual half-dozen local Annies in the lobby corner of Leamington Hotel in Minneapolis, where teams visiting the Minnesota Twins stayed. My best friend Art Simon and I, autograph hounds, would come to the Leamington several times a week to gather the signatures of major league baseball players. We were always unceremoniously hustled by the concierge to the lobby's farthest corner and ghettoed with the Annies, who, of course, were there to have sex with the same players.

They were nice women, teenagers probably, who talked to us while we all waited for the elevators to come down with players. "Who cares about their autographs?" a blond woman named Tammi told me. "Why don't you boys get girlfriends?"

By 1972, both Art and I understood what she meant. But before, when the ballplayers did come down the hotel's only elevator bank, Art and I got their autographs. Often, the player went straight to the Waikiki Room and its faded Polynesian decor in the hotel lobby and got plastered. We watched as Billy Martin, who was then the manager of the Detroit Tigers, entered the bar, drank seven Seven and Sevens, ate one handful of pretzels, and then weaved out like Crazy Guggenheim.

Meantime, other ballplayers lounged in the Leamington's lobby, opening up the centerfolds to publicly inspect the *Penthouse*s and *Playboy*s they'd just purchased at the hotel gift shop. Dressed in expensive disco-era synthetic fibers, the boys put their feet on the lobby's table, flicked their cigarette ashes on the floor, yet always remained coolly aloof from the hoi palloi around them. They were major leaguers; you could smell it.

Other members of the visiting team went down the road apiece to the Bangkok Sauna, a nefarious massage parlor that city Comstocks had been trying to close down for years. "Handjobs on sale," one of the Annies told me disdainfully, referring to arts performed by women pros who worked the local massage parlors, taking away fun nights for girls like herself who "really like these guys as *people.*"

She cracked her Wrigley's Spearmint in our inconspicuous holding pen in the hotel lobby corner. "The players go there for twenty-dollar handjobs," she went on. "They've got sex slaves working there or something, I heard. Yah, sluts for sure."

"What's a sex slave?" I asked, eleven years old and holding a clipboard of baseball cards to be signed.

"Tell you later," she said, reapplying her white lipstick, straightening her miniskirt, and pushing up her breasts just as her ballplayer and tonight's boyfriend, who'd left her tickets to that afternoon's game, sauntered off the elevator. Seeing his Annie, he strolled toward us with the bored mien all ballplayers use when dealing with their Annies.

Depending on the team, a half-dozen players would leave the elevator bank, sign autographs for Art and me, then walk toward the night's catch. The players would walk a few steps ahead of the assembled Annies, their dates, as if they were the king of Prussia. The women—were they girls?—said not a word as they followed their men either out the door or back into an elevator.

Whether you were in the bigs or the deepest of the minors, ball-players had long considered Baseball Annies as part of their constitutional rights. Babe Ruth once slept with seven in one night. So Saints manager Marty Scott, himself a practicing Texas Baptist who read the Bible each night before bed, did not plan on impinging on his ballplayers' inalienable rights to chase tail, especially during opening weekend in a foreign city like Duluth.

"I'll give them a lot of rope, unless their galavanting at night affects their play," Marty explains. "At the same time, I realize that a lot of our kids are rookies, young men experiencing their first year as a professional, and they are eager to experience the . . . experiences."

"Life in the carnival," I said.

"Exactly," Marty said.

According to Penn Gillette, a scholar of carnivals and their lore, those in The Life called themselves "fucklets." It had, he wrote, nothing to do with sex.

We're all fucklets on this bus, I thought to myself.

Marty Scott, meantime, was thinking about the futures of some departed Saints players. In some ways, Darryl Strawberry was only his second-most-important reclamation project. Strawberry would make it or not by his own volition; all Marty could do was play him, sit back, and talk when Darryl wanted one of his ever-increasing man-to-mans.

At first, the player the manager most wanted to see make it was the other Daryl, Daryl Henderson. For the first several days of camp, Henderson had been a model student and teammate; bowing down to Marty, smilingly chatting up all his teammates, gofering anything Darryl Strawberry wanted him to get. There was no sign of the player who only a few years before would slug a teammate without any provocation.

Best of all, Henderson was pitching like a dream: keeping the ball down in practice, taking extra throwing practice on the mound when practices were over.

"You ever had an arm injury?" Marty Scott had asked him as he threw another several pitches in spring training.

"No, never. I'm invincible," laughed Henderson, tossing another few.

"Okay," said Marty, "but don't throw too many more. It's still early in training."

The manager was impressed. "Daryl Henderson was pitching like the old days a couple of years ago when he had definite major league talent," said Scott. "When he was with Texas, I thought he was going to be the next Vida Blue; he was *that* dominating. But emotionally, he was stuck in the street. Maybe a couple of seasons away from the game did him some good."

Near the end of spring training, Marty had wandered onto the field to tell Henderson the best news he'd heard in years.

"You made the team, Daryl," he said. "Congratulations."

Henderson broke into a smile that could have spanned the Mississippi.

"Yessss!" he said quietly. "I made it."

"One other thing," Marty said. "I want you to start the Opening Day regular season game in Duluth." Marty wanted to hold out Jack Morris for that three-game series so he could start the Saints' home opener.

"Oh man," said Henderson, beaming, gleaming, afraid it was all a joke. "Oh man."

Marty inserted Henderson in the Fargo exhibition game, and things were progressing nicely for the pitcher until he walked off the mound, cried for help, and began pointing to his elbow. "Oh no," Marty Scott said as he and pitching coach Ray Korn ran out to the mound to check on their pitcher, who was taking himself out of the game.

Gone within microseconds was the all-purpose grin that Henderson had worn all spring; in its place was a thousand-yard stare of hurt, anger, and wonder. When Tom Tisdale wrapped his throwing elbow in tape on the training table, Henderson looked as though he were about to enter life-threatening surgery.

After the game, Marty Scott called the Saints' team physician and briefed him on the situation. "I probably jinxed him," Marty said. "He told me he'd never been injured, then I go and tell him he's our starting day pitcher."

The manager listened on the phone to the doctor for a few seconds, nodding. "If there's no tear in there," he said, "then Daryl will be back on the mound for the Saints. If there is a tear, then he gets released. That's sad, because he's got a major league arm." There are no second chances in the Northern League, even for the players you like most.

Henderson, Scott had been told by the doctor, would need an MRI—a highly expensive magnetic resonance imaging test that would determine what exactly the damage was—and whether Daryl Hender-

son's life was essentially over. The doctor on the phone paused. "MRIs are expensive," he said. "Will Mike Veeck approve the thousand-dollar cost?"

"*I'm* approving it," Marty said. "And Mike would too."

When word came to Henderson back on the training table that he would be going in for an MRI tomorrow, he remained mute. "Baseball is like life," he finally said. "You do what has to be done." His face was now set in a permanent frown.

Two days later, Marty Scott and trainer Tisdale got the news over the phone. "It's a torn ulna collateral nerve, clean off the bone," Marty repeated over the phone, looking crestfallen. "A Tommy John-type injury," he said into the phone, speaking the name of the major league star pitcher who'd spent years having his wrecked arm completely rebuilt, courtesy of major league doctors and orthopedists.

That would not be an option here. "Let's tell him tomorrow," Marty said, sighing with the weight of bad news undelivered.

Marty sat directly across from Henderson on a bench the next morning, and made no small talk, just gave him a sympathetic rendering of his arm injury.

"That isn't going to heal by itself," Marty said. "That's the bad news. Basically, you can't throw."

Henderson looked at Marty as if he'd just explained that two plus two equal five. He was silent, staring straight ahead. "You're awful calm," Marty said to his wounded pitcher. "What are you thinking?"

"Not much."

While his teammates packed their bags in preparation for heading to Duluth and the start of the regular season, Henderson quickly gathered his belongings, received his ticket home to Chicago from Saints general manager Bill Fanning, and headed out to the Twin Cities airport.

He appeared to be in a walking coma. "Things happen for a reason," he said over and over as he packed his locker, with barely a word to any of his teammates to whom two days earlier he'd been the clown prince. "I've just got to stay on top of things."

A day later, Henderson's name went fishing. "You never want to get too close to anybody in baseball," said Tisdale, who had to look at the GON' FISHIN' wall everytime he taped somebody up, "because they very well might be gone tomorrow, and you didn't even get to say good-bye."

May 31, 1996

The next morning Marty Scott said, "Okay, let's go," and the team bus pulled out of the Midway Stadium parking lot. I had asked him if it was okay if I hitched a ride with them.

"Suit yourself," the forty-one-year-old manager said, waving me in. "I'm not responsible for you inside. Okay?"

"Okay," I said. "Thanks." I was in.

But shit, I discovered at that moment Darryl Strawberry has decided at the last second to skip the Saints' bus ride to Duluth and get there with Charysse, his one-year-old baby, Jade, and Rodney, who has rented a nice vehicle. I had been looking forward to stalking Strawberry from the bus: many of his worst acts had come while sitting in the back of the New York Mets' private airplane (where reporters were barred.)

Drunk from a seemingly endless supply of booze provided by charter flight attendants, he'd taunted some of his teammates with a viciousness that had astounded others. He would tease and tease, toasted and mean, calling, for example, second baseman Tim Teufel "Richard Head"—dickhead—for nearly an hour during one flight.

Minutes after I board the bus that will take me the 156 miles to the Saints' opening series with the Duluth-Superior Dukes, it becomes clearly evident once again that the Saints aren't in the big time. Crematorium heat, not air-conditioning, is blasting from the inside vents this hot late spring day, and the bus driver doesn't know how to fix it.

Saint Paul Saints

Saints ✳ Northern League   WAYNE TERWILLIGER

COACH

Wayne Terwilliger may have enjoyed his second season with the St. Paul Saints even more than his first. Terwilliger was first in the Saints' employ in 1952 when he hit a career high .312 while playing second base. Last year, "Twig" coached first base and worked with the infielders, a role he will have again this year. It's Twig's 48th year in a baseball uniform in a career that started in 1948 in Des Moines in the old Western League. Twig played 666 games for the Cubs, Dodgers, Senators, Giants and A's before retiring in 1960. He then spent 15 years as a minor league manager or a coach. Twig has also coached with the Yankees, Senators, Rangers, and Twins. From 1986-94, Twig coached first base for the Twins. There, he was part of the team's only two World Series titles. As former Twins' manager Gene Mauch put it, "Twig is as good a baseball man as there is, period. End of discussion."

Nor does the sound work on the jerry-built video monitor at the front of the bus. Manager Scott always picks the movies and is now standing, but there will be no Jackie Chan film today unless the problem is corrected. It will be. Scott has a keen understanding of morale.

There is a strict seating plan on all transportation bearing baseball teams, be they at the bottom of the bottom or the top of the majors. In the Northern League, the bus driver, whose true name is never known, is called "bussie." The manager sits alone behind bussie, able to stretch out and spot fast-food joints faster than anyone.

Across the aisle from Marty Scott, also granted his own two seats, is the venerable first base coach Wayne "Twig" Terwilliger. Twig fought at Iwo Jima, was sitting in the Brooklyn Dodgers' dugout the moment Bobby Thomson hit his "Shot Heard Round the World" to win the 1951 pennant for the New York Giants, and actually ran the Washington Senators for Ted Williams when the great one was lured out of retirement to officially manage the team in 1969.

Twig is the Zelig of baseball, somehow making himself present for some of life's most moving happenings. "Never got to manage in the big leagues, though. That was always a dream," Twig says. "But you get over it. I'm seventy-two and I still get a kick out of hitting fungoes and pitching batting practice and telling guys, 'Go on to second; your hit rolled all the way to the wall.'"

Behind the manager, sharing adjoining seats, are the Saints' radio broadcasters. Dave Wright, the play-by-play man for Saints home games, has a great library at home of recorded baseball from the past. Driving in *his* car with the cracked windshield, he listens to the likes of Vin Scully with the Brooklyn Dodgers, Bob Prince with the Pittsburgh Pirates, and, most of all, his boyhood hero, Ernie Harwell, the voice of the Detroit Tigers. Dave, in his early forties, still dreams of being discovered and landing an announcing job in the majors.

Dave, the team scapegoat, is typically tortured by everyone in the Saints' organization. His current torment also stems from the fact that after a lifetime of bachelorhood, his five-minute marriage to a very nice woman named Francine just ended in a divorce. Dave takes it all in stride, be it at home or at the office; he was raised in an orphanage. Like Radar O'Reilly, however, Dave often gets the juiciest pieces of management gossip before anyone else, information he guards like precious gold.

Dave also keeps the Saints' scorebook, compiles daily lists of team statistics, and knows an alarming number of batting champions dating from the 1920s. In his private life, all of Dave's non-Saints friends simply refer to him as "Stats."

Sitting with Dave is the Saints' play-by-play man, Greg Harrington, who is killing time this summer until he hears about a major league hockey radio-announcing job out west. He bides his time for the present, announcing for St. Paul and selling souvenirs inside the Metrodome during Twins games. It's a living.

Greg prefers rubber pucks to leather-stitched baseballs, and on upcoming summer nights on the road when I'm not chasing after whoring, boozing ballplayers, I will often sit with him as he pounds postgame beers in cement roadhouses seemingly plunked in the middle of hay fields. "Hockey players are the nicest athletes," Greg tells me at the bar as I nurse my sissy drink in a Fargo establishment filled with menacing men and their bad-girl girlfriends. "They're nice because they are the only athletes left who still can't believe they get paid to play the game they love. That'll probably end in the next couple of years."

After Greg and Dave's aisle on the bus comes no-man's-land— no reporter's-land, at least—where the players sit, many uncomfortably four to a row, packed into their seats with extra pillows brought along for a more comfortable ride. The very back of the bus is somehow automatically reserved for the African American and Hispanic members of the team; all of the Saints simply call those last few aisles "the 'hood."

This invisible demarcation is exactly the same in the majors: players sit in the back of the plane, civilians sit up front. But all the action happens in back and, for my purposes, I needed to get back there to watch Darryl, who had told me he'd be riding mostly with the team on the bus.

A few days before, I'd seen from the bus's reporters' seat as the team headed toward Madison that Strawberry liked to ride alone on the last seat of the bus, next to the bathroom, where he could stretch his six-foot-six legs, where no one could come up from behind him, and where he could stare wordlessly up the aisle. Before the end of the season, I vowed, I would be granted permission to sit in the 'hood.

The bus and plane management of players is key for a manager at any level. Ed "Singin' Ed" Nottle, the beery Zen master and manger of the league's Sioux City Explorers, put it thusly: "Anybody who coaches Little League can call the plays on the field for a professional team. Everybody knows when to bunt. A real manager is someone who can walk down an aisle of a plane or bus and with just a glance, not a word, shut a player up. That's a manager."

Still, to keep the peace, there were these rules about who was allowed to sit where. But to spy and to get any shit at all on Strawberry, I would need to routinely go past that barrier of ballplayers and the rest of the team officials.

So after I boarded the team bus to Duluth, I went straight to the middle, sat down, slunk down in my seat, and stared out the window. It was important at this moment for me not only not to be a jerk, but to become invisible. Too late, I noticed several players noticing me and grimacing, but nobody said anything—yet.

It was strange for them to see a reporter back here. It went against the Laws of Nature. Good, I thought. Let them get used to me. Let me buy them drinks and make them like me. Let me watch them pick up groupies and spy comfortably on Strawberry when he rides the bus. I would eviscerate Billy Murray on my own.

Across the aisle, Stanford grad and outfielder Steve Solomon put down the morning *New York Times* and looked straight at me. I knew this fellow was, as they say in the Midwest, *different*. The fact that he was reading *The New York Times* made him immediately suspect among his teammates, who, if they were intellectuals, satisfied themselves daily with the sports section of *USA Today*.

"You shouldn't even be sitting back here," he said. "It's okay with me, but some of the other guys might not be too happy with it."

"It's okay. I'm with *Rolling Stone*," I whispered back, proffering all sorts of letters of credential and my old photo ID signed by Jann Wenner. Solomon nodded and put his nose back in his paper.

"So . . . Steve," I said, racing through my press package for his name and history, "tell me more about what got you to St. Paul." If I pretended I was taking an interview, perhaps the other players would relax and not object to having a reporter in their midst. Solomon put down his paper.

"You know, a lot of people think you're old if you're not in the major leagues and you're not twenty-five. I'm twenty-six. Two years ago I lead the entire Phillies' organization in batting. Last year I bat .228. Everyone has a bad year. But they let me go. Maybe to try and bring along a player a year or two younger than you. A lot of the players here are just around for one last go, one great final hurrah, but I'm determined to make it to the major leagues."

"By major league standards," Solomon said, "I'm getting kind of old at twenty-six. But this team attracts a lot of national pub."

Ouch. Old at twenty-six. I felt as old and battered as Steve Solomon, used up in earlier times before I'd lost my spirit. As Yogi Berra said about the afternoon shadows that darken Yankee Stadium's left field, "It gets late early out there."

"Maybe if I play hard and well in St. Paul, put up some numbers and get some good pub," Solomon says, "some club might remember my name and give me a little more time to make the major leagues. "The major leagues, yeah, that's what it's all about," Solomon said, lifting up his copy of the paper to check the day's news, markets, and who was getting the good pub in the major leagues.

"Pub" is baseballese for any form of publicity accrued to a player. To a ballplayer, there are only two kinds of pub. "Good pub," which was a flattering piece, and "bad pub," which is a hatchet job about a player's abilities. In a world of binaries—out/safe, ball/strike, out/safe, there was no room for so-so pub.

Unstated in the midst of all this was the fact that Solomon is Jewish, a species in baseball that is almost as rare as a Hindu. Less that two hundred Jews have made it to the majors, and a few have become cultural heroes: Sandy Koufax and Hank Greenberg outshadow anything written by Maimonides. Steve Solomon could go down in history.

The other players had noticed the Star of David around Solomon's neck and were already gossiping about how he made the team. Marv Goldklang, it was said, had been searching for an adequate Jew for his team for years and had finally found one in this Stanford honors grad who'd been labeled a head case by the Phillies.

It did not help that Solomon refused to go out with his teammates and drink and whore. But organized baseball had never liked Jews, let alone blacks. In *Lords of the Realm,* the *Wall Street Journal*'s John Helyar reported that owners regularly referred to the players' negotiator Marvin Miller as that "gimpy-armed Jew bastard." And if Walter O'Malley didn't like one of Miller's proposals, he would say, "Tell that Jewish boy to go back to Brooklyn."

When Solomon's father visited later that summer, he would insist that the reason why his two sons had been cut from the Phillies and Seattle was "those anti-Semitic motherfuckers of baseball."

"He's from a different generation," explained Solomon, embarrassed.

African Americans fared even worse among owners, except for Bill Veeck. They never understood how to lure black fans into ballparks. In the late 1970s, Minnesota Twins owner Calvin Griffith was asked why he moved his team from Washington, D.C., to Minnesota, depriving a home team for *The Washington Post*'s Shirley Povich, the best newspaper baseball beat writer and columnist ever.

"It was when I found out you had only fifteen thousand black people here [sic]," Griffith said. "Black people don't go to ball games, but they'll fill up a rassling ring and put up such a chant it'll scare you to death. It's believable. We came here because you've got good hardworking white people here."

The white players said worse. But on that ride to Duluth, I began meeting some of the nicest people I'd ever met. There was starting pitcher Jeff Alkire, twenty-six, who'd made the U.S. Olympic baseball team, pitched brilliantly at the University of Miami, been drafted by the St. Louis Cardinals in the fifth round in 1992, and was dropped this spring.

As I moved to Alkire's seat, I asked him idiotically what his dreams are. "I want the call," he said. "Even for one day, I want the call to the big leagues. Players say you don't really know how great it is until you're there, even if it's for a day. You are treated like a God. You don't touch a bag. You get chartered flights. You don't deal with ticketing. And you've got money. I was just in Cincinnati, and I saw Kent Mercker just walk into this restaurant where I'd been waiting an hour and a half to get in. And they immediately gave him a table. He probably slipped him a couple hundred bucks, but

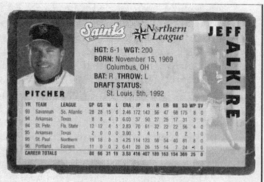

he had his own table. In St. Paul, we get free Jackie Chan movies on the bus, hah-hah. I still want to get there, the bigs."

Alkire was a good buy. But Wenner would hate him and cut him out of any piece. Too boring. He was no Strawberry.

Meantime, real trouble was afoot two rows back in the form of Kevin Garner, nearing age thirty-one, height six-foot-two, weight 220. As a former number-one draft choice and can't-miss prospect who tragically missed, he still had his pride.

There are ways things are done in baseball, Garner said loudly to me, and reporters sitting with players was not one of them, not even when he played in Mexico. Garner, the most muscular fellow on the team, stood up, walked to my aisle, and began half-yelling, "Who are you? Why are you sitting here?"

I gave him my papers, my photo ID autographed by Jann Wenner.

"How do I know you didn't forge these papers? How do I know you really write for *Rolling Stone?*"

"How do I know you're even a baseball player?" I shot back.

Experience has taught me that if a ballplayer yells at you, yell back. If you don't get punched, chances are the rest of the team will back you in humiliating one of their own. It's part of the credo of being a ballplayer to humiliate their buddies, even if by hot foot or sticking toilet paper on their shoe. Getting even vaguely one-upped by a five-foot-nine *Rolling Stone* reporter was a bad thing.

I riffled through my roster and found Garner's statistics. "Oooh, a *designated hitter*," I went on meanly. "Nothing more valuable on a major league team than a thirty-one-year-old designated hitter. There aren't a *lot* of those around."

As a matter of fact, it was the worst, most useless thing to be, unless you were Albert Belle himself. Garner laughed, the joke on him. But he just wouldn't let things be with me.

"And just don't take any shits in the bus bathroom. It stinks up the bus for the entire ride!" he yelled, regaining the upper hand.

Actually, a ballplayer yelling at you could be very good copy. A couple of years before, Willie Mays, in full spring training uniform, had kicked me out of his sports car (vanity plates SAY HEY) when I gently provoked him into being as bitter a prick as everybody said he was.

"I promise," I said to Kevin Garner, whose pride in keeping the rules of the big leagues that he would never make I still sort of admired. "What was life like playing in the Mexican League?" I asked Garner.

"No comment," Garner said. "Ever."

Garner would spend the rest of the summer calling me either a "fake" or a "fag," trying to retain face.

Fucking ballplayers. Baseball players, I'd learned in the old days, were the worst to deal with. Many hadn't been to college and truly believed that the meaning of life was women, beer, baseball, and The Life of a baseball player. They took rudeness to anyone outside of the fraternity of ballplayers as worthy of cheers. At least professional football players had all been to college and perhaps read a book or two. Pro basketball players were generally very nice and cooperative—and strangely shy. Most grew up as giants, feeling like freaks, and their quietness often traveled with them into the locker room.

Greg Harrington, the Saints' play-by-play guy, was right—hockey players were the nicest. But I had to make my stand on the Saints' bus, or I would spend the summer up front talking to bussie for the eight-hour trips up to Thunder Bay, Ontario. I needed dirt on the men in the back of the bus to fill in my story of doom at the end of the line.

"Whoa, Kevin was pretty angry at you," Solomon said to me from across the aisle. "His arm got hurt pretty bad way back when, and I think he's one of the ones just playing for The Life."

With Solomon, about fifteen other Saints are harboring hopes, insane or not, of making it to the Show. For inspiration, they use the example of Rey Ordoñez, an unknown Cuban who joined the Saints in 1993 and is now the starting shortstop of the New York Met. Ex-Saint pitcher Mike Mimbs made it all the way back up to the Philadelphia Phillies, though he was loathe to admit to reporters that he had to play independent minor league ball with the St. Paul Saints to do it. And then came the rejuvenation of Dan Peltier. In 1995, Peltier had made $1,800 a month with St. Paul; in 1996, he made $18,000 a month with the San Francisco Giants. Their names— Ordoñez, Mimbs, Peltier—which are repeated like Hail Marys by the wannabes, are enough to keep the players here. For the average salary for a major league baseball player is $1.336 million a year.

"I don't want to waste my time on the bus if I'm not going to make it," says Solomon. "There are other things I could do besides baseball. I'm not sure what . . . but I know they're there."

Marty Neff, the Saints' most famous head case, hears Solomon and paints another picture. "I knew I'd never get back after the Pirates released me and started talking trash about me," the twenty-six-year-old says. "So I'm just here to have fun and enjoy doing something I don't have to get up at seven A.M. to do. I like The Life."

The Life. Sleeping until noon. Playing ball at night. Guzzling beer until closing time and chasing what ballplayers still call "puss" after the game. The Life, be it baseball, rock & roll, or the carnival: where time is turned upside down, and the straight nine-to-five world is looked upon with contempt.

The Saints' rookies seemed most excited, especially Dan Thomson, a twenty-two-year-old pitcher from Bensonhurst, Brooklyn, who was dressed like a Seattle nightmare right down to his grunge beard, earrings, and shaved head. While his teammates favored country music almost exclusively, Thomson preferred to play Nirvana and Nine Inch Nails over the rickety CD player he'd brought onboard.

"Hey, Thomson, turn that shit off, it's leaking out of your headphones," shouted Country Stewart as Thomson bangs his hands in rhythm on his lap. "I am a professional baseball player for the first time this year," Thomson says as he takes off his headphones, "but I will have much fun this year."

Settled into my seat for the moment, having averted a true crisis, I listened in. "Anyone for cards?" Solomon called and, within seconds, a gaggle of players had joined in back as a deck appeared.

Gin rummy was another beloved prop of baseball, as beloved to ballplayers as the pine tar rag or the practice still known as "beaver

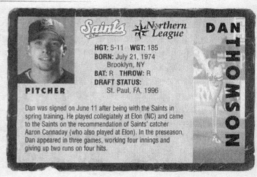

shooting"—looking up a young woman's dress from the playing field, a habit first publicly identified in Jim Bouton's *Ball Four.*

Often, even in the low-paid minors, players bring out all their money for gin rummy and may even gamble their entire salary on one card game. In the Northern League, where the average pay is $400 week, one could be shot within minutes of a new gin game. Cards are so potentially dangerous that Maury Allen announced in *Bo Pitching and Wooing,* his biography of satyr/pitcher Bo Belinsky of the early sixties:

> Extramarital sex is a proven, harmless pastime for most play-
> ers: what the little woman doesn't know won't hurt her. But
> card losses are a lot harder to hide. Johnny Superstar has an
> awful tough time convincing the old lady his pay is a thousand
> dollars short because he was fined for not running out a
> ground ball.

Marathon bus rides in the minor leagues are a rite of passage for virtually every player who makes the Show. Being on the bus meant paying your dues, and Saints manager Marty Scott had even written a country and western song about it when he got his first gig managing at the Class A level with the Burlington Rangers of the Midwest League.

Marty would only sing the song if pushed hard and repeatedly, someone had an acoustic guitar with which he could accompany himself, and an audience that hopefully didn't include any of his ballplayers. With a country voice that was one part Hank Williams to one part Oak Ridge Boys, Marty wrote the song during a two-hour bus ride to Cedar Rapids in 1982. He called it "The Bus Driver's Song," a tale of the minor leagues as seen through the eyes of bussie. He sang it for me in a private performance later that season:

> Winding roads, a full busload
> On my way to Cedar Rapids
> Passing cornfields on my left and right, hazy rainy skies above me
> Happy cuz I know I will be
> Driving back to Burlington tonight
> Going near or going far
> Stopping at all railroad crossings, clearing bridges that are low
>   in height
> Screaming directed at me
> But I'm happy cuz I will be
> Driving back to Burlington tonight
> Only thing I know above all
> Driving for the Rangers is all right.

But this is the opening weekend, and nobody is singing. Three hours later, the Saints' bus pulls into the Best Western Motel in downtown Duluth, and some players scramble to the windows to see the local talent waiting for them outside the motel. Sure, the largest city on Lake Superior is fogged in, so it's hard to tell who is outside the bus's tinted windows. But the veterans knew there would be women for those ballplayers who wanted one, even for players so low-down as to play for the Saints. "Women follow a uniform—whether it's a soldier, musician, or ballplayer," announced a hotel manager where segregated Negro League teams stayed in the 1940s.

Peering at potential sex partners, several players size up the young and willing of Duluth and its twin city, Superior, Wisconsin. Generally, baseball players talk about sex at least as much as they talk about baseball. Many ballplayers talk about it using an almost quaint 1940s tough guy patois of the kind seen in early Norman Mailer novels.

Here on the bus, one hears references to women's breasts as "guns" (as in "She's got a set of guns on her") or "rack." "Beaver" remains a favorite, while a coach known for chasing women is still called a "cooze hound." The emphasis remains even on the field: a perfect unhittable pitch thrown right below the belt, explained third baseman Chris Evans, is called a "cock shot" by ballplayers.

As written in *Diamonds in the Rough: The Untold History of Baseball* by Joel Zoss and John Bowman:

> Ballplayers today are virtually all presented as monogamous young men, whether single or married, more interested in the heft of the bat than the curve of a female. It is hard to imagine an article revealing that a player is as dedicated to bedding women than Dwight Evans was shown to be eating his wife's pesto.

Finally the players amble off the bus and begin searching for ways to spend their $15-a-day meal money (major leaguers receive $67 per diem, with a yearly cost-of-living increase). The motel is tiny and dingy and reminds one of Norman Bates. Darryl Strawberry and his family, as well as Jack Morris, have opted for more glamorous surroundings downtown (at their own expense).

The Saints unlock their doors, with fog coming knee-high off the lake. Twig, who along with Marty Scott is the only Saint with his own room, reminds them to be ready to go back to the ballpark via the bus at 4 P.M. for a 7 P.M. start.

By 4:15 P.M., the team bus hits Wade Stadium, a crumbling Works Progress Administration brick edifice that bears a frightening resemblance to Shawshank Prison. The outfield, dotted with potholes and lumps, has a decidedly non-major-league feel to it. To get out of the tiny dugout, an angled aluminum contraption with only a foot of headroom, a player has to duck deep to avoid decapitation.

"Welcome to the Northern League," says Twig, not bitching at all. "Doesn't smell like they've fixed the bathroom from last season."

The players, meantime, kill time, hoping the game will be canceled on account of fog so they can hit the nightspots of Duluth and especially Superior. "All the women in Duluth and Superior are either tens or ones," explains a player, "but there are enough tens for all of us."

But it's Opening Day in Duluth, and the Dukes' owners want to wait until game time when much of the capacity crowd of over three thousand has filtered in before calling the game. "Fer chrissakes, let us at least sell some beer," one says.

"This Duluth weather is nothing," points out Dave Wright who has come to Duluth in his role as press relations director. "Last year, a game was canceled here with us because there was a seventeen-degree windchill."

Meantime, Jack Morris, who is slated to pitch the opener now that Henderson is gone, warms up with weights in the shower because, as in St. Paul, there are no training facilities. When it becomes obvious that Morris won't be pitching that night because of the fog, he puts down the weights.

He walks past Marty Neff and rubs the twenty-six-year-old's big belly. "What is that?" Morris demands. "I'm forty-one and I'm in better shape than you. You want to move up, don't you?"

Neff is silent, furious.

Morris then starts regaling his teammates with stories of the big leagues. A major league batter nicknamed "Champ" among the players had drunk thirteen beers before a game, he said, not believing he was playing that day. Unexpectedly penciled into the game, Champ according to Morris, went four for five with four doubles. Kevin Garner, sitting at Morris's knee, forces a weak smile—he, more than anybody else in this room, once deserved to tell stories like these, gleaned from the major leagues.

Darryl Strawberry, meantime, gives a forced laugh, then looks straight ahead with a straight line for an expression. The story is not funny to him. In the 1980s, he was famous for not playing with hangovers, sending word to manager Davey Johnson from the training table that he wouldn't be available for the game that night because of the liquor he'd consumed the night before.

Finally, after enough beer has been sold to the sellout crowd that has come to see Darryl and Jack to ensure the owners of not a total washout, the game is called. A doubleheader will be played tomorrow, with Jack on the mound and Darryl in an outfield as lumpy as gravy.

Also in attendance is Tom Keegan, the respected national baseball writer for the *New York Post*. If Darryl goes back to the majors, melodrama suggests it only makes sense that it would be with the New York Mets or Yankees, towns big enough to hold his magic—or fuck him up. Keegan is here to see what is up and headlines his first article: DARRYL'S "EXILE IN HELL."

Strawberry disappeared immediately after the called game with his family. A few of the players, however, are ready to blow their meal money in Superior and wave on the team bus back to the hotel. For while standing on the field, in the bullpen, admiring the fog, some

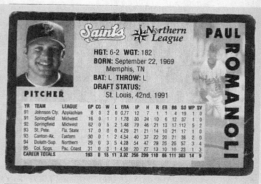

women had thrown notes at relief pitcher Paul "Roma" Romanoli and another player.

Roma is the team's closer, as well as its Romeo. Dark, suave, and six-foot-two, he made it all the way up to AAA last year before being released. Word of Roma's exploits had traveled the league when he played for Duluth in 1994, and the word was that he could pick up any woman, at any time, with any line.

"Hell, come along, I'll do it on the record," he said, the only player willing to use his name while whoring.

"But, Roma," I said, "you have a girlfriend in St. Paul. What about Marie?"

"That doesn't matter. Marie loves me," Roma said with a wink. "I'll just tell her that you mistook me for somebody else. Or that you just made it up."

But now it was down to business. The notes said to meet the women at a country and western bar across the Wisconsin border, so the players pooled their money and chipped in for a cab. "I didn't like the looks of those two," Roma said, "but let's see what kind of other talent they have."

When they get to the club, one of the Saints yells to another, "Whoo-whee! I can smell that pussy!" A beautiful woman walks by in country gear, all fringe and tight skirt, and the players' eyes bulge. "Roma," he says, "if I could get a piece of that, I'd be batting .400."

Once again, most ballplayers have an obsession about sex and performance. Wade Boggs once went to the trouble of figuring out that he hit .333 with his mistress in Fenway Park and only .229 when his wife was in attendance.

"Never mind that," says Roma. "Look at her. Five feet away stands trouble with its midriff bare. What about her?" he asks. "Gimme that, and I'll have a 104 mile per hour fastball." Roma looks around the pulsating country bar.

"Thank God those women who threw us the notes at the ballpark aren't here yet," Roma says. "I'm going to have to work fast."

The collected Saints nod in agreement. "Let me," Romanoli says, "show you all how it's done."

Approaching the firecracker in the blouse that looks painted on, Roma walks behind her, pulls the tag out from her shirt, and inspects it. "What do you think you're doing?" she says, turning around, pissed off.

"I just wanted to see," says Romanoli, "if you were made in heaven."

"Oh God," says the woman, shaking her head at the corn.

"Are you tired?" Roma goes on.

"No," says the woman. "Why?"

"Because you've been running through my mind all day."

"What are you, crazy?" she continues.

"No," Roma says, "I'm Paul Romanoli, closing relief pitcher for the St. Paul Saints. Pleased to meet you."

They shake hands. "Oh, one more question." Roma asks, "Do you have a quarter?"

"Why?" asks the prey.

"Because I want to call my daddy," he says in his deepest Southern accent, "and tell him I've met the woman I want to marry."

"Oh God," she says, laughing and finishing her beer. Five minutes later, they are out the door, before the girls who threw him the note arrive.

"Amazing," says a Saint who has witnessed the proceedings. "Fucking Roma."

It takes a few hours, but the few other gathered Saints round up their evening's quarry. It is to be a six-person orgy back at the motel, with the women paying for the pizza because the players have already blown their meal money on cabs. The Life.

"Why didn't you wake me up?" demands Scott Stewart the next morning, who had turned in after the game and didn't wake up when the party started.

"Being with a woman all night never hurt no professional baseball player," the venerable Casey Stengel once said. "It's staying up all night looking for a woman that does him in."

All Saints are present and accounted for, though, and look reasonably well rested the next day as Jeff Alkire, not Morris, takes the mound on June 1 for Duluth's rescheduled Opening Day. Jack, it turns out, wants an extra day to get in shape. But the highlight of the show comes before the game, when Strawberry takes batting practice, and all action on the field and in the stands stops. He quickly hits four out of the park, including a home run that hits the scoreboard so hard it careens all the way back to the infield before it stops rolling.

Most of the Duluth fans are now convinced that Strawberry is a mighty spirit and cheer every movement the exiled player makes. Still, there are random calls of "Dar-ryl! Dar-ryl!"—the mean-spirited chant sent his way by 1986 Boston Red Sox fans in the World Series. The chant will follow him wherever he goes. As he will all season, Darryl ignores the fans who mock him.

Out in the outfield, things did not go so well for him. A ground single into the hilly outfield turned into a two-base error for Strawberry, who had to chase it down to the fence. Then, with the score tied in the ninth, he struck out on four pitches, and the Saints lost 7–6.

Still, he did get two singles. "I've just got to adapt, get used to the surroundings, make baseball fun again," he says, dragging on a Newport. "I know I can still play, and that's why I made the decision to come to the Northern League. To make baseball fun one more time, even if I don't get back to the major leagues."

The next afternoon before the game, I go to the library in Duluth, where I find out that the city of 100,000 is considered the politest, proudest city in Minnesota. Duluth is famous as the birthplace of Bob Dylan and as a major port on the Great Lakes. In fact, some of the great mining and shipping fortunes in the world still reside in Duluth. I went down to the city boat canal; it was remarkably relaxing to watch 700-foot boats filled with iron ore come in via the internal waterway of the entire Great Lakes, causing the rise of the Aeriel Lift Bridge.

But to the readers of *Rolling Stone?* Booooring. Since people were also a little stuck up about being nicer and tougher than folks from Minneapolis or St. Paul, I wanted to stick it to them.

The biggest dirt I found was a 1920 lynching by 10,000 people convinced that a Duluth white woman had been raped and nearly killed by some black men. Three blacks working for a nearby carnival were quickly strung up from a lamppost. No evidence of a crime was ever firmly found, and five months later another carnival worker was tried, convicted, and sent to jail for five years.

The lynched men, meanwhile, were buried in unmarked graves. I went to see them in Duluth's Park Hill Cemetery and found that Duluth, which prides itself on being more civilized than either Minneapolis or St. Paul, had indeed tried to make amends. In 1991, a local church put up headstones for the three men with an epitaph of DETERRED BUT NOT DEFEATED.

Before the game the next day, Sunday, June 2, Strawberry and I head to the bullpen while Jack Morris warms up on the sidelines. It's time for "Baseball Chapel," a little church service run in bullpens throughout the bigs and minors on Sundays for the devout believers.

"Lord Jesus," the preacher begins, "thank you for dying on the cross for me. I am a sinner and need to be forgiven."

Strawberry knows the words by heart, but I still wonder. He was "born again" in 1991 and tested positive for drugs several times since. "I really don't care if you think it's real," Strawberry says. "It's real to me. I made my mistakes, and I've paid the price."

Many in today's crowd seem to be booing Darryl before the game, and he's hearing it in little Wade Stadium. "Pay your alimony!" several yell. But Darryl's revenge comes in the fifth inning when Strawberry hits a 522-foot home run to center. The ball clears the fence, the backstop of a nearby Little League field, and leaves a divot in the miniature park. The crowd of Duluth fans sitting behind the Saints' dugout begins doing the "We are not worthy" wave from *Wayne's World*.

Home run number one for Darryl Strawberry, and it looks . . . redemptive. Jack Morris is not so lucky, battered around by a corps of no-name Duluth players before exiting to the PA sounds of "Hit the Road, Jack."

After leaving the game, Morris uncharacteristically goes to sit in the stands and chat with fans and sign autographs. The headline of Tom Powers's column the next day in the St. Paul paper was SAINT JACK HAS CHANGED. According to Powers, he saw the astounding sight of Morris making small talk with fans as almost an act of God. "This did not appear to be the Jack Morris I remembered. For example, not once did he open wide and spew a torrent of fire. . . . Mr.

Morris apparently turned charming while he was out [in Montana] farming."

Time would tell. I'd read that Morris had left the Reds, his last big league team, in tears.

The Saints win 9–6 and sweep the doubleheader with a strong performance by Scott Stewart.

But then, in the locker room after the game, a reporter from Winnipeg approaches Strawberry. He's been scouting Darryl for an upcoming game with his team and has chased away the Duluth cold with what smells like several beers.

Tom Keegan, the *New York Post* reporter likens the appearance of the reporter to Otis the town drunk in "The Andy Griffith Show" in his column.

"Why are you here?" the drunk asks Strawberry. "You had a decent year last year, Darryl. Why aren't you in the major leagues with the others?"

Strawberry glared at the man, the mean old Darryl stare that he hadn't shown anyone since he'd gone sober and decided to take this last chance with the Saints. "Why don't you ask major league baseball?" Darryl said softly. "Maybe they'll tell you."

The reporter wouldn't let up. "Did this park remind you of Candlestick Park? Did you ever play much in Candlestick?"

"I played in the National League for ten years, man," Darryl shot back. And then he gets a whiff of the reporter's *boozy* breath. "Man, you been drinking?"

"Well, I did have a couple beers out there. Gets mighty cold some nights in Duluth."

"Man," Darryl responds, "don't you know the rules? You're supposed to start drinking *after* the game. Why don't you let the reporters who haven't been drinking ask the questions?"

"Like I said, Darryl, it was awful cold out there."

Other reporters crowd around, but the drunk feels the need to shout out one more question. "Darryl, why are you a guy who everybody either loves or hates? Why is that?"

Darryl stops his response to another reporter and looks the drunk reporter right in the eye. "I know God loves me, so it doesn't really matter what anybody else thinks of me."

And then Strawberry is gone—back to his family and the drive to St. Paul. Jack Morris takes off in a sports car. The rest of the team, meantime, boards the team bus for the ride home. There is one stop made at Kentucky Fried Chicken for twenty-five minutes, then it's back on the bus and blessed sleep.

Tomorrow it's on the road again, this time an eight-hour bus ride to Thunder Bay, Ontario, to play the Whiskey Jacks (the league's best nickname, inspired by an indigenous bird). Thunder Bay is the Devil's Island of this Devil's Island league, and the bus ride is an unmitigated hell for too many players, with not enough space and far too much time to contemplate their highly uncertain futures.

The solitude of Thunder Bay is almost frightening; there is not another major town within 470 miles of the Ontario Circle where it sits. Except for the fact that Paul Shaffer from the "Late Show with David Letterman" hails from here, there isn't even history: Thunder Bay was created in 1969, when the lonely cities of Fort William and Port Arthur decided to cling together for good.

When the players got to their hotel in Thunder Bay on June 4, however, some found a few perks. A handful of girls from Superior had made the drive also and made sure their favorites weren't too lonely in what felt like the worst place in the world.

Darryl, at six-foot-six, looks like he might not survive the long drive home to St. Paul from remotest Ontario. Mute, wearing his rarely seen penitentiary face, Straw sits in his accustomed spot in the back of the 'hood, trying to stretch his legs. He hits a home run, his second of the season, but goes only one for six for the series and the Saints lose two out of three.

Neither cigarettes, nor pleasant conversation, nor idle chatter from other players seems to mollify him. All he wants is to go home to St. Paul, and his family, and the next stage of his peculiar adventure.

Time has passed, the season is over
Snow will come
Stay at home and dream of baseball
Only thing I know above all.
—Marty Scott, "The Bus Driver's Song"

6

Sister Roz Explains It All to Me

O! how this spring of love resembleth
The uncertain glory of an April day!
Which now shows all the beauty of the sun,
And by and by a cloud takes all away.
—William Shakespeare, *The Two Gentlemen of Verona*

June 6, 1996

Finally it was Opening Day at home, and I had to be ready for Bill Murray to arrive unannounced—just in case. He'd done that before: shown up at Midway Stadium on Opening Day in Saints attire, thrown out the ceremonial first ball straight over the press box and into the parking lot, and then gone on to goof his way through the entire game with fans, players, and even the umpires.

Mike Veeck, dummying up, said he had no idea if Murray was coming. Meantime, before the game, he could be found painting fences and garbage cans, planting flowers, talking with his late father, and remembering how Bill Veeck used to come bail him out of jail after a burglary arrest in Mike's lengthy troubled years. "At least be a *good* punk," his father told him. "Now, when I'm tense, I paint things instead of burning them down," Mike said.

Mostly, however, Mike gleamed at the spectacle around him as the gates prepared to open at 6 P.M., when he himself would be manning a turnstile. From his position inside the ballpark, Mike could see the parking lot full of tailgaters who'd turned the asphalt outside into a party for St. Paul. "It's like Woodstock or old home

Mike Veeck, in tux, tails and tophat, at the turnstiles, Opening Day, 1996
Courtesy of St. Paul Saints

week out in the parking lot," he said. "People who haven't seen each other all winter are finally able to say hello."

Inside the action was frenzied. The inflatable sumo suits, to be used as a between-inning promotion, were readied, as was the outfield hot tub, the chair where patrons could get a haircut while watching the game, and the massage stations where fans could get a rubdown during the game delivered by a genuine nun with hands as strong as Sonny Liston's.

Two man-yoked chariots for between innings *Spartacus* races were being readied, and a Saints representative was out in the parking lot, looking for the dirtiest car: the winner would be announced over the PA and win a free car wash.

Somethings could not be perfectly controlled, like the number of trains that would rumble past the left field fence every game (the average was thirteen). If a Saint was batting, the crowd would chant, "Hit the train! Hit the train!" and the engineer would toot his horn. Another train was set up and running atop the Saints' dugout, by Saints saint Annie Huidekoper. "It's the rally train," she explained.

"We're just testing it out; it'll start running if we're behind by the bottom of the eighth."

There were other traditions. No one was allowed to wear a tie in the stadium, in memory, perhaps of Bill Veeck, whose nickname was "the Shirt" for his refusal to ever wear neck gear. The Wave, that noxious crowd waving stunt, was permanently banned—and a sign was posted declaring Midway Stadium a NO WAVE ZONE. Any foul ball caught by an adult would be met with chants of "Give it to a kid! Give it to a kid!" If an opposing batter struck out, a chant of "One-two! One-two!" followed his trudge back to the visiting dugout. Bags of peanuts would be thrown out of the press box during the seventh-inning stretch.

There were other variables peculiar to St. Paul and the Saints, like the outfield tree house where local talk show celebrity Tom Mischke would broadcast his call-in radio show, with topics having nothing to do with baseball, every time the Saints were in town. A home run could fly into his tree house while Mischke was discussing NATO on the air. "I'm from St. Paul, and I can't tell you how badly this town needed this team at this time," says Mischke, a New York talent who decided to stay home here in St. Paul.

Indeed, in three short years, the Saints had become St. Paul's beloved. Never mind that Minneapolis had the major league baseball Twins, football Vikings, and basketball Timberwolves. Who cared that downtown Minneapolis jumped by night, while downtown St. Paul snoozed? Who gave a shit that CBS News correspondent Morley Safer once called St. Paul "the most boring city in America"?

Still, "that town across the river" is how St. Paul's old world aristocracy referred to what is considered nouveau riche Minneapolis. St. Paul also prides itself on its memory. It was no coincidence that it took over three quarters of a century for the city to forgive F. Scott Fitzgerald for cracking wise about his hometown, nor that his pardon was spurred by Garrison Keillor, another writer who's long been wrongly pilloried locally for making Minnesotans look like prairie simpletons.

Memories also stretch far back for less literary-minded St. Paulites, the ones who remember or heard about the old St. Paul Saints of the almost-major American Association. This is where many of the old Brooklyn Dodgers made their last stops before heading to Ebbets Field: Duke Snider and Pee Wee Reese got their final seasoning here, and St. Paul is where Hall of Fame catcher Roy Campanella became the first black man to play in the American Association.

Yet long before Walter O'Malley ripped the heart out of Brooklyn and St. Paul, the Saints were feeding St. Paul's historic abandonment and inferiority complexes. Founded in 1884, the team bounced around the professional bushes until it was purchased for the 1895 season by Charles Comiskey, who installed the St. Paul Saints in the Western League. Comiskey and Western League president Ban Johnson, however, had plans to take their circuit into the majors. Unfortunately, challenging the long established National League would mean moving a couple of Western League teams to major metropolises.

So, in March 1900, Comiskey quit St. Paul and moved the Saints to Chicago, where they immediately became the Chicago White Stockings, by 1901 charter members of the American league. Karma came back; Comiskey became infamous as the tightwad owner who indirectly caused the fixing of the 1919 "Say it ain't so, Joe" World Series.

The Saints were soon reborn as a minor league team. In 1902, they joined Minneapolis and six other mid-size cities as charter members of the American Association. There the Saints stayed for fifty-eight straight seasons, with the likes of Dizzy Dean, Babe Ruth, and Satchel Paige all making appearances at the Saint's minor league home.

All are still fondly talked about by people who weren't nearly old enough to have been there. But it's been a long time for highlights for those from St. Paul: the major league Minnesota Twins moved into the Minneapolis suburbs in 1961, and the Saints eventually packed up and moved to Omaha, where the team's name was changed to the Royals. The town's inexorable decline to second-class mill town began.

But that was before. Now the biggest party St. Paul had ever seen was being thrown out in the parking lot at every home game. The music blared, the beer flowed, and the broilers worked to capacity on behalf of friends and strangers who supped and danced with each other as if they were relatives. Saints players, manager Marty Scott, and co-owner Bill Murray (when he was in town) routinely worked the parking lot before games, rubbing elbows, taking bites, shaking hands.

"Here," said a large chef named Vince Jeannette, pushing a load of barbecued shrimp onto my plate. "Join the party." Around Vince, a special education teacher, swirled several dozen Saints fans who

Vince and his famous tailgaters
Courtesy of Bonnie Butler

were reconnecting after the long winter, as well as Rosie, Vince's girlfriend.

"Who are these people?" I asked Vince, who had gone back to manning his grill.

"I don't know half of them," he said. "Earlier in the afternoon, we fed the entire Winnipeg team. Nice boys, big appetites. But what the hell? This is St. Paul. Everybody's welcome—unlike in Minneapolis, where you're nobody unless you've taken a bubble bath with Prince."

"Booooo!" yelled the line at the grill at the mere sound of the hated rival city. "Hey," Vince said, "why don't you go say hi to Sister Roz? She's sitting under that umbrella under our tent, staying cool until the game starts and she has to work. You know Sister Roz, right?"

Indeed. Who didn't? Sister Roz was the septuagenarian Benedictine nun who provided professional massages for a few bucks in the grandstand each game. Featured in every feature about the team, a blessed guest on the doomed "Joan Rivers Show," she was for real, I found. She was alone now, slowly sipping a beer and going over her travel plans to India to visit with Mother Teresa after the season ended.

SISTER ROSALIND GEFRE
SAINTS' STRESS RELIEVER   1996

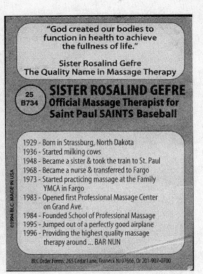

"God created our bodies to
function in health to achieve
the fullness of life."

Sister Rosalind Gefre
The Quality Name in Massage Therapy

25
B734   **SISTER ROSALIND GEFRE**
Official Massage Therapist for
Saint Paul SAINTS Baseball

1929 - Born in Strassburg, North Dakota
1936 - Started milking cows
1948 - Became a sister & took the train to St. Paul
1968 - Became a nurse & transferred to Fargo
1973 - Started practicing massage at the Family
        YMCA in Fargo
1983 - Opened first Professional Massage Center
        on Grand Ave.
1984 - Founded School of Professional Massage
1995 - Jumped out of a perfectly good airplane
1996 - Providing the highest quality massage
        therapy around ... BAR NUN

BLC Order Form: 265 Cedar Lane, Teaneck NJ 07666, Or 201-907-0700

"Come sit down here," she said in a strange accent that she traced to her birthplace only a few miles from where Lawrence Welk grew up. "Yah, sure, everyone knew the Welks," the sister said. "Peggy Lee also came from around there, although her name back then was Deloris Engstrom."

Yes, she was real. "Could I ask you a few questions?" I inquired.

"Yes, but first let me ask you a question," she said. "Why do you look so sad? Is there anything more beautiful than an Opening Day of baseball on one of God's most splendid evenings?"

"I'm not into baseball too much these days, Sister," I said. "I used to love it, live for it. But not anymore."

"Why?" asked the sister.

"Long story," I said.

"Come see me during the game and I'll give you a massage," she said. "You look so sad."

"What about you?"

"I was an ordinary farm girl," she began, sipping her beer, "who always felt the call to the sisterhood. I came to St. Paul and lived in the convent, cooking for the other sisters, but then I had to go home to Fargo to take care of my dying mother. It was there that I saw how much better she felt when I massaged her. Until that time, I'd always be up at night with internal chest pain, but then I too got massage, and the pain went away."

But the sisters back in the convent in St. Paul were not impressed with Sister Rosalind's idea of massage as a healing tool. "God called me in the 1970s to the massage, and when I started there were days I didn't know if I could live through the night because of the pressure from within the convent and from laypeople," she remembers. "Massage wasn't accepted then, and I felt lots of rejection. Many laypeople called my convent and said, 'Get rid of her.' But I endured."

She paused for a sip of beer. "But God kept calling, and I waited through the rejection. Now people come to me for a massage and talk, no matter what their religions. They tell me their problems, right there on the third base line in front of thousands of people. I hug them as often as I can, because often I wonder if I'm the last person who can touch their soul before they put a bullet through their head."

"I see," I said, turning off my tape recorder and rising. "Good luck, Sister."

"Come see me during the game," she said, hugging me good-bye. "You look like you hurt, you're sad. I'll give you a massage, and if you want to talk, we'll talk. If you want to pray, we'll pray. You don't have to be Catholic."

Whatever, I thought. What I needed was Bill Murray to show up, not a nun to tell me why my life had gone down the toilet. Well, Bill Murray wasn't here, but shortly before game time, columnist Patrick Reusse flopped up the steps to the press box like a walrus performing at an aquarium. After four innings, he left, claiming, "I've got my story—it's an overview."

What he saw was Jack Morris pitch most of five innings before leaving with a 9–3 lead. What he wrote about was "baseball's most profitable sweatshop" and patrons "so full of beer" that they might have been hallucinating. The Saints ended up losing ugly, 12–10, but nobody complained; the fireworks show after the game more than made up for the messy ballplaying. "It's a feeling I'm after, something you remember from when you're young," said Mike Veeck, watching the fireworks with his three-year-old daughter Rebecca. "And besides, I always liked setting things on fire and blowing up things."

I had skipped visiting Sister Roz, who was working away under her STRESS REDUCTION CENTER billboard in the grandstand, during the game out of embarrassment. It didn't seem seemly to me for a reporter to take comfort and a massage in the middle of a game.

"You owe yourself a try," said Sister Roz as she nabbed me after the game and took me to her massage table, a contraption featuring an upward reclining board for one's torso and a doughnut-shaped hole for one's head. The last fans filed out after the fireworks and the grounds crew took the field.

The old woman put her hands on my shoulders. I couldn't remember the last time I'd cried, but suddenly I started sobbing.

"It's okay," said Sister Roz, "a lot of people start crying here when I press on a muscle or touch something hidden. You make lots of jokes with people, but you seem so sad. Do you want to tell me what it's about?"

"I don't know if it's appropriate," I said between my own gasps. "It's about a woman. It's why I hate baseball. It's why I no longer really believe that things work out in life the way you think they will."

"Tell me," Sister Roz said. "Anything you say, believe me, I've heard worse."

"I'd thought Sasha [not her real name], you see, was my soul mate," I told Sister Roz. "It wasn't just that she looked like an angel and read the French postmodernists for fun."

"I don't know the French postmodernists," said Sister Roz.

"No problem," I said. "But no, what made me sure I'd found my partner for life with the notorious Baddest Girl in the Twin Cities' was that our courtship was bonded by baseball. I'd never before kissed a woman who knew the starting lineup of the 1955 Brooklyn Dodgers."

"A good team?" Sister Roz asked. Her hands were incredibly strong as they moved down my spine. I took my head out of the hole to make sure none of the Saints' staff was watching and started sobbing anew.

"A very good team," I said. "Anyway," I went on, "the first time I said, 'I love you' to Sasha, I gave her my prized Harmon 'the Minnesota Fat Boy' Killebrew autographed baseball to show her I meant it; the instant I knew I had to marry her was when she referred to a lousy Twins pitcher's heater as a 'Peggy Lee fastball.' How could I not fall in love with a woman who knew this inside baseball term for a fastball so feeble that the batter must ask, 'Is that all there is?' "

"You loved this woman," Sister Roz said as she crinkled my neck. "You really loved her."

"Yes."

"Did I mention that Peggy Lee grew up not too far from me in North Dakota?"

"Yes."

"So you really loved her."

"I really did, Sister. Ten months after our first Twins game together, Sasha and I got hitched. As we stood before the judge, I patted my right breast pocket where I'd put an index card bearing Satchel Paige's autograph."

"Satchel Paige?" the sister asked.

"He was an old pitcher from the Negro Leagues who pitched forever. He didn't get to come up to the major leagues until Mike Veeck's father signed him to the Cleveland Indians."

"I see," she said, attacking my lower back as I cried out in physical pain.

"I'd sent away to the old Negro League pitcher for his autograph when I was twelve. What better good-luck totem for an enduring and passionate marriage could I carry in my wedding suit than the signature of the man who pitched longer and more artfully than anyone?"

"You're a romantic," said Sister Roz. "That's nice."

"Anyway, we went to Vegas for our honeymoon."

"That doesn't sound so romantic."

"It was," I assured her. "The only bet Sasha and I placed all week was at the Golden Nugget, where we wagered five dollars on the Twins to win the Series. Then, six weeks after we got home to Minneapolis, I discovered that I hadn't married my soul mate, but an utter stranger. My heart broke, I filed for divorce, and I knew I would never go to another ball game."

"But now you're here," said Sister Roz.

"I'm working," I said. "I'm supposed to . . . never mind. Anyway, sitting on my kitchen floor a couple of days after signing my divorce decree, I cradled my autographed Harmon Killebrew baseball against my chest."

"I'm sorry," said Sister Roz, driving my clavicle somewhere deep into an unknown patch of nerves in my body.

"I also realized that an autographed baseball of the slugger known as 'the Minnesota Fat Boy' is a terrible companion on Valentine's Day. And most of all, it dawned on me that one could love baseball, but you shouldn't fall in love over it."

"I see," said Sister Roz. "You're blaming baseball when you should be happy that God spared you a lifetime of misery. Do you know that saying from St. Teresa? 'More tears are shed over answered prayers than unanswered ones.'"

"Yes? Do you know the first words of Nick Hornby's book about soccer where he says, 'I fell in love with football as I fell in love with women: suddenly, inexplicably, uncritically, giving no thought to the pain or disruption it would bring with it'?"

"No," said Sister Roz. "Don't know him. But I know you. It wasn't that you prayed wrongly for love, you just prayed for the wrong love. You know what they say: be careful what you wish for because you might get it. You just wished for the wrong thing and got it. Baseball has nothing to do with it."

"Well, I guess so," I replied.

"Go on with your story," she said.

"Anyway, 'I hate baseball,' I told my friends when the new season started. For the first time in my life, I paid no attention to the game. Instead, I spent my summer in the fetal position, listening to Patsy Cline and Peggy Lee from the floor of my apartment. Not even the chance to see Dave Winfield's three-thousandth hit could get my ass to the Twins' ballpark. 'I hate baseball,' I reminded my friends, who began calling me a weenie to my face."

"A weenie?" Sister Roz asked.

"Sorry. A weak person. Finally, packing up the apartment where Sasha and I were going to live for a move down the block, I came across my forgotten copy of *The Dickson Baseball Dictionary*. I turned to Satchel Paige, whose entry consisted of his six famous rules for staying young, hopeful, and alive. I'd repressed all Satchel trivia since my doomed marriage. Now I stared at the last item on his list as if for the first time. It said:

I Don't look back.

"Interesting philosophy," said Sister Roz.

"Now, when people ask me about my ex-wife, I begin by saying, 'We had a Peggy Lee marriage.' When they look puzzled, I say, 'You know, the kind of marriage where you have to ask, "Is that all there is?" '

"Usually they laugh, and sometimes I do too," I told Sister Roz. "What's lasted, though, is that I still loathe baseball and feel paralyzed in every other part of my life. I feel like used goods, yesterday's news, an old man playing a young man's gig."

"No you're not," Sister Roz said, finally taking her hands off my back and hugging me. "I'm seventy-four and I've never felt better. Just come back to the ballpark and pay attention to what happens here that is joyful. This is where your happiness was—and will be again. Be grateful that you get to work here, just like me."

"My work isn't so devout," I confessed. "My job here is to be mean."

"Do you have to?" she asked.

"I think so," I said. "I'm broke and meanness pays my bills."

"Don't worry," she said. "The answer for you is here."

And then she pointed to the sign that is the slogan of the St. Paul Saints on a stadium wall: FUN IS GOOD.

"You know when the last time I saw my ex-wife was?" I asked as Sister Roz folded up her massage table.

"Tell me."

"The night before I started working on this article for the Saints. My front two teeth are fake, and I immediately chewed off my bridge and swallowed it. I was supposed to do my first interview with general manager Bill Fanning the next morning. It's the only interview I've ever done with my front two teeth missing."

"See? That's funny!" Sister Roz said. "Funny is good. But if you ever want to break down, feel free to visit me. I hope your article is good. Feel better now?"

"Much," I said as Sister Roz refused my money.

"Good," said Sister Roz. "Now let's go down and see what Vince has got on the grill. He likes to cook things up after the game too. I heard a rumor he's been saving some shrimp for the true believers."

7

Zen and the Art of Minnie Minoso

June 8, 1996

The morning after confessing my grief and paralysis to Sister Roz, I felt slightly happier and lighter, if not quite happy. And the following afternoon, for the first time since I'd been following the team, I actually laughed. I showed up three hours early for the game, hung out in the parking lot, and ate a healthy hunk of Vince and Rosie's grilled kielbasa.

Sadly, I'd locked my keys in my "Northern League car" with the shattered windshield, and the mechanic from the AAA couldn't open the door. Vince finally took matters into his hands with a monkey wrench, which he used to break the back corner window so I could reach inside and unlock my door. "Here, let's get some plastic over that hole in your window," Vince volunteered, leaving his grill. "Now you got a real fine-looking ride."

Meantime, over the loudspeakers booming out of the stadium, which wouldn't open for another couple of hours, came a generation-old tune sung by comedian Phil Foster in which Brooklyn's biggest booster begged the Dodgers not to abandon the borough for Los Angeles.

By the time the gates opened at six for the seven o'clock game with Winnipeg (as they would all summer), "We're a Happy Family," a tune about happy dysfunction among a huddled family of misfits, was blasting from the speakers. Then came Joey Ramone barking out the anthem titled "I don't Want To Grow Up." The Ramones wouldn't stop playing until autumn.

"Saints fans," says Mike Veeck as he stands at his usual turnstile, ripping tickets and rapping with the fans, "appreciate the misfit, the underdog, the guy at the end of the line with a perhaps ridiculous dream."

Mike is at his personal best here, most like his father in his happy interactions with the fans who line up to say hello. Here Mike is *on*. Once a game starts, however, he can often be found sitting alone in his office, watching the game on television. Or he might watch from his friend Tommy Mischke's radio booth/tree house in the outfield. Or he might stand alone and silent a few feet from the dugout, smoking a cigarette and looking worried.

But at the turnstile when the gates open, Mike transmogrifies from the sometimes brooding promotional genius into Will Rogers, Jr., a man of the people ready with an ad-libbed quip, joke, or memory for every single fan whose ticket he rips. His raps are a fascinating monologue that circles the sum of human knowledge from Jerry Garcia to stadium voodoo to eighteenth-century politics to the meaning of modern photography. And the fans love it.

This is why the walkway to the team's ticket office is lined with stark black-and-white artsy photographs commissioned by Mike of a North Carolina beauty parlor, an Amish farmer plowing, a desiccated drive-in movie theater, and a dog at the Gateway Arch in St. Louis. "I wanted pictures like these, and artists from the community, to get the chance to make sure Saints fans take time to think about more than just baseball," he says.

Economics, however, is one topic Mike keeps away from. Some estimates have the team's four partners splitting a $2 million profit annually, with a $7 top-priced ticket. Every ticket, all season, is sold.

But even fans who don't have tickets to the always sold-out games are given a chance by Mike to talk their way in—if they can come up with a good enough whopper of a tale. If so, he will let about a hundred gate crashers into each game. "Their stories don't even have to be good," Mike says "just done with enthusiasm. My dad understood this: let the fans have some fun with the ballpark environment, and not only will they behave themselves, they'll have a great time. Did you ever hear of 'Joe Earley Night'?"

In the 1948 season, just as Bill Veeck's Cleveland Indians were about to win the World Series and set an all-time attendance record, he received an angry letter from an Indians fan named Joe Earley. Every player seemed to be getting a special "night" thrown on their behalf at the Indian's Municipal Stadium, Earley wrote in protest. "What about the average Joe? When is it his turn?"

And so, Bill Veeck decreed, "Joe Earley Night" would come to be. Joe came onto the field and was showered with gifts both goofy and valuable. It's a funny story, and Mike tells it with the relish of one who was there.

"Tonight I'll be honoring my father in a way too," he says, "in the form of Minnie Minoso."

Minoso, a popular Cuban player of indeterminate age, had been one of Bill Veeck's favorite players. He led the league in steals three times, triples thrice, and being hit by pitched balls six times. In the 1960 Chicago White Sox home opener, the aged Minnie hit the game's first two home runs, allowing Bill Veeck his initial chance to set off the $350,000 exploding scoreboard he'd put up in the off-season, much to the mortification of his fellow owners.

Minnie was brought back for at-bats with the White Sox in both 1976 and 1980 by Bill Veeck so Minoso could claim to be the only player to play in five decades. When Bill Veeck died in 1986, the ancient Minoso showed up at his funeral in full White Sox uniform. Afterward, Minoso discovered he'd locked his keys in his car, which was parked directly in front of Chicago's Church of St. Paul the Apostle. A nun produced a coat hanger. Minnie picked the lock, signed dozens of autographs, and left burning rubber in his ancient uniform. "My dad would have loved that," says Mike Veeck. "He would have laughed, which was something he did better than anyone."

The Veeck-less White Sox tried to get Minnie again in 1990, when Minoso was at least seventy. But Commissioner Fay Vincent said no, Minoso could not bat; it was a mockery to baseball's dignity. But the independent St. Paul Saints, who Fay Vincent had no more control over than he did the U.S. Marines (or baseball's owners, it turned out) gave Minnie his at-bat the summer before.

Now, tonight, minutes before the Saints' game, a helicopter appears over Midway Stadium's center field, always one of Bill Veeck's favorite ploys. The chopper lands at second base, and Minnie Minoso hops out wearing Saints regalia and holding the bat he swung for the Saints last year that made him the only man to play in six decades of baseball (he grounded out).

There to receive the bat was a befuddled man from the Hall of Fame, who accepted the bat and promised the Hall would take good care of it. "Call it cheap theatrics if you want," said Mike. "I call it proper respect."

Minnie then threw out the Saints' ceremonial first ball, already giving Saints fans more of a daffy thrill than they could have expected all year across the Mississippi River with the major league Twins. The helicopter, Mike said, was also a bow to the promotional genius of his father. The last time Bill Veeck hired Eddie Gaedel, the midget who batted for Veeck's Browns in 1951, was as a Martian popping out of a helicopter in the early 1960s before a White Sox game.

The Saints' game wasn't bad either, the Saints beating the Goldeyes 8–3, with Darryl Strawberry going three for four, raising his average to .379 while singling in a critical go-ahead run in the fifth. "I'm still not in my groove," he said, sucking down one of my menthols after the game, "but I feel it coming."

The team was 6–4 through the first couple weeks of the season, in first place in the Northern League's Eastern Division, and Darryl was batting .390 with an RBI a game. Mike was sanguine. "Darryl will be gone in weeks. There is no way major league baseball can ignore him for long."

Minutes away, however, the woeful Twins didn't even send a flunky across the Mississippi to check out Darryl Strawberry. Though the team was desperate for a left-handed power hitter like Straw, the Twins were not interested in either St. Paul's hero or St. Paul's team.

Minneapolis's paper, meantime, continued to heap abuse upon Mike. He said he didn't care when they ridiculed him publicly, though he pointed with pride to the day last September when the Saints outdrew the Twins when both teams were at home, and he continued to pin every insult directed toward him on his bulletin board. "I just think there are people on the other side of the river who just naturally hate my guts," said Mike. "When my father was around, the other major league teams hated his guts too."

But this season, detente finally seemed to be brewing. The Twins had hired Pat Forciea, a forward-looking promoter of other professional local teams, to help with marketing, and he and Mike had cooked up some ideas to show there was peace. At Midway Stadium, for starters, the Twins' Hall of Fame announcer Herb Carneal threw out the first pitch of a game against Winnipeg during a day game.

Across the river in Minneapolis that night, meantime, Mike and Tobias the pig were invited to sit in one of the Twins' luxury boxes. The Saints, of course, had no luxury boxes—just one futon behind home plate where winning contestants were served free Cokes and peanuts.

More importantly, Wayne "Twig" Terwilliger, so shoddily dismissed from the Twins after helping them win two world championships, was finally going to get his day on the field at the Metrodome.

"I don't know why they're doing this for me," Twig said, "except that I've been riding buses for forty-eight years. Maybe if I do it another ten, they'll put me in the Hall of Fame."

Still, Twig seemed uncharacteristically subdued as he entered the Twins' Metrodome, where he hadn't been since being abruptly discharged in 1994, with nary an official farewell or thank you, so he could be replaced by young Scott Ullger. "I don't feel well," Twig said, claiming to have caught a cold on the bus ride back from Thunder Bay the previous week.

Finally he was led down an elevator: ESPN was broadcasting the Twins' game live starting at seven o'clock, and the Twig event was supposed to be done by 6:46. But Twig couldn't escape the eyes of his former teammates as he passed by the locker room.

Twins manager Tom Kelly, filling out his lineup card, stopped his labors and shook Twig's hand. "How are you, Twig? We miss you. Come on into the locker room. There are a lot of people who want to see you."

"No thanks, T.K.," said Twig pridefully, invoking the manager's initials and nickname. The Twins had kicked Twig out of that locker room, humiliating him, and he sure as hell wasn't going back in.

Suddenly Kirby Puckett comes out of the locker room. "Twig! Come in here! Everyone wants to see you! Come on in and see [Chuck] Knoblauch."

"No thanks," says Twig.

"Scared?" says Puckett.

"Yes!" says Twig.

"I'll go get everybody," says Puckett, ducking back into the locker room "Hey, everybody, it's Twig!"

"How you doing?" Twig asks Puckett, who is fighting an eye condition that will shortly end his career.

"I can see," Puckett says. "I just can't hit. Wait a second. Let me get the guys."

Within seconds, the runway leading from the locker room to the dugout is filled with Twins, shaking Twig's hand, pounding him on the back, and saying they miss him. All-Star second baseman Chuck "Knobby" Knoblauch, along with Puckett one of Twig's major projects, comes out and hugs him.

"You look good, Twig! You feel good? I looked for you on TV last night! C'mon, let's go into the dugout. There are some guys in there."

"No way!" says Twig. "I'm not going in there."

Despite his pride, Twig is touched as the dugout empties to say hello to him. "I still see Twig at second base, turning double plays like he was still twenty-one," says Denny Hocking, who joined the Twins as a shortstop in 1993 and was tutored in turning the double play by a septuagenarian. "Twig wasn't going through the motions; he'd throw the ball and leap over imaginary players sliding into second," Hocking says. "It was so much fun to watch."

"Hey, Twig!" says Knoblauch. "What are they giving you for your day, a car?"

"No," Twig says, laughing. "A painting."

"Aw shit, Twig," says Knobby.

Finally Twig is introduced with his wife-of-forever Lin; the crowds lustily cheers the old man who still hits fungoes as hard as he hit the beach at Iwo Jima. His wife gets roses; Twig gets a painting of himself in the uniforms he wore during his major league career. He's off the field before ESPN begins its national broadcast, and while Mike and Tobias the pig sit in a luxury suite, Twig takes a regular seat near the press box. He hasn't been to a Twins game since they fired him, and he probably won't be. As soon as he's over this cold, he says, he can't wait to be throwing batting practice back at Midway Stadium for the team that still wants him.

By the middle of June, it seemed that Strawberry was finally hitting his stride. Playing at home before Thunder Bay on June 10, Darryl smashed a homer at least forty feet from the ground, helping the Saints to an ugly 10–9 lead and continued control of first place over Madison. Strawberry hit two more home runs at home against Thunder Bay, the first a shot that cleared the right field fence, then a fence behind that. After a dozen games, he was tied for the league lead in homers with five and batting .408. Still, he seemed curiously detached from his teammates, none of whom he'd especially bonded with since Dave Stevens left training camp. He was polite to everybody, signed autographs for all comers, posed for every camera, yet still seemed like he was serving a curious sentence, like Malcolm McDowell in A Clockwork Orange. His best friend on the team now seemed to be manager Marty Scott, the latest in a series of surrogate fathers. By now, he was even calling Marty "Dad."

"I just tell him to take it one day at a time, like he's learned," Scott said. "He's proving his head is where it should be, and that's what will get him back."

The big breakthrough for Strawberry seemed to come in the next series, away at Sioux City, Iowa, to play the Explorers. There, in the eighth inning of the second game of the series, Strawberry shot his sixth homer of the season far past deepest center field to bring the Saints within 4–3. Trotting around the bases, the always graceful Strawberry's feet suddenly became tangled up in themselves as he neared home plate, and he fell on his ass to touch home. Completely out of character, Strawberry leaped to his feet and began shouting like a Little Leaguer, "That's baseball! Now that's baseball!"

Knocking fists with everybody on the team, Strawberry finally seemed like a member of the team. The next two pumped-up batters, Marty Neff and Kevin Garner, each added solo home runs, and the Saints had a 5–4 victory and remained tied with Madison for the season's first-half lead with a record of 8–6.

With pitchers forced to throw around Strawberry, Garner and Neff were seeing the meatball pitches of their lives and were also both in the league running for home runs and RBIs. Garner was philosophic about his success: "I led the league in home runs last year, and I still ended up in the off-season living with my parents. This is my last year of this shit. It's time to move on."

Garner also tweaked Marty Neff for the protection offered him in the lineup by Strawberry. Marty Neff, however, was riding high on his own inflated statistics. As a member of the Sioux City Explorers last year, the right fielder always made a point of chatting with the nearby Midway Stadium grandstand fans whenever his team was playing St. Paul. He would come over and talk with Saints fans between innings and game breaks and throw balls into the crowd at every opportunity. He was a beloved foreigner in Midway Stadium, and when he was traded to the Saints over the off-season, his fans cheered.

This season, several Saints fans in the right field stands even formed the Marty Neff Fan Club to honor their hero. There would be weekly meetings at which Marty would answer questions, and production began on T-shirts that said MARTY NEFF FAN CLUB, complete with his number 36 and a facsimile autograph. A large banner would be hoisted during each game proclaiming the fans' allegiance to Marty. "Our goal is to have our presence felt for Marty at every game, be it home or away," said Wendy Herbert, the president of the fan club.

The Saints' players, meantime, were not impressed. To them, Marty was the consummate "hot dog." Worse, Marty was a difficult teammate. When happy, he was a prince; when angered, an ogre.

He would swear at umps. He would kick his helmet to manager Scott's disconcert and not run out his ground balls. No one went and called Marty lazy, but there had to be a reason he had a protuberant gut at his tender age. He also had the habit of keeping close track of his personal statistics in full view of his teammates. This pissed them off, but so far, with Darryl Strawberry protecting him, Marty Neff was doing very well.

June 12, 1996

Jack Morris, however, was not fairing as well, and cracks were beginning to show in his until now uncharacteristically polite behavior. In mid-June, *USA Today* sportswriter Mel Antonen came to St. Paul to watch Morris and came away with a story headlined: WITH EYE TO MAJORS, MORRIS RESUMES STEWING ON MOUND.

The article was filled with the Jack of old, whose record with the Saints stood at 0–0 with a 5.19 ERA, allowing fourteen hits in a little over eight and two-thirds innings. "Jack Morris glares at infielders who misplay grounders," Antonen wrote. "A bloop hit means cursing and dirt-kicking. He even yells at an opposing manager, [Winnipeg's] Hal Lanier, for running the bases too much."

"Obviously, the defense is not what I'm used to," he said, bitching about the Saints behind him. But, he added, "if I'm ticked off, that's a good sign. I didn't have that when I retired."

The key, Morris said gruffly to me and all reporters, was building up his arm strength so he could properly throw his forkball. That meant lifting weights in the Saints' shower, because there wasn't enough space in the high-school-sized team locker room. He could live with having to get a beer by having the clubhouse attendant go wait in line at the Saint's concession booth; what he couldn't survive without was that forkball.

"It's coming back, my arm," he said. "And come the middle of summer, some major league team is going to need pitching." Then, uttering a string of profanities, he shoos reporters away so he can resume hitting on some women leaning over the guard rail of the stadium.

"You must be pretty sick of people talking about you pitching that shutout in the last game of the 1991 World Series for the Twins," I offered weakly.

"Yeah, I do," said Morris. "Especially right now."

"How many times have you watched that game on video?" I continued.

Jack Morris
Courtesy of Bonnie Butler

Jack looked up. "Never," he said. "No one taped it for me, and I've actually never seen my performance."

"If I get a copy," I said, "will you watch it?"

"Maybe," said Morris, walking away. I knew about five thousand people in the Twin Cities with a tape of that famous game; the next day I brought my own to the ballpark to show after practice. As the players took off their uniforms, Marty Neff took the tape and inserted it into the locker room's VCR. The tape was wound to the ninth inning of Game 7 of the World Series with Jack Morris on the mound.

"Hey, Jack!" Neff yelled across the lockers. "Come over and look at this!"

And there he was, five years younger, pitching one of the guttiest shutouts in World Series history. Within seconds, the entire team was huddled before the VCR, watching an event that they could only dream about. Darryl Strawberry also watched. He'd been there too, but his face revealed nothing.

WORLD SERIES ANNOUNCER JACK BUCK: Seventh game, ninth inning, no score. And through it all, Jack Morris is still on the hill for the Twins.

WORLD SERIES ANNOUNCER TIM MCCARVER: Let's watch Jack Morris work. That guy right there is a warhorse.

Morris, watching with a shit-eating grin in front of pitcher Jeff Alkire, suddenly breaks down in tears and walks to the other side of the locker room, vainly stifling the waterworks that no self-respecting bastard would let his teammates see.

He walked back shortly thereafter as Jack Buck announced, "The Twins have won it 1–0 in ten innings," accompanied by a picture of Morris rushing out of the dugout into the bear hugs of his teammates. Morris begins bawling again a few minutes later when the VCR shows him accepting the Most Valuable Player of the 1991 World Series.

For the first time in a while, Jack seemed almost like a normal human. "I wish I could just sit you down and *give* you my feeling," he says. "If I could just give you a piece of me, because then you would be totally zoned into what happened. If I could do anything in my whole life, it would be to give them what I felt that day."

Jack wiped his eyes, and I offered him the tape. He took it without saying thank you and never mentioned the incident again. He didn't need to: he was finally beginning to pitch in the Northern League like the diva he used to be. His next start was June 18 against Thunder Bay at home, and he did better, giving up four runs in six innings and scattering six hits while battling the flu.

And finally, in Sioux City on June 17, Jack Morris had the moment he had wanted and needed. If things didn't pick up soon, he'd said privately shortly before, he'd just up and quit, maybe by the end of the week, rather than embarrass himself. Pitching against the Sioux City Explorers, he'd twirled a beautiful seven innings, giving up no runs and only five hits. He had his first win in two years, since the days his arrogance seemed earned, his prima donna act accepted as part of the package of a great pitcher.

"I really almost quit that first week with the Saints," he said. "You don't have any idea what it's like being forty-one and coming back after not pitching for so long."

In his first few games, he said, he'd thrown nothing but fastballs and sliders. Now, in Iowa, he'd finally let loose with his forkball (his bread-and-butter pitch) and his changeup. "All of a sudden I have this four-pitch arsenal, and I'm thinking this might be fun after all."

The Saints' route through Iowa was torturous and long, but oddly calming and reassuring. Later in the season, on the way again to Sioux City for Explorer games, I would search out the field where Buddy Holly fatally crashed in 1959 in Clear Lake, Iowa.

But on the team bus in Iowa that afternoon, there seemed only contentment. In a book of travel essays published by the literary magazine *Granta*, Iowa native Bill Bryson explained it thusly: "I come from Des Moines. . . . I had to. When you come from Des Moines, you either accept the fact without question and settle down with a local girl named Bobbi and get a job at the Firestone factory and live there forever, or you spend your adolescence moaning at length about what a dump this is and how you can't wait to get out, and you settle down with a local girl named Bobbi and get a job at the Firestone factory and live there forever and ever. . . . Everybody in Des Moines is strangely serene."

In Iowa, Des Moines is considered more cosmopolitan than Sioux City, where life seems even more serene, despite the smell emanating from the steer slaughterhouses of Omaha a few miles away. Indeed, Sioux City is famous among Northern League ballplayers as having the most beautiful young women and fattest older women in the world. After the games, Saints disappeared in all directions, to all kinds of country and western bars, with the best-looking women they'd ever gone out with.

Some of the players never went out. Steve Solomon, still determined to show his talent and get picked up by an organization, continued to go straight back to the motel after the game. Then he would call his girlfriend, Lisa, in Los Angeles, or perhaps his father, or maybe his older brother who was cut by the Seattle Mariners because he got the bad rap that he was slow.

On June 22 at home against Duluth, meantime, Strawberry hit two majestic home runs for the third time this season, giving him ten. Suddenly it began dawning on the men in the Saints' clubhouse that their two most famous stars might not be around much longer.

Major league scouts, those oddly dressed creatures bearing radar guns, notebooks, pinkie rings, and white shoes, were beginning to show up at Midway Stadium to have a peek at what in the hell was going on with Strawberry and Morris.

Who, for instance, really knew what was inside Jack Morris? In the parade after he'd pitched the great World Series game in 1991, he'd ridden on the back of a convertible alone. He was in the middle of an ugly divorce, and his wife and kids did not join him.

Earlier in the summer, Morris had asked for a particular day off so he could get remarried. "Sure," said Marty. But when the day came, Morris told Scott he was ready to play and that he wasn't getting hitched after all. "She didn't want to sign a prenup," explained the multimillionaire starting pitcher.

Morris looked even better his next time out, at home on June 22 against Duluth. Pitching six and two-thirds innings, he allowed only an unearned run and six hits. "Someone is going to want me when the major league pennant races heat up," he said.

Strawberry himself was not coy about where he wanted to go: New York. His bridges to the Mets had all long ago been burned, but he felt most of the Yankees had treated him with respect. They also desperately needed a left-handed power hitter.

A quarter of the season had passed, and considering Madison's candlepower, it was surprising that the Saints were only two games ahead of the Black Wolf. But it was a comfortable two-game lead— each 84-game Northern League season is divided into two separate 42-game pennant races. At the end of the summer, the divisional winners of each half would qualify for the league playoffs that would determine the league champion.

It was a complicated formula, but it ensured that no matter how badly a team sucked in the first half, they would always have a chance in the second. The two teams that won the first-half season divisions, meantime, could coast until September. Marty Scott would prefer to coast, so he was already churning talent in an attempt to find the equation that would bring home that first-half crown.

And then, out of nowhere, came the news on June 25, apparently from hell. Darryl Strawberry missed a payment for $300,000 in overdue child support and spousal support to his ex-wife, Lisa. "Darryl is not denying he owes it," said his lawyer. "But you can't get blood from a stone. Hopefully, he will gain employment with the major leagues in the near future, which will enable him to pay a substantial amount of the support."

In any case, the headlines ran from coast to coast. Strawberry the deadbeat was due in court in Los Angeles in two weeks to answer the charges and plead his case. In his office, Mike Veeck seemed unconcerned. "My understanding was that this had all been taken care of before," he said. "Darryl is still going up to the majors real soon, where he will hit a home run for everybody, me included, who's screwed up their lives and come back."

Before the game, however, Strawberry accepted a cigarette and looked bereft. It was no secret that his first wife, Lisa, hated his guts and would like to see his ass in jail. He had long ago pointed a gun at her; now she pointed a lawyer at him.

While his lawyer argued from New York that Strawberry had set up $600,000 in trust funds for the children from that first marriage, it appeared to the reporters in the Saints' locker room that Straw's current financial status shadowed him as closely as the tattoo of his ex-wife's name on his shoulder.

"I want to pay what I owe," Darryl said as he took a deep drag off his cigarette, "but I need to get back to the majors to do that. I've tried talking to her, but talking to Lisa is like talking to a brick wall. It sounds mean, but she's money hungry."

Had it only been a decade since the original Mr. and Mrs. Strawberry played New York like they were Scott and Zelda, the tabloids had reported, bathing in money? There were mortgages on two houses, multiple sports cars, and several relatives on the payroll back then. When they divorced in 1993, Lisa received one home, $300,000 in cash, and three luxury cars: a late-model Porsche, a Mercedes, and a BMW. She also got $95,000 in lawyers' fees, $50,000 in monthly spousal support, and $30,000 in monthly child support. Darryl was fucked, and it had been his own fault.

He took another drag on his cigarette in the Saints' locker room. "I can't believe that this incident will hurt me over all," he said. "If people only knew how much money I'd put out to that woman over the years, if they understood what my money situation is right now, they might not judge me so harshly. I will honor my obligations as soon as I make it back to the majors and can."

Whatever. This news was not playing well in New York, where the Yankees were keeping close tabs on Strawberry's rehabilitation. Marv Goldklang had been keeping in constant personal touch with George Steinbrenner, telling the ship builder with the savior complex that Darryl had done everything his manager, teammates, family, fans, and community wanted. His drug tests were clean, his home runs of the kind never before seen in the Northern League.

Still, the *New York Post* sent ace reporter Tom Keegan out again just to see what the hell was going on. Only two days before, Yankee general manager Bob Watson had exposed a soft spot in his soul—maybe there was a little room for Darryl on the Yankees after all, Watson implied. Now, accompanying the Yankees to Minneapolis for a series with the Twins, Watson wouldn't even bother to cross the river to scout Strawberry, who was playing only twenty minutes away.

"What I hear is that there is nothing new with Darryl," said Watson. "He's hitting okay, but not doing much in the field."

Marty Scott begged to differ. "Darryl has caught every ball he's gotten to, and he's gotten to a lot of balls others wouldn't because his legs are so long and his strides are so broad."

Still, Bob Watson was not interested. "He doesn't fit," Watson said. Then Watson added for emphasis, "He doesn't fit. He doesn't fit. He doesn't fit. He doesn't fit."

Told of Watson's words before the game, Strawberry asked for another cigarette. "Why would he suddenly say he's not interested? Does he hate me? Why is he doing this?"

If he didn't get called up by someone in the next couple of weeks, he said, he might just pack up and head home to California for good. "I don't feel like I'm done, but what else can I do?"

What he did on that day of hideously bad national pub was go out and hit two dingers against Sioux City to lead the Saints to a 5–2 win at home over the Explorers. They were his eleventh and twelfth homers in twenty-two games; his most important came in the eighth inning, when he broke a 2–2 tie with a 440-foot homer to center.

Up in the stands, his wife Charysse promenaded the aisles like a just-crowned prom queen. Back in 1994, when Darryl was with the Dodgers, still using drugs, and dating the then Charysse Simon, he'd struck her. Charysse stood by her man back then, though the Dodgers wanted her to press charges so they could get out of their contract with Strawberry. And she stood by him now.

"I'd hate her, if she only wasn't so nice," said Randi, Marty Neff's girlfriend, a bartender at a place called the Hog's Breath in St. Paul. "A Major League Wife," Randi said, her voice trailing off.

Mike Veeck remained sanguine that that was exactly what Charysse would be shortly. "Darryl will be in the majors in two weeks. It's going to work out. Tomorrow the Cincinnati Reds are sending assistant general manager Gene Bennett and Jerry Radatz, their top scout, to look over Darryl and Jack."

The next day, however, Gene Bennett, sitting in the stadium before the game, denied everything. "I'm not looking at anybody. In fact, I'm not even here. And that's off the record."

There had also been an Opening Day for the single women who dreamed of being, like Charysse Strawberry, a Major League Wife. Now, though the season was well under way, some of the Saints still hadn't centered on one local summer girlfriend or had already dumped their first. And though these often-beautiful women's dreams of riches were as realistic as those Saints who actually thought they would ever make the major leagues, they all tried.

The place for these women to go after every game was Gabe's bar, which is located only a few hundred yards from Midway Stadium. After tonight's game, most of the team but Straw and Solomon headed there, the semiofficial tippling spot of the Saints, to use whatever was left of the $5 drink and food coupons the bar gave them and to look at the ladies. The queen of the scene was Jill Muellner, a woman in her early thirties who worked behind the bar as Gabe's night manager and mother confessor. Beloved, blue-collar beautiful, and untouchable by mere mortal men, Jill has paid her dues.

Finally sober after twelve years of hideous alcoholism, Jill says, she watches after the girls, keeps an eye on the boys, and tries to keep her eye on who is going in and out of the door. Jill is grateful, she says, that she is no longer playing the game of getting wasted, getting laid, and waking up to an empty bed that had been filled by a guy who didn't remember her name.

"The women in Gabe's, by and large," she says, "aren't groupies. They want love from these ballplayers—and then they want to go to the major leagues with them. They always think the ballplayer who likes them is going to make it."

And the players? "They're here for sex, a one-night stand," she says. "I can tell the women the truth, but often they have to find out the hard way. Then they come up to me crying the next night, and I put my arm around them."

"What should I do?" they always want to know the next night from Jill.

"No more ballplayers," Jill will say. "Next time you'll find a *real* man."

The ballplayers, meantime, make no excuses. Paul Romanoli, the relief pitcher who spends most of the game on a folding chair out in the bullpen, sees the women every day at Midway Stadium. "Their boyfriends go out for a second, and these girls come up to the gate separating them from the bullpen, and they'll just stare at us for twenty minutes. No mere boyfriend can compare with a ballplayer."

Meantime, Roma's girlfriend, Marie, sits at Gabe's and wonders where her beloved is. "Tell her I'm out," Roma says from another part of the city. "Tell her this is my last year of professional ball, and I'm going to enjoy myself."

Marie is back the next night, cheering Paul and wishing she could somehow break his heart—or at least have the strength to break up with him. "After this season," she promises, "no more ballplayers." She'll start over.

"I started over, in my own way," says Jill Muellner, observing the scene at Gabe's and shaking her head. "And these guys are starting over too. Then you talk to some of these girls, and they think this is their last chance to find a ballplayer and live the fairy tale."

8

Bill Murray Gets Set Up
for His Hatchet Job

Like the credulous widow who wakes up one day to find the charm-
ing young man and all her savings gone, so the consenting subject
of a piece of nonfiction writing learns—when the article or book
appears—his hard lesson. Journalists justify their treachery in vari-
ous ways according to their temperaments. The more pompous talk
about freedom of speech and "the public's right to know," the least
talented talk about Art, the seemliest murmur about earning a
living.
—Janet Malcolm, *The Journalist and the Murderer*

July 3, 1996

And then, at the end of the fourth inning of a home game a few
days later against the Sioux City Explorers, Bill Murray walks, un-
armed, unannounced, and in untied sneakers, into the runway under
Midway Stadium next to the Saints' dugout. Running past is Sioux
City manager Ed "Singin' Ed" Nottle, spitting dugout tobacco juice
as he traipses from the third base coach's box back to the visiting
dugout.

"Hey, fatso!" yells Bill Murray from his perch.

"Hey, Bill!" says Nottle, a man who understands show business.
As a top pitching prospect with the Chicago White sox in the mid-
1960s, Nottle cost himself a position in the majors by staying out
all night after games by crooning Frank Sinatra-like tunes at fancy
restaurants. "I'd get great free meals, and the women were great,
nothing like a ballpayer who sings," Nottle remembers. "I have no
regrets. I just loved The Life."

St. Paul Saints

1	~~BANETT~~ / EVANS ②	OF / LF
2	SOLOMON ④	CF DH
3	~~STRAWBERRY~~ / LIEDER	OF / 1B
4	NEFF ①	RF DH
5	~~GARNER~~ / McNALLY ⑤	DH / DH
6	D'ALEXANDER ③⑥	SS
7	FLEMING	2B
8	CANNADAY ⑦①	C
9	KONIGSMARK	3B
PITCHERS	MORRIS	P

vs. Sioux Falls

1	POWELL ③	CF
2	~~DUFAS~~ / SEAL ①⑥	DH / LF
3	DAVIS ①	SS
4	CAREY ④	1B
5	HOSEY ②	RF
6	LANTIGUA	3B
7	ALLEN ①②	DH
8	LOUVIER ⑤	C
9	~~PEREZ~~ / GUERRERI	2B / 2B
PITCHERS	~~MOGART~~ / SHEETS / SERNA	P / ~~LOVATO~~

EXTRA MEN

LH	RH	LH	RH
~~LIEDER~~	~~EVANS~~	~~SEAL~~	~~GUERRERI~~
	~~McNALLY~~		

SWITCH HITTERS

PITCHERS

LH	RH	LH	RH
ROMANOLI	MANFRED	~~LOVATO~~	~~SHEETS~~
CORDEIRO	WESTFALL		~~SERNA~~
	THOMSON		

Years later, after winning three International League championships, only one step from the majors, Nottle was hired by the Oakland A's to be a coach. He thereupon hired the Oakland Symphony
Orchestra at a cost of tens of thousands of dollars and cut an album
with him singing tunes ranging from the theme from "New York,
New York" to "That's Life."

"I literally lost my house on that project," Nottle had said earlier.
"The bank repossessed my home. But big deal. Everybody's got a
house. My wife understood my point."

Murray trills a raspberry at the enemy manager, then yells, "Hit
the road, meat!"

The gathered Saints brain trust and crew know enough not to
make a big deal about their "czar" and team psychologist's first
entrance of the season. He would have been here sooner, Murray
explains to the staff watching the game from the decrepit "owners'
box," but he's been in Butte, Montana, helping to ready the stadium
for Mike's latest minor league adventure, the low-down Butte Copper Kings.

In Butte, everybody is in—even Saints employees. Saints general
manager Bill Fanning, community relations director Annie Huidekoper, and lawyer/operations manager Tom Whaley have been allowed to buy percentages of the Copper Kings, as has GQ writer
Peter Richmond, who became friends with Veeck after writing per-
ceptively about him in the past.

"Getting the Butte stadium ready was like moving your mother-
in-law in," says Murray of the ramshackle Montana ballpark. "We
were scrubbing out filthy sinks and making things look nice for days.
I served beer, and man, those Montana women know how to drink—
I'd be pouring out a dozen glasses for each of them at a time."

I watched Murray from twenty yards away while he briefed the
Saints' staff, waiting for the moment to break in and make my spiel.
I was nervous, as usual, around intimidating subjects; I relied on the
tactics of Joan Didion, who wrote in Slouching Towards Bethlehem:

> My only advantage as a reporter is that I am so physically
> small, so temperamentally unobtrusive, and so neurotically
> inarticulate that people tend to forget that my presence runs
> counter to their best interests. And it always does.

But you never know it will until it happens, and so I sweated and
spied, doubting by now that I would be paid my fee or my already

over-the-top expenses, even if I did get Murray. I would have no second chances with either Bill Murray or Jann Wenner.

After greeting everyone in the Saints' family, Murray came up to general manager Bill Fanning, a job title which in the minor leagues translates to business manager.

"Is the Builder's Square lot full?" Murray asked, inquiring about the Saints' satellite parking lot that they rented from a local lumber company.

"Totally," said Fanning.

"Do the players still get a prize if they hit a ball into the hot tub?'
"No."

"And how is the bratwurst?" Murray went on. "Is it prepared in the traditional manner?"

"As always."

Murray then surveyed the billboards on the outside wall and was particularly impressed by a huge facsimile bottle of liquor that hung on the fence. "Where'd you get that Phillips vodka bottle?" he asked and then paused. "At least it's Phillips."

Murray then takes out a brand-new Saints fitted cap. "The key if a cap is too big," he says to no one in particular, "is to put some newspaper in it."

I took more notes than a Fed. "That Bill Murray carries the weight of a celebrity Job is no revelation," I wrote. "For years, tales have circled Hollywood that he no longer *enjoys* being Bill Murray. He'd grown bitter and mean under the tonnage of his own fame, it was said, and had evolved into an angry drunk who would verbally dice any face that displeased him."

My only source for this was a guy Murray supposedly kicked out of a team party last season in Winnipeg. "Murray had been," as they say in St. Paul, "*overserved*," the source told me, but that account would be enough to get by the *Rolling Stone* fact checkers.

I added a quick observation. "Murray: pot-bellied, balding, wearing raggedy-ass pants and Saints hat."

Meantime, Homer and Luke, Murray's teenage sons, then wandered into the runway from the Saints' dugout to see what was cooking with their dad. Murray led them back to the dugout, where they watched Darryl Strawberry set up at the plate to the strains of the PA's blasting version of the Ramones' "I Want You Around."

And indeed, all of St. Paul did. Strawberry, after his epiphany in Sioux City, had become beloved by his teammates. The town, meantime, had taken him up as their phoenix weeks before, when he began hitting two homers a game, continued to sign autographs for all comers, and began telling newspapermen that he'd never had as much fun playing baseball as he was now in St. Paul.

Mike Veeck was right when he said St. Paul had an inferiority complex; how could it not, after Morley Safer called it "the most boring city in the country"? Or Henny Youngman, who once told a heckler, "You're a real gentleman. You remind me of St. Paul, one of the dullest towns in America."

And then there was glitzy Minneapolis, which had always treated its Twin City as an unwanted stepchild. Until now, when the Saints were the hippest, most spiritually uplifting ticket around—and nobody in Minneapolis seemed to be able to get a ducat to see the rise of the Straw Man.

In the dugout, Murray watched with his sons as Darryl Strawberry set, swung, and sent a thundering blast to the edge of the right field warning track. "I met Darryl in L.A. a few years ago," Murray tells some of the Saints players. "He actually has a great sense of humor. Maybe he's here because he's like a great musician who needs to go back to the woodshed and work on all his chops. The Yankees really made a big mistake when they let him go." It was a sentence Murray would say time and again, not as a George Bush-style bumbler, but as a mantra. He repeats himself often, he says with a laugh, "because a lot of times I just don't remember what the question was in the first place."

In minutes, one of his sons begins acting up on the bench, and Murray takes him back to the locker room for some disciplinary words. As Murray is talking to his kid, he looks up and for the first time notices a young man with a camcorder taping the exchange. The cameraman is from FX, a cable channel in the vast Fox Network, which has paid the Saints to film a documentary-style television series on the team. Bill Murray, when he heard of the scheme, made sure everyone knew he wanted no part of it.

Now he was furious. "Do you *mind?*" he asked the cameraman. "I'm talking privately with my *son!*"

The cameraman, working for cable scale, slunk away. Murray, meantime, returned to the runway next to the dugout.

When Murray came back, happily discussing baseball, I knew it was time to put myself into the comedian's face. But before I could get to him, another handheld camera is shoved into his face by a young New York filmmaker named Joe who, he says, has moved to

Iowa to shoot a still-unnamed new wave documentary about the minor leagues. Murray immediately turns to frost.

"Hey, Bill, can I have a minute?" the *auteur* asks, tape rolling. "Why did you get involved in this crazy league?"

"Next question," Murray says, simmering.

"There's a lot of weird stuff that goes on here," the director says. "What are the nun and pig all about?"

Murray is now pissed off. "Joe, you said you wanted a minute, and now you're out here improvising stone-cold," he says, lecturing. "Do your research! Forget about the pig and the nun, Joe! Just look at the field! That's where the answers are! Go outside the ballpark and look in. Tell me what you see, and then maybe you'll begin to understand!"

"But . . ." interjects the filmmaker.

Several hundred yards past the right field fence is the burnt shell of a building that the St. Paul Fire Department continually sets on fire to train its troops. Sometimes the Saints are allowed to set it ablaze for some *Towering Inferno*-type cheap theatrics. "Do you see that building, Joe?" Murray says. "We set fire to it three times a week, and we put guys like you from Iowa in there just to keep it going."

Joe is wobbling from the force of the wasting and Murray walks on, shaking off the bad vibes. Now that the major leagues have all but dissolved in the brine of labor strife, negative karma, and the overreverent blathers of George Will types, the masses have now discovered the bush leagues. That's fine, Murray says, just as long as the attendant camera crews stay away from him.

Good shit, I think. Which, if spun nastily, would help provide the big hit I need to deliver. Finally I approach, credentials in hand.

"You're from *Rolling Stone?*" Murray says, laughing. "No thank you."

"But it would be about the Saints and Mike Veeck," I say. "It would be a way to get them some attention. All I need is five minutes of you to stick in at the beginning of the story to make Jann feel like he's got his celebrity quotient."

"Jann. . . . How is *Jann?*" says Murray, disgusted.

"Thinner," I say. "He thinks *Rolling Stone* has 'a special relationship' with you because of the coverage they gave you back during your 'Saturday Night Live' days."

"I don't think so," Murray says, laughing. "Jann Wenner and I, I can assure you, have *no* special relationship. What does he want?"

"A story and some pictures," I say. "They'll fly in a hot-shot photographer from New York, spend an afternoon in a shoot with you in a Saints uniform, you know, the usual."

"No way," says Murray. "I come to St. Paul to get *away* from Jann Wenner."

That and every other reporter who wants to know why he long ago abdicated his role as number-one male box office star in America and as one of *People* magazine's Most Intriguing People of 1984.

Murray hates and distrusts reporters and always has. In his first appearance on *Rolling Stone*'s cover in 1978, flush with his first taste of fame, he explained how he'd come up with "Bill Murray's Celebrity Corner," a recurring "Saturday Night Live" segment in which he played an unctious show business newshound who seemed to be on a first-name basis with every movie star from Greta Garbo to Marlon Brando.

"Now get *outta* here, Woodman, you're a *nut*, you're *tremendous*, and I *love* you," he'd say into the camera as if he were best friends with Woody Allen. But to Murray the on-screen parody was no joke.

"I really hate critics," he said in the story. "They're usually wrong, and when they're right, they're right for the wrong reasons. It's like because they've seen this guy's movie, they're on a first-name basis with him. They imply that they know everybody when there are all sorts of people who won't even talk to them and think of them as the sleaziest sort of person."

"Please?" I beg, for real, eighteen years later. "It's my job if I don't get something from you on the record. Five minutes, and I'll be out of your face."

Murray looks me over. "I don't want to cost you your job," he says. Then he goes on for several minutes about how the hero of the Saints is Mike Veeck and that he isn't going to say a word unless he is sure I am here for Mike, not him. "Mike deserves the credit for putting this together, and the odds are a hundred to one you'll leave him out and just hose me."

A smart man. Still, I talk and yammer about how not all reporters are skunks and liars, and he begs to differ. "You know who the worst is?" he says. "Bob Woodward. Can you believe what he just wrote about Hillary Clinton? Someday a big truck or a meteorite is going to hit Bob Woodward."

He pauses and continues his diatribe. "But the worst was that book he wrote about John Belushi, *Wired*. I read that and said, 'Holy shit, this Bob Woodward is a total fraud.' The people he interviewed for his story were all in the outer circle, four degrees of separation removed from John's life and the truth."

He is on a roll. "The thing about John Belushi is that Woodward never understood his sense of humor," Murray says. "He didn't understand why he was funny, or what funny is, or that John was as great an onstage actor as Richard Burton. Woodward had a mean bent from the beginning, and I know why. Bob Woodward is jealous: he is only the third most famous person from Wheaton, Illinois. The first is John Belushi, the second is Red Grange, and the third is Bob Woodward. And Woodward is a distant third and is never going to get any closer."

Almost as bad, he says, was the history of "Saturday Night Live" in which he *himself* was pictured as a violent maniac. "That book was ridiculous, absurd," he says. "It was written by guys who came to work as interns and again interviewed people in the fifth rung of what happened."

I have about two minutes left, and I have to think fast. In my pocket, I have an old baseball card showing the midget Eddie Gaedel, sent to the plate by Bill Veeck in 1951, standing in the batter's box. I give it to Murray. "Here," I say, "I'm here to talk about Bill and Mike Veeck and baseball." Means to an end.

Murray looks at Gaedel, who would have to be cast in his making of *Veeck as in Wreck.* "Midgets can be real mean. I wonder who'll get the part," he says. "It'll probably be someone I've worked with before."

Murray tucks the Eddie Gaedel baseball card into his pocket, leans against the field tractor stored in the runway, and finally says he'll talk to me. But, he says, he won't sit for any set-up studio pictures. There, I realize, goes my last chance of writing a nice piece about Murray and the Saints and sneaking it past Jann.

At *Rolling Stone,* even the coolest flavor of the second celebrity must pose for hours. Most of them like it. For Murray to say no, I know, thereby will only increase Jann's rage. And since Murray won't pose, I am informed later by *Rolling Stone,* my article will be accompanied by grotesque cartoons of the comedian. For Murray not to at least play along with the photo game is tantamount at *Rolling Stone* to Gary Gilmore begging for the cigarette and blindfold.

Unless, that is, I won't do it. Fat chance. I'm a reporter with few illusions: my first boss told me that the best elements to look for in a story were "tits, tots, pets, or vets."

Or a celebrity meanie. "Tell me about baseball," I say. "Tell me about Bill Veeck. Tell me abut growing up in Chicago with him. Tell me about meeting Mike Veeck back then when he worked for the White Sox and you were in Second City with John Candy. Didn't they call the troupe 'the Seven Giant Goyim,' because everyone was Gentile and over six feet tall?"

"Say," Murray says, "you have been doing your research." He leans back.

"Well, growing up in Chicago in the sixties was like an armed camp," he says. "The 1968 Democratic Convention boiled over, paddy wagons were wall to wall for a year, and then the Weathermen, 'Days of Rage' came.

"What finally broke the tension in the city was the 1969 Chicago Cubs. They had my all-time favorite player, Ernie Banks, and almost pulled it off. When the team finally lost, the town was finally reunited again. My father died that year, right after he got promoted as a lumber salesman and was about to make real money for the first time in his life. There were nine kids in the family, and he was the funniest of all."

Murray pauses to think about his father. "At the dinner table, he was the hardest guy to get a laugh out of," he remembers. "One of the things that bonds Mike and I is that our dads died before we made it."

Murray stops talking and looks straight ahead. "We must assume the lump of coal we are given. Santa leaves a lump of coal in some stockings, and that's all you are given. It doesn't mean, however, that he's given up on you totally. I also got my grandfather, a role model who had a pocketful of magic and tricks, a manner that still touches me."

Murray catches himself and quickly returns to baseball, pausing to remember the chronology. "Anyway, then in the seventies, Bill Veeck bought the Chicago White Sox, and things got real funky over at Comiskey Park. Everything that I love about baseball is embodied in Bill Veeck. I met him the way everyone met him—he'd sit in the bleachers, take off his wooden leg and shirt, drink beer, and flick his cigarettes into the ashtray he'd built into his wooden leg. He'd just lay there in the sun, almost naked, talking to fans. That's how I'm going to play Bill Veeck . . . as the naked fan."

Like Bill Veeck, Murray now spends much of his life as a nomad, filling his time buying and selling dreck baseball teams populated by has-beens and losers. Then, just like Bill Veeck before him, the actor turns his ballparks into equal parts Fellini film and Coney Island geek show.

"I like rejects, and I like the carny part of minor league baseball," says Murray, whose millions could easily buy him a place in his own major league owner's sky box. Here in St. Paul, Murray sits on a folding chair set next to the inflatable sumo wrestling suit and the tractor that smooths the infield before and after the game. Officially, this hole in the wall is known as the "owners' box."

"Hey, Bill!" Murray yells again to Bill Fanning, who is sitting alone a few feet away, intently watching the game. "Do we still have the K-Man?"

Fanning says yes, and resumes watching the game.

"The K-Man is a great promotion and it was Bill Fanning's idea," Murray explains. "Each game, a guy on the other side is designated as the K-Man. If he strikes out, everybody in the park gets a Coke. People go nuts. At first, everyone in the league was pissed off by the K-Man—they said it showed up their side. Now every other team in the league is using it."

It's a promotion that Bill Veeck would have approved. And Mike agrees that Murray is the perfect choice to play his father in the upcoming bio pic. "Bill loves baseball, and he knows what Bill Veeck stood for," he says.

"But such nuttiness as the K-Man," I say, "would never be countenanced in the major leagues."

"That's the carny element that makes the minor leagues so great," Murray says, "where the fans know they'll get a good price and some bang for their buck."

The inning ends with Twig arguing a call with the umpire at first base. As Twig kicks the dirt and heads back to the Saints' dugout, Murray yells, "Hey, Twig! Why don't you go tell him to do the right thing?"

"I'll do that, Bill," Twig says, cracking up. "You bet I will."

Murray nods. The sun is shining, his sons are with him, the Saints are winning, and the Ramones' "Blitzkrieg Bop" is blasting over the PA. It's a full, exuberant house, and Bill looks happier than he has in ten years' worth of "Entertainment Tonight" clips.

Between innings, Murray walks out a few feet where the fans can see him and drop items to be autographed. Every second he is out in the open, someone above is shouting out a line from some movie of his.

"It's in the hole!" (from *Caddyshack*)

"Gimme, gimme, gimme, I need, I need, I need!" (from *What About Bob?*)

"Cinderella story!" (from *Caddyshack*)

"It's just another deadline. I'll just lash together a few raw facts, a little bit of old Negro wisdom, and this nightmare is over!" (as Hunter Thompson from *Where the Buffalo Roam*)

Murray, for the first time, looks me over closely. "So did Jann fly you out from New York?" he asks.

" 'Don't hassle me, I'm local,' " I say, quoting the T-shirt Murray wore through most of *What About Bob?*, a film in which he played the world's most neurotic patient torturing the planet's most self-centered psychiatrist, portrayed by Richard Dreyfuss. Not being from New York or Los Angeles seems to give me a dash more credibility with the movie star.

"You know what was fun about *What About Bob?* was actually *torturing* Richard Dreyfuss during the filming," Murray says. "He drove me nuts with his stage precision, so I returned the favor with anarchy. That's cinema verité you see up there."

Murray then steps back into the owners' box as the inning starts; he isn't yet ready to start goofing with the thousands of fans above him with whom he will soon intermingle. But one woman above wants a second autograph this second. "Wait until the break between innings, okay?" Murray asks.

"No, I want the autograph now!" she declaims.

"Please wait," Murray says.

"I want it now!"

"I promise," says Murray. "Between innings."

"You're a jerk, Bill Murray!" she says, storming off.

For the rest of the game, a worried Murray asks everyone he comes in contact with: "Am I a jerk?"

I hammer out more notes as if they're nails in his coffin. "Murray, the story has always gone," I write, "has always seemed trapped by his own fame. In Hollywood, stories have long circulated that he'd turned bitter and mean, a star more than willing to bite the heads off of fans or studio executives. 'There are probably fifteen hundred people in the world who actively hate my guts,' he says."

But hanging out in Midway Stadium with his team, Murray is, in fact, as genial as a game show host. Ever since he bought his first club in 1976, he explains, he's favored players dredged from the bottom of the barrel. "I've always owned teams of players nobody wants," he says. "There's a lot of goodwill that comes from being the mutt."

Over the railing, someone yells a line from Murray's film *Stripes*. "We are the wretched refuse! We're the underdog! We're mutts!"

"See what I mean?" says Murray.

Murray, full of bonhomie, heads back to the dugout, his favorite vantage point to watch the game.

Within moments, a scream comes from where the players sit.

"It's wired!" Bill Murray says, noticing for the first time that FX, the Rupert Murdoch-owned cable station doing a TV show on the Saints, has strung cable throughout the dugout to spy on the players and anyone else who might wander in.

"My last oasis!" Murray yells, genuinely pissed that his Eden has been violated. Murray leaps up from the bench and descends deep into the bowels of the stadium. In the basement, he whips open the door to Mike Veeck's windowless, cramped office. Out billows the smoke of five men puffing stogies as they count out today's gate receipts. Murray sits down disconsolately and addresses Mike.

"Mike," he says, "I told you it was a terrible idea to let cameras in here. I told you, I *told* you. The cameras are all over the players! They tell me the cameras go on the road with them, they're in the hotel, there's no brain there with those cameras, Mike, they're just shooting *nothing!* I *told* you that they'd be invading, that you would end up hating them, that no amount of money they're paying you is enough."

Mike drums his fingers and says nothing. Behind him is the Folgers coffee can with Bill Veeck's ashes. Murray doesn't seem to mind his friend's apparent disinterest and silence. The lack of verbal communication goes both ways; usually Murray doesn't let Veeck know he'll be attending a game until half an hour before the opening pitch; when he does come, it's not unusual for Murray and Mike to barely speak.

"There's nothing for us to talk about. Bill Murray and I just don't have long conversations about anything," Mike says, then echoes the comedian. "Our greatest form of communication is to get in a car for a road trip, blast cassettes, and just drive like crazy."

Not once during this weekend will either of the friends mention that Murray will shortly be playing Mike's father in the movie *Veeck as in Wreck* or that Sigourney Weaver has been cast as Mike's mother. "We never talk about the movie," Murray says. "I don't worry about it, and neither does Mike. He thinks I'm similar in so many ways to his father, though he won't tell me how. But Mike wants me to play him, so I'll do Bill Veeck as just a fan who made it all the way to the Hall of Fame."

Like an artist with an exciting new role, Murray goes on and on about Bill Veeck. In the meantime, I wonder if I can make a point in print that the comedian is so bitter with his own life that he's decided to *become* Bill Veeck. I think, I could make it sound a little spooky and, true or not, perhaps concoct a pseudopsychological theory of celebrity self-loathing for my hatchet job.

Mollified in minutes from the FX onslaught, Murray heads back to watch the game and again talk comfortably. Just then, a train rumbles past on the tracks just behind the outfield fence, and the engineer blasts his horn several times to say hi to rocking Midway Stadium.

"Isn't that just *great?*" Murray says, pointing to the train, enthusing over the corny, lovely nostalgia of it all. "Whenever a train goes by here, it just shakes everybody in the ballpark to their *gizzards*. He pauses and looks into the sky. "Isn't this how you remember baseball when you were young?"

Yes. But what about corrupt, desiccated major league baseball, which gave us Bill Murray's Ernie "Let's Play Two" Banks and my own beloved Harmon "the Minnesota Fat Boy" Killebrew? Murray laughs when he is reminded how the venerated *New York Times* columnist Robert Lipsyte nominated the comedian in his lead sentence for commissioner of baseball not too long ago.

" 'I will accept the job,' said Bill Murray, who is also part-owner of the St. Paul Saints of the Northern League, to *The New York Times*," the column began, " 'if you give me unlimited powers.' "

"Can you imagine if elements of this carny came to the big leagues?" he asks. "I went to see the Twins play last night at the Metrodome, and I fell asleep." But there are more important tasks at hand for Murray beyond the fate of major league baseball. Though he could afford a major chunk of a major league team, he likes the boonies. And now, it's time to do some public relations work for the fans in Midway Stadium from here in Flyoverland.

"C'mon, let's go get a bratwurst out at the concession stand," Murray says. He will spend much of the next several days mingling, serving, swerving into, dancing, hugging, and just generally connecting with the people of St. Paul. "The key is to keep moving, or it will take two hours to get our bratwursts," he says. "But it is important to me that they are prepared in the usual manner."

He makes his way among the people, who scream when they see him, who want dozens of pictures and hundreds of autographs and frequently a personal moment or three with the movie star whose fame has not diminished in the years since he virtually walked out of Hollywood to make the smaller, weirder, better movies he wanted to make. Sure, he'd pop up in a big-budget *Tootsie* every once in a while, but even there Murray gave Hollywood a little tweak.

Given a major supporting role in the Sydney Pollack–Dustin Hoffman–Elaine May collaboration and smash, Murray nearly stole the show. He also preferred to work uncredited.

And so he did, his name as invisible on screen as his own life has been to pesky reporters. Lately, his only big-budget film had been in a supporting role in *Space Jam*—the party animated major studio confection in which Murray did all of his on-camera work with the star Michael Jordan while wearing a St. Paul Saints cap. Mostly, he's since preferred appearing in small off-beat films like *Kingpin, The Man Who Knew Too Much,* and *Rushmore.*

And now, in Midway Stadium, land-locked among people screaming his name and his most famous movie lines, he seems happy. "A real *Day of the Locust* scene," I write in my notebook, but it isn't, really. He is not living *The Day of the Locust*'s Hollywood horror and stampede, but that of an icon who long ago overcame the fear and amazing sensation of hundreds of people rushing toward you, shrieking your name.

At the concession stand, Murray flirts with old ladies and pauses for pictures with giggly gangs of girls with braces on their teeth and shakes hands mock-gravely with boyfriends who tell Murray how much they like him. He is downright likable as he wanders the stadium, going up to the press box to announce an inning of the game on the Saints tiny radio station. Done with that, he takes bites out of several people's hot dogs and bratwursts, always with permission.

Gee, I think, I almost hate to hatchet him. He is already easily giving up to me the material that I could twist out of context to make him look like a mad artist who can only flee his own anger in the hinterlands of America's ballparks, yet still thrusts it upon other people by fingering their food. As I continue to figure out how I am going to do it, I begin to realize again that maybe I shouldn't.

Murray came to low-down minor league baseball via "Saturday Night Live." In the mid-1970s, cast members made home movies with director Gary Weiss of what they did on their summer vacations. Murray had hung out with the Gray's Harbor team in Washington state, the lone independent team of the low-down Northwest League. In the coming days, he gave Lou Gehrig's "luckiest man" farewell speech to the crowd, sang the national anthem, and even batted twice.

"The first time, the guy from the Walla Walla team threw me a strike and I hit it hard for a single," he says. "It felt great. But the next time up, they threw me a real slider, which I'd never seen before, and I went out."

Charmed by an independent team fighting in the mostly corporate minors, Murray bought the team. "The teams I had over the years never made money. It was a friendship thing," he says. "I wanted friends to come and be company. Gray's Harbor was in that part of Washington where it always rains, there's no work, and there's a lot of depression. They have the highest alcoholism rates in the country. When I found out that Kurt Cobain was born and grew up around that area of Washington, I understood what eventually happened to him."

Still, he loved the ball. "It was cool," remembers Murray, "because the whole ballpark was made out of timber—it was a monument to crazy four-by-twelve pieces of wood you never see anymore. They even had an old wooden steam bath there that had been built during the WPA before World War II."

Using bush league baseball to meditate, Murray found a way to "return to the feeling of your own past. Minor league baseball is very seductive. The magic is that this is how you remember baseball from when you were young. And the fact that we're independent from organized baseball meant we could make our own rules, with no interference. There was nobody telling us what to do. [We had] the mutt's edge."

After Gray's Harbor, Murray bought into the Utica Blue Sox, an independent team of nobodies in a minor league otherwise populated entirely by clubs all hooked up to major league organizations. "At Utica we had to play teams like the Oneonta Yankees, who had bonus babies with hundred-thousand-dollar contracts and other prospects getting paid real money. They had an actual payroll—their bonus baby got paid more than our entire team."

From there, it was on to the Salt Lake City Trappers, which Murray helped build from scratch. "Salt Lake hadn't had a team in years, and that was really a gamble because suddenly we were dealing with real money. We won a lot of games, though—we set the organized baseball record of twenty-nine straight wins one year—but we never made any money. Since we were the only outsiders in the league again, I started making up grudges against the other teams to get fans in. I invented a grudge with the Dodgers' affiliate in our league, telling people on the radio to come out and see a completely independent team take on the hateful Dodgers. I coached a lot at Salt Lake during games."

Murray pauses to watch the action on the Saints' field. "None of the other teams in the league liked us," he says of Salt Lake City. "And every year they'd change the rules so we couldn't win. But we always did and even set a minor league attendance record, which I'm very proud of. It wasn't about money and we never made any dough, but it was a lot of fun. I liked that 'us' and 'them' mentality."

And then came the Miami Miracle, which begat the Pompano Miracle, both run on other people's recommendation by the notorious Mike Veeck. Murray, with his button-down partner Marv Goldklang and the Zen scout and documentary filmmaker partner Van Schley, now had their own empire of teams nobody in the majors wanted, stocked with players all released from real organizations.

But battling the stiffs of baseball isn't the reason Murray owns baseball teams. "Mostly, it's for fun," he says. "I find this a calming, relaxing, soothing environment. All you have to do is find a quiet place at the park, and it's like your life stops."

Forever refusing to be interviewed or photographed at the ballpark, his teams became Murray's last public refuge from the celebrity locust. "For me, owning baseball teams was maybe like Danny [Aykroyd] and John [Belushi] having a blues band," Murray says. "It was a fun way to disappear. It's magic to play catch with your sons in the outfield. This year, after all the fans go home, we'll all go out on the field and play ball. It's great."

Murray recoils, however, at the idea that owning a minor league team is suddenly hip just because actress Heather Locklear and singer Jimmy Buffett recently bought teams. For Murray, owning scruffy teams mostly provides a place to sit down. "This is a refuge for me," he says. "Because here, sitting in Midway Stadium with the St. Paul Saints, I'm with the home team. I'm home. And in life, people don't mess with you too much when you've got home-field advantage."

The next afternoon Murray heads out with manager Marty Scott and pitcher Jeff Alkire into the Saint's parking lot to do the

Courtesy of Neal Karlen

goodwill tour of the barbecuers and tailgaters who began arriving hours before the Sioux City game. Allowed into his entourage, I follow along like a lapdog and begin taking notes, once more spinning the facts, interpreting isolated moments in Murray's life in order to make him sound like a lost prick. I feel sick.

If I go through with the hatchet job, I figure I will probably lead with a paragraph saying something like: "Bill Murray shuffles into the eye of a St. Paul mob with the lead-foot enthusiasm of Sean Penn taking his dead men's walk. 'This can be fun,' Murray says doubtfully. As he is caught in the celebrity glare," I scribble into my notebook, "he looks embarrassed to be himself."

Actually, Bill Murray seems quite happy hopping from tailgater to tailgater in the parking lot. "This *can* be fun," he says with feeling as he stops with the uniformed players and manager at every barbecue for a howdy and a bite.

I can't just make up my hatchet job—I have to explain the fact that Murray is, in fact, talking with and enjoying his fans in St. Paul. Easy. "Murray has a goofy quip for every stranger," I write, "that lasts exactly as long as it takes him to scribble his name and move on—but not so long that he actually has to communicate. 'I hate insincerity of any kind,' Murray tells an obese man dripping ketchup who wants a pennant signed, 'and I don't mean that,' he says as he autographs and moves on. 'I was reading the Gettysburg Address the other day,' he tells the next, 'and, you know, that guy was really on to something.' And then he is gone."

I'm taking the classic approach of writing a mean profile of a celebrity. Begin by repeating unattributed gossip early on, distancing oneself from the dirt by just saying, "This is just the conventional wisdom and gossip." My job, I know, is to make Murray look like a jerk. I have the sentences, I figure, that just might work.

If I go through with it, I will probably show him verbally wasting the abrasive cameraman that I witnessed, in which he jokingly threatened to set the documentarian on fire. Irony, untranslated, is a perfect way to make someone look mean and/or like an idiot.

I'll paint him as a celebrity out of touch with his own reality. "Even now," I write, "Murray seems only dimly aware of his projects outside of a picture in which he'll play Bill Veeck, his favorite baseball hero."

Then I'll waste him with one of his own quotes, maybe when he says, "Besides doing Veeck, there's this thing I just signed to do written by some young guy who did *Twelve Monkeys* or *Spanking the Monkey* or something. He had some hit movie in the last year or two." Murray sounds disinterested in the topic. "I think there's a book behind it that's got something different. I read the script last week, and they're never good, but this was one was," he continues,

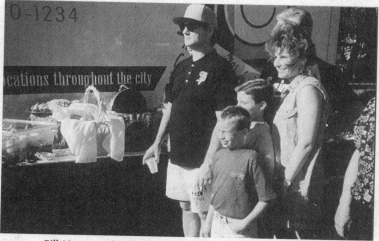

Bill Murray with tailgaters in the Saints pre-game parking lot
Courtesy of Neal Karlen

now barely sounding interested at all in his own movie career as he heads from the Saints' parking lot to the underground cavern where he will watch the game.

With some variation of this tack, I figure, I'll begin crucifying Murray in print as some sort of Hollywood-style Howard Hughes, cut off from his own world, able to find peace only in the middle of nowhere, missing, unlike Howard, only fingernails several inches long and pop bottles filled with urine. I let on nothing to Murray or the Saints, of course, thanking Murray for his time, grateful that Jann Wenner will now be likely to sign my check. I have the goods.

"Why would you hose me?" Murray asks. "You live here in Minnesota, right? You'd be hosing me where you *live.*"

Uh yeah. I'd be doing, I realize, exactly what I left New York for in the first place.

Murray, meantime, goes back to remembering the Saints' first two games ever at home in 1993. "It drizzled the first and second nights of those games," Murray recalls, "and by the eighth inning of that second game, the rain was really coming down hard. But no one in Midway left the park. Then the PA announced that there would be fireworks after the game."

Murray sighs happily and laughs, remembering the scene. "Suddenly there was this deep-bellied laugh all across the stadium from the fans, and I knew right then that this experience with the Saints was going to be great. After the game, Mike put on one of his spectacular fireworks shows and this recording of Judy Garland singing 'The Battle Hymn of the Republic.' Still, no one left because you could already feel the joy in that stadium with this team."

Within a few minutes before game time, Murray takes the mound in his Saints cap, holding a baseball and being introduced over the PA as "The Ayatollah of hilarity, Bill Murray." With that, he heaves a ceremonial first pitch over the grandstand and out of the ballpark, missing only by inches the open window and exposed heads of the writers in the Saints' tiny press box. He then hugs the Saints catcher who was supposed to catch the ball. From there he embraces all the umpires, then kisses them on the lips. As the crowd goes mental, Murray trots back to his hiding spot under the stands, a few feet away from the Saints' dugout.

I join him there and continue to set him up as all good magazine feature writers on nefarious missions do. Unable to get it up to discuss his other film projects, Murray grows animated once again when the subject of Bill Veeck and his starring role in the *Veeck as in Wreck* movie comes up.

In my notebook, I scrawl some more sentences I might use to indicate a man before me who has lost his bearings. "Murray is so much more animated talking about Bill Veeck than himself that it's almost certain he'd rather *be* Bill Veeck. It's all a little spooky, especially since one of his great friends is Bill Veeck's son, Mike."

It isn't spooky at all, but I keep scribbling as Murray talks about Bill Veeck's place in baseball history, and what a visionary Mike was. A couple weeks before, Libby Veeck had shown me her wedding album from when she'd married Mike in 1996. There were pictures of Murray at the St. Paul wedding, dressed shabbily in a Salvation Army-style coat, no tie, and some pants that looked like they'd been fished out of a Dumpster.

Back then, I will note falsely or at least guess in print, Bill Murray seemed to be inhabiting in real life the character of Charlie Chaplin's tramp, whose style, Chaplin once said, was one of "shabby gentility." Now he has switched personas to a dead baseball promoter with a peg leg who was loved by virtually everyone he came in contact with.

"It is sad to see such a gifted clown in a run from himself," I write in my notebook, though Murray seems like he is on the run from nothing but the FX cameras as he describes his different ventures into minor league baseball. "Mike and I both have the same idea when it comes to promotions, no matter how ludicrous they may sound," he says. "It's like doing improv—instead of saying no to an idea, you say, 'How?' "

So no, Bill Murray was not a meanie or schmuck, no matter what I had to write about him. My notebook, though journalistically valid with real events and quotes, seemed like an exercise in fiction writing. I had the goods, but morally could I write in the hippest magazine in the land that my facts proved Murray, the hippest icon to a major portion of America, was a dick?

Kind to fans, he seemed especially happy and comfortable with the team itself, always willing to fill a new water cooler in the locker room, always respectful of even the most ornery, talentless ballplayers.

Today Murray has once again decided to wear a Saints uniform for an on-field coaching stunt. Wandering midway into the game into the locker room, he grabs a Saints T-shirt out of the locker of Chris Evans, the hotheaded, good-hitting right fielder who is riding the bench while Darryl Strawberry takes his position.

Suddenly Evans is in the locker room in full game face, angrily demanding to know if Murray is stealing his equipment. Murray, meantime, emotes terror as he's cornered by one of his own enraged players. "I was going to give it back," the millionaire Murray says with embarrassment and conciliation to the scrubeenie Evans, almost pleading for absolution for violating the locker room. "Here, take this," Murray says, beginning to peel the crisp polo shirt he's wearing off his own back to give to Evans.

What could I do with this? Writing in my notebook, I came up with: "And where does grouchy, bitter old Bill Murray fit into this carnival? 'I find minor league ball a calming, relaxing, soothing environment,' I will quote him. 'All you have to do is find a quiet place at the park, and it's like your life stops.' "

" 'Life stops'?" I would opine in print. "Who but the most unhappy of superstars would want life to stop?"

Murray, meantime, is checking on the status of Tobias, the trained pig kept behind the grandstand where the movie star hides. "You look good, Tobias," he tells the pig. "You're a gamer." Each year brings a new baby pig to be trained to deliver balls to the umpire; swollen by the end of the year, the Saints' mascot is then retired to a Wisconsin farm.

"We should do a poster of the three pigs we've used so far," Murray tells Tobias's trainer, Dennis Hauth. "There is history and tradition in these pigs."

No way, I realized again. I couldn't do this. There would be no more inner discussions of my perilous finances or wish to see my name again in *Rolling Stone*. I hadn't grown into a weenie; I'd grown up.

I knew Bill Murray wasn't Dale Carnegie: he'd yelled at obnoxious people as had Mike (Darryl Strawberry never could afford to). But he was realer than virtually any celebrity I'd interviewed or stalked over the last fifteen years, less focused on himself than any "star" I'd encountered for a few days for a phony baloney celebrity profile.

And now, all he wanted to do was watch his ball game in peace. I slipped away, knowing it was okay to stay and get more material with which to kill Murray if I decided to. But I was afraid that I might fall back into the trap of the hatchet man and do what I'd been ordered to do at great remuneration.

"I'll see you later. Thanks," I said. "Are you coming back?"

"I'm driving to Madison with Mike tomorrow to see the Black-Wolf series," Murray said, "and then I'll be back for the playoffs."

"I'll try not to bug you," I promised.

"Thanks," he said. "Say how *is* Jann?"

I shrugged.

"And if you're going to hose me," Murray reminded me, "please don't hose Mike."

Or all my new friends in the tiny Saints' organization. They'd smiled and waved to me every day of the season and were sure, I knew, that I would do neither them or their team any harm. They were from St. Paul, not Minneapolis, and they believed more.

After the game, Murray got into a car with Mike and barreled down the I-94 Interstate for 253 miles until they hit the mosquito-infested Warner Park, built on a swamp and home of the first-year Madison Black Wolf. Just as Mike had said, they blasted tapes the entire way, saying only a few words to each other the entire trip.

At the Madison ballpark, meantime, Monica Toppen, was shaking with rage. Up in the press box, someone had left a sexually harassing note about her attire and had invited others in the box to write their own comments. "I don't want to complain," she said. "I want to own a minor league team someday and I don't want to get a reputation as a troublemaker, especially on an expansion team. But I'm not going to take this."

The game, played on June 28, was won by the Saints, 8–7. Afterward Monica related that she had called every team in the Northern League, asking, she said, for a small donation to put up a small memorial, but she had been rebuffed everywhere.

"Say, didn't they find some marijuana on his body when they fished him out of the lake?" one executive for another team asked Monica as he begged off. Nor did the Black Wolf seem excited about memorializing a man who, apocryphally, is still supposed to be at the bottom of the lake. When strange stirrings in the sky, water or atmosphere were spotted, it was said by locals to be a Loch Ness-like "Otis."

An "Otis," I learned, was Redding's ghost at the bottom of the lake, trying to make it up and out for his gig with the Bar-Kays on December 10, 1967. "They recovered his body, so I don't believe in the 'Otis' at the bottom of the lake story," Monica said, "but I believe we should remember and mark the spot where one of the greatest R&B singers ever got killed."

I said nothing, as she whispered/sang Otis's "Respect." " 'Attention must be paid,' " she said, quoting *Death of a Salesman*.

"You're pretty smart," I said. "I think the Most Beloved Woman of the Northern League is one day going to own her own minor league team, finish her law degree, and then make it all the way up to president of the National League."

"I hope so," she said. For the next several minutes, we discussed ancient baseball books that we either wanted or had found cheap at used bookstores. She talked about Christy Mathewson some more, how she'd just read a new biography of him by Ray Robinson called *Matty: An American Hero.* Christy was, she said, just as perfect in real life as in his legend. He was a gentleman with a wicked old time "fadeaway" pitch.

But he was long dead. And even if Monica waited for Christy and he never showed up, she assured me again, she would only marry a man who would name their child after him. "But I'm waiting for Christy." And I was waiting for . . . nobody. I didn't care.

And then it hit me. Monica hadn't healed my heart, but she had finally succeeded in rekindling my long-lost love of baseball. That love had fallen apart only because I'd married the most beautiful woman I'd ever met as much for her appreciation of a well-turned double play as for her soul, so when she broke my heart, baseball took the blame, "wore the jacket," as Mike Veeck liked to say.

But after Monica and a half a season in the Northern League, I could at last appreciate a nicely turned double play again. I could talk about Christy Mathewson, no longer marveling at the existential waste of keeping score of each play in the program during a game or cheering athletes who almost universally touched their genitals several times an inning.

The green grass on the freshly watered infield looked beautiful again. That was the kind of love Monica gave me back, and the Most Beloved Woman of the Northern League only became more beloved.

Back in St. Paul the previous day, Murray had been talking about the meaning of independent baseball. He'd become an increasingly hands-on owner; the previous winter he'd even gone to the Northern League owner meetings in Los Angeles that had been called to hash out and remind each other of why they'd gotten involved in the first place. Everybody also wanted to bitch.

And that was fine, Murray said, because the point of the Northern League was to make sure that all the teams were united in the spirit of fun and fond memories. Infighting between teams, however, had caused some rifts in the last few years, Murray went on, which is why Mike gave such a fire-and-brimstone speech at the league meetings.

"All the team presidents and owners were there to air their gripes. It was like a war conference," Murray remembers. "I, of course, was a fashionable two hours late, so I missed all the weeping and Mafia kisses." He also missed Mike's speech.

"Mike stood up and said we'd all gotten caught up in the competitive myths, and that wasn't what this league was about," Murray continues. "Mike pulled down the pillars of the temple, and by the time I got there, it was like talking through clouds of dust. I'd never met most of these owners, but I liked them. They don't wear their ownership on their sleeves, while these fantasy baseball fruitcakes, who [instead of] dealing with real teams, drool it off their sleeves."

So the Northern League, it was decided, would remember its mission.

"Even if the major leagues think your promotions and idealism are nuts," I said, "and you would never be allowed in the bigs?"

"That's the carny element that makes the minor leagues so great," Murray says one more time, "where the fans know they'll get a good price and some bang for their buck."

9

Darryl Goes to the Show

Son, be of good cheer; thy sins be forgiven thee.
—Matthew 9:2

With the great Yankee teams of the past,
You stay awake,
And you dream,
And you think of what might be,
If you are the hero or the goat.
—Phil Rizzuto, "Hero or the Goat"
  (Yankees pregame show, 1976)

The best place to check out women in Midway Stadium during a game, it was generally agreed by the players, was from the makeshift bullpen next to the St. Paul dugout. There, sitting on folding chairs placed right next to the fence on the third base grandstand, the Saints' relief pitchers could carry on the wooing that helped make life in the Northern League bearable.

They had to be discreet. It was the middle of a game, after all. The women who came down to the fence to stare at the relievers, however, were under no such restrictions. At home against Madison in mid-July, reliever Paul Romanoli, the best closer (with women and ninth-inning batters) in the league, couldn't help but notice the tanned and beautiful woman in the tight black summer dress staring directly at him from across the stands and behind the bullpen.

"Well, well," says Roma, turning his head over his shoulder.

"She's married," Rod Seip tells him, not as a warning but a challenge.

"Tell me she isn't checking me out," Roma retorts, a man for whom no conquest is impossible, a ballplayer who can pick up beautiful women in bars with lines like:

ROMA: Did it hurt?
WOMAN: What?
ROMA: When you fell from heaven.

"Turn around, Roma, you're turned around way too far!" says Seip, who meantime has got some action going on his own. Directly in front of him, a curvy young woman in a tight white T-shirt is broadly smiling directly at him and won't turn away.

"She's straight checking me out," Seip says to Roma. "Her boyfriend's up there somewhere, and now she's trying to keep a secret thing going while he's gone. I got to beat them off me!"

"Ah, the life of a relief pitcher," Roma says. "I wonder what it's like to get a good night's sleep. In a fifteen-minute period last night, I had a Captain and Coke, a glass of white Zinfandel, and a Jim Beam and Coke. That'll get you!"

Suddenly a Scandinavian madchen comes down to the fence and announces to Roma, "I don't have a boyfriend."

Nice. But later. Roma is up, warming up in seconds, and in minutes has added another save to his league-leading total of nine.

June 25, 1996

Ancient domestic relations, meantime, looked as if they'd be Darryl Strawberry's bete noir. Still owing $300,000 in spousal and child support to his first wife, Lisa, he was due in a Los Angeles court in days. Needless to say, he didn't have the money: even his 1986 championship trophy from the Mets had been sold.

"You can't get blood from a stone," explained Darryl Strawberry's agent Eric Grossman to the press as to why his client was so behind in maintenance to the woman he divorced in 1993. "He doesn't have the money right now."

But with Strawberry leading the league with ten home runs and a .378 average, Grossman said, and with the scouts of the world looking upon him, he would soon be making a major league salary with which to make restitution. "Two weeks," Mike Veeck estimated. "Darryl Strawberry will be back in the big leagues in two weeks, hitting a home run that will be very meaningful for a lot of people who've screwed up their lives and managed to come back. We knew there was a court date coming up for him, but everybody also knew he couldn't make that payment by that date. He has to make a major league salary first—and he will."

Or would he? No major league teams were calling, but Strawberry seemed accepting of the bad news without the veneer of arrogance that had dogged his career forever. True, George Steinbrenner had a savior complex, but Darryl had to look, as he'd done up until now, like a soul worth saving. Lisa's claims, which hit the New York newspapers like a cold shower on what might have been a sunny comeback story, didn't look good.

Yet he labored on. The next night, at home against Sioux City on June 26, he hit two home runs to win the game 5–2 and raised his average to .400. The following evening in Madison, he hit three home runs in an 8–7 victory, and the Saints rose to a four-game lead over the upstart second-place Black Wolf. But sucking on one of my Newports after the game, Darryl looked sad, if not sullen.

"I'm still having fun doing this, just playing ball with these kids," Strawberry said. "But I'm a veteran." And so far, he went on, he hadn't heard from one major league team looking for someone with a left-handed home run swing like his. Rumors still abounded among major league scouts about more than the constantly analyzed content of Darryl's pee—word remained that he'd lost a key fraction of bat speed that had once made him seem a shoo-in for Cooperstown.

"If nothing happens in the next few weeks," he said, "I don't know if I will still be having fun. I'll see where I am in ten days. If nothing comes up, I'll have to sit down and think everything over."

"Fine, think about your career, Darryl," manager Marty Scott kept telling him. "Just don't quit. Better times are coming—the major leagues will soon be expanding by two teams, further diluting the talent pool. If you can just keep productive, clean, and safe," Scott told him, "you'll have a good chance to make it back up."

When I asked Scott about this, he told me, "Darryl and I talked about this the other day, about how he still has to go out and play hard and sign autographs—even if he is hitting .411. He can't get discouraged when it seems no one wants him. We had a guy last year, Dan Peltier, who was hitting .370 and nobody called. But he hung in there, and today he's with the San Francisco Giants, batting .350 and making over a million dollars."

And then Marty repeated the mantra said by every player, manager, or coach in the Northern League who was praying for magic. "You just don't know what's going to happen," he said, "when you're inside a professional uniform."

So Darryl hit two home runs in the next game. Then he hit another, his seventeenth, two days later on July 3 at home against Sioux Falls. It was an ugly 14–9 loss for the Saints in front of a sold-out crowd, but they made up for it the next night when Jack Morris pitched a nine-inning shutout, raising his record to 4–0, with a 2.38 earned run average. Strawberry, meantime, hit his eighteenth homer, a franchise record.

The game ended 12–0 for the Saints, and the crowd cheered each one of Morris's outs or Strawberry's hits like they were celebrating a birth. Or a survival. Their very presence on the ballfield, it seemed, said that growing old in a young world wasn't so bad after all. But in sensible, don't-judge-a-book-by-its-cover underdog St. Paul, they already knew that.

In the dressing room after the game, Morris waxed sanguine, recalling the days earlier in the season when he talked of quitting the team because he couldn't get by without his forkball and breaking balls, pitches that he'd only recently started comfortably using. "It's tough to get by on two pitches, but that's why I needed to build up my arm strength early in the season," Morris said. "I'm right where I want to be."

Where he wanted to be, it went unsaid, was ready for the majors. The attention that night, however, would be going to Strawberry, not Morris. Jack had gotten the shutout, but Straw had gotten the call.

The earth had moved in New York—or at least under the feet of George Steinbrenner. Humiliating Bob Watson, Steinbrenner took Darryl off his shit list and set a place for him with the New York Yankees. For their trouble, Mike Veeck, Marv Goldklang, and the Saints received a check for $3,000, the standard fee Northern League teams got when one of their players signed with a major league organization.

It happened on the night of July 3, with the Saints leading Sioux Falls, 12–0, in the fourth inning. Suddenly the standing-room-only crowd saw Strawberry being waved in from right field by manager Marty Scott. The crowd seemed to sense something was happening; they rose in mass with the loudest ovation of the season for the man who had proven so much to them over the short summer.

Saints co-owner Marv Goldklang, the Wall Street investor who also owned a sliver of the Yankees, had been updating Steinbrenner for weeks on Darryl's rebirth in St. Paul. He'd been living quietly, Marv said over and over to George, with his second wife and batch of kids. Not once, Marv told Steinbrenner, had Strawberry refused the autograph of one starry-eyed child holding out a baseball in Fargo, Sioux City, Thunder Bay, or St. Paul.

When Steinbrenner had first signed Darryl in 1995, it was a public relations disaster prompting negative comment from President Clinton's drug czar. Now, only six months after he'd released Strawberry, the Boss decided to sign Strawberry again. "I know a lot of you recall statements that he didn't fit," Watson backpedaled to reporters. "I stand by that statement, but I can change my mind. The man has put up some serious numbers."

Yes. In twenty-nine games with the Saints, Darryl had batted 108 times and led the Northern League in home runs (18), batting average (.435), and slugging percentage (1.0000).

"All that I'll say is that it's time to heal and to move on," Steinbrenner said. "I was impressed with the way Darryl conducted himself in St. Paul and the way he treated fans. He was devoted to his family and that was important to me."

As he'd done for so many ballplayers and managers he'd banished then reclaimed, Steinbrenner let Strawberry come back on a short leash. His one-year deal for $700,000 would garner Darryl $350,000 for his half-season in the majors. He also got a signing bonus of $260,000, which, it turned out, was almost precisely the amount of cash the Los Angeles court was demanding that Strawberry pay to his first wife for marital and child support.

Steinbrenner also had his respected general manager Bob Watson, who wanted Strawberry like he wanted ebola, eat shit in public. In the press release on Yankees stationery announcing that New York had bought Strawberry's contract from St. Paul, Watson was quoted immediately after it was noted that Darryl had homered once every six at-bats for the Saints. "Our scouts have regularly covered Darryl and, especially in the last two weeks, have reported that he can help this club offensively," the release said. It ended with Strawberry thanking the Saints, Mike, and Marv Goldklang.

Steinbrenner, however, was not up for any last grandiose display of affection for or by Strawberry and St. Paul on behalf of each other. He wanted him up to the majors fast and immediately dispatched the right fielder to Columbus, the Yankees' top minor league team, for a three-game warm-up before he hit Yankee Stadium.

Mike, however, had wisely put together a night before Independence Day fireworks show for after what proved to be Darryl's last Saints game. As Darryl held up his children, hugged his wife, and stared into the prairie pyrotechnics, he tried to explain what St. Paul had meant to him. Maybe, he proposed to manager Marty Scott, George would let him play one more game with the Saints.

"I don't think so," said the manager. "You got the call. You've got to go."

"It goes so deep down inside, what the St. Paul Saints mean to me," he said in the locker room after the game, taking his Saints jersey off for the last time. "Those players gave me the energy and lift to go out there every day. We became a unit together."

He handed Tom Tisdale, the team's trainer, his jersey. "Send this back to me. I want to get it framed," Strawberry said, rushing to get packed and to the airport that night. "And when we win this championship, I want my ring sent to me," he demanded.

Strawberry then took two of his own bats out of his locker and asked everybody on the team to sign them as a memento. For that last moment, he was still a Saint.

And then, in front of everyone's eyes, Darryl somehow alchemized in the pint-sized Saints locker room back into a major leaguer: a guy headed for the bigs, a New York Yankee. He seemed suddenly taller, broader, somehow more mighty and less approachable. There wasn't a swagger, but an air that preceded him that said, "*This* is a man who no longer needs to dress in a shit hole, ride a bus all night to Thunder Bay, or tell his woes to a Cigarette Boy."

I held out one more Newport menthol to Darryl as he stuffed his gear into a bag and hugged his teammates. "One last cigarette?" I asked. I had a fantasy that Darryl would say, "Cigarette Boy, come with me. I'm taking you back to New York, to the Show." I saw myself wearing a Yankees uniform with c.b. written on the back, and I'd hand him his Newports whenever Darryl wanted a smoke in the clubhouse.

Not to be. For the first time all season, he turned down one of my smokes.

"No thanks," Strawberry said, licking his lips over something, but waving off the cigarette. "I have to go to New York." Cigarette Boy was dead.

Darryl saved his fondest locker room greetings for manager Scott. "I want to stay in touch with you," Darryl said.

"You will. Just call me, I'll be there," said Scott. "I'll be waiting on you."

"Who knows?" said Marty privately. "Maybe he'll go oh for four one night up there, and he can call me up and say, 'Help!' I won't be able to tell him how not to go oh for four, but I can talk to him and at least make him feel good about himself."

Darryl headed off to Gabe's, where the entire team had gathered to toast and say good-bye to their leader. "Hey, Chris, take care, man," he said to outfielder Chris Evans, who would take his place in right field. "And watch that temper."

"Temper?" said Evans, renowned for having the shortest fuse on the team, who'd been vocally bitching ever since Darryl Strawberry had taken away his position. "Yeah, your temper," Strawberry lectured, giving Evans a hug, then hugging everyone.

He shook Kevin Garner's hand, the man who, more than anybody in the room but Strawberry, should have made the Show. But that was a long time ago. "I'm proud of you, man," Garner said with a smile that looked both sly and sad as he took Darryl's hand. Pictures were taken all around, and Darryl only left Gabe's after he was told he must get to the airport immediately if he was going to catch the plane that would get him to Columbus for the game the next day.

At the Twin Cities airport, Darryl's baggage handler, an old black man with a broad smile on his face, said simply, "So you're going back to New York."

"Going back to New York," Darryl said. "Going to take care of business."

The next night, July 5, began with Charysse Strawberry walking out onto the Midway Stadium field to address the crowd wearing Darryl's number 17 jersey. "Darryl, what do you want me to say?" Charysse had asked right before he took off for Columbus. "Give me ideas, Darryl." And he had.

Now it was time to start the first game of the post-Strawberry era. When Charysse came out of the Saints' dugout looking like a prom queen wearing her boyfriend's jersey, the crowd cheered lustily. Charysse then started talking, using the notes she and Darryl had gone over the night before.

"Darryl felt bad that he just had to leave without saying good-bye," Charysse began before reading the sold-out crowd his final good-bye. "To the St. Paul Saints fans and organization," she said, "I would like to thank you for your kindness at all times, for allowing us to have a dream and allowing it to happen. To Marty Scott and my teammates, thanks for your support and encouragement. I love you guys and will miss you greatly. Thank you and God bless." And then she ended with the sign-off: "Darryl Strawberry and his family."

In the girlfriends-of-the-ballplayers section, there was astonishment at how good Charysse looked, even wearing her husband's way-too-big Saints uniform. She was a major league wife, no question, top of the line, and the few rows of Saints girlfriends smiled wishfully and clapped politely.

Then it was over. As soon as Charysse was out of town, the name DARRYL STRAWBERRY was ripped from his locker and put on the GON' FISHIN' wall. Darryl then played two games for Columbus, the Yankees' top farm club, hitting three home runs in eight at-bats. Finally, on July 7, he was back in pinstripes. "He looked gentler in the face," a couple of New York reporters printed, "humbled by all the years of drugs and drinking and back-page controversy."

On his very first pitch against the Milwaukee Brewers, Darryl slammed a deep drive to right that looked like it would clear the wall. It didn't, barely, and was caught on the warning track. But the crowd was on its feet and Straw was back where he belonged.

Things, however, were not going nearly as well back on the field in St. Paul. The Saints lost the Independence Day game after Strawberry left to Sioux Falls 7–3, looking as if they were playing on downers. St. Paul was still in first by two games, with twelve left to play in the first half of the season, but the slide had begun. "It's natural that the team would feel a tremendous letdown after losing someone like Darryl," Marty Scott said, "but someone else is just going to have to be the leader."

To fill Strawberry's veteran slot on the roster, the Saints signed third baseman Chuck Jackson, thirty-three. Marty Scott had known the infielder with the Ricky Ricardo pencil-thin mustache through most of Jackson's 1,088 games in the minors with the Texas Rangers' organization, where he had been a career .289 hitter.

Jackson had also come up for cups of coffee with the Rangers and Houston Astros for 82 major league games. Those were cherished cups: in his briefcase, Jackson carried eight-by-ten color glossies of himself in his Texas Rangers uniform.

"Jackson's a good talker with a good bat," Marty Scott said, "and I'm hoping he's willing to lead."

Still, some of the Saints were realistic about replacing Darryl Strawberry with Chuck Jackson. "There's a difference between getting hits," said Steve Solomon, "and dominating the game."

Chuck Jackson
Courtesy of Bonnie Butler

But Jackson, despite his ability to keep the clubhouse loose and the hits coming, could not keep the team from disintegrating. A cloud came over the team like the one over the head of Lil' Abner's jinxed Joe Btfsplk. Certain players were beginning to act like infants as Madison began creeping up to the Saints in the standings. The Saints lost two out of three at Fargo in the series after Straw left, leaving them with a 19–14 record, one game ahead of Madison with nine games left in the half-season.

Except for Morris—who was sure he'd be called to the majors when the big league pennant races heated up and arms up there became sore and tired—the whining continued. Worst of the babies was Marty Neff, who, if he went out on the way to first, had a tendency to sail his batting helmet over Twig, whose hand was out to take it, or bounce it on the ground in front of the proud old man. The habit made manager Marty Scott furious, and for the first time he began calling team meetings where he would yell. This team, he said, was no longer acting professional.

Now it was on to Winnipeg, "the Sodom of the Northern League." In the opening game on July 8, Jack Morris lost his first game 4–3 and looked more pissed off than in his entire career. The sun had been in his eyes in the first inning, he bitched at reporters, when a ball came back through the box, barely missing Morris's face.

"I didn't see it until it was two feet from my face," Morris claimed. "If I had been hit, that would have been it." It had been a hideous first inning for Jack; blinded by the sun, he gave up three runs. He then put down fifteen Goldeyes in a row, until he yielded a home run in the seventh that lost the game 4–3.

"It was the fucking fence's fault," Jack groused mightily after the game. "A guy hits a fly ball three hundred and twenty-five feet into the power alley and gets a home run. This is the only park in baseball where you can do that."

But Jack wasn't through. "I don't want to play in Winnipeg again," he said. "If I'm not able to attract any offers soon, I'll go back to farming in Montana. I think I'm ready right now."

But there was a grim reality that Morris had realized ever since Strawberry left. The scouts just didn't seem to be showing up with their radar guns to test Morris's speed the way they eventually did to check out Strawberry's bat. He'd always known he'd go up later to the Show than Strawberry, but he expected that scouts would at least be *looking*. "I doubt if there were any baseball scouts in the crowd tonight," he said. "Maybe hockey scouts."

The Saints lost the next night too, July 9, their fourth straight, a bumbling loss featuring four errors by second baseman Carlton Fleming that dropped them to a half-game lead over Madison. Chuck Jackson, however, was finding his groove. He hit his first home run and was hoovering up the balls at third base. He was leading off the field too, even sharing his massive CD collection with the players in the 'hood in the back of the bus. Though not Darryl Strawberry, Jackson looked just like the leader Scott wanted.

Unbidden, Jackson talked to Marty Neff about his penchant for throwing bats and helmets and for telling umpires to constantly go fuck themselves. "If I were an umpire, I'd toss you out in a second," Jackson lectured Neff after another bat-throwing incident. "You're supposed to be a professional."

"I look at leadership as a way to maybe be prepared for the other side of baseball, when I'm done playing and can pass on what I've

Saint Paul Saints

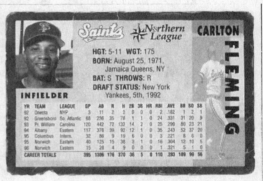

learned to young players coming up," said Jackson. "But right now there is nothing that compares to the feeling of hitting a baseball."

But for now the thirty-three-year-old married father of three wasn't ready to give up his swings, not as long as he was still wanted by someone, somewhere, be it in Taiwan, the Mexican jungle, even Fargo. The simple act of hitting a baseball, as Hall of Famer Reggie Jackson once explained, was better than sex.

Manager Marty Scott agreed with Jackson about the beauty of just being able to put on a uniform and *play*. "There isn't one of those players I wouldn't trade places with," said Scott.

The team, having lost four in a row, stood at 19–16, only half a game ahead of Madison in the Eastern Division. Enraged by his team's swoon, Marty Scott finally found it necessary to play the bad cop in the minutes after the Saints, playing at Winnipeg, dropped their fourth straight game. "Nobody shower!" he yelled as his team entered the clubhouse. "I got something to say."

What had finally set the manager off was, naturally, Marty Neff. After grounding out to end an inning on July 9, Neff had bounced his batting helmet off the ground instead of handing it to coach Twig, who was standing there with his hands outstretched. "No one does that to Twig," the manager said shortly before he exploded. "Nobody on any team of *mine!*"

Neff's frustration emanated in large part from the fact that he no longer had Darryl Strawberry protecting him in the batting order.

Before Strawberry left, Neff was leading the league in batting and RBIs. Now, as the Saints lost the first seven of eight without Darryl, Neff had slipped badly, unable to count on the meatballs that had been thrown his way when Strawberry hit in front of him.

Neff's homer total now only inched up, and most of them seemed to be solo shots when games no longer mattered, while his batting average went down for the first time all season. Still, back home in Midway Stadium, the members of the Marty Neff Fan Club cheered for him as their hero. Marty still tossed them balls and went to talk to the fans during pitching changes. He attended the weekly gatherings of the fan club at a local meeting hall, where he would give monologues about the meaning of being Marty Neff, and autograph his fan club's T-shirts, which featured his name, number, and facsimile signature.

The manager and players of the Saints, though, continued to stare in disbelief at Neff's on-field behavior; one day, in early July, a dozen players made the not-so-subtle ironic point of wearing MARTY NEFF FAN CLUB T-shirts during batting practice. His fans, however, couldn't hear Neff screaming obscenities at umpires after being thrown out of games, didn't see him studying the daily stat sheets in the locker room to see exactly how he was hitting, weren't aware of the major disrespect Neff was showing his teammates every time he failed to run out ground balls or threw his batting helmet at the feet of the venerated Twig like he was some ordinary ball boy. To Marty's fans, however, he was the kind heart and karmic soul of the Saints.

But now, in the Winnipeg visitors' clubhouse, in the eyes of the other players, he remained a major head case, a lazy man/child with terrific baseball skills and a pot belly at twenty-eight. No one doubted why the Pittsburgh Pirates' organization cut him, and Marty himself said he bore a ruined reputation in organized baseball.

And so, finally, in Winnipeg, Marty Scott had enough. As he slammed the clubhouse door closed, the Southern Baptist with the gentlemanly mild manners and the judicious way of cutting players began a tirade filled with so many staccato cuss words that it was like listening to a David Mamet monologue.

"From now on, there will be 'effing' fines," Marty shrieked, "for misbehavior on and off the field!" He threw a large garbage can against the wall and told them, "If you guys are waiting for fucking Darryl Strawberry to come back and save you, well, it 'effing' isn't going to happen."

As Marty raged, the players tried to disappear into their lockers, looking like altar boys who'd been nabbed drinking the sacramental wine. Finally Marty screamed his final epithet, threw open the clubhouse door, and walked back toward the field. He was planning some changes, some big fucking collective changes with this team at the end of the first half-season.

Unknown to the players, Marty had already phoned around the league about getting rid of Marty Neff, but the only nibble had come from Ed Nottle, the manager at Sioux City, who never minded a good head case on his team; he *enjoyed* one as a matter of fact. But not even Ed would give the Saints anything for Marty Neff . . . alone. Singin' Ed wanted more. He wanted the Saints to throw in Kevin Garner, one of the most popular players among the players. Marty had also tried to peddle Chris Evans, he told the moody right fielder, but nobody had offered "more than a box of balls."

As Marty wound down, a collective sigh of relief from the players in the Winnipeg locker room was palpable. They were in Winnipeg, after all, and it was time to party in the get-down capital of the Northern League.

In the film *Jesus of Montreal,* a priest who commits a grievous error frets that his punishment from the archbishop would be banishment to boring, bland Winnipeg. Baseball players, however, knew better. For ballplayers, if not priests, Winnipeg was the best, easiest place in the league to get laid, as well as the only stop on the Saints' season-long itinerary where they would stay at a nice hotel, the downtown Delta.

Throughout that evening's game, groupies had been throwing pieces of paper with invitations to a few Saints players in the dugout and bullpen. As the game progressed, all the female prospects were surreptitiously analyzed by the athletes for hotness and easiness of picking. Sexual intrigue seemed an aphrodisiac to the players; out in the visiting bullpen, as at home, the first question Saints players asked pretty-looking women preening at them was: "Are your boyfriends here?" It only added to the game: "Ditch the guys and we'll meet you later."

Boarding the team bus that night back to the hotel, meantime, a phalanx of groupies on either side of the vehicle spread out as players walked by, making their choices. "You," "You," "You," said three Saints, giving the name of their hotel. Several players, however, led by Romanoli, weren't going back with the team, but were headed immediately to a Winnipeg rock and roll bar.

Though cab fare there would just about eat up everybody's daily meal money, the players all agreed there would be puss tonight.

I was allowed on some of the players' whoring expeditions because they felt that a *Rolling Stone* reporter, replete with photographic credentials, would make the players somehow look more important to their would-be conquests. I followed along as a sidekick to the country and western bars that served as the players' primary hunting grounds; several times a night I'd be asked by one of them to produce my *Rolling Stone* ID and the piece of paper saying I was writing about their team for a female mark. The ground rules were simple: I would name no player whoring unless I had their permission.

That night in Winnipeg began at a rocking roadhouse as big as a roller rink that was lit up with neon beer signs. Meantime, five ballplayers were putting in an hour scouting prospects and sizing up the boyfriends of the women they were working. Roma continued to work his magic with his tried-and true lines like "I think the alphabet should be rearranged so *u* and *I* are together." Within minutes, Roma was out the door with the best-looking woman in the humongous bar, a minute ahead of her boyfriend.

After that night's search for the others, an actual gang bang seemed to be in the offing. A couple of ballplayers and women huddled and then headed out, waving me to come along. Although I had no interest in participating even if they'd invited me, I came along as an unwilling witness outside the room to verify the debauch to the rest of the team at the next day's clubhouse bull session.

I made small talk in the next room with some of the women as they rested between bouts. A gap-toothed woman of twenty-two named Judy asked me, "You here as a voyager?" (mispronouncing "voyeur"). "Or you here for sloppy seconds?"

"No," I said, "I'm a writer."

"Oh."

In *Sportin' Ladies: Confessions of the Bimbos*, sportswriter Herb Michelson's 1975 tome on sports groupies, a Californian named Marianne (not her real name) explained that she would cross continents to sleep with a baseball player simply because they were the most dynamic bedmates of all professional athletes. Football players, she continued, were often at a loss with what to do with their massive bodies. True, she said, the college-educated men of the gridiron were smarter than the boys of summer, who "you can get hung up just talking about baseball and that's it. In bed, though, it's different."

In any case, she continued, virtually any jock was a far better lover than your average Joe on the street. Practice, she suggested, made perfect. "They lay so many different women, you know, so many days a week and in so many different towns. And they learn techniques."

Yet Marianne had no illusions about the character of the athletes whose names she mentally notched on her bedpost. These men, she said, are "not humanly mature. They're spoiled; they're moody. They want to be pampered and fondled."

I read the book's quote to Judy, who was about to get ready to go get boinked again by an infielder whose name she couldn't remember. "Yeah, that's baseball players," she said. "I've been with a few of the Winnipeg Blue Bombers football team and I've got an eye out for someone on the Toronto Maple Leafs. They're all the same. 'Suck me. Fuck me. Don't let the door hit your ass on the way out.' Hockey players are a little nice."

"So why do you do it?" I asked.

"Cuz I like it," Judy said. "Cuz it gives me stories to give my girlfriends. Cuz maybe I'll meet one who's real nice one day who will be for real."

For the players, looks were not the only prerequisite. One of the most famous groupies of all time, known to the ages as "Chicago Shirley," plied her trade with hundreds of major leaguers in recent years despite the fact that she was over forty, fat, and had a six-foot-six-inch-tall policeman for a husband. Her goal was to fuck every player in the major leagues, men she kept track of in a little black book. Chicago Shirley had a heart, though—if a player got dropped to the minors, she would follow his minor league team whenever it came near Chicago.

"I'm no 'Baseball Shirley,'" Judy said as she headed back in for more action. "I'm no slut."

That evening's shenanigans apparently lit a fire under the entire team, which ended its four-game losing streak the next night, July 10, by beating Winnipeg 12–5, highlighted by sixteen hits and five home runs, including a four-for-four performance by Kevin Garner, who had not taken part in the previous evening's festivities.

Still, it had been a mighty fall. On June 30, the Saints had held a five-game lead over second-place Madison. Now, the lead was down to half a game, with only two series left in the first half of the year. If the Saints could win the first half, they could cruise through the second half of the season—their spot in the league playoffs would be assured.

"A season divided in halves is good for the fans and for the teams that struggle early on," said Marty Scott. "So if you win the first half and are automatically in the playoffs at the end of the season, you can really have fun."

But not yet. On July 12, Fargo, the leaders of the Western Division, came to Midway Stadium and beat the Saints 7–5 after St. Paul started the game leading 5–0. "Pretty ugly," said Scott. "There were times this year when I thought we were playing at AAA level. Now we're down at Rookie League level."

The loss sucked; what seemed less worrisome was that veteran Chuck Jackson, Darryl Strawberry's replacement, had apparently sprained his ankle running out a ground ball and probably would be out for a few games.

The Saints fought back to win 5–2 the next night, but then hell came to visit Midway Stadium. Fargo beat St. Paul 11–9 on July 14 in the last game of the series, despite outhitting the RedHawks fourteen to seven. The fourth inning was the main hideosity; trailing 3–1, Saints pitchers gave up seven runs on three hits and six walks. Five of the walks were in succession, and twenty-two pitches in a row were balls, with two wild pitches thrown in. It was so bad that I'm sure the fans were thinking, Can it get any worse than this? The half-inning lasted forty-five minutes, and after the game, manager Scott looked like he'd been weaned on a pickle.

Now, with one three game series left against Madison at Midway, the Saints were in the kind of free fall through the standings that seemed unstoppable without an act of God. The Saints had lost eleven out of fifteen, and Chuck Jackson, their new leader, was hobbling around the bases like Fred Sanford. Jackson was hurt—hurt bad—but already in his thirties, denial and some bandages were the only things he used to mend himself enough to get put back in the lineup for the big series that would determine who was first-half champion of the Northern League.

And so the Madison Black Wolf, now trailing by a game, came into Midway Stadium for the last series of the half-season and a chance at the championship. The Black Wolf destroyed St. Paul 8–0 in the first game on July 15, tying the standings with two games left. Madison's Monica Toppen had accompanied the team to St. Paul. But strolling nervously through the stands, she was unable to even nod toward me.

Our palship, which she still called a baseball "romance," if it became known, would make her look terrible around the league, where any woman who worked for any team was still rumored to be there for unsavory reasons, usually sexual. She wanted to be remembered as the first woman to buy her own minor league team. Taking my advice, she also eventually wanted to finish law school. She did not want to be gossiped about as the "chick" or "babe" or carnival "fucklet" who rumor had it might be fucking the *Rolling Stone* reporter.

Though there was nothing prurient about the two of us, she walked past me a dozen times in the ballpark that night, her nose buried in her scorebook, her hands shaking with the nerves that her underdog team might actually beat the Saints and make it into the league playoffs at the end of the year.

The next night, July 16, the Black Wolf beat the Saints 3–1, dropping St. Paul a game behind Madison, with falling slugger Marty Neff failing to get a hit for the second straight game. If St. Paul didn't win the last game of the first half, Madison would be half-season champs. If the Saints did, there would be a one-game playoff the next day, July 18, between the Black Wolf and the Saints to determine the first half's winner. I met Monica under the grandstand before the last game, and she acted like it was an act of espionage.

I'd been traveling with the Saints all season and was considered one of "theirs." By hanging with Monica, I was engaging in fraternizing with the enemy of the worst sort. "I'm rooting," I told her truthfully, "for the Black Wolf." I even had proof: the Black Wolf polo shirt I'd worn to Midway Stadium that day, for which I'd received an ungodly amount of shit from the home fans and the Saints' players I'd come to know during the last months.

"You mean it?" the Most Beloved Woman in the Northern League said.

"Don't tell anyone," I told her.

"It doesn't matter," Monica said, "even if we win today, Jack Morris will pitch against us tomorrow in the playoff, and we're not going to beat Jack Morris."

"Jack's an old bastard," I said, "and old bastards can be beat."

I'd already seen Morris hit on Monica that night from the field in the hours before the game. I observed her rebuffs and marveled that I'd found friendship and a tutorial on loving baseball again through a woman who would tell a future Hall of Famer to go fuck himself right before my eyes. It was a great day.

And the playoff game with Morris pitching would come to pass, as Monica predicted, with the Saints beating Madison 3–2, giving

Glenn Davis
Courtesy of Bonnie Butler

each a 22–20 record at the end of the first half of the season and a tie for first place in the Eastern Division. Fargo had won the West with an impressive 26–16 record, only one game ahead of Winnipeg.

But back in St. Paul, Marty Neff finally came out of his coma, hitting a double on the last day of the half-season to start a rally in the eighth inning and force the one-game playoff that would ensure Jack Morris his big game.

But even so, a fog of cockeyed karma had swept across Midway Stadium. Then came fear from the players for their jobs, as Marty Scott summoned for a tryout Glenn Davis, a power-hitting former All-Star with the Houston Astros who'd been playing for two seasons with the Hanshin Tigers in the Japanese major leagues. Or maybe Marty was crazy as a fox, trying to shock his players into realizing that changes would soon be made.

Davis, who'd hit 190 lifetime major league home runs, had been hurt a few years earlier outside what he now termed "an adult entertainment complex" in Baltimore, where he'd signed as a big bucks franchise player. Released by the Orioles after years of injury, he'd headed to Japan. Davis had held on to his major league dough, but he was homesick for a chance to make it back to the Show, which was why he was taking batting practice cuts, unannounced to anybody, in the Midway Stadium infield the afternoon of the day before the Saints were to play their championship game.

Scott "Country" Stewart thought Davis looked familiar as the former All-Star dressed in the Saints' locker room, but couldn't place him until he saw him on the locker room television that beamed action on the field. "Hey!" Country said. "That's Glenn Davis on TV out there!"

The arrival of Davis, a veteran, would mean that under league rules another veteran would have to go if he were to be signed. Maybe the locker room rumors that Marty Scott was planning wholesale changes in the team were true. Or maybe he was just getting ready for the departure of Jack Morris.

Morris, who had been actively dickering with the New York Yankees for a major league contract of his own for the last week, had promised he would pitch that final playoff game for the Saints against the Black Wolf, even if he got the inevitable call-up to the majors. He'd proved the motherfuckers wrong, he said, it was just a fluke that during his last two years in the major leagues, 1993–1994, his earned run average was 5.93.

When he'd walked out of the Cincinnati Reds' training camp in 1994, claiming to be a mentally drained old-timer who'd lost his desire to pitch, he was a different man, he said. He'd arrived in the Saints' camp this spring able to throw only three minutes of batting practice before his elbow began throbbing. But now, two months later, he'd built up his strength to the point that he led the Northern League in every pitching category with a 5–1 record and a 2.17 earned run average.

In any case, Morris said, acting his usual cocky self before the big game, this was his last game with the Saints. The Yankees, he said, had offered him a deal. There was one sticking point; the Yankees wanted Morris to take three starts in Columbus before joining the major league team. Darryl had played a couple of games for the Yankees' top minor league team, and before they came up with the several hundred thousand dollars they were offering Morris, they wanted to see a little warm-up, à la Strawberry.

But Jack would not have it, and it had nothing to do with the money. Proud and determined as a kamikaze, he would only agree to pitch one game for Columbus, and *then* join the Yankees. His agent was now fighting with the Yankees for a compromise, but Jack didn't even want to bend. In any case, Morris made broad hints that after this game he would never pitch for the Saints again, even if the Yankee deal fell through.

Strutting around the dugout and locker room, Jack Morris looked like a pitcher with the exact kind of arrogance one would want pitching a playoff game like this one. "We shouldn't be in this position right now. We shouldn't have lost eleven of sixteen to let the Black Wolf catch us," Morris said. "But that happened. And certainly I want to pitch that final game. But every pitcher on our staff should want to pitch that game."

But this was the Saints, after all. A few pitchers privately would say they, in fact, wanted to be nowhere near the ball that day. Jack Morris, however, would pay attention to the ball, pitch until his lungs heaved, then take off his uniform and shortly be a New York Yankee. Maybe.

"Whether I get that big cherry at the end," Morris said to me, "remains to be seen. Hey"— he pointed to Monica Toppen in the stadium—"can you get me her phone number?"

Morris would pitch another ten innings of playoff game that was just as gutty and gritty a performance as his World Series triumph over the Braves in 1991. The game, and the first-half division crown, were ultimately won 7–6 by the Saints, who prevailed in twelve innings after infielder Carlton Fleming bounced a single over a drawn-in Black Wolf infield. Morris had not pitched prettily or artfully, giving up eleven hits in ten innings, striking out nine and walking three. But his gutty performance had kept the Saints from choking the title away.

Among those watching his performance at the stadium were Gene Michael of the New York Yankees and several other scouts. That night, in fact, one of the Twin City papers would announce that Morris had signed with the Yankees.

But Michael was bothered by how Morris labored slightly that night, and the Yankees still wanted him to pitch three games at Columbus. No, Jack insisted. One game for Columbus, then up to the Yankees. Or, Jack said, it's good-bye baseball.

No, said the New York Yankees, and then Jack Morris was suddenly gone forever from the Saints and baseball. He cleaned out his locker in approximately two minutes, said good-bye to nobody,

Steve and Lisa
Courtesy of Bonnie Butler

including manager Marty Scott, and gunned out of the parking lot on his motorcycle. He would not to be seen again by anybody anywhere for the rest of the season.

He had saved his money, still had that farm in Montana, and George Steinbrenner could go screw himself. Jack didn't even say farewell to Kristina Schatz, the FX camerawoman and Minnesota filmmaker who'd befriended Morris and then followed him all season with a minicam.

The next morning the tape above his locker that read JACK MORRIS would be ripped off and placed on the GON' FISHIN' wall. No matter what life he rode off to, he was dead in St. Paul.

Out on the field, meantime, the Saints were making the usual we win mayhem of exploding champagne and bear hugs and butt pats. Steve Solomon, using a portable phone, called his girlfriend, Lisa, in Los Angeles from the field to let her know they'd won. But still there was a sense of impending doom among the team. Beyond the mysterious arrival of Glenn Davis from the Japanese leagues, the chemistry of the Saints had changed, and it was obvious that this wasn't all Marty Scott wanted to change for the second half of the season.

Beyond the shock of Jack's sudden departure and the elation of the Saints winning, Scott that night had had to make a painful confession to two other players. That morning, before the game, he had made a deal with the Sioux City Explorers for Marty Neff, who Scott could no longer stand. Sioux City, run by the easygoing Singin' Ed Nottle, would also be getting Kevin Garner.

The uncomfortable dilemma Marty Scott faced was that Garner and Neff had hit the two balls that had begun the rally that had led to the Saints' final rally. They had won the half-pennant for the Saints, and moments later, as the cheap champagne exploded on the field, Marty called the two into his office and told them they had been traded to Sioux City, effective immediately. It was bad timing, Marty Scott said, but thank you very much for your contributions to the Saints.

Marty Neff's girlfriend, Randi, heartbroken by the trade of her man, was crying as hard as Monica had been under the grandstand after her team lost the first-half playoff game. "I am *never* going out with a ballplayer again," Randi sputtered in the parking lot of Gabe's, where Marty was inside drinking beer. "I can't take it any longer. I can't take not knowing where they're going to be traded the next day."

That night she would help Marty Neff pack for the trip to Sioux City. There would be hell to pay for the Saints with the Marty Neff Fan Club in the coming days. But back in Gabe's tonight, after the Saints' greatest victory of the year, the mood was, at best, that of a good wake. None of the players was sad that Marty Neff with his showboating ways was gone; what had destroyed the spirit of the party was the fact that Kevin Garner, universally admired (even by me, his half-season-long feuding partner), would not be with the team for the rest of the year.

"Now do you believe me when I say that the name of my autobiography is going to be *In Pursuit of a Nightmare*?" he said as he downed a beer inside Gabe's. "This game will break your heart. That's all it's here for: to break your heart."

I knew what he meant, but in a different context.

Marty Neff, meantime, was ready to carve up something or somebody. Hadn't he hit .330 for the Saints, with eight home runs,

eighteen doubles, and forty-one RBIs? Wasn't Marty Scott fucked—
especially since news had leaked to Neff *during* the playoff game
against Madison that he'd already been traded? Word of the swap
had originally come from somewhere outside the Saints, but was
common knowledge on playoff day to the BlackWolf, their players,
and the league office.

Then, during the last game when Marty was hitting like the prospect he once was, going two for six with a homer and four runs
batted in, Madison first baseman Darin Everson asked Neff, "Why
are you doing this to us when you are being traded after the game?"

Neff had kept it together for those final innings, even scoring the
winning run in the twelfth inning after reaching on a three-base
error. But once more, he felt, he'd been screwed by baseball.

Marty Scott was sorry that it had come down to this, mortified
that news of the trade had leaked during the game, and sorry that
he'd have to say good-bye to Garner. "I wanted to trade Neff, but
the only deal we could get was if we threw you in," he said that night.

Garner, building into a slow rage with each beer that evening
inside Gabe's, announced he was retiring from baseball, which had
no need for thirty-one-year-old men with permanently injured shoulders who could only play designated hitter. "No, I will not go to
Sioux City," Garner told his former teammates around the bar. "I
am finished. My nightmare is over."

But Garner wasn't. He could still lead The Life of sleeping until
noon in Sioux City. He still had a good shot at leading the league
in home runs. It might be nice being out of the Twin Cities, where
major league players (who he'd once been a better prospect than)
always called him up when they were playing the Minnesota Twins.
They'd pay for dinner with the million-dollar salaries he was once
supposed to get, while Garner sat there grinning, the tragedy of his
life written in the several-hundred-dollars-a-week paychecks that he
played for with the St. Paul Saints.

"Baseball, shit," said Garner, unable to give up the uniform for
good. "It gets in your blood like a snakebite, and unless you get
someone to suck out the venom, you're dead." Within twenty-four
hours, he was in Sioux City, ready to play.

In St. Paul, meantime, the Marty Neff Fan Club was in open
rebellion against the Saints for trading their hero. Members defaced
their MARTY NEFF FAN CLUB T-shirts, drawing a Sioux City logo where
the Saints' standard used to be. Signs damning Mike Veeck were
lifted in the right field bleachers, and field trips were planned to see

Marty play in Sioux City. "We'd like at least one of our members at every one of his games," said Wendy Herbert, the president of the organization.

Even with the first half of the season over, thoughts in the Midway Stadium stands constantly returned to Darryl Strawberry: his daily statistics with the New York Yankees were reported each day in the *Saint Paul Pioneer Press*. Across the river, even the Minneapolis *Star Tribune* was beginning to take fond note of the rebirths happening on the field and in the parking lot of the St. Paul Saints.

All except Patrick Reusse, that is, the powerful and mean as he was morbidly obese *Star Tribune* columnist who continued his screeds against the Saints and Mike. Yet Reusse, known in the Saints' press box as "that fat fuck," wouldn't stop the nagging and know-it-all whining he'd begun when the Saints signed Darryl Strawberry.

Now Reusse checked Strawberry out during an Orioles–Yankees series. Even to Reusse, Strawberry continued to wax nostalgic: "[St. Paul] reminded me how much love for the game you can have. The opportunity there brought me back . . . made me free inside, to let my talent come out."

Still, Reusse wouldn't let go, asking Strawberry and dissing the Northern League as he inquired whether "overmatching a low-budget independent league for five hundred bucks a week would have gotten frustrating had he stayed much longer."

"I don't think so," Strawberry said to Reusse. "It was a humbling experience, riding the buses, and the humility was one of the rewards for me. . . . The manager, Marty Scott, became like a father to me."

Strawberry was back, showing flashes of his old brilliance with the Yankees that returned his status as a valued power hitter. In Baltimore on July 13, he hit two high and long home runs, gamboling around the bases like the Darryl of the eighties and the Mets. The Orioles, managed by his old nemesis Davey Johnson, had been one of the teams that had decided that Straw's bat speed was too slow to merit another look. Now, reported John Harper and Bob Klapish, the two just stared at each other on the field.

On August 6 at Yankee Stadium, Strawberry blew out three long-distance, parabolic home runs against the White Sox that brought the jaded Yankee fans back to their feet once again. New York was in the pennant race, and Darryl Strawberry was going to help.

In St. Paul, meantime, every at-bat of Strawberry's in the Show continued to be reported as if he were a beloved native son. "Darryl Strawberry bats for all of us who've screwed up, screwed up, screwed up, but still made it off the canvas and made it on their last chance," said Mike, repeating one of his most heartfelt litanies. "He's hitting for me, and for St. Paul, and for the nostalgia of how a baseball hero hitting a home run—albeit a hero with scar tissue—is the most beautiful thing in the world."

In Baltimore, Reusse rumbled off to type up his lazy man's report. Back in St. Paul, meantime, a new Saints' team was forming. Now that he'd won the first half, Marty could experiment for the next forty-one games for the right combination of players to bring him the season championship.

Marty thought the second half would be fun. A religious Southern Baptist who could be pushed in the dugout to talking with the vocabulary of a hard-core rapper, Marty would, in fact, spend the next part of the season in hell.

10

A Jew in Fargo

Well, I'm a skinny Jew,
one of the few,
from Minnesota.
They had a quota.
—Richard Belzer, "The Ballad of Bob Dylan"

The previous season, FX, the new cable station started by Rupert Murdoch's Fox Network, had offered the Saints thousands of dollars to let them film a serialized documentary on the wackiest baseball team in the world. The show about the Saints would be the station's only original programming; the rest of FX's schedule was taken up with reruns of dreck like "Wonder Woman."

Rupert Murdoch was not worried, however. FX, it was generally known, was in a holding pattern until the vulgar Australian could purchase the Los Angeles Dodgers from the selling O'Malleys. Then, word went, he would turn FX into a superstation that would broadcast Dodger games across the country. Look what WTBS had done for Ted Turner and his Atlanta Braves: "America's Team."

In the meantime, while Murdoch waited to be approved by the other major league owners, FX would keep the company's toehold on the cable dial. Until then, it was reruns of "Miami Vice"—and, if Mike Veeck agreed, a cinema verité television show called "Baseball Minnesota" about the running of his baseball team.

By the following season, FX was, in fact, already bidding on and televising major league games. But first would come this Saints show, which, its makers promised, would be no ordinary dopey one-hour television show or a three-hour Frederick Wiseman-like documentary of an American phenomenon.

Rather, FX proposed that Mike Veeck allow their production team's cameramen to film the Saints doing whatever baseball teams do, for twenty-four half-hour episodes, the same cumulative time it took Ken Burns to tell the entire history of baseball in his recent documentary. From the season's first pitch to its last out, FX would be there. The Saints' dugout would be wired for sound, manager Marty Scott would frequently wear a microphone on and off the field, and many of the players would sometimes be fitted with a wireless mike.

Mike would later say the only reason he assented to the proposal wasn't the money from Rupert Murdoch being thrown at him. Rather, he was intrigued that such an episodic documentary had never been tried before. Mike always liked the danger of the new, so he mulled the proposal. If he said yes to the documentary, it would be a go.

Plus, such a series might show the magic of a well-run minor league team. The Saints would make a little money, and the piece of the world that received the FX cable channel would discover, the Saints' office staff thought, what a promotional genius Mike truly was. Mike himself denied that he wanted proof on film that he had reformed, but he didn't mind the idea of showcasing some of his more inspired and offbeat ideas that he thought could help the major leagues save themselves from themselves.

His decision made Bill Murray furious, but Mike agreed to the deal with the network proviso that the FX crew was responsible for getting the notoriously uncommunicative Murray to talk. If Murray told the film crew to fuck off, so be it; they would have to back away. As part of the deal Mike worked out, the network was also not to use Bill Murray's picture or name in any ads or credits for the show.

Furthermore, the contract read, there would be no shots of Saints personnel actually counting the day's cash in Mike's office during each home game. No one, Mike knew from the lessons of his own father, likes to think of the carnival as a business.

And so, as in Albert Brooks's film *Real Life,* an army of fifteen ill-paid cameramen and -women were hired from the Minneapolis College of Art and Design and other local Twin City funky filmmaking terrains. Their job was to follow the team everywhere—literally.

Many were attractive women; all were told to get close to the players and not to miss a thing.

FX rented a huge recreational vehicle to follow the Saints on the road. Inside, the local performance artists and musicians outfitted with minicams called the RV "the mother ship" and laughed at the idiotically smug New York producers who'd flown in to run the show.

All of the Twin Citians transformed into cameramen were great. Most beloved by the players was Catherine Whyte, an art student and rock & roller who was as pale as Casper the Friendly Ghost. On the road, Catherine, twenty-one and exotically beautiful, sang her angry Courtney Love-like songs while she accompanied herself on guitar. The players just scratched their heads and tried to figure out how to bed this exotic creature who knew more about the lineup of the Smashing Pumpkins than she did of the St. Paul Saints.

Home and away, every day of the season, she wore a tight white T-shirt tucked into funky black pants, a pair of shitkicker motorcycle boots, and a facial expression that was both friendly to the ballplayers yet said *Don't Fuck With Me*. Meantime, the players plotted on how to make a move on the woman they'd secretly nicknamed "Lilith," after the character on "Cheers" with the translucent skin.

Their efforts were for naught, however, because Catherine already knew who, if anybody, she would fuck on the team and when. It would be Jason McNally, the second-string catcher who was built somewhat like the Colossus of Rhodes.

But Catherine sensed he was a box of rocks. C'mon, he was a baseball player, for God's sake! Plus, he was a baseball player with a girlfriend in Florida. In any case, Catherine didn't want to have a deep season-long salon of conversation with McNally. Instead, she wanted to shtup him once, then say good-bye. So she would wait, she decided, until the last night after the last game of the Saints' season.

"She a lezzy? She looks too pretty to be a lezzy," asked and opined twenty-year-old Scott Stewart when he saw Catherine for the first time. In the piney woods of the South, Country had never seen a woman wear motorcycle boots day after day or sing songs on her guitar about women not taking shit from pig-dog men anymore.

Put in charge of filming the always irascible and horny Jack Morris was Kristina Schatz, another beautiful local who had line-produced for several major films. She was doing this job for chump change until her boyfriend returned from California, where he had a big gig on a feature production.

For a woman who made it known from the start that she wouldn't be having sex with Jack Morris, Kristina got surprisingly close to the reporters' nightmare. Like a horse whisperer, she was able to approach him out in the field when he was stretching and get him to talk about what it's like to be old, your talent eroded by time, and to think you didn't do things in your life the way you wanted. He opened up to her not for her journalistic empathy, the players gossiped, but simply because he couldn't believe that this camerawoman wouldn't give it up to him, the famous Jack Morris.

In any case, sex seemed to be the point of the entire FX documentary. Specifically, the producers wanted to catch the players having it or going to it. Meantime, the players wanted to do it with the FX crew. And the network brass, whenever they flew in from the coasts for one of their project look-sees, did it with everyone: barmaids, ballplayers, and anyone who looked Scandinavian Minnesotan. The season dripped with sex, none of which made it to the television show, which proved as hilariously squeaky clean and bowdlerized as the 1948 biopic howler *The Babe Ruth Story*.

Wedding rings on both sides came off, as players did it to these strange business babes from the coast, while the bored collegiate camerapeople merely picked someone interesting on the scene or a good-looking ballplayer and fucked them. Reality, it seemed, had won out over Columbia Journalism School morality around the time Eisenhower was president.

But was I any different? Hadn't I had a romance with the Most Beloved Woman of the Northern League, an important source? Yes, I thought to myself as I watched a married man from New York wooing a barmaid at Gabe's, but I was going to cop to it. Monica had given me permission to write about us, so I figured I was still kosher.

Only two outsiders toted minicams for the New York producers. First there was Walter, an arrogant twenty-one-year-old Ivy Leaguer with no social skills who hailed from Newport, Rhode Island. He was hired to be "the Badass Minicam Man," the person responsible for walking into the middle of the gnarliest, most personal, and embarrassing scenes of the Saints with the film rolling.

It took courage, gentry hubris, and a willingness to be despised to do what he was supposed to do. In fact, he was despised, by both the players and the local crew, which is why he got so few of the killer shots that would have made the show more than a one-dimensional time waster for Rupert Murdoch's greater plans.

And then there was my "Evil Twin."

I didn't know he was my Evil Twin then, of course. For months, I thought he was my pal and lantzman who would one day accept my multiple invitations to go out for a friendly beer or come over the river for dinner at my place in Minneapolis so we could tell each other war stories and exchange clubhouse gossip. I felt neither a grudge nor a glimmer of the truth then.

When the New York producers weren't screwing folks from St. Paul, they treated them as yokels. All, that is, except Anthony Horn, the soft-spoken creator of the show, who went out of his way to show respect. But the rest? With their Columbus Avenue designer baseball hats, the producers told everyone how their "concept" had been "shopped," how then Fox "passed" and then "green-lighted" the show for its FX channel. This would be art, they promised, the first episodic documentary in the history of the world, more real, they promised than even PBS's acclaimed 1970s documentary on the Loud clan, "An American Family," which showed above everything else a camera's ability to break up a marriage.

These New Yorkers, I knew from working among them, were laughable in the utter contempt they held for their subjects, be they the locals or players around them. They didn't want the real stories of the young men who couldn't give up a dream; they wanted Bill Murray yelling at people. They wanted to befriend Darryl Strawberry, so if he did light up the crack pipe, they'd be there to film it (like myself, I had to admit).

In return, some of the yokels saw the producers as central casting New York Showbiz Jews, even when they weren't. It is not a favored archetype in the Midwest, especially among Midwest Jews. We Yids in the provinces are tougher, we know, than New York Jews. We ice-fish and throw punches if ethnically insulted, and we know the mores of the people around us, some of whom still believe we Jews have a yellow stripe on our backs. It was only 1945 when the country's most eminent sociologist, Carey McWilliams, wrote in *The Nation* that "Minneapolis is the capital of anti-Semitism in the United States."

And so, I told the Saints' front office that I was "the Jew who paid retail," a tag that stuck. I liked it and was happy to fork over what the fans paid for Saints memorabilia. There were so few Jews out here, I learned long ago, that we have to fight cultural stereotypes wherever we can, be it with our fists or by refusing wholesale.

Unfortunately, the only actual New York Showbiz Jew who was with the team the whole season looked and talked vaguely like me.

As a result, many people, especially the players, confused the two of us. They had never seen more than a handful of Jews before, so they sometimes thought we were each other. It was fun.

He was also New York Showbiz Paranoid, terribly afraid that I would scoop him via our mutual friend, Darryl Strawberry, with my Newports—and get cheaply what his army of camerapeople couldn't get with their network equipment and big-time TV Land attitude. I began jestfully calling him to his face my "Evil Twin" and my "doppelganger." My twin, sure I was out to get him, did things like make me rewind my tape recorder in Fargo to make sure I wasn't secretly recording him. He told his crew to stay away from me (they didn't) and dissed me to the players (who dissed him back to me).

And because his crews often stole my scenes and interviews, I would tease him about faking filmed scenarios and paying the Saints for access, a practice no real news organization would countenance. Enjoying how the goyim, Marty Scott especially, got off on the sight of the two Jews fighting, I'd have mock shouting matches in the locker room with my Evil Twin. Or at least *I* thought the tussles were all in good fun. Oops.

My Evil Twin, who I actually really liked and empathized with for the impossibility of his task, stewed and refused my invitations to go privately to Gabe's or to my home in Minneapolis and make peace. For him, we were locked in a turf battle, and he wasn't going to fuck around with anybody interfering in his access to the shots he wanted.

Sorry.

So he kept pecking at me in that annoying New York Showbiz Paranoid way, and finally I decided to torture him some more. I made subtle comments to him on how it looked like this wasn't a real documentary they were shooting because they were setting ball-players up: buying them drinks and then shooting them hitting on women.

To piss him off even more, I'd remind him that the players let me hang around because I didn't have a camera, had promised to keep my mouth shut to their girlfriends back home, and never asked for a piece of their action. Most important, my affiliation with *Rolling Stone,* some players felt, helped them get laid. I was loyal *and* useful; my Evil Twin was neither.

FX, which wanted players whoring at night, did everything they could to catch the fleeing Saints after the game with their cameras, which is the very reason they missed most of the action. Meantime, my Evil Twin explained again to me one night in the stands in Winnipeg about how "real" this program was.

They knew, he said, what was fake. One of them had worked on "The Real World," the MTV original series in which several demographically correct strangers were made to live in a house together, the results captured by camera crews "24/7," the industry buzzwords for the number of hours in a day and days in a week a subject is shot in order not to miss anything. Scenes were scripted or made up, he told me, and the first "Real World" was as bogus as the Marty Neff Fan Club.

"But the Marty Neff Fan Club is real," I replied. "Those grandstand fans in Midway Stadium really do love their pot-bellied hero."

"Nah," he said, unaware, putting down Neff like he himself was a member of the Saints' roster.

In any case, he went on, the show was different than "The Real World." This was groundbreaking documentarianism, the next step beyond the work of Albert Maysles and D. A. Pennebaker. Now the New York Showbiz quarry would be this baseball team and the surrounding Midwesterners who had made the St. Paul Saints the most famous team in the minor leagues. At first, the ballplayers liked the cameras, the attention, and the questions from the camera people, which provided all the spectacle they'd missed by not making the Show. But as soon as it became obvious that the FX people also wanted to catch ballplayers drinking and whoring, they became as distant and one-dimensional as a jock cliché.

Almost all of the ballplayers, after all, had girlfriends in St. Paul, and very few didn't fuck around on the road. So when it became obvious that the filmmakers weren't going to get the verité they'd come for, they stepped up their efforts to ply ballplayers with free booze in bars and film them from across the room while they weren't looking.

"They got me drunk, had me talk to girls, and told me the camera was off," said pitcher Dan Thomson. "But the camera wasn't off; it was on at the other side of the room. I looked like the biggest dick in the world."

The New Yorkers were comical in their attempts to inject art into the most banal of situations. At one point on a long team bus ride, an FX producer played a tape of a performance artist he'd directed in downtown New York on the vehicle's videocassette player.

The players hooted the artsy crap off the monitors in minutes. On the bus, they much preferred a home movie made at a bachelor party by one of the players' buddies. As real prostitutes pleasured in real unusual ways the real people at the party, the team sat entranced.

And then there was another New York producer's patronizing fascination with Jill Muellner, the head barkeep at Gabe's, who knew every secret of every ballplayer and girlfriend in the club. Jill was about to become an exploited cable star.

During her time as an alcoholic, she explained to the camera, she'd fallen down so many times that her nose had been broken more times than your average hockey player's. Now she was going in to have her nose redone. So in a television show ostensibly about baseball, but which was really about producing proletarian art from the prairie, the filmmakers included Jill's new nose in several episodes. And so, over several episodes, baseball fans watched her choose it; they sat at the edge of their seats as a doctor inserted a probe deep into her current proboscis and performed surgery; they cheered when she came out looking like Robert De Niro after 15 rounds in *Raging Bull.*

As the swelling went down and Jill stayed away from Gabe's until her beauty returned, the camera followed her to her trailer home. She lived there with several relatives, who were presented on-camera as if they were extras in *Deliverance.* It was a shameful, mean, and exploitative scene, made only more ridiculous by the fact that this producer, over the weeks, had truly come to believe he was a Saint.

"I feel like I am a member of the team," he told me. "I *am* a member of the team." At the end of each Saints win, the producer would run out onto the field, alone with all the players, and slap the butts of all the Saints, just as if he was, well, a member of the team.

"There he is, my Evil Twin who thinks the ballplayers think of him as a ballplayer," I'd say to whoever I was sitting with up in the stands at the end of the game. Almost always, I tried to stay out of the dugout and off the field in foul territory during the game, simply because this was the ballplayers' office. They'd like me more and give up their stories more easily if they weren't aware of my presence while they still had on their game faces.

The ballplayers laughed at the faux-Walter Mitty, but the New York producer didn't care about his hubris in thinking he was so close to them that he was a ballplayer. For he thought he had caught America on film, real America, Jack Kerouac's America. He had overseen the filming of the Flying Elvises exhibition that followed the game in Fargo. He had seen the casino riverboats of Iowa. He had seen it, filmed it all, and—damn it—he would make art of it.

But people knew it was baloney. Both locals and ballplayers knew he thought they were rubes, and they laughed when the cable station started showing episodes in the middle of the season.

Still, my Evil Twin and I kept at each other. Or at least he kept after me. Their documentary was in trouble, I knew, because they'd even started following me around the ballpark with their cameras, interviewing people I was talking to there, filming me taking notes. It was hideously banal footage, and I knew that with their failure to get Morris leaving, Strawberry talking real, ballplayers having sex, and Bill Murray at all, the only thing left for them to shoot was the life story of everybody with even a whisker of a connection to the team.

They had turned into Bill Murray's description of the terribly soured Bob Woodward.

The New Yorkers didn't mind, or even realize, the fact that they were ridiculing people. Tom Mischke, he of the tree house, was profiled as some Midwestern Buddha, a village idiot who somehow spoke the people's truth with his homilies over the airwaves. In fact, Mischke is one of the most acerbic, ironic, and intelligent hosts in Radio Land. And Mischke's occasional comments on the game being played below him were uniformly brilliant, even though the topics discussed on his radio show were totally unrelated to baseball.

Finally I couldn't put up with the shenanigans of my Evil Twin anymore. There was nothing left to do but challenge him to a duel, Saints style, on the field, during the game, wearing inflatable sumo suits. The battle, performed between each home game's second and third innings, was sponsored by Mother's Strawberry Schnapps and featured two adults in sumo costumes bouncing on a mat in front of the Saints' dugout. Complete with appropriate headpiece, the weighted suits lower one's center of gravity to somewhere in the knees.

Each game someone in the stands, who is dubbed "Minneapolis" and consequently booed, faces off with another fan, who is announced as "St. Paul" and cheered. The two then try to batter each other to the mat with their uncontrollable suits. Once one of the combatants fell, he would be unable to get up in his bulky suit, and the winner would take this golden opportunity to add insult to insult (if losing an inflatable sumo match weren't bad enough) by pouncing on the loser. Then it would be time to start the third inning.

Courtesy of Bonnie Butler

The sumo contest was a suckers' bet—if all you wanted to do was win. The secret to winning was to simply do nothing besides sidestep your opponent and let him throw all the punches. Gravity took care of him for you, since the puncher inevitably lost his balance and fell to the ground. Doing nothing on the mat was a cowardly strategy, but I sensed that my Evil Twin might use it.

Manager Marty Scott, who had watched the "battle" between me and my doppelganger all summer long, arranged for us to fight after the second inning of a game against Fargo-Moorhead. At the end of the first inning, I went down to the appointed runway under the grandstand and found that my Evil Twin had already laid claim to the red "St. Paul" sumo suit and was now being zippered in.

I hurried into the "Minneapolis" suit, which was never washed and was rank with years of sweat (all sumo participants were warned to bring two sets of clothes). Zippered in, a human dirigible, I was led out to the mat at the end of the second inning. My Evil Twin took his place, our names were announced, and I went after this schmuck from New York who was making fools of the natives with Rupert Murdoch's dough and his squadron of underpaid camera people.

I punched him and punched him and punched him and punched him again, and the doppelganger grimaced, then just stood aside, throwing nothing, protected by his suit. He watched gravity take me down a little more with each of my roundhouses, right crosses, and left jabs, finally moving when I hit the ground and he jumped on me like a schoolyard weenie. He had technically won the battle of the Jews, I told the goyim under the grandstand who work for the Saints, but I had *fought*. I'd done something on the mat while all he did was back off and let nature fell me.

"Whatever," Mike Veeck said from a few feet away.

"That was pathetic," Bill Murray, who was at the game, told me. "I'm not talking to you for fifteen minutes."

"No," I said, "it's like Billy Conn winning on points in the fourteenth round against Joe Louis and refusing to play safe and win the championship. He lost by taking chances, but he was game. Doesn't that count?"

"Okay," said Murray, who only penalized me for ten minutes, long enough for me to change clothes.

My Evil Twin, convinced I was furious by the result and by his own cowardice, hurried over with the certificate granted each sumo winner by the makers of Mother's Strawberry Schnapps. He wanted me to have it, this piece of paper saying I'd actually won the match. I took it.

"You should have taken a punch at me. It was bad for the Jews," I said. "Made us look bad in front of the cowboys."

"The secret to winning the sumo contest . . ." he began to say.

"Yeah, I know the secret," I said.

"Whatever," said Mike Veeck, who was still standing at the gate, looking onto the field. Now he was smoking a cigarette, chewing his fingernail, and listening to our argument.

"You could have thrown a punch like a man," I said to my Evil Twin. "It doesn't look good."

Solomon's father would understand.

FX showed Solomon as the nice Jewish boy, calling his girlfriend in Los Angeles after every game when all the other players were out whoring across the Midwest. Wayne, "the Badass Minicam Man," had roomed the entire season with Solomon and Chris Evans.

With Solomon, alone on the team, he captured a picture of a man who watched what he ate, taped every Saints game, and stayed up until two or three every night going over his at-bats from that day's contest. He read *The New York Times,* which marked him as a freak with the other ballplayers. *And* he got enough sleep.

Steve Solomon, almost alone among his teammates, really believed he could make it to the big leagues after the Phillies cut him from AA ball at Reading. It wasn't a pipe dream: Mike thought Solomon was the only Saint from this year's contingent likely to be picked up by a major league organization. By hitting .300 all season for the Saints and playing the kind of heads-up, serious, and hustling baseball rarely seen for an entire season in the Northern League, he was, thought manager Scott, "Mr. Perfect."

If he did make it all the way to the bigs, Solomon would be more than an anomaly as a Jew in the majors. He would also be a cultural hero more beloved by his people than Saul Bellow or Jonas Salk. By showing that a Jew could outhit or -pitch Gentiles at their own game had been a rare point of honor ever since Hank Greenberg threatened Babe Ruth's single-season home run record in 1938. OI OI, OH BOY! HAIL THAT LONG-SOUGHT JEWISH STAR the *Sporting News* headline ran when Greenberg first came up, accompanied by a cartoon of a large-beaked man who looked like Fagin saying, "Oy yoy-yoy."

Even Nobel prizewinner Bellow understood. He wrote in *Humboldt's Gift* that the Jewish

> Humboldt could hit like a sonofabitch on the sandlot. With his shoulders, just imagine how much beef there went into his swing. If I had my way, he would have ended up in the majors. But he started hanging around Forty-Second Street library . . . first thing I knew he was printing highbrow poems in the magazines.

The Jews, like every other group of newly arrived immigrants, had clung to their baseball heroes as proof not only that they were Americans—but that they weren't necessarily the bookish weaklings of early century popular lore. It was a prejudice, at least in baseball, that lasted far longer.

It is extra tough being a Jewish player in the Northern League. Take the bizarre case of Barry Goldman, a Sioux City and Winnipeg pitcher for a couple of seasons. One spring training he arrived demanding to be called Barry Nelson. Saints' co-owner Marv Goldklang, enraged by Nelson's alleged cave-in to baseball's rednecks, ordered the Midway Stadium PA announcer to always introduce the chicken to the St. Paul crowd as Barry Goldman. Up Fargo-way, meantime,

North Dakota hadn't had one rabbi in residence for ten years, and a woman activist from Minot has a suit before the U.S. Court of Appeals in which male circumcision would be outlawed. If Jody McLaughlin had her way, there would never again be a *bris* in North Dakota.

My maternal grandfather had moved to the Midwest and North Dakota to farm early in the century, but had split when he blew his small grubstake on crappy land purchased from a wily North Dakotan. The Ku Klux Klan held marches down Main Street in Grand Forks, North Dakota, during the Depression, and generations later, many people in the smaller towns of the Midwest could count on one hand how many Jews they'd ever met and were astounded when I fessed up.

Even in Fargo, where I met some of the nicest people in the league, an old man at the ballpark looked me up and down and said, "Yer a Jewish fella, ain't cha? Well, I'll be, yer from New York, right? What's a Jewish feller doin' in Fargo?"

"I live in Minneapolis," I said.

"Well, I'll be damned," said the old man.

But if Solomon could make the majors, he would be an icon. As such, he might stir up a paradox for Jews that has tortured everyone of my religion from Maimonides to Morey Amsterdam: What am I first, a Jew or a citizen of the place in which I live? It's a paradox that first tortured me when, as a six-year-old growing up in Minneapolis, I unaccountably found myself rooting for Sandy Koufax and the Los Angeles Dodgers to beat (or at least not humiliate himself) my then-beloved Minnesota Twins when he pitched against them in Game 7 of the 1965 World Series. (Not only was Koufax a Jew, he bore a startling resemblance to my Uncle Eddie.)

Until that game, which my father and I attended, I had thought Koufax to be the epitome of weeniedom. After all, hadn't he sat out the Series opener in order to observe Yom Kippur, much to the delight of Twins fans, myself included. The price Koufax paid for being such a nice Jewish boy was that he had to pitch that final game of the Series on only two days' rest instead of his usual three or four. But Koufax threw a shutout, the Twins lost the Series, and I learned the meaning of "mixed feelings." As we filed out of old Metropolitan Stadium, my father muttered, "Well, you got to admit that the Yid's got *batzim* [balls]."

Bill Veeck understood the appeal of the Jewish baseball player: in the early 1970s, when he owned the Chicago White Sox, he tried to sign ex-Yankee slugger Ron Blomberg so he could claim to be the first team ever with three Jews (Ken Holtzman and Steve Stone were the others). Veeck gave up his quest when he learned that years before, the Dodgers had briefly gotten to three with Koufax and those nice Sherry boys: Larry and Norm.

Even Sandy Koufax, however, had not survived the slings and arrows. He'd retired in 1966 at only thirty-one with a still-unhittable fastball, claiming that inflaming his chronic arm trouble wasn't worth winning another several Cy Young awards. In a 1998 article in *Elysian Fields*, a scholarly baseball journal, Peter C. Bjarkman wrote:

> The handsome and refined [Koufax] at first seemed to wipe away a common notion about Jewish athletes as essentially inferior, second-rate, and feeble; then his sudden retirement at the pinnacle of glory seemed to confirm a popular conception and also certify a time-worn myth.

Eventually, I learned that *shtetl* chauvinism is normal when you, the Coen brothers, and Bob Dylan were apparently the only Jews who were ever born in Minnesota. My love of religion, however, extended only as far as a fetish for Jewish baseball players. Today one of the few things I remember from Hebrew school was the day Rabbi Younger brought Mike Epstein, the Washington Senators' first baseman, to class. I can still recall how Epstein blanched when the rabbi opened with "So, Mike—may I call you Mordecai? I understand that your nickname in the big leagues is 'Super Jew.'"

To learn what exactly it would mean if Steve Solomon were to be picked up by a major league organization, as Mike Veeck predicted, and then make the bigs, I contacted the Jewish Sports Information Center, an eleven-year-old organization of several hundred people that is devoted to keeping track of those rare Jews who have managed to make it in the major leagues. When I joined, the center sent me a list of all known Sandy Koufax and Hank Greenberg memorabilia and a complete run of the JSIC newsletter for my $5 membership fee.

The highlight, however, was a four-page printout filled with the career stats of the around 150 Jewish ballplayers, from Cal Abrams to Larry Yellen, ever to make it up to the Show (that's 141 out of an all-time total of over 13,000 major leaguers, Jews and Gentiles alike—or 1.2 percent, compared with the Jewish 3 percent of the general population).

The first thing I noticed was that modern sportswriters have lost the knack of nicknaming: contemporary handles like "Straw" or "Doc" seem flat and uninspired compared with old-timers like Barney "the Yiddish Curver" Pelty and Moses "the Rabbi of Swat" Solomon.

Moses Solomon had played in four games for the New York Giants in 1930. The Saints' Steve Solomon wanted to play for anybody who'd give him the chance. "With all the publicity the Saints get," he said, "I thought maybe I'd get noticed. You know what they say: 'As long as you've got the uniform on, you don't know what might happen.' Right place, right time, you're there."

I called the Jewish Sports Information Center and its founder, Louis Schonfeld, a Parma, Ohio, businessman, for a hint of the importance of Steve Solomon's quest. Schonfeld's own contributions to the newsletter are chatty, equally single-minded schmoozes. "I was too hasty in deleting John Lowenstein from the list," he began one article. "Notwithstanding the fact that he is from Montana, John's father is Jewish; coincidentally, John is married to a Jewish girl. Another major leaguer who is married to a Jewish girl is Ron Cey."

Each new Jewish ballplayer to reach the majors, Schonfeld said, was in very select company. But the goal is inclusionary, he says, not to separate. "The biggest problem in identification is going solely by last names," he says. "I heard about a minor leaguer named Brian Abraham, and I sent away for his baseball card. The card came, the guy was black. Not that that in itself rules him out—remember, we *know* that Elliott Maddox [who is black] converted."

Schonfeld urged me on to do a research project of my own. "You're from Minneapolis, huh?" he inquired. "Isn't that where Andy Cohen finished up his career?" I said I'd check it out.

I lost my stomach for research soon after turning to the chapter on Andy Cohen in *Jewish Baseball Stars,* a seminal text for JSIC investigators. When Andy Cohen, nicknamed "the Great Jewish Hope," arrived to play for the New York Giants in 1928, I read, a parody of "Casey at the Bat" was printed in a New York tabloid.

> And from the stand bleachers
> The cry of "Oy, oy" rose.
> And up came Andy Cohen
> Half a foot behind his nose.

Cohen was good, but not the superstar Giant manager John

McGraw hoped would profitably lure the masses of Jewish immigrants who lived in New York City to the Polo Grounds. McGraw tired of Cohen in a couple of years, and the Giants began shuffling in the undistinguished yet enticingly surnamed likes of Goody Rosen, Phil Weintraub, and Harry Rosenberg.

Cohen, meantime, wandered off to the Midwest, where he killed seven years playing out his career with the Minneapolis Millers, the archenemies of the St. Paul Saints in the American Association. "Cohen was great," my father remembered from his own youth when I called him with the fruits of my research. "The guy had *batzim*."

I then received Schonfeld's twenty-three-page list of every known baseball card ever issued of a Jewish ballplayer and checked to see if there had ever been any Jews on the Minnesota Twins.

On page 5, I read:

Ike Goldstein. 1987 Procards Issue. Visalia Oaks.

The Oaks, I knew, had been a minor league team in the Twins' organization. I called the Twins' office and asked for a report on Ike's career. Had he made it to the big leagues?

"Let's see," said the nice woman checking the records in the Twins' office. "Ike Goldstein. Yes, here he is, a catcher. He played in fifty-five games for Visalia in 1987. He batted .174."

She paused. "Ike Goldstein," she said, sounding sorry, "was released at the end of [that] season."

Steve Solomon had been released too after a season that wasn't quite as shitty as Ike's, but Steve had decided he had enough tools to maybe—just maybe—make it where his brother had failed. "This is a last chance," he said. "I need to know whether to go on with my life. I'm realistic—I don't have the shiniest armor, but it works. I'm fundamentally sound. You don't have to be a big home run hitter or base stealer in the majors. I believe I can be a role player there who can steal twenty to thirty bases and hit ten home runs."

Maybe—just maybe—he could. He hit .300 all year long for the Saints, never made a baserunning error, and fielded his outfield position flawlessly. Homers and steals came, and even Marty Scott became impressed with the man with the *Little Engine That Could* work ethic. "I call him Mr. Perfect, [and] he deserves to be in the majors for what he puts himself through," Scott said.

Eleanor Mondale Does the
St. Paul Macarena
(The Second Half of the Season)

The arbitrator of despairs,
Just death, kind umpire of men's miseries . . .
—William Shakespeare, *Henry VI*

The use of methamphetamines is on the rise in North Dakota. Offi-
cials say they got suspicious when they noticed everybody did noth-
ing much more quickly.
—Gary Shandling as Larry Sanders, "The Larry Sanders Show"

July 10, 1996

Chuck Jackson was among the most likable, productive Saints on the team—for a while. He'd been to the Show, was hitting home runs, and was genuinely funny. He played the team leader with gusto. He knew music, could sing Jackie Wilson, had the best CDs on the team, and always invited me to sit with him back in the 'hood, where white men (and especially white reporters) weren't supposed to be. I felt honored, and Jackson was my favorite player.

But then Jackson jammed his ankle at Winnipeg near the end of the first half of the season and life slowly unraveled for the man who'd always been able to feed his wife and kids back in North Carolina on the strength of his bat. He had once made major league dough and had been paid bounties to play in Mexico and Taiwan. But he wanted back up, he was sure he would make it, and then his ankle went out shortly before the Saints' half-pennant drive.

It was a horrible sight to watch Jackson hobble out there to third base on one leg. His average dropped precipitously, and he was missing ground balls he had easily scooped up only days before. Though his ankle was responding to no known cure, he refused to take himself out of the lineup.

Manager Marty Scott had liked Jackson from his days in the Rangers' organization and thought he'd done a good job in leading the Saints. Now the manager dreaded having to tell the man that if he didn't get well soon, he would have to be cut several weeks after his injury. "If you work through it, fine," Marty told Jackson during a mid-August three-game stand at Fargo. "At the same time, if I see what I see in two weeks, I can't go with it."

Jackson understood. At home against Madison a week later, soaking his foot in ice, he heard the clock ticking and laid it out. "I don't see how they can go with a guy with one foot. I was supposed to hit homers, and here I am, hitting two bills [.200]."

Weeks before in Winnipeg, he had secretly felt that he had hurt himself badly. By the time he got to Madison, Chuck's anger was joining reality. "I don't know what I did," he said, "but I can tell you I didn't [just] sprain my ankle. Something is telling me I'm not going to be here come crunch time, and that's the only reason I came here." And then came pride. "I was not hired to go out there and be an average player, or what I consider now to be a less than average player. I'm supposed to be out here controlling this thing. I just want to play like I did before I got hurt."

It was over.

Marty Scott waited another week, until Fargo and the beginning of the second half of the season, to give Jackson the news that he was being cut. Marty did it in a beautiful, spacious setting in the empty new ballpark in the middle of August. There the two would have time to talk in the hours before the game.

Sitting on folding chairs to the side of the Fargo visitors' dugout, Marty looked Jackson in the eyes. "Based on your ankle and based on your performance, I've been trying to find another veteran." Marty paused. "Okay?"

Jackson, leaning back in his chair, simply said, "Un-hunh."

Still, Marty had a carrot. He liked what Chuck had done with the younger kids on the team and wanted him to stay on as a coach. "If I find that veteran in the next few days," Marty said moments later as Chuck stared, oblivious, into the Fargo skyline, "then you will continue to be a member of this team as another one of my able-bodied assistants."

Chuck Jackson leaned back on his chair and looked straight ahead at the empty infield.

"Talk to me, Chuck," Marty said.

"Wow," Jackson finally said. And then he cracked a sickly smile. "Uh . . . do I get a pocket watch?"

Minutes later, it was Marty's turn to talk sadly about his team. "A lot of these guys think, 'Wow, Marty, you were head of the Rangers' farm organization. Now you're a manager in the Northern League, where they treat you pretty good. It may not be where you want to be, but it's a pretty good gig.' "

Jackson nodded.

"And they don't realize I'd trade places with any one of them right now," the manager said. "Because they don't realize there's nothing like playing. It's hard on me too."

Jackson nodded. Scott slapped his knee and walked away. Jackson then took several minutes to contemplate what he was going to do. "I'm going to take them up on being a coach," he finally said. "But I'll tell you what. It's going to be harder and harder to watch these guys go out and play."

Jackson, Marty realized, had agreed to step over the line, from player to management, and that was a moment Chuck had always secretly dreaded. Chuck had prepared for this day, gone to the University of Hawaii on a full baseball scholarship, and had been in the army. But in his heart of hearts, Chuck had never thought he'd have to actually stop playing ball.

Sadly, as the half-season progressed, Chuck Jackson the coach began acting out in ways that he'd never done as a player. Marty Scott would soon worry whether Jackson was suffering a mental breakdown, but the anger Jackson began showing seemed perfectly reasonable for a man whose life, in a way, had just ended.

Yet all was not gloom in the Saints' dugout that mid-August day in Fargo as they continued their swoon in the no-incentive second-half standings. After the game, a sharp young woman in her early twenties, wearing a dress but no underwear, climbed on top of the St. Paul dugout. From there she promenaded up and down, asking the Saints for autographs.

Most of the team spilled out of the dugout to look up her dress, beaver shooting the old-fashioned Mickey Mantle way. Giggling like little boys, they pushed and shoved for a better vantage point as the exhibitionist—in Fargo, no less!—gave every player who wanted a peek up her skirt, one, then another, then one more.

Doug Simunic, the RedHawks' manager with a beer gut as big as the Black Hills, was meantime explaining why Jack Michaels, his team's radio announcer, shouts, "Track it down, Marge" every time a Fargo player hits a home run. "Track it down, Marge," said the manager, "seemed so much more thoughtful than 'Lick my vagina, it's gone.'"

Simunic had no reservations about his reputation around the league as a crybaby and jerk. He was, after all, also a damn good manager who reigned as the popular king of Fargo. "In St. Paul, they'd throw pacifiers on a string over our dugout," he said. "Last year in Winnipeg, fans would dangle dead fish over the roof. It's a good thing that some people hate me, because it takes the pressure off my players."

Besides St. Paul, Simunic said, he had to "endure the worst ribbings in Sioux Falls, Thunder Bay, and Winnipeg." Maybe he likes it, I suggested, maybe he needed the abuse in some Freudian way. Simunic looked at me as if I were from Pluto and said, "I don't like getting heckled. I especially don't like people who yell, 'Hey, Simunic! You sober?' That's out of bounds."

In Fargo, one sensed that everything was just a tad different from the rest of the world—and this is coming from someone who spent each day with the Saints. When I went to lunch at a Fuddruckers hamburger joint near the Comfort Inn where the Saints were staying, a nice woman in her twenties took my order, then asked for my first name when my burger was done.

When I told her, she said, "Is that *N-e-i-l?*"

"No," I said. "My name is spelled with an *a* instead of an *i.*"

"Oh, my parents misspelled my name too," said the waitress, telling me that her name, pronounced Danielle, was spelled *D-a-n-n-y-e-l.*

"Why did they do that?" I asked her.

"I guess," she said, "they just didn't know how to spell it."

I joined a table of giggling Saints with my tray. Despite their lunchtime bonhomie, it was obvious the team was suffering from some uncomfortable personnel problems. In the next couple days, for example, it became clear that Chuck Jackson was not making a smooth transition from player to coach. Instead of taking his place up front with the manager and Twig on the Saints' bus, he still sat

in the 'hood of the bus with the black and Hispanic players, regaling
all with tales of rock & roll and his time in the Show.

He couldn't stop acting like a player. Days later, back at Midway
Stadium, I was standing on the field, spacing out before the game
in foul territory. Sneaking up behind me, Jackson took a pie tin full
of whipped cream and tossed it in my face, a gag that ranked with
the dugout hotfoot as the baseball player's favorite practical joke.

Even Bill Murray had suffered the infamous hotfoot, as well as
some toilet paper stuck to the bottom of his shoe. It was a sign that
Murray was meat, one of them. Being a good sport myself, I put
the pie back in Jackson's kisser.

I loved Jackson's pie face. I found out later that a video camera
had caught the act and that a tape of the gag had found its way
onto the nationally syndicated show "This Week in Baseball." To be
humiliated on television via one of the game's great broadcasters,
narrator Mel Allen, was one of the proudest moments of my life.
And for a moment, like my hapless Evil Twin, I too could pretend
I was meat.

Reality soon returned. Jackson, however, turned some sort of an-
guished corner soon after the arrival at Midway Stadium of Pat
Jordan, a fiftyish former minor league pitcher who'd once written a
terrific book about being a busher called *A False Spring.* For the past
two decades, however, Jordan was probably most notorious as the
magazine writer who'd hatcheted Cyndi and Steve Garvey's marriage
with a 1980 piece in *Inside Sports.* In the piece, Jordan made broad
hints that Mrs. Garvey had fallen for him and described scenes that
the couple said never happened.

The Garveys sued *Inside Sports, Newsweek,* and Pat Jordan for
libel. The icky couple apparently had a good case, and *Newsweek*
settled out of court.

Now, fifteen years later, Jordan waltzed into Midway Stadium
wearing his omnipresent and garish Hawaiian shirt and smoking a
cigar that never seemed to leave his mouth. Well over six feet tall,
he announced, "The players respect me because I'm taller than
they are."

Jordan was in St. Paul, like myself, to write a magazine article
about the cuckoo Saints, albeit post-Strawberry and sans Murray, for
Men's Journal. Accompanying Jordan was a busty New York woman
in her late twenties wearing a T-shirt a couple of sizes too small and
a pair of short shorts—his photographer.

"Look at those *guns,*" said a player from the dugout. "I wouldn't mind a piece of that." Although the players had been putting their *schvantzes* inside some of the prettiest girls of the Midwest all summer, the photographer was a revelation.

"*Look* at those guns," said another player shagging flies in the outfield. "I would love to shag her."

"She likes the ballplayers," said Pat Jordan as he watched his photographer walk right into the faces of the players in the field and begin shooting. Just about everyone on the team made their best play for her, but rumor had it that the only one she eventually gave it up to was a certain outfielder who she'd partied with later that night at Gabe's.

I, meantime, was focusing on Jordan. Old, gray, arrogant, and as Hawaiian as a Shriner listening to Don Ho, he looked like a knock-off Hunter Thompson. He was also, for me, a vision of the Ghost of Christmas Yet to Come, a name-dropping picture of the gossipy hatchet man in deep middle age. "I'm married to Meg Ryan's mother," he told me, although mother and daughter were no longer on speaking terms.

Impossibly full of himself, his article on the Saints would be entitled "The Craziest Team in America." But first Jordan had to stir up a ruckus.

He did this by walking into the Saints' locker room, before a game, smoke billowing out of his stogie and into the players' tiny dressing quarters. Finally coach Chuck Jackson had enough and began screaming at Jordan to get the fuck out of there with his smoke and bad vibes, and the two moved toward each other to mix it up. Jordan, I knew, would be dead in seconds, but players moved to separate the two.

Afterward, Marty Scott wondered if Jackson, growing ever more manic by the day, was losing it. "He was always a leader when I knew him in the Texas organization," Scott said. "I've never seen him go around the bend like this."

With Jackson fighting his demons, Jordan continued in the coming days to take his notes inside a large blank hardcover book that looked like a king's diary. In the piece that finally came out, trumpeted on the magazine cover as BASEBALL'S CRAZIEST TEAM, it looked suspiciously as if Jordan had fallen for Jody Beaulieu, the pretty young woman five seconds out of Texas Tech who ran the Saints on-field promotions during the game. In his article, Jordan somehow managed to mention Jody four times, ending his piece with a rhap-

Jody Beaulieu
Courtesy of Bonnie Butler

sody of "in the owners' box, Jody Beaulieu doesn't even bother to look up. She's busy stacking the sumo suits for next season."

For the next year, everyone in the Saints' front office would tease Jody unmercifully about the apparent crush the writer had had on her. "He was a creep!" protested Jody. "I didn't even *talk* to him."

To me, while he was in St. Paul, Jordan remained my Marley's ghost, warning me of what was to become of me if I didn't change. Was his Hunter Thompson getup Marley's chains, shaking me awake? Would I spend my middle-aged years writing peculiarly obsessive articles focusing on young pretty women? No. God no.

On the field, with Chuck Jackson having trouble coping with his coach's role, the leadership role on the team fell to the mostly silent, once-famously dysfunctional Glenn Davis. During his glory years with the Houston Astros, much was made of Davis's troubled youth. A suicidal teenage alcoholic who was beaten by his parents, Davis finally found refuge during his high school years in the home of his cousin Storm Davis, who went on to a fine career with the Baltimore Orioles.

Redeemed, Davis became a great ballplayer, hitting 164 home runs from 1985 to 1990 with the Astros. But after joining the Baltimore Orioles, he got into a fistfight, injuring himself for the rest of the season, and word started circulating that he'd quite simply gone mad.

According to Davis, Thomas Boswell, the esteemed baseball writer of *The Washington Post,* wrote that the ballplayer had turned into a flake, a mild insult that the injured slugger still hasn't forgotten. Released by the Orioles in 1993, he came back this spring from Japan when Darryl Strawberry's example led him to believe he too could return to the big leagues if he played for St. Paul.

The prospects of this seemed good enough that soon after he arrived *in* midseason to the Saints, Davis was sent a gratis shipment of top-of-the-line hardwood bats. Athletic gear distributors make sure that all real (and potential) major leaguers are outfitted with their wares. So while most of the Saints had to do with a couple oddly matched pieces of lumber, Davis now had dozens of the finest bats being hewn and carved.

Opening the box, Davis immediately began handing out the bats as gifts to his new teammates, as well as the batting gloves and other assorted equipment he was being sent as swag by the athletic gear companies. For a ballplayer to give up these kind of weapons was enormously generous; his teammates beamed at Davis for days.

"I have never seen so many guys walk up to the plate with Mizzunos," said Anthony LaPanta, the Saints' cable TV broadcaster. "That is one happy clubhouse. Those bats are made of some kind of hard wood. We will be seeing some prodigious knocks."

Yes, at least from Davis. In his first twelve games in a St. Paul uniform, he had twenty-eight RBIs, hitting two grand slams in five days. On the road, he would read piles of financial magazines taken out of a locked Wall Street briefcase, keep unlit cheroots in his mouth, drink an occasional red wine poured out of a bottle with a screw cap, and discuss how he would give up one of his kidneys to know which stock would be the next Tommy Hilfiger. "I need to know the next trend," said the only Saints player who seemed to have any money.

And so, mostly hanging out alone, Davis pored through his *Wall Street Journal, Forbes,* and assorted financial newsletters. But Glenn, more than making a financial killing, wanted one more chance at the Show. If he got back to the majors, he promised himself, he would enjoy himself this time. "I was so nervous every second up there that I didn't take the time to enjoy the major league experience," he said in Winnipeg in mid-August, right after the Fargo series. "In some ways, it was like I was never there. I want to go back up there and for the first time just *enjoy* it."

And still, there were signs of the wild man Davis of yore. Country Stewart, the youngest player in the league, turned twenty-one while the team was just in Fargo. To celebrate, several members of the team took him to a country bar where he downed nineteen straight shots of whiskey, one more than the rumored amount that killed Dylan Thomas and twelve more than the actual count.

Stewart was then dragged back to the Saints' Comfort Inn, where out in the parking lot behind the team bus a couple of players were smoking pot out of a pipe made out of a soda can. Upstairs, meantime, Glenn Davis was hog-tying Country Stewart with belts and then overseeing a galaxy of teammates who were shaving the young pitcher from eyebrows to testicles. The next morning Davis was back in the motel coffeeshop, talking softly and reading *The Kiplinger Report,* while Stewart stuck his hangover and shaved head in a bucket of hotel ice and wondered aloud what had happened the previous night.

Fargo itself remained an astonishment out of time. After a night game won by the RedHawks that mid-August, I retired to my motel room, too tired to impress the Saints' potential dates at the country and western bar they were attending.

Back in my motel, I heard the sounds of hundreds of people nearby. I also heard screeching truck tires, shitty music, and screaming, happy youth. Raising my motel blinds, I looked down the road a piece at a Hardees fast food restaurant. The Hardees parking lot, it turned out, was the Studio 54 of Fargo for the town's teenagers. It was "American Graffiti," with Randy Travis and Shania Twain providing the soundtrack.

The townspeople were uniformly friendly, except when discussing the movie *Fargo.* They thought the film, made naturally by Twin Cities smartasses named Coen, unfairly tarred their city because only a couple of scenes of the movie were supposed to have taken place

Dakota Sadie and Hillory
Courtesy of Dave Wallis/The Forum/Fargo, N.D.

there. Ever since, the mere mention of Fargo, they felt, was a slur
that implied that the entire town was made up of village idiots who
said nothing but "Yah sure, you betcha."

Calvin Trillin, originally from Kansas City, called this phenomenon "rube-o-phobia"—the fear in the Midwest that someone slick,
from somewhere even slicker, might think you are a rube. And so
in Fargo, the city, they don't want to talk about *Fargo*, the movie.
They'd rather talk about their team and beautiful brand-new baseball
stadium, perhaps the best in the league, which was built as a scaled-
down model of Yankee Stadium.

One of the most charming of the Bird's Nest's attributes was its

old-time, non-electric scoreboard, where numerals had to be hung
by hand to mark the progress of the game. For that, Fargo had the
two most beautiful women in town, "Dakota Sadie," a twenty-one-
year-old with a pierced nose and a baby, and Hillory, a soft-spoken
twenty-year-old pal of Dakota Sadie's who spent most of her time
when she wasn't sitting on the scoreboard turning down dates from
the finer bachelors of town. They were the Fargo "Scoreboard Girls"
and, as such, were Fargo celebrities.

Despite the growing homogenization of low minor league baseball
promotions—who now doesn't have a "dizzy bat spin" or a "dirtiest
car in the parking lot" contest?—Fargo had come up with something
new and, for this chaste city, sexy. It involved Dakota Sadie and
Hillory, who moments before each game would meet at home plate
wearing short shorts and baseball jerseys with logos that read LIFE IS
GOOD on the back.

Like boxing ring girls announcing the first round, the buxom two
would stand in the batter's box, each holding scoreboard signs above
their heads that read: 1. The crowd would rise and scream, then the
PA announcer would announce their presence and say, "Are you
ready to rumble?"

Then over the loudspeakers would come the first strains of a
techno hit that signaled the start of the Scoreboard Girls ritual. Sadie
and Hillory, their signs still held high above their heads, would separate, then shimmy down each of the foul lines all the way to the
outfield fence. There they would exit the field and climb a ladder to
the scoreboard. And there they sat for nine innings, accompanied
only by a walkie-talkie connected to the press box that was used to
get scores from other Northern League games to hang on the old-
fashioned board.

To the conservative men of Fargo, it was the equivalent of a lap
dance; for the good women of the town, it announced the beginning
of the RedHawks game, the best show in town. In Fargo, they take
their baseball more seriously than any other stop in the league—if
you are talking from a seat during the game, it is likely you will be
shushed by a fan nearby who, leaning forward to spot the action on
the field, will mutter under his breath about "big-city twerps from
St. Paul."

Unlike at every other stadium in the league, no smoking was
allowed anywhere in the ballpark; at Midway Stadium, smoking a
stinking cigar in the grandstand was considered an inalienable right
(though to avoid fistfights, the Saints eventually instituted a no-

smoking section). Also different from other teams was that Fargo fans actually seemed to know the names of their ballplayers, even new ones who Doug Simunic had churned, like Marty Scott, out of the baseball netherworld two days before.

After the game, something special was always scheduled. In St. Paul, Mike Veeck favored fireworks, rock shows, or something deliciously ridiculous and purposely cheap. In Fargo, they leaned more toward the Flying Elvises impersonators parachuting out of a plane and landing in the infield. Inspired by the movie *Honeymoon in Vegas,* the Flying Elvises were cheered as if they were the Flying Wallendas performing a death-defying feat as they landed safely and signed autographs. Fargo definitely had an Elvis jones, with the parachutists adding just the right note of happy absurdism.

Elvis, I found, remained alive all over the Northern League. In *Elvis People,* a sociological examination of the cult, author and BBC correspondent Ted Harrison reported that

> a recent American guide to Elvis impersonators lists sixty-four leading acts. It is just the tip of the iceberg, for there are hundreds of amateurs. They describe their "calling" in many ways, but repeatedly express a deep commitment and seriousness of purpose.

And so it is with Rick Dunham, a beefy, open, and Southern-friendly Elvis impersonator hired by the Sioux Falls Canaries to perform in mid-June when the Saints came to town. "Singing is the important thing," he says as he puts on his white jumpsuit amid boxes underneath the Sioux Falls stadium. "Lord knows that's my forte," a word he pronounces "fort," full of American blood.

It is not an easy life, traveling the minor league circuit with two jumpsuits, a handful of rhinestone jewelry, and a fake gold belt buckle, all representing the King's Vegas years. "Here's my pinkie ring," Dunham says, slipping on a shiny plastic bauble. "I'm always afraid I'm going to lose that—I've already lost three pinkie rings."

He looks in the mirror and stretches the white cape attached to the jumpsuit. Sewn on the back is an eagle made out of rhinestones. "Some of the stones are missing, but it's still pretty nice," Dunham says. He's going to buy a nice new one, he says, "if I get that agent I'm hoping to get."

On goes Elvis's famous red neckerchief, but Dunham is not happy with his hair, which he doesn't think is slick enough. "I don't have any Dippity-Do, so I guess I'll have to go with it," he says, slipping on the silver shades Elvis wore in his declining years. And finally Dunham sprays some cheap perfume over himself. "My mother picked this out for me. Elvis has got to smell good, you know?"

One last look in the mirror, and Dunham notices how tired his white jumpsuit is beginning to look. "I've been bleaching that suit a lot lately, which you're not supposed to do, but it's so hard to keep clean on the baseball circuit."

And now it's showtime. Dunham is down for seven songs as old Elvis, including "The Star-Spangled Banner" and "Take Me Out to the Ball Game" during the seventh-inning stretch. Going out the back and reentering the stadium gates in a limousine, he lowers the window and starts waving at Canaries fans. "How's it going?" he asks with a perfect Elvis twang. "I'm back, I'm back!"

Dunham as Elvis is cheered every step during the game as he wanders the stands, switching in the middle innings to a black jump-suit bearing black rhinestones in a sunburst pattern. Back downstairs while changing, he takes another look in the mirror and notices that the Ronald Reagan black is running in his hair. "Look," he sighs, "the dye's coming out. I don't think he's leaving it in long enough!"

But then it's back upstairs to sing "Are You Lonesome Tonight?" on the dugout to a pair of giggling little girls. After the game, back in his cubby hole below the stadium, Dunham talks about his dreams of being the most famous Elvis impersonator ever. Considering fail-ure as he puts his jumpsuits on hangers, he says only that "My biggest fear is that somebody will steal these things [jumpsuits], cuz I got so much in 'em. And I don't have any insurance right now." Does anybody in the Northern League? And then Dunham is gone.

The Saints, meantime, kept coming up with the funkiest game promotions in the league. Besides having Minnie Minoso descend from the heavens, there was "Seventies Night," when all 6,329 fans were given smiley face masks to wear during the game. They did, creating a bizarre sight that looked part John Waters, part Ingmar Bergman. Most of the crowd wore polyester and wide bell bottoms; on top of the dugout between innings, the Saints' staff danced the Hustle as the PA blasted an entire game's worth of seventies music that ranged from George Clinton's Funkadelic to arguably the sappi-est white boy song ever, Terry Jacks's "Seasons in the Sun."

There was "Phantom of the Ballpark Night," when each woman at the game received a rose from a man dressed like the opera specter, and "Drive-in Movie Night," when fans were invited to

bring blankets onto the field after the game and watch flicks on a
screen set up in center field until the wee hours. And who could
forget "Mascot Mania Night," when humans inside the corporate
logo suits of every company from Subway sandwiches to the Pillsbury
Dough Boy to UPS would do gladiatorial battle on the field.

During the season, men proposed to their loved ones as the entire
stadium watched and cheered; later, marriages were held at home
plate. A bar mitzvah had once taken place on the field before a
Saints game, and a request had come in from a fan who wanted to
be buried under home plate. The most romantic proposal of 1996
came when a woman was called to the field to accept a prize drawing,
to be presented by the Saints' fully geared catcher. When he took
off his mask, it wasn't starting catcher Aaron Cannaday, but a man
who fell to his knees and offered a ring. She said yes.

A few of the promotions went unannounced and a couple were
strictly personal for members of the Saints' staff. On the anniversary
of the 1979 "Disco Demolition Night" in Chicago that ruined Mike
Veeck's life, Annie Huidekoper had an idea to pep Mike up. All day
long, she'd been going to used record shops in the Twin Cities,
looking for albums featuring the likes of K.C. and the Sunshine
Band, Van McCoy, Donna Summer, and other seventies disco acts.

At the end of the game, she took about twenty albums and Mike
to the outfield, whereupon the vinyl was thrown into a garbage can
and firecrackers thrown inside. It was purposefully one of the dinkier
displays of the season, but Mike understood the meaning. The ghosts
were gone and, seventeen years later to the day, he had survived.

Not so with his team itself. Since they were guaranteed a spot
in the playoffs, the Saints played the second half of the season as if
they were distracted by more important matters elsewhere. A four-
game winning streak against Sioux City and Sioux Falls would be
followed by a four-game losing streak in Winnipeg and Fargo, and
the manager fumed as his team went up and down, seemingly depending on how they felt that day. Yes, they were already in the
playoffs, but Marty Scott was pissed. "You smell like a distillery," he
beefed at nice guy rookie pitcher Dan Thomson when he reported
to work one morning after a long night of midseason partying.

But what could Marty do? If the Saints won the East's half-season
title again, they would face the second-place team in their division
in the league semifinals. If they didn't, they would play whoever won

the second half. This time it looked like Duluth, which had gone ahead of the bipolar Saints by August 18.

Four games behind was Madison, and I thought again of Monica, wondering if she was crying under the grandstand about the Black-Wolf's folding. But I knew she wasn't. She'd toughened up over the year and wasn't going to let any one see her vulnerable. Instead, she continued taking care of the reporters and running her between-innings "dizzy bat spin." As I daydreamed about her, I hummed a few bars of Otis Redding's "(Sittin' on) The Dock of the Bay" to myself.

So by August 18, Madison looked dead. If the Saints got past first-place Duluth in the Eastern finals, they would probably then face Fargo in the league championship. Fargo, which had run away with the first half of the West Division standings, not only hated St. Paul, but also boasted better pitching than anybody in the league. Their ace was the ancient yet still effective Jeff Bittiger, who'd once been up for cups of coffee with the major league White Sox, Phillies, and Twins, but whose fame came as the winningest pitcher in minor league history.

Their acerbic manager, Doug Simunic, had already sent his teams to the three league finals. No one else had done that, though Marty Scott had only been around for two years. But in Fargo, Simunic was lionized as a local savior who defended their city from all the slights that had come their way from the rest of the *Fargo*-watching country. Living year round in town with a long-term contract to manage, Simunic was settled down as the local domo.

Simunic won the Northern League championship in 1994 while managing Winnipeg; his two other teams had lost in the league's World Series to the St. Paul Saints. And so Doug Simunic hated the Saints (for the unfair advantage, as he saw it, of the team's publicity magnet that drew ringers like Darryl Strawberry). His city, meantime, despised St. Paul because it represented the Sodom they imagined the Twin Cities to be, the closest big city where Fargoites might lose their children to easy drugs, prostitution, and atheists.

Still, Simunic was a good manager; not as good as Marty, but a winner. In the four-year history of the Northern League, only Fargo had a winning record against the Saints. Now Fargo was coming into Midway on August 19 for their final series against St. Paul, unless both teams saw each other in the league finals. Fargo on top again in the West, looked ready to stomp the inconsistent Saints and take all the momentum into the playoffs.

The first game, on August 19, was the kind that makes Northern League officials wince, the type that when it occurs, belies all their statements that their league plays at the AA minor league level. Fargo beat St. Paul 14–12, overcoming two Glenn Davis home runs, including his third grand slam of his young season. Thirteen pitchers were used; there were twenty-nine hits and four errors. At one point, Fargo sent twenty-eight players to the plate in a three-inning span. The Saints had now fallen to 12–12 for the second half, while Fargo stood happy in the other division at 17–11.

What happened the next day, August 20, was one of the great moments of the season, an event that could never happen in the major leagues. And why should it, for the performance art piece that went on between managers Scott and Simunic the next night at Midway Stadium really had nothing to do with baseball.

It was another badly played ball game, with the Saints finally winning 10–9, drawing within one game of division-leading Duluth. What made it so special was what happened after the RedHawks manager was thrown out of the game in the sixth inning for arguing a call with an umpire; an inning later, the Saints' Marty Scott too was tossed for demanding in un-Baptist terms an explanation from the home plate umpire about a called third strike.

The managers, both banished to the bowels of the stadium, ran into each other as they roamed the inner halls, wondering what was happening in the game outside. Suddenly Simunic had an idea that would get them back on the field incognito, tweak the umpires, and also give them both a chance to do battle with each other, mano à mano. "Let's sumo," Simunic challenged the Saints' manager.

Scott agreed it was a terrific idea for the two to replay in the middle of the eighth the promotion typically run in the second inning. They approached Mike Veeck with the scheme, who agreed it was a stunt worth trying.

Under the grandstand, the two portly managers (to put it mildly) were zippered into the rubber suits, the fake sumo headdresses locked around their chins for further disguise. Upstairs, meantime, the PA announcer asked the fans if they were interested in having a second sumo match that evening. The crowd cheered yes.

That is when Mike Haiduck, the PA announcer, made his tragic error. Haiduck, who'd hiply turned the Ramones into the punk rock "house band" of Midway Stadium and who announced batters with an hysterically woozy, boozy imitation of Harry Caray, leaned into his microphone The match, he told the crowd, would not be between "Minneapolis" (boo) and "St. Paul" (yea), but would pit the evenings's "two ejected managers."

Oops.

Their cover blown, Scott and Simunic rushed onto the field as enormous sumo wrestlers while Mike Veeck helped drag out the wrestling mat. Just as the umpires were realizing what was going on, the two managers they'd ejected from the field minutes before were bouncing bellies against each other against a soundtrack of the screaming crowd. The match ended when the sumo managers fell to the mat at the same time, making the contest a draw.

As the managers exited the field, third base ump Don Grimaluskus ran into the runway, shoved the managers deeper into the stadium, and screamed. The two manager bastards, he said, had shown up the umpire squad, and the matter was not over. The umps refused to talk after the game, but could be heard shrieking in their dressing room that they would seek "maximum penalties" for these crimes against the baseball order.

Even for the Northern League, this incident may have gone too far. Yet Mike, shaking hands with departing fans after the game, seemed unconcerned that he would once again be labeled a promotional troublemaker. "The ball game was already a bit," he said, using a theater term for a shittily played 10–9 game. "The last couple of games have been kind of a travesty," he went on. "I don't think we're mocking anything. It isn't mocking because it wasn't sponsored. There wasn't time."

And so he would gladly confess his crime to the league office. "I okayed it and helped carry the mat," Mike said. "I can't say I didn't."

And anyway, Mike went on, it was nice to see Fargo's Doug Simunic, whose mere presence in Midway Stadium made thousands of fans wave plastic baby pacifiers at the RedHawks manager every time he came out of the dugout to argue about how he was being cheated by the Saints, do something positive. According to Veeck, "The sumo thing was the first human thing Doug has done in a year and a half."

The next day league founder and commissioner Miles Wolf— former owner of the Durham Bulls and owner/publisher of *Baseball America*—fined the two teams $150.

If there was one matter generally agreed upon in the Northern League, it was that in general the umpiring sucked (the same thing was generally said by players in the majors about their umps too). Yet it was especially hard being an umpire in the independent Northern League, home to no union and little more hope.

Like the players, most of the umpires were here for a reason, many of them bad. Several umps, like many of the players, had washed out of organized baseball's minor leagues when the major league supervisors deemed them no longer prospects to be umpires in the Show. Others, having already spent thousands of dollars at accredited umpire schools run by former big league arbiters, couldn't let go and were as sure as the players that if someone just saw them in action, they could get on the right track and out of this league.

Other umps were free agents with a dream, unconnected and unwanted, amazed that the Northern League would pay them approximately $1,700 a month to call balls and strikes and maybe get onto a road leading to the major leagues. Some big league umps earned over $200,000, a year, while rookies began in the $60,000 range. Umps in the Show also had dental insurance and were guarded by a union that kicked butt if one of their men in blue was abused on the field (à la the Roberto Alomar spitting incident).

But here in the Northern League—hell, just here in St. Paul— they had to deal with sumo-wrestling managers who they'd just thrown out of the game, white-faced mimes running up the basepaths as an instant replay of the last at-bat, a male movie star kissing them on the lips after throwing out the first ball, and a pig delivering them fresh baseballs. Yet still they came, fanning out across the Midwest to call their games in teams of two. When they hit a Northern League city, they would be joined on the field by a third ump, a putatively competent local who could call a fair game, who was picked by each home team.

In fact, a few of the umpires had a shot at moving up to organized baseball's minor leagues. The best was John Ramsey, a tall, blond, handsome man in his late twenties with a teacher's degree and a bone-crushing handshake. Around the league, it was said that he might have the right stuff to move up. At the very least, he would work the league championship in September with his season-long partner, A. J. Lastaglio.

Sure never to stay in the same motels or frequent the same bars as players, the umps I came to know had their own motels and tippling spots in each town around the league. Off the field, they always dressed more conservatively than the players they were judging, with most teams of umpires favoring nice khaki pants, dress shoes, and argyle socks. Some teams of umps traveled in suits and ties, others in matching polo shirts.

Theirs was a calling of tradition. For hours before each game, umpires in all professional leagues remove the gloss from fresh baseballs by rubbing them with mud taken from the shores of the Delaware River. It is a ritual of all umps everywhere that dates back to 1930; the goo is called Lena Blackburne Rubbing Mud and is still sold to umpires by the same family who began the tradition.

Soon after a bush league manager named Lena Blackburne started the habit, no balls would be put into professional play until they had been carefully rubbed down for hours with this mud schlepped around the country by umpires as if it was holy water. Indeed, there was something almost priestly about the umpires.

Since most of them were on the road all summer, with no home on the circuit, they had to fold their on-field uniforms and street clothes into tiny origami that would always come out looking fresh. Almost all carried their entire gear and belongings in cases that looked just like the trunks priests use to carry their vestments.

And they got laid.

Umpires, it seems, have their own groupies, women who like the order and power symbolized by a man who can call you out in a uniform. Like the Baseball Annies, the umpire groupies know the right bars to catch their quests and reacquaint themselves with umps they met on the last time through. "Basically," confided one umpire, "they're the same women who like cops."

So there were some benefits, the umpires thought. But even usually easygoing St. Paul manager Marty Scott was often repelled by the choked calls of the league's umpires. And he was unrepentant about his role in the absurd Beckett-like on-field sumo managers comedy that entertained the fans when both teams stunk up the joint. "I would rather the theater was good baseball," Marty said, "but we aren't executing very well right now."

To put it mildly. The next day, in the team's last scheduled game of the year against the RedHawks, Fargo spanked the Saints 11–3, winning the season series, seven games to five. St. Paul made four errors in the game, didn't score until it was 8–0 in the seventh inning, and looked like they, well, *sucked.*

Marty Scott, though still not yet panicking, hit the August 20 twenty-two-man playoff roster freeze date with some quick changes in mind. He signed Hector Villanueva, a jovial and philosophic ex-Chicago Cub and St. Louis Cardinal in his early thirties who had hit

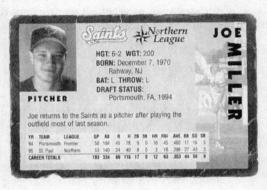

25 homers and had 72 runs batted in during his stay in the majors. Since then, he'd bounced around the high minors, but mostly Hector had supported his wife and three kids living in Puerto Rico by playing as a short-time ringer for the private baseball teams of Mexico.

Victory-mad owners in Mexico, he claimed, would pay him $25,000 for a week of work. It was well worth the dough, Hector said on the bus in the 'hood, even if it meant living under virtual house arrest in the luxury hotels where the owners kept their teams.

Now he would play for the Saints for a few weeks and hopefully hit some playoff home runs. Listed at six-feet-one and 220 pounds, Villanueva, in fact, seemed to weigh least thirty pounds more and stand two inches less. Within days it was said that Hector had the biggest ass of anybody in the Northern League, even Doug Simunic.

Scott also brought in strikeout pitcher John Burgos, who he'd signed with Texas and had since spent eleven years climbing to the high minors, just short of the Show. Another baseball soldier of fortune, one who averaged seven whiffs per game, Marty thought, might be the stopper that the team would need in order not to disintegrate in the playoffs.

Churning his roster, Marty spent hours each night going over lists of players just released from other organizations and players who'd seemingly reappeared after falling off the earth. The Saints were now virtually an entirely different team than they'd been at the beginning of the season, and the GON' FISHIN' wall in their locker room, filled

Saint Paul Saints

By the time the Saints hit the field for their May 31 season opener at Duluth, pitching coach Ray Korn already has a full season under his belt. The New Jersey native serves as athletic director and baseball coach at Elizabeth High School in Elizabeth, NJ. In 1989, Ray coached at the Olympic Sports Festival in Oklahoma City, OK. Before joining the Saints last year, Ray worked with Erie and in Niagara Falls in the NY-Penn League and Huntington in the Appalachian League. He also has worked with the 1990 U.S. National team and spent four years as pitching coach at Seton Hall.

COACH

RAY KORN

with the adhesive-taped names of this year's departed, began to take on the image of a Scotch-brand war memorial.

Despite the Saints' generally lackluster play, there still remained beautiful moments on their ball field. On August 25, Saint Joe Miller threw a masterful 10–0 no-hitter at Midway Stadium against the Thunder Bay Whiskey Jacks, the second no-hitter in league history. What made the game so peculiar was that Miller threw his gem in the first game he'd ever thrown as a starting pitcher—*ever*.

In fact, the outfielder had never pitched at all until this year, when manager Scott and pitching coach Ray Korn had decided his arm was better than his bat and had turned Miller into a pitcher. From there, he had worked only in relief, compiling an unimpressive 1–5 record with a 7.01 earned run average. Never all season had he worked more than four and a third innings in a row.

The St. Paul crowd was on its feet from the seventh inning on, chanting, "Joe! Joe! Joe!" When he came off the field after finishing off the Whiskey Jacks and his no-hitter, there were tears in Miller's eyes. "Those aren't real tears, they're from the sting of champagne hitting me," he contended, but it was obvious bullshit.

The next day someone in the Saints' organization would call the Hall of Fame research library and learn that never before in baseball history had a player starting his very first game thrown a no-hitter. Cooperstown wanted the game-ending ball.

"It's no big deal," jested Marty Scott. "Everybody knows that Joe and Nolan Ryan have eight no-hitters between them."

Miller still seemed stunned. The fist thing he thought he'd do, he said, was call his father in New Jersey. "I'll say, 'Dad, I made my first start and pitched a no-hitter,'" Miller said. "It's a routine story."

Not for the Saints, who would look great one night and like semiprofessionals the next. The season, if not doomed, was in serious question.

And so was my absolute sureness about not hatcheting Bill Murray, who I knew would be coming back to St. Paul for the playoffs. I realized again that if I didn't get my dough and expenses from *Rolling Stone* and Jann Wenner, I'd probably have to move into my parents' basement. What was next—a job at Arby's? But my moral hesitancy disappeared during a visit to Midway Stadium from CBS correspondent Eleanor Mondale, my only famous friend and the daughter of the former Vice President and ambassador to Japan.

I had met Eleanor years before, when I wrote a hatchet job in a magazine about her entitled "Wild Child," an article that got her fired from her job. I'd only known her since the end of the 1980s, when we'd simultaneously moved back to our native Minneapolis after both our lives had blown up in the big city.

The plucky Eleanor, who had the style, smarts, and mouth of a successful gun moll, had snagged a high-profile job with the local CBS affiliate, and I'd been quickly assigned by a local city magazine to profile the state's most famous daughter. And so I did, using the journalist's proven techniques for celebrity profiles that I'd learned in New York. For weeks, I'd followed her around town to parties and dates, gathering enough quotes that when picked and rearranged would paint a picture of a Midwest Holly Golightly, a scandal waiting to happen.

We'd become an odd pair for the months I was reporting my story on her. Eleanor would check out the women I was dating in my new life, while I would dissect for her the strengths and weaknesses of the boys courting her.

I never become friends with people I write stories about after the fact, usually because there is no longer anything for either of us to say. If I hatcheted someone, they hated me; if I puffed them, I hated feeling like a celebrity suck or a part of anybody's entourage. But Eleanor, I realized only later, actually had become a friend in that dark season for both of us.

Still, I wrote the story the way I'd been trained and didn't even try to talk her out of wearing the scanty French cocktail dresses and black bustier she'd brought along for her photo shoot. I'd forgotten the Midwest rules: while these clothes might be fine for New York or L.A. hipster magazines, they would be scandalous in Minneapolis for a Vice President's daughter for whom the fatted calf had been sacrificed.

The "Wild Child" story ultimately appeared with Eleanor on the cover, her hands on her hips, in a black camisole that showed ample cleavage. I should have warned her, but I too was new back then. Days later she was fired from her local television news job, unemployable in town, not only because of the pictures, but because of the remarks she'd made to me that a friend would have told her to put off the record. But I was a reporter, not a friend, I thought, and she ended up having to leave town. She moved to Los Angeles, where her career has flourished all the way up to the network level. Hah!

Weirdly, we stayed in touch. She never blamed me for virtually destroying her life and I never asked why she forgave me. I was too amazed.

Skipping ahead several years, Eleanor was back in Minneapolis for one of her brief visits during the first summer I followed the Saints from town to town. Word had already reached her in Los Angeles that the Saints had become the most fun ticket in town, and she made me take her to a game in early August against the Sioux Falls Canaries. She'd only been to one pro baseball game before, she said, in 1969 when her father was a U.S. senator and he took her to a Washington Senators game.

I gasped at Eleanor. Here was another Wayne Terwilliger as Zelig connection. In 1969, Twig was the third base coach for the Washington Senators, managed by Ted Williams (but actually run, everybody knew, by Terwilliger).

Eleanor was impressed that Twig had been in the first landing wave of Marines at Iwo Jima, much less by the fact that he'd been on the bench for the Brooklyn Dodgers in 1951 when Bobby Thomson hit his "Shot Heard Round the World" at New York's Polo Grounds. But when I explained he was the Zen master of the fungo, she was intrigued and demanded to be taken down to the field to meet this Yoda-like figure who I promised was as nice as he was deep.

Unfortunately, to get to Twig before the game, I had to walk past a dugout full of Saints who began thrusting their pelvises skyward and shrieking like sex fiends as the well-proportioned Eleanor walked by in her Melrose Avenue outfit. They wanted to do her. Hadn't her ex-husband been with the Chicago Bears? Several players attempted to pick her up in the locker room after the game.

Eleanor shook Twig's hand, we went back up to our seats directly under the press box, and all was quiet until the third inning when the inevitable rendering of "The Macarena" blared over the PA. It was one of the Saints' few bows to ballpark convention: the other was playing "YMCA," a 1970s-era song about anonymous gay sex by the Village People, during the seventh-inning stretch so the fans could sing along and dance to it. The practice, allegedly begun by the Yankee Stadium grounds crew, was now as ubiquitous at the testosterone-heavy ballparks as "The Star-Spangled Banner."

Eleanor arose to the first beats of the hot sun that summer and began the ritual dance in a way that had never before been seen in conservative St. Paul. It was no big deal; in Dodger Stadium, few people would have even looked up at her gyrations; few people would have even *called* them gyrations. But here, at Midway, virtually everybody in the ballpark turned to Eleanor Mondale as if she was Little Egypt doing some never before seen dirty dancing.

Usually about half the crowd, some three thousand or so fans, tried to do some version of the dance. Tonight about twelve did. The rest stopped dancing and looked up toward the press box to watch Eleanor sexily pound to the beat like Madonna. Men's jaws dropped and women glared at their husbands; adolescent boys dropped their bratwurst buns and little girls came up to Eleanor and asked her how she did her hair. Over the rest of the year, at least twenty people told me that her dance was the highlight of the entire season.

Still, Eleanor was a visitor, and the Most Beloved Woman of the Northern League would have her moment in Midway Stadium too. On July 16, she entered the ballpark after the game had started for a big Saints series at home against her visiting BlackWolf. "Monica Toppen is in the house!" declaimed public address announcer Mike Haiduk.

The home crowd erupted as Monica, a member of the *visiting* team's front office, quickly made her way to a seat along the grandstand's main walkway. Later in the game, while busy keeping play-by-play score in her notebook and talking to the Madison home office on her cellular phone, Monica discovered that she had lost her purse.

When Monica told St. Paul policeman Steve Golden, who besides working security in his cop's uniform for the Saints for several years had also bought a piece of the Madison team over the off-season, he immediately began doing some detective work. Over the loud-speaker came an announcement that Monica had lost her purse; within minutes it had been found.

The crowd cheered lustily again when it was announced a few minutes later that the Most Beloved Woman of the Northern League had found her belongings. Her face turned beet-red from the atten-tion when about forty men in the section below the press box and PA booth began chanting, "Monica! Monica! Monica!" as she reen-tered the stands from the Saints' lost and found department.

For the Saints, however, the rest of the season looked like it might be lost for good. By August, so much had the team changed from the first-half championship squad that it was almost like starting over. Yes, I would still ride the bus and occasionally assist the players after games by impressing their dates with my old *Rolling Stone* press card from the eighties. But since the team's place in the playoffs was already assured, I decided to pull away for a little bit or at least take more time to look at the scenery as we traveled from game to game and city to city. Now I would also spend more time taking Greyhounds and driving my beater city to city, windshield still unfixed, detouring as often as I pleased to see the sights and profound weirdness of the rural Midwest that I'd always avoided as a city boy from Minneapolis.

Such visions as I could pick up along the way, I hoped, would bear the same carnival sideshow oddness and Midwestern good karma that the Saints' edifice is built upon. There were Grand Kleagles of the Ku Klux Klan and Michigan Militias out there too, I knew, but that was part of the midway experience.

Inspired by Monica's campaign on behalf of Otis Redding, I began trying to reach sad, anonymous places and visions of happy oddball citizens dancing in cornfields. They wouldn't be hard to find, espe-cially in my own Minnesota backyard. In the book *Eccentrics: A Study of Sanity and Strangeness,* English psychologist David Weeks and journalist Jamie James wrote:

We were surprised to find that there were more eccentrics in the Minneapolis–St. Paul region, per capita, than in any other area of the United States.

So, detouring about fifty miles outside Minneapolis on the way to see the Sioux Falls Canaries, I came upon the life's work of bachelor farmer Francis Johnson. Sometime during the Truman Administration, he began rolling twine into a ball—though no one was quite sure why. Johnson's creation, forty feet around and weighing several tons, ranked as the largest ball of string in the world.

When he died a few years ago, the nearby town of Darwin had the twine ball removed from his barn on a forklift and brought to the center of the little town, where it was enshrined in Plexiglas for all to marvel at. Each summer, for three days, Darwin now celebrates "Twine Ball Days," a festival in honor of a benignly mad local citizen who was allowed the courage of his craziness.

Later, taking the long route to Sioux City to check in with banished former Saints Marty Neff and Kevin Garner, I veered toward Clear Lake, Iowa, home of the Surf Ballroom where Buddy Holly, Ritchie Valens, and the Big Bopper played their last concert on February 2, 1959, before flying off in bad weather for the Fargo airport (where else?) and their next concert.

Their plane had crashed in a field only miles away from Clear Lake and everyone on-board was killed. "I'll never forget seeing Buddy Holly up on the bandstand, and he died a week after that, it was unbelievable," recalled Bob Dylan a few decades later. Dylan, who'd caught Holly's show as a pimply, teenaged hipster the week before in Duluth, said the deaths never stopped influencing him. "The singers and musicians I grew up with transcend nostalgia. Buddy Holly [is] just as valid to me today as then."

Likewise, a teenaged Gary (later Garrison) Keillor drove straight down to Clear Lake after the crash to see what had happened in that field to the young man who had invented rock & roll. Over a generation later, one of Keillor's best radio monologues was about that cold night in a wrecked Iowa cornfield. It was almost a religious shrine; I had to find that field.

This would be no easy task in a city where Holly searchers are routinely directed to the Surf Ballroom, home still to the pay phone where Holly and Valens made their last phone calls. Isn't that enough?

No. As the poet Thomas Lynch write in *The Undertaking:*

"I'm OK, you're OK, and by the way, he's dead!" is, for the living, a kind of comfort. It is why we drag rivers and comb plane wrecks and bomb sites. . . . It is why we have open caskets and all read the obits.

So only the exact spot would do.

My research told me that to find it one must take I-35 straight toward Clear Lake. Highway 18 going west leads right into town; from there, one needs to turn onto a road named S28. Going north for five and a half miles on S28, one should make a right turn onto 310 Street, then make an immediate left onto a gravel path called Gull Avenue. Going north for half a mile, one should stop at 315 Street and get out and start walking west into the cornfield past the 315 Street Sign. Half a mile down, on the north side of a wire fence, are four oak trees.

The trees, planted by the cornfield's owner to commemorate the four people who died right there—even among three luminaries, the pilot wasn't forgotten—are accompanied by a small marker. The farmer doesn't mind pilgrims, as long as they act normally and don't trample his corn. At the spot, I said *Kaddish* and, unbelievably to me, cried.

But there were also happier sites in Iowa; for about 75 miles, I followed the route driven in the last several years by a septuagenarian farmer on a John Deere riding mower; his driver's license had been revoked because of his poor eyesight. When the farmer's brother became ill in Wisconsin 250 miles away, he mounted his mower and made the journey along the road at five miles per hour. His was a heroic act, a lesson in real family values.

And even in the middle of who knows what, I found the most beauty from another time and, sometimes, place. In Vermillion, South Dakota, I ran into the University of South Dakota's Shrine to Music and Center for the Study of Musical Instruments, dedicated to documenting the history of music. Their collection of dozens of ancient violins, lutes, cellos, and guitars was breathtaking, especially in a setting that reminded me of a Kellogg's Corn Flakes commercial.

The center's last big purchase was a $3 million buy of seventy-five violins in 1993, which the London-based *Strad* magazine, the arbiter of all that is cool in the old violin world, considered "the world's finest assemblage of Baroque violins." All this in a place New Yorkers would call "Bumfuck, America."

And then there was Fargo, birth- and resting place of the late Roger Maris, for the last thirty-five years the only man to hit more home runs in one year than Babe Ruth. Those 61 dingers in

1961 had cost Roger dearly. He broke the record with his hair falling out in patches from nerves, while reporters all over the league badgered the North Dakota-reserved Maris to act it up for their copy. But that wasn't Roger; he far preferred the Midwest mellowness he found playing for the Kansas City A's early in his career rather than the blinding glare of Gotham.

Never forgiven for not coming close again to his magic Yankee season, for not being as colorful as Ruth or majestic as Mickey Mantle, Maris went to his grave early, generally unloved by an outside world that didn't understand that good Fargo boys like Roger liked to perform their heroics with a minimum of hoopla. In baseball lore, Maris was long thought of as the beneficiary of a freakish season, a gruff and humorless man who never forgave the press for not appreciating that he was an actual ballplayer with admirable skills. "Roger was sort of colorless," his biographer Maury Allen said on the "Today" show in 1988. "He was a laconic person, and we sportswriters were angry at him for not being a Babe Ruth character, for being what he wanted to be."

Indeed. Maris never understood why Mickey Mantle, who fucked strangers for all his career, was lionized, while he, a good, decent Fargo boy, was sometimes booed by his own fans in Yankee Stadium. New York tired of his lack of flash; he was traded to the St. Louis Cardinals for the 1967 season for a journeyman infielder named Charley Smith. In Fargo, though, they always understood Roger and the majesty of his 1961 accomplishment.

And in the summer of 1996, when Ken Griffey, Jr., Mark McGwire, and Tino Martinez were all threatening to shatter their homeboy hero's single-season homer record, no one in Fargo has anything but nice things to say about Maris. And nobody, it seemed, wanted any of the nineties breed of ballplayer to break Roger's mark.

"In Fargo, we don't want to see a guy with an earring beat his record," Nick Coleman of the *Saint Paul Pioneer Press* quoted Wayne Blanchard, one of Roger's classmates in town. Maris's national reputation would rebound by 1998, when Mark McGuire, then Sammy Sosa broke his record. But here "61" is and always will be the magic number.

I went to visit Maris's grave in Fargo's Holy Cross cemetery, where the caretaker said at least a person a day came to see the headstone that reads under Roger's name the notation 61–61. And then there is Fargo's rather spartan Roger Maris Museum, located in a mall near a gift shop and Foot Locker shoe store.

Kevin Garner, at peace in Sioux City
Courtesy of Bonnie Butler

The museum seventy-two feet long and behind glass, features Roger's football jersey from Fargo's Shanley High. Home run ball number 60 is there; number 61 is at the Hall of Fame in Cooperstown. A tape of Mel Allen describing Roger's accomplishments is played on eternal rewind, and there are pictures of Maris shaking hands with Truman and Kennedy. Also on display are his American League Most Valuable Player awards from 1960 and 1961, but given the setting, the most moving object is Roger's trophy for being the Fargo American Legion MVP for 1951.

He was a Fargo boy born and bred until the day he died, said everybody I talked to, and those New York writers who made his short life such misery should, as one Fargoite put it, "take a flying leap at a rolling doughnut."

But then I realized that it was time to get back with the living. In Sioux City, I met up with Kevin Garner, who had made peace with the fact that the St. Paul Saints had traded him to the edge of Iowa. The beautiful women of the surrounding townships swarmed around him the leading home run hitter in the Northern League now that Strawberry was gone. The women wouldn't leave the beefy Garner alone, even when he explained that he had a permanent girlfriend elsewhere.

I found Marty Neff, meantime, actually *living* in the Sioux City trainer's quarters. "It's great," he said, pointing to the rubdown table, which doubled as his bed. "It's rent-free, and I'm never late for practice."

I mentioned the name Marty Scott, the manager who'd traded him away, and he scowled. I then mentioned Singin' Ed Nottle, manager of Sioux City and the only manager in the whole league who wanted him. "I love Ed, because I've played for him before and he understands my approach to the game," Neff said. "I might have made the majors if I'd had a manager like Ed along the way."

Nottle, meantime, would have been a major league manager twice, for real. All he had to do was play the organization man for the Boston Red Sox or Oakland A's, whose AAA minor league teams he'd taken to championships. But he refused to fill out the daily reports he was supposed to send up to the major league home office. "I hate filling out reports," Nottle says, an unsurprising sentiment for a man who lost his house after financing a record of himself singing the nightclub classics.

"I'd rather be here, where I can call all the shots, become part of the community and be a big wheel in town for all my kids to see," says Nottle. "When I'm done, I'll buy a bar, and be with all my friends, and tell them how if I had been the one picked for the Boston Red Sox job, which I thought was mine, how I was going to throw this huge concert atop Fenway Park's Green Monster. We'd put all the acts up there, Lionel Richie, whoever, and maybe I'd sing '[Theme from] New York, New York.' We'd sell worldwide rights and give it all to charity. Whaddya think of that?"

I'd originally asked the king of Sioux City about Marty Neff, but with Singin' Ed Nottle the questions don't matter, it's the stream of usually funny, always smart answers that do.

"Right. Marty Neff," Nottle said. "You see, I understand Marty Neff. He doesn't want to work out or really stay in shape, and he's an idiot when it comes to running the bases. But he'll always hit for you, and he'll always try for you, and I think he's a hell of a nice kid. I used to stay out late when I was in the minors too, would have made the bigs if I hadn't spent so many nights singing and chasing the girls. You're young, and you do what you want to and have to do. I have no regrets that I didn't make the majors."

And, Marty Neff, do you have any regrets?

"Hunh?" he says, a twenty-six-year-old with a pot belly rising from his trainer's table-cum-bed. "Baseball has always been my life. My family moved me to California so I could play more baseball when I was young," he repeated. "But the Pirates tagged me as a head case, and that's that. They say everybody is in the Northern League for a reason, and that's mine."

Back in St. Paul, meantime, the season wore down. The only question was who the Saints would face in the playoffs: the Duluth-Superior Dukes or Madison Black Wolf, who'd made a late-season surge into second place. By the time of the last series of the year, in early September in Thunder Bay, the Saints were all focused on the playoffs.

On the way up north, though, I wanted to find Marvin Staples of Roseau, an old mining town near the Canadian border. Staples, I'd once read, had walked backward—only—for four straight years. All I could locate, however, was sad news from his brother, Art: Marvin, it seemed, had died in a house fire in the mid-1990s. "He was going for the record," Art said, "and he came pretty close."

So it was back on the road, hundreds of miles toward Thunder Bay, which proved exceptional only to the Saints who discovered that three groupies they'd met in Winnipeg had secretly made the trip to bang their heroes here in the loneliest of Northern League outposts.

Thunder Bay, in last place in the hearts of the league and the standings, was also playing on auto-pilot. They had the most loathed manager in the league, Jay Ward, a former Marine who'd been up to the majors for a few cups of coffee. Running his club like a Gulag, the buzz-cut Ward refused to let his team play music in the locker room, keep any food in the locker room, or in any way question his authority.

He was such a prick that he even disrespected his own league, saying the Saints' Joe Miller's no-hitter against his team earlier in the season wasn't any big deal because the league sucked so bad. "So how come no one else will hire him?" asked Saints manager Marty Scott. "Why did he have to come begging to the Northern League for a job?"

The Saints took two out of three in the league's Alcatraz, squeaking into a first-place tie at 21–20 with Madison. Duluth had fallen apart in the second half and Madison had tied the Saints for first place on the last day of the season, meaning they would play the Saints in the league semifinals (best two out of three) in the coming days.

When I heard the news, I phoned the Most Beloved Woman of the Northern League to congratulate her.

"Who are you going to root for?" she asked.

"I'm rooting for you," I said truthfully. One day she would own her own minor league team, I knew. After the season, I even made plans to meet her at the baseball winter meetings, the annual convention of the front office staffs of all professional teams everywhere, where jobs are offered and everyone gets to see who is doing (or not doing) what and where.

At the winter meetings, Monica would be ogled by hundreds of men who would want to know why she had so many questions about minor league team ownership, fight off the advances of armies of baseball executives high and low, and reemphasize to all that she really wasn't into the major leagues.

"If they want to talk about Christy Mathewson or the major leagues of the dead-ball era, fine," she said. "But I have no interest in Mark McGwire or George Steinbrenner or anything else in the bigs. Baseball is what I love, and real baseball is in the minors."

In Sioux City, Kevin Garner walked into the town's most hopping country-and-western bar and ordered a beer. A few minutes later in walked The Prettiest Girl in Sioux City, Kristen Pfeister. She was not a groupie; she'd just stopped in for a beer with friends from her job crunching numbers for a health insurance group. In any case she had too much self-respect; The Prettiest Girl in Sioux City was too big for Sioux City, she'd decided and was moving to Minneapolis.

And then she looked across the room, and Kevin Garner was looking at her.

12

The Mutt King Returns
for the Coronation

All right, this is it,
The whole season coming down
To just one ball game,
And every mistake will be magnified
And every great play will be magnified,
And it's a tough night for the player,
I'll tell ya.
—Phil Rizzuto, "Hero or the Goat (Part 2)"
  (Yankees pregame show, final game,
  American League Playoff Series, 1976)

The end crowns all.
And that old common arbitrator, Time,
Will one day end it.
—William Shakespeare, *Troilus and Cressida*

September 7, 1996

Word had come back to Mike Veeck that Bill Murray would not be attending the Saints' first playoff series against Madison. He was in Ireland finishing a play and then was supposed to report immediately to London to begin filming *The Man Who Knew Too Much*, directed by the esteemed Jon Amiel, who'd overseen the even more acclaimed *The Singing Detective*.

But Murray had also made it known that if his team made it to the championship round, there was no continent he wouldn't cross to make it back to Midway Stadium. No matter how many film days would be lost or esteemed directors pissed off, he had to see his Saints, even if just for a game. Though as an actor he was a consummate professional, Murray *had* his priorities.

Mike, meantime, wasn't overly worried about the fate of *Veeck as in Wreck,* the filmed bio pic featuring Murray as his father. Signourney Weaver was still on as Mike's mom, and in Hollywood, *Daily Variety* reported that *Veeck as in Wreck* was a go, that it had been green-lighted by the money men. It would begin shooting, the show-biz bible reported, as soon as the screenplay was approved and Bill Murray and Ms. Weaver could coordinate dates.

That could be in a few months or two years; fer chrissakes, it was Hollywood. Veeck, meantime, said what would be would be.

Among Hollywood insiders, the movie seemed to be another typical "fuck you" from Murray. An obscure movie topic among the major ticket-buying audience of young women—Bill Veeck?—it was common knowledge that baseball movies were now out.

Still, the cycle that had begun with *Bull Durham, Major League,* and *Field of Dreams* was showing signs of returning. Ron Shelton, writer/director of *Bull Durham, White Men Can't Jump,* and *Tin Cup,* was finally making another baseball movie. Soon the baseball movie cycle would be back, said the studio, so maybe *Veeck as in Wreck* would sell some popcorn.

It couldn't make any less money than *Kingpin,* which was debuting that summer, where Murray plays a shyster on the bowling circuit out to fleece Woody Harrelson and an Amish bowling prodigy played by Randy Quaid. The small-budget movie, written by real writer and Murray's friend Roy Blount, was hysterically funny, but it died over its first weekend. Saints fans were duly rewarded with hundreds of water bottles shaped like bowling pins with KINGPIN written on them.

They were movie swag, abandoned by the studio when *Kingpin* didn't open as a smash. Yet the very good movie's commercial failure was the fans' delight: it became "*Kingpin* Night" at Midway Stadium, and everybody seemed happy with their free bowling pin.

The championship was in early September; my editors at *Rolling Stone* told me that if Murray came back by then, there was still time to trash him before the World Series. Fuck Bill Murray, they said. We'll fly in a photographer and ambush him. All I would have to do is call the editors and tell them I had him cornered.

All I had to do to drop a dime on Bill Murray was call, said the devil in New York, and $7,500 and an expensive summer of expenses would be mine. Now more than ever, I needed the dough; Visa was starting to treat me like Vegas treats a high roller with an ice-cold hand and empty wallet. No sale.

I talked to *Rolling Stone* several more times, but I didn't make that particular call. I had learned a lot that summer, and weren't the Saints about healing and reformation? For Monica, the Saints' Marty Scott, and heaven's Otis Redding, Roger Maris, Bill Veeck, and Buddy Holly, I would not hatchet Bill Murray.

I'd rather declare bankruptcy, then go to hell.

I was almost positive I wouldn't crack.

On September 4, the first league semifinal game against Madison was played in St. Paul.

It was a crisp and close game, ultimately won by the Saints' biggest stars, the final score 6–4. Glenn Davis hit a bases-loaded double in the fifth inning, allowing St. Paul to rally from a 3–0 deficit, and Jeff Alkire, the team's best starter, went almost eight innings and picked up the win. Then there was closer Paul Romanoli, who led the Northern League in saves this year (19). He got one here too, shutting down the BlackWolf in the ninth inning to end the game.

Monica had accompanied her team to St. Paul, and though she always looked cool in front of every civilian at every ballpark, she now looked as distraught as I'd ever seen her. "It's not fair that St. Paul wins," she said. "We're an expansion team, and we have a *nicer* team."

Now the Saints needed to win only once more against Madison to proceed to the league championship, set to begin on Saturday, September 7. Fargo was beating Winnipeg in the Western playoffs, so it seemed likely that it would be a St. Paul–Fargo final, which meant that Bill Murray would be back.

Should I hatchet him? I wondered again that day, something I hadn't considered in the weeks since I'd last seen the movie star. But then, racing to Madison the next day for the next playoff game with one of the team's announcers, we stopped at a Stuckey's truck stop to pee. I was thinking of Bill Murray when I absentmindedly picked up a copy of *Hoard's Dairyman,* a publication which I learned is to the milk industry what *The Sporting News* is to baseball.

The dairy producer's bible in the dairy state of the nation, the magazine was named after William Hoard, the father of modern dairy farming, who, in the late 1800s, began convincing Wisconsin farmers to switch from growing their failing wheat to doing dairy. Hoard's sayings, it turned out, are often reprinted in *Hoard's Dairyman.* One of his ancient credos reads:

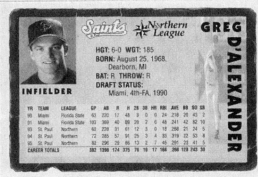

Notice to the help. The rule to be observed at all times toward the cattle, young and old, is that of patience and kindness. Remember, this is the home of mothers. Treat each cow as a mother should be treated.

Hmm. Though Bill Murray wasn't exactly a mother to the Saints, I also knew that to live with myself I couldn't paint him as the motherfucker some magazine editor in New York wanted. Though I sensed the Saints would be out of Madison and into the championship round in hours, I still couldn't make the call for an ambush photographer from New York.

The ultimate fate of the second game of the series, played September 5 in Madison, lay in the ears of Saints manager Marty Scott. Madison's Jim Vatcher hit a two-run home run in the sixth to move the BlackWolf ahead 3–2, but in the next inning, Scott played a trick with the help of Saints left fielder Joe Biernat, a former University of Minnesota star who was right in the middle of his final examinations back in Minneapolis to become a licensed chiropractor.

Greg D'Alexander, the Saints' shortstop, opened the inning with a single, and manager Scott, coaching from third base, flashed the bunt sign to Biernat. Biernat tried once and failed to get bat on ball; the next two pitches from Madison's Michael LaPlante were so far outside that the squared-around outfielder couldn't even try to sacrifice his man to second.

Now, with the count two and one, Scott began eavesdropping on Black Wolf pitching coach Ken Medlock. "Lay one down the middle, Michael!" Scott heard him yell. "*Let* him bunt it!"

Scott immediately changed the sign. "I figured if the pitch was coming right down the middle," Scott said, "I would let Joe hit away." And so he did, and Biernat responded by smacking a double to left-center, starting a rally that put the Saints back in front 4–3.

It was too nerve-racking, and I started walking. Out behind the center field fence, I found the mysterious and vaunted Van Schley, an artist, filmmaker, baseball scout, and godfather in many ways to the Saints, the Black Wolf, and Mike Veeck's rejuvenated career. "I bought a team for a hundred bucks in 1976 at a Hamburger Hamlet in Los Angeles," Schley says, watching the action, his heart torn because one of these two teams would lose. "I got hooked on the scouting and player procurement end of minor league baseball and stayed with it. I have a lot of friends who are scouts, and they will tell me info on players, and once in a while I'll get to sneak in and sign someone."

In time, he hooked up in his minor league journeys with Bill Murray, who he'd originally met while filming a comic documentary short early in the comedian's career.

It was also Schley who acted as the middleman in bringing Mike Veeck back to baseball. Van was the one on the plane with Roland Hemond, a great friend of Bill Veeck's, who told him that Mike had finally cleaned up his act. "We'd just bought the Miami Miracle, so I mentioned Mike's name to Marv, and weeks later he was hired. At our very first game, Bill Murray was there with Jimmy Buffett, both dressed up in Panamanian pimp outfits."

Then came the Northern League in 1993, and the three partners offered Veeck a quarter ownership for the sweat equity of running the team. Schley, Murray, and Goldklang each had another quarter. "Because the Saints and the Northern League are really about recovery and getting a second chance, it's all very American in a positive way," Schley says, as mellow as Malibu, California, where he now lives. "It's very Norman Rockwell, and not at all like the major leagues with their sound bytes and high-tech baloney. I have a nine-year-old daughter who loves the minor leaguers, but thinks all the big leaguers are jerks."

Now, while Van holds on to his Saints stock, he has concentrated this year on helping the expansion Madison team with scouting, signing good players, and getting the team off the ground. "I mostly want the league to do well overall," he says, "which is why I kind of want the Black Wolf to win, even though I own a share of the Saints. Madison is a better story."

But it was not to be. The Saints' John Burgos pitched a complete game, struck out seven, and the team won 5–3 to take the series, two games to none. They were in the league championship with Fargo, which had withheld a late charge from Winnipeg in the play-offs to win their division in three games.

After the game, Monica said, "I feel like someone has just stepped on my face." She went on, "The saddest day of the year, they say, is the last day of the baseball season. This team doesn't exist any-more, because it will be mostly new players next year. Now that it's over, the players will soon act as if each other is dead. They put a protective seal around themselves so they won't get hurt."

And she, the Most Beloved Woman in the Northern League? Does Monica think she's overcome the Northern League consensus at the beginning of the season that she was, above all else, the finest piece of ass on the circuit?

"You know," she said, "a season ticket holder told me yesterday that I'm one of the most beautiful women in the league. I said, 'Thanks,' and he said, 'No, I mean you do something that no one else does . . . you help make baseball fun.' And I thought to myself, 'Gee, so there *is* a difference between me and Dakota Sadie.' I liked that."

From there, for Monica, it was over to a big end-of-the-season party on the wooden deck the Black Wolf had built down the left field line for midgame tipplers. "Some of the people out there at the party will be players, others will be girls who like to watch young guys in tight pants," she said. "I'll be out there having a beer so I don't have to think about the end of the season. I never want the season to end. It reminds me of death, like a love that's gone away for the winter."

She paused. "And then, after the party, I'll go home to my empty apartment in a town that isn't mine, and I'll cry and say, 'Why do you *do* this?' And then, in ten days, I'll remember. I'll recall that this is the right path I'm taking, that there's a reason I'm in baseball and not law school. I think of owning my own team in the minors, and then I think of Christy Mathewson, and what he meant, and how I someday want a son named Christy. And then I'm okay."

I kissed her . . . good-bye? And I said, "Thank you." And then I drove home to Minnesota, smiling as broadly as I had in a few years.

The Northern League championship series (three out of five) would begin in St. Paul for two games, then move to Fargo for as many days as necessary for a team to win the necessary third. Bill Murray, from whatever part of the planet he was now inhabiting, would be in Midway Stadium for Game 1.

It's September 7, and Bill Murray reclines against the fence just a few paces from the plate and shouts his usual pregame insults at Fargo manager Doug Simunic. "Hey, fatso," he says when Simunic steps out of his dugout, "you ever heard of a situp?"

"Hey, Bill, nice to see you," Simunic says, the mere appearance of his belly on the field causing the Saints' crowd to erupt in boos. "You're meat, meat," Murray says, dramatically shooing away the enemy manager (who he actually kind of likes).

It is Game 1, and Murray, wearing a gray Saints cap and assorted team attire, cuts through the home dugout to the locker room to hang out with his players, where he is most comfortable of all. The team, relaxed as you can be while wearing a game face, looks ready. Murray, ever-respectful of the players in their office, looks around for a way to be helpful. Centering on an empty watercooler next to the showers, he picks up a large new jug and manhandles it into place.

He then begins kibbitzing with the players, who are milling about in the locker room until the game begins in a few minutes. "Can I see your stick?" he asks Glenn Davis, who duly hands over his bat to the comedian.

"Sure, Bill," says Davis, who then hands Murray a ball and asks him to sign it "for my wife." When he's done with the autograph, Murray takes a few cuts with Davis's lumber. "No wonder you're so good, man," he tells Glenn. "You've got the bat!"

He then turns to catcher Hector Villanueva. "Hector," Murray says, "why don't you use this bat?"

Villanueva looks up and shakes his head. "My bat needs a little more head," the chunky former major leaguer says. Murray nods his head. "Who wouldn't like to have a little more head in his life?"

The locker room cracks up, and someone asks Murray to do a riff as one of his crazed characters: Carl Spackle, the greenskeeper in *Caddyshack*. Murray nods and begins an extemporaneous rap about the game, the Saints, and the Northern League championship that has the entire team howling. Whatever pregame tension hung over the locker room has been dissipated; the co-owner and official "team psychologist" has done his job.

Twig then enters the locker room from the dugout and walks past Murray with a wave and a quick handshake. The coach, who has seen everything, sees Murray, smiles, and simply says, "Hi, Bill, funny man. Glad you made it. Terrific!"

Murray then remembers that any second he is once again supposed to throw out the ceremonial first ball of the game, an orb that would be delivered to him on the mound by a parachutist now hovering in a plane circling Midway Stadium. "I've got to seriously warm up before I do that," Murray says, feeling his arm. "Hey, Glenn, can I borrow your glove?"

"Sure," says Davis, handing it over.

"You sure you can handle a first baseman's mitt?" the ancient Twig tweaks Murray, something no other man on earth could do with impunity.

"Sure, Twig," Murray says, looking mock-hurt, "it's me!"

Asking Villanueva to play catch with him out in left field to warm up, Murray then runs out of the dugout to the screams of the crowd. I run up next to him, counting on the fact that he is living in clockless star time and that he isn't quite consciously aware that the game can't start without him. Meantime, everyone in the ballpark waits, clapping and shouting, "Bill! Bill! Bill!" as he winds up and sends a ball Villanueva's way.

He wishes, he says, that his acting schedule hadn't been so hectic this summer that he had to miss so many of the season's best moments. "Wherever I am, I try to keep up with what's happening with the team," he says. "Sometimes I'm a week behind, but I get the news. Wasn't that hysterical about Marty Scott and Simunic, the two *managers* for God's sake, sumo wrestling each other? That kind of thing should happen in major league baseball, but it couldn't. It's too different and weird and new for them. But that kind of thing was just what any fan would have wanted—a 'Let's settle this outside' type of thing. In independent baseball, it was *possible*, it was *spectacular*."

Murray continues to limber up, and the plane bearing the parachutist with the ceremonial first baseball continues to fly circles around the ballpark. As Murray tosses the ball back and forth to Hector in left field, he continues to play back the entire Saints season.

"Darryl Strawberry leaving the team and going to the Yankees and having success was a great story. Jack Morris leaving the team and disappearing was a big story. The no-hitter Joe Miller threw was a great story. That Madison, an expansion team, could make the playoffs was a great story that Van Schley should get more credit for, just like he should get more credit for getting me, Mike, and Marv together to put together baseball teams. I couldn't get this crazy over an indoor game, or football, or hoops."

Murray is on a roll and continues to seem unaware that 6,329 rabid fans, two teams, three umpires, several reporters, and a parachutist above Midway Stadium await him. "The litmus test we all have before we do a promotion is 'Is this fun?' " he says. "We're not Rotarians, so if someone has an idea that sounds like we ourselves would enjoy or laugh at, we try it. It's like the Saints' slogan: 'Fun Is Good.' Well, fun *is* good. I don't think anyone necessarily knows why humans want to laugh, but we do. It's something we need, and I have no idea why that is. The people who work for the Saints and this league understand the fun and entertainment quotient—and if it isn't fun, it doesn't work right."

Murray, still trying to limber up, windmills his arm like a pitcher from the 1920s. "The major leagues have completely lost touch with that notion of fun and laughter," he says. "And though I might say, 'I'd like to take these ideas of entertaining people at the ballpark by buying the New York Yankees,' it's not feasible, and not just because I don't have a quarter of a billion dollars. No one's asked me to get involved with any major league team, so me saying, 'I'd like to own the Yankees' is the same as me saying, 'I'd like to be the Queen of England.' "

Thwunk. The ball cracks into Murray's hand. Hector is throwing hard. I suggest to Murray the unremarkable notion that his life in showbiz is necessarily filled with the slickness of Hollywood, and here at the ballpark he can live in an unslick world. With this he takes umbrage and flashes a scowl at me, the dark side I'd been warned about but hadn't seen all season. The look quickly disappears as he tosses a rainbow to Villanueva.

"I don't know if my life is slick or not," he says. Still, he describes the simplicity of minor league baseball compared to the horrors of Hollywood. "I do know that there's a different attitude in showbiz than to baseball," he says. "There's an attitude here among the players, but it's one of 'I can get this guy, I can get this guy out, I can hit this guy, I can help win this game.' It's pressure, but a different kind of pressure."

A few feet away in right field, Annie Huidekoper of the Saints' front office is waiting patiently to tell Murray that it might be nice if he stopped warming up and made his way to the mound so the championship could begin. "They want you to ham it up while the parachutist is coming down," Annie tells Murray.

"God bless the skydivers, and God bless the work they do," says Murray with a laugh as he runs to the mound to the strains of "Wooly Bully" in the voice of Richard Nixon.

The plane circles and drops its man, who lands a few feet away from Murray. Accepting a baseball, Murray then throws it over the backstop and right into the open window of the Saints' press box. He runs off the field into the owners' box, and the crowd starts cheering as the Saints run onto the field.

"See?" Murray says, listening to the roar, realizing his work is done that day, that all the handclaps will be for the players. "It's a very nice feeling as an entertainer to be entertained. I can enjoy myself without having to do anything. So why do I come? Because here they're not clapping for me."

Chris Powell of Fargo steps up to the plate to start the game, and Murray is amazed. "That guy looks just like Sean Penn. Maybe that guy *is* Sean Penn."

No, he's isn't. But owning a minor league team has become hip; Jimmy Buffett owns a piece of the Madison team, and Heather Locklear has purchased shares in a low-down minor league team herself. When I point this out, Murray just shakes his head like I'm one more dopey reporter who just doesn't get that this isn't about being cool.

"I *know* Jimmy Buffett," Murray says, "and he just likes baseball. He was down in Florida and came to our first game when he had the Miami Miracle. I don't think Jimmy Buffett thinks about hipness. He's a musician who's sold a quarter of a billion records, while Heather Locklear has been on twenty-five TV shows and is a rock babe known across the world. I don't think she relies on her team for hipness. It's a release, a relief from that higher profile. It's a higher, decompressed sort of fun, a refuge."

A refuge? From what? From himself, as my editors would like me to write? Murray ponders the question and gives an answer similar to the one he gave in July when I first met him, when I was still determined to do him in. "This is a refuge," Murray says, "because we're the home team. People don't mess with you when you've got home-field advantage. This is home, where it's always safer."

The game starts badly as Saints starter Joe Miller is rocked for four quick runs in the first inning and is yanked. Murray wanders into the dugout to console the disconsolate Miller, then quickly edges back out.

Murray is now deeply into the game. Sitting on a futon a few feet from home plate, he rises when Fargo DH Darryl Motley, a member of the 1986 Kansas City Royals, comes to the plate. Stepping over a table bearing peanuts and beer, he begins whispering loud enough for Motley to hear a few feet away.

"Darryl, it's Bill," Murray says with the stage monotone of a hypnotist. "Join our side. Don't swing. Join our side. You'll be happy with us." Motley flies out, and Murray steps back onto the futon.

Slowly the Saints begin edging back from their 4–0 deficit. St. Paul's Kevin Dattola, a power-hitting outfielder picked up from Winnipeg in the second half of the season, steps to the plate and Murray whispers a secret. "Fargo doesn't know, but Dattola has got a separated shoulder," he says. "The guy is insane—he doesn't want to be taken out because it's the championship series. He can't even make the throw from the outfield, but we don't want Fargo to know."

Dattola then fouls off seven balls in a row, wincing each time as wood meets horsehide. Murray winces with him. "I don't have a favorite player," he says. "They are all my children. My favorites on the team are Twig, Marty Scott, and Ray Korn. I sympathize with the adults in charge."

I nodded and left him alone for a little while. I'd volunteered again with the Saints to do the sumo wrestling gag between innings. Still angry that I'd gone down swinging against the FX producer who'd refused to fight earlier in the season, I allowed myself to be zippered in one more time. Introduced as "St. Paul," I was cheered on the field, while the man dubbed "Minneapolis" bounced up and down on the mat to boos and awaited what I promised him aloud would be another stupid, illogical charge.

Sadly, he knew the secret, and as I punched him two, three, then four times, he stepped to the side, never tossing a blow, waiting for my own weighted suit to bring me to the ground. It did. But I was pleased. Once again the Jew had proven himself worthy in combat.

"That was pathetic!" Bill Murray said, reprising to me what he'd said when I thought I'd manfully lost the sumo contest. Murray shakes his head, much less than impressed, and goes to Mike Veeck, who is sitting alone, biting his fingernails at the gate separating the owners from the dugout.

As usual, they say nothing to each other and watch the Saints battle back to 4–3. I'd ripped tickets next to Mike at the turnstiles that day, seen him greet fans and shake hands and throw out one-liners as if he were the happiest man in the ballpark. He was—nothing makes Mike more happy than being there to bring the fans into the tent. But during the game, he remains eerily quiet.

Fargo went ahead 5–3 in the third, and Bill Murray seemed to be the only one in the stadium not nervous.

"Hey, Mr. Murray!" shouts a fan above. "Can I shake your hand?"

"Well, since you called me 'Mr. Murray,' okay," the movie star says, reaching up to grasp palms.

"Hey, Bill!" a young man in his twenties then yells down. "It's my mom's birthday today. Will you come up and sing her 'Happy Birthday'?"

Murray considers the request. "I'd rather shove a piece of cake in her mouth," he tells the guy. "Where is she? Get a piece of cake, and you can get a picture of her nose in the frosting. And then I'll buy her a bratwurst."

"All right!" says the kid, hurrying off for supplies.

I keep trying to goad Murray, my instincts as a hatchet man forcing me to ask questions I don't want to write or print the answers to. One key to the craft is to get the subject sounding bitter; turning the key with Murray, I'd discovered, was as easy as bringing up the topic of no-nothing reporters.

"What about the players down here?" I ask Murray, lobbing a softball. "You seem to have so much fun goofing around with them."

"It's more fun to hang out with these players than major leaguers," Murray said, "and I think it's because of all the media attention up in the big leagues. The players have more space at this level. I don't think fans know how annoying sports reporters and radio guys are."

He pauses. "These reporters are completely unenlightened about the game. They're no smarter than any drunken fan who comes up to them in a bar, but because of their zealousness they got their gig, and now they can ask every dumb question of the players. So the players, surrounded by these morons after every game, have to bear with any guy with a tape recorder. If you're a major league player, you can't just tell these fifteen guys at once, 'I hit a home run.' You have to tell each of them what you hit, what you were looking for, what it all *means*, and all that—over and over."

Murray takes a breath. "When I see that, I think, 'Give it a break.'

It takes a little joy out of their accomplishments when major leaguers have to replay entire games via these stupid questions."

And *you*, Mr. Murray, I ask, setting him up for a story that I could still get in the magazine before the World Series—if I lost my soul. I wouldn't, I was almost positive, but why can he be such a tough guy around reporters' tape recorders? "If someone asks me a dumb question," he says, "I'm free to just say, 'You know the answer; answer it yourself.' I don't have to explain everything. This year, with those goofy cameras all over me here, all I have to say is: 'This is about the players, not me.'"

And then came some sweetness, which of course I would leave out of the article. Indeed, there are major leaguers he brings up several times as major influences in his life. He talks of Ernie Banks of the Chicago Cubs, again. And then, he continues, there is the recent saga of Stan "the Man" Musial of the St. Louis Cardinals, now in his mid-seventies, who he met while filming *Larger Than Life*, another funny Murray movie gone in the flick of an eye this summer. It was a movie where Murray played a sleazy, low-rent Tony Robbins-type motivational speaker who inherits an elephant from a dead uncle and must transport it across the country to get the money due him.

"We were in St. Louis," Murray recounts, "and we got a phone call from Stan Musial, who asked if he could come by the set. 'Well,' I thought, 'He's "the Man," he can do whatever he wants.' So he came down and we fed him breakfast. I loved the story of this great athlete—how he'd been this fantastic pitcher who hurt his arm early on, then turned everything around by becoming one of baseball's all-time best hitters.

"After we had our eggs, I said, 'Stan, old man, it's time for you to ride the elephant.' He said okay, climbed on my back, and all I could think about was that I'd be lynched in St. Louis if Stan the Man should fall off and hurt himself. But he made it up on the elephant, and I have the photos."

Murray, it turned out, could still be stagestruck. "But the main thing that made this especially charming," he says, "was how delightful this superstar was. Here was a guy who'd truly been to the other side, for good and bad. He'd seen the happiness and liked it and brought some of it back for all who were fortunate enough to meet him. Too bad, though, that I always hated the Cardinals."

With that begins the excruciating opening beats of "The Macarena" from the PA. Murray immediately begins the dance, not missing a step. "I learned this in a bar late one night," he says. "It's the over-forty version of 'the Macarena.'"

When it's over, he slinks out on the field and into the Saints' dugout as the "Saturday Night Live" character from the seventies he invented called "the roadie." It is his expert impersonation of a too-cool instrument technician at a rock concert, running onstage like a turtle to fix a microphone, pretending he doesn't want to be seen, when, in fact, he wants *everybody* to see him with the rock & roll superstar.

"Jerry Aldini [the sleazy A&R guy from Polysutra Records] was one of my favorite characters from the show," Murrays says, "but I always loved 'the roadie.'"

It is a role he plays well with the Saints, helping out with manual labor in the locker room, cheering with vigor from feet away as his charges come to bat or take the field.

After Miller got shellacked in the first, Country Stewart, his eyebrow and pubic hair not yet fully grown back from his birthday bacchanal, was called in to take over. Stewart pitched an effective six and two-thirds innings while the Saints tried to catch up. They did, 5–5 in the fifth inning, but in the top of the eighth the RedHawks took a 6–5 lead. Runners were now on first and second with two out, when the Sean Penn look-alike, Fargo leadoff man Chris Powell, hit a sharp single to right off Saints pitcher John Burgos.

Out in right field, Joe Biernat charged the ball to try and save the game. It was Saturday, and Biernat had only gotten an hour and a half of sleep after finishing a nine-hour chiropractor test the day before. He picked up the ball and nailed a perfect strike to catch Hector Villanueva, who tagged the RedHawks' Matt Rundels out. "Every time there's a runner on second, you think about making that throw," Biernat said. "I just tried to throw it as hard and accurate as I could."

True, television replays would later show that Rundels had touched home before the tag. But what the hell. This was baseball.

Bill Murray was beside himself that his team had fought back to come so close. But looking at his watch, he realized that the plane he was supposed to catch back to London and his movie star life was due to leave in minutes. The game was running way long and he wasn't supposed to be anywhere near America, let alone St. Paul in the first place. But despite being needed that second in London for a movie, he wasn't about to run out on his team when they were down by a run coming into the bottom of the eighth inning.

Murray walked over to pitching coach Ray Korn and told him of the problem. Emergency phone calls were then made to the Minneapolis–St. Paul International Airport, which agreed to hold Murray's plane, and to the St. Paul police, who arranged for an escort of prowl cars to take him to the airport with sirens screeching. Celebrity has its privileges.

Murray mentions none of this, simply that it breaks his heart that he can't stay the whole series and see the Saints win the championship. He'd made it to Winnipeg when the Saints had won an earlier Northern League title, but his new set in London, commanded by a director Murray respected, had no interest in the outcome of the championship series between St. Paul and Fargo.

"We won the championship our first year with Grey's Harbor, Washington," Murray says from about twenty years later. "The team got its trophy in a local doughnut shop. The whole team was sitting there with the doughnuts, waiting for the trophy to show up. Finally it came, and everyone touched and rubbed it a few times. Then it was *bang*—the season was over—and twenty-five guys immediately headed for the bus station to head in twenty-five different directions."

And then Murray said the exact same thing Monica had said to me a few days before when the Saints had eliminated the Black Wolf for the year. "The saddest day of the year," he said, "is the last day of the baseball season."

That would be today for Murray, but not the Saints. In the bottom of the eighth, trailing by a run, Biernat started the inning with a double to center. Within minutes, Glenn Davis, already having gone three for three that night, stroked a two-run double to put the Saints ahead 7–6.

Burgos got the last outs, and the Saints had won the white-knuckler opener, an exhausting, mentally excruciating game. The contest, said widely respected *Saint Paul Pioneer Press* staff writer Mike Augustin, the beat writer who'd seen almost every pitch since the St. Paul Saints came into existence, was the finest championship series game ever played in the Northern League.

Nevertheless, things got literally ugly a few minutes after the game. Fargo manager Doug Simunic came out of his dugout with his shirt off, belly protuberant, screaming toward the Saints' dugout that his team had no hot water for showers. Murray, packing up to go, heard the yells and went to get Marty Scott.

And then Murray was gone, surrounded by police cars. "Send me my ring!" were his last words. But no one knew where to send the ring if the Saints, indeed, prevailed.

The next game, September 8, was a blowout, with the Saints kicking Fargo's ass 12–2, taking a 5–0 lead after only two innings. It was the last game of the season at Midway—the last three games of the championship were scheduled for Fargo. The fans of St. Paul, denied for so long, stood and cheered for fifteen minutes as their team lingered on the field to wave good-bye. Signing autographs, they all promised to bring back the trophy to the city that has had almost zero to cheer about since Walter O'Malley fucked Brooklyn by moving their Dodgers and dropping the original St. Paul Saints as a farm team.

As the crowd cleared out, looking back over their shoulders for one last look at the ballpark, I stopped by Sister Roz's massage table. I'd been almost embarrassed to see her ever since I had sobbed about my broken heart and how much I hated baseball earlier in the season. I had told no one else on the scene but the seventy-four-year-old nun of my assorted ills, and she hadn't brought them up once whenever we'd pass each other in the ballpark.

"Have a good winter, Sister," I said, about to walk past. "Any plans?"

The elderly sister hugged me, as she hugs everyone she comes in contact with. "I'm making a pilgrimage to India to see Mother Teresa," she said in the North Dakota voice that sounded uncannily like a female version of Lawrence Welk. "And you? Have you been healing since we last talked?"

"Sure, Sister Roz," I said, inviting her to accompany me to Vince's final postgame barbecue and beer bash out in the Saints' parking lot. "In a minute," she said. "First I want to give you a minute of massage."

Unwilling to deal with the bad karma of fending off a nun, I put my head through the hole in her massage table. Suddenly her strong hands were upon my neck and Sister Roz was taking my psychological temperature through the feelings in her fingers. "You're having fun again," she said. "You know once more what it feels like to be happy and appreciate all the beautiful things God has laid before you: a beautiful day, a wonderful baseball game, the kindness of strangers."

"Yes," I said, "you're right."

Sister Roz drew pause, however, as she worked her magic fingers down my back and around my ribs. "But you are still hurting down here. Your heart is still broken by something that happened to you before you ever came here."

I said nothing, rising off Sister Rosalind's table, realizing the truth (again) of her pronouncements. "C'mon, Sister," I finally said, helping her fold up her shop. "Let's go get that beer."

The Saints, up two games to none in the series, still had to win one game in Fargo, never a sure thing. The bus ride that night was quiet all the way up to North Dakota and the usual Comfort Inn.

The game was as good as Game 1. Both ex-Olympian Jeff Alkire, the Saints' best starter, and the RedHawks' Jeff Bittiger, the winningest pitcher in minor league history, pitched eight and two-thirds innings of tense, terrific ball.

As the middle innings went on, with Bittiger meeting Alkire pitch for pitch in a tie game, the Fargo fans looked upon the field as if it were some sort of gladiatorial contest between good and evil. They'd been made fun of by so many people for so long that their team represented what seemed like their first hope of redemption in years. Never mind that Doug Simunic, their beloved manager, was booed in every other park in the league; every time he walked to the mound in Fargo, the PA blasted "Hail to the Chief."

Around the seventh inning, I decided to watch the end of the game up on the scoreboard in left field with Hillory, the junior sign girl with the pierced nose. I climbed the ladder to the catwalk where Hillory sat amid neat piles of numbers from 1 to 9 and explained that Sadie, her best friend, the righteous pal who'd gotten her this job, was too sick to attend the most important game of the year.

So Hillory, twenty, was stuck up there alone with her walkie-talkie. "I like it up here because you have the best seat in the house and nobody's bugging you," Hillory said. The attendant fame in Fargo, however, she found disconcerting. "It's weird when strangers who know you from the ballpark come up and say, 'Hi, Hillory, I saw you on the scoreboard last night.' Everybody says hello, which makes me feel strange, because I don't like to be in the spotlight."

It all began when Sadie got her a gig as the woman who walked around the ring announcing the next round with signs at a local boxing match. The RedHawks then signed up the local cutie to do her walk up the foul line and then hang the numeral signs on the scoreboard.

"Sadie was here first, so she told me what to do," says Hillory. "It's pretty easy. Sometimes I'll get really into a game and forget to

GAME #3
CHAMPIONSHIP SERIES @ FARGO
St. Paul Saints   Date 9/9/96

#				#			
1	FLEMING	2B		1	POWELL	CF	①②③
2	SOLOMON	RF	④⑤⑥	2	AKERS	3B SS	②
3	LEARY	1B	①②	3	TRAXLER	1B	①
4	DAVIS	DH		4	MOTLEY	DH	
5	VILLANUEVA	C		5	KNOTT / MANWAL	3B SS	①②
6	DATTOLA	CF	①②	6	IATAROLA	LF	①②
7	ROBBINS	SS	①②	7	RUNDELS	RF	
8	D'ALEXANDER	3B		8	COSTE	C	
9	BIERNAT	LF	③	9	MIGITA	2B	
PITCHERS	~~ATLURE~~ ROMANOLI	P			~~BITFIGER~~ ALAZAUS	P	

EXTRA MEN

LH	RH	LH	RH
LIEDER	MCNALLY CANNADAY		~~MANWAL~~

SWITCH HITTERS

PITCHERS

LH	RH	LH	RH
~~ROMANOLI~~ MILLER	MANFRED THOMSON LETOURNEAU	~~ALAZAUS~~	LUKAS

put up the numbers, but they'll remind me with this," she says, pointing to her walkie-talkie. "And sometimes I've hung up the wrong number. It happens, and even if the walkie-talkie goes out, somebody from the press box can run over and tell me the other scores around the league."

There is only one thing about her job she doesn't particularly like. "I feel dumb doing that walk at the beginning of the game," she says of her amble up the sidelines immediately before each contest with a 1 sign held high over her head and the crowd going nuts.

Hillory excuses herself to hang up some more numbers on the scoreboard, but says it's fine if I stay up there with her to watch the end of the game. It was the most peaceful landing spot, offering the best view, that I'd enjoyed all season.

It was 3–3 with two out and nobody on in the top of the ninth when the Saints' Joe Biernat lofted a routine can of corn toward RedHawk third baseman Johnny Knott, one of Fargo's best and most-liked players. It looked like the inning was over, with the RedHawks up. Knott drifted back, put up his glove—and crumpled to the ground as the ball hit him squarely in the right eye, Charlie Brown-style.

It was horrible but great, and Biernat ended up at second base. Knott's eye was bruised black and soon swollen shut, and he was taken out of the game to a stadium of silence. Carlton Fleming, the Saints' next batter, tried to bunt and missed. Marty Scott, coaching at third, waved Fleming toward him and said, "What are you doing? Do you want Sol [Steve Solomon, the next batter] to be the hero instead of you?"

Fleming got the point, hitting Bittiger's next pitch into the right field gap that center fielder Chris Powell just barely missed. It was a triple, the Saints were ahead 4–3 going into the bottom of the ninth, and all looked well.

Not so fast. Fargo set the table during their last at-bat, but they were unable to put the tying run across. Paul Romanoli closed out the game for the Saints by getting Chad Akers to fly to left.

The Saints rushed out of the visitors' dugout like a riptide while the Fargo fans filed out of their beautiful stadium as if at the end of a funeral. Hillory arose silently from her seat on the scoreboard and began stacking her numbers into nine neat piles. "Oh well," she said, "it was a nice season."

Would she be back? "If Sadie comes," she said, "yes. Like I said, I can live with, but don't really like, walking up the foul line with the sign. But I've come to love baseball, just sitting up here removed from the planet."

Down on the field, Glenn Davis, three-time ex-major league All-Star, doused his corpulent manager Marty Scott, a former executive with the Texas Rangers, with the requisite Gatorade, just as if they were still in the big time.

"Even if I'd gotten picked up by a major league organization, I would have insisted on staying with the Saints through the championship," said Davis, who besides his many RBIs and record number of grand slams, was perhaps best remembered on the team for hog-tying Country Stewart with belts in a Fargo motel for his twenty-first birthday.

Once the Saints were showered, they were taken by team bus to the best bar in Fargo, cleared out for the occasion, all expenses on Mike Veeck. One of the heroes of the final championship game didn't go to the party: he preferred to have sex back at the motel with one of the same groupies who'd last followed the team up to Thunder Bay. The rest of the team, it seemed, made the party.

There was joy, real rapture, as the broke players, none of whom had yet been offered a contract by a major league organization, got sloshed in honor of their championship on somebody else's dime. Carried away with the joy and wanting to see as many happy faces as possible, I jumped over the bar and began serving shots and beer with the bartenders so I could get a load of every happy, loaded smile.

"He's a pushy Jew," my Evil Twin said at that point to Libby Veeck, Mike's wife. Libby told me and said I wasn't. I edged up to my Evil Twin and simply said something about him being a *shanda* for the goyim. It was Yiddish for "motherfucker" and he knew it.

Marty Scott, the devout Southern Baptist who himself wasn't above saying "motherfucker" when the dugout-related occasion demanded, slowly sipped a beer with a look that was part relieved parent, part proud grandfather. It had been a wicked season.

There were twenty-two Saints players when the team won the championship; only eleven had been there at the start of the team's spring training. Those who made it the entire year got a $400 check for winning it all, while those who came for half the year got $200.

Such movement among players in the Northern League was common because immediate victories, not player development, was the aim of this league. Fuck up once more on the field or in the club-house, it was understood everywhere around the league, and it was up and out, your name on the GON' FISHIN' wall located in every team's locker room from Thunder Bay to Sioux City.

The team had had a remarkable series of ups and downs this year: Darryl Strawberry had left the team on July 4, playing in only twenty-nine games but hitting 18 home runs for a Saints' single-season record. Jack Morris, a bastard to the end, had turned down the offer tendered by the New York Yankees and disappeared on July 19. By the end of the month, Glenn Davis was at Midway from Japan with his bats, cheroots, and stock portfolios. In August, Joe Miller, an outfielder making his first start ever, threw a no-hitter. The Saints were as popular as ever, having dawn 267,099 for the season, the highest of any minor league short-season team in the country.

Yet there had been shitty times too. The team has blown major leads in both of the season's two halves, having to win the last two games of each half-season to win their semititles. They lost season series to both Fargo and Madison; Fargo, at 53–31, had a season-long record that was eight and a half games better than the Saints'. And, most galling to Saints fans, Doug Simunic was named Manager of the Year in ceremonies held minutes after St. Paul beat him for the championship in his own ballyard.

But the Saints were the champs, so fuck 'em. It was the end of the season, and as soon as the team bus got back to St. Paul, the team would disperse forever. Pouring beer down each other's throats in Fargo, they didn't want to go home.

But Catherine Whyte, the FX minicam operator and punk rocker from the Minneapolis College of Art and Design, had been looking forward to the last day of the season more than anyone. It was time to nab the Saints' Jason McNally, and she didn't care if he wasn't the sharpest tool in the shed or he couldn't be shown to her friends at a punk rock concert. He was handsome and nice and sort of a gentleman. He liked that she always wore biker boots to Midway Stadium and that she never, ever, got any sun on her alabaster rock & roll face.

He was also a *second*-string ballplayer, I pointed out to Catherine, trying to fake-dissuade her. And worse than that, I continued, he was a *catcher*. Guys named Yogi were catchers, and even other ball-players called their protective gear "the tools of ignorance."

But she didn't care. She boarded the team bus and scoped out where McNally was sitting. Soon the rest of the players were on the bus too, out of Fargo, and back home in the middle of the night.

Bottles of Bourbon and cases of beer began appearing, and some

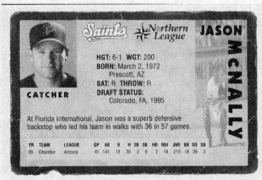

players talked about what was next. "If I don't get picked up, I'll use my Stanford degree to help me get some financial job," said Steve Solomon. A few sheepishly said that if they didn't get picked up by a major league organization, they were going home to live with their parents and sort out their lives.

After an hour, small puddles of vomit obstructed two patches of the bus's aisle, but I was safe back in the 'hood with Chuck Jackson, Kevin Dattola, and Hector Villanueva. Hector said he would probably head immediately back down to Mexico to play winter ball or maybe Europe. Good offers kept coming in for the former major league catcher who made several hundred thousand dollars a year as a worldwide baseball soldier of fortune.

Yet he was a little tired, Hector said, of the baseball life. He then took out pictures of his wife and kids at home in Puerto Rico. "But I have to make them a living. Pretty good, hunh?" he said, pointing out furniture and faces in the photo. "That's my own house, a hundred percent clear." In the foreground, his beaming family stood before furniture fully encased in plastic. It looked pretty good, indeed.

"Hector," I said to the man with the biggest butt and smile in the league, "what is the answer again to women?" Villanueva put away the pictures and stroked his belly like a Buddha. "Okay, remember this," the thirty-one-year-old said. "If the pussy gives you singles, go back to her the next night. If the pussy gives you home runs, marry her and make babies. Maybe get some sons."

Got it. The team howled, then it was quiet for the last 100 miles of the middle of the night trip. As heads bobbed in sleep, up front Catherine Whyte was sitting next to Jason McNally. Twice she turned around to give me the high sign. When the team bus hit the Midway Stadium parking lot, they took off for McNally's room at the nearby Holiday Inn.

For St. Paul, the Saints' victory lifted the anonymous city's spirit for days. St. Paul gave the team a parade, and Mayor Norm Coleman sat on the back of the convertible with Mike Veeck. Coleman, a potential candidate to be Minnesota's next governor, had been born in Brooklyn when the Dodgers and their original St. Paul Saints were still around. Now he speechified for the citizens of the Twin Cities' Brooklyn.

"The Saints have given us back the game we love," he told the crowd. "Every orchestra needs a maestro, and Mike [Veeck] is the maestro of the Saints. He is a St. Paul treasure, and the Saints are one of our assets." City council president Dave Thune then took out a proclamation designating the day, Wednesday, September 11, as "St. Paul All-Saints Day." Always forgotten as the other Twin City, St. Paul was, at least for a day, the headline.

But the best remarks were saved for Garrison Keillor in *Time* magazine.

In St. Paul, America's fifty-seventh largest city, we have our own ballpark, next to the railroad tracks south of the State Fair Grounds, where our baseball team, the Saints, plays against teams from Duluth, Sioux Falls, Sioux City, Fargo-Moorhead, Madison, and Thunder Bay. We wave at the trains as they go by, and we always have a good time, regardless of what happens on the field. Between innings, a man walks up to the home plate ump, leading a pig with a bag of fresh baseballs on its back. Once, a player from an opposing team was offended by the pig and turned to the umpire and said, "That is so bush league," and the ump said, "This *is* the bush league."

In St. Paul, America's fifty-seventh-largest city, we're all right with that. Nobody who sits near me at the ballpark seems to feel personally diminished by living in a minor league city. We do not consider ourselves fundamentally so different from Duluthites or Sioux Fallsians of Fargo-Moorheaders. We

all eat the same brand of corn flakes, and one size fits all.
However, in Minneapolis, the forty-second-largest American
city, there are people who imagine it to be the "Manhattan of
the Midwest," "the Paris of the Prairie." This is embarrassing
to us St. Paulites, like knowing a small man with a bad toupee
who thinks he's Tom Cruise. What can you say to him, other
than "Stop that."

Keillor was right. A lifelong Minneapolis snob, even during those
crazy eighties in New York when I made my living doing dirty work
for Jann Wenner and smoking my body weight in marijuana. However, this summer, as I crossed the Mississippi each day into St. Paul
and Midway Stadium, I looked at the niceness and decency of St.
Paul like some quaint Glocca Morra. It wasn't until the end of the
season that I learned how to get to the airport from St. Paul or even
got a St. Paul phone book.

True, the town could break your heart. My ex-wife grew up in
St. Paul, went to an exclusive prep school there that F. Scott Fitzgerald attended, and then went to a liberal arts college in town that is
famous for its rich kids wearing Birkenstocks. "In high school, she
had been a skating cheerleader for the Minnesota North Stars," I
said, like I was telling a joke, when my friends would ask me why
I'd married "the Baddest Girl in the Twin Cities." "I had to marry
her," I would continue. "She gave me her North Starlettes satin
jacket, with her name stitched in white above the green and white
logo. How can you *not* marry a woman who gives you her Northstar-
lettes skating cheerleader jacket?" I would ask.

Men I told this to nodded their heads and understood. Women
friends shook their heads and muttered under their breaths about
"tits and hair" and "pathetic men."

Outside of that, I loved St. Paul.

But the end of the baseball season in St. Paul didn't really end
until the saga of Darryl Strawberry and his return to the major
leagues was complete. It had begun with Yankee general manager
Bob Watson, who never wanted Darryl, calling him in for a chat.
"We had a nice little heart-to-heart," said the Yankee GM when the
season was almost over. "We set up ground rules. I'm not going to
get into what they were. But he did what we hoped he would do."

Catherine Whyte did fuck reserve catcher Jason McNally once,
as she'd planned, on the last night of the baseball season. In the

morning, the phone rang in his Holiday Inn room. Jason was out of the room getting some ice, so Catherine picked up the phone and said hello to Jason's full-time girlfriend in Florida, who as she understood it looked like an astronauts' wife or prom queen or something.

The girlfriend asked for Jason, then hung up on Catherine. Catherine, meantime, began looking for her clothes. When Jason walked back in, she said, "See you later, alligator." She told me later that she had marveled as she pulled on her motorcycle boots that she, no slut at all, had actually slept with a *baseball* player.

13

Strawberry Fields Forever

FIRST WITCH: *When shall we three meet again*
In thunder, lightning, or in rain?
SECOND WITCH: *When the hurlyburly's done,*
When the battle's lost and won.
—William Shakespeare, *Macbeth*

July–October, 1996

Darryl Strawberry, the reborn New York Yankee, mentioned his
stint with the St. Paul Saints every base hit of the way for the rest
of the year. His was to become a classic Gotham comeback and
success story, as the Yankees went on to win the World Series that
year, often via a well-timed Strawberry blow, or miracle of miracles,
a *catch* (finally, after years of indifference, he'd been working every
day with Yankees coach Jose Cardenal on his fielding).

In modest St. Paul, his was the rise of the phoenix. In cynical
New York, he'd become breathing proof that sometimes you can go
home again.

On paper, what he did for the rest of the regular major league
season was hit .262, with 11 homers and 36 RBIs, in 63 games. But
his presence meant more than statistics or the last stand of the man
who other major leaguers still watched taking batting practice before
every game to see Strawberry, with his still beautiful, looping swing,
hit balls into the highest decks of every stadium.

"Strawberry made the Yankees look smart," wrote sportswriters
John Harper and Bob Klapish in *Champions*, the story of the Yan-

kees' year. "In just one swing," they went on, he could "recapture his crown as New York's most charismatic player."

While watching Darryl on television with friends, I would melodramatically look closely up and down the Yankees' bench to see if he had a new Cigarette Boy, saying I had to know if he'd left me behind for someone flashier who had better menthols in the big city that used to be my own. I saw no one, even though I'd been told by reliable sources that Darryl still puffed away in the locker room.

It wasn't the thirty-six-year-old legs that Darryl had damned on the Saints' bus rides to play the Thunder Bay Whiskey Jacks that eventually let him down, it was a broken toe. Still, he labored on, an infamous slacker who had been alchemized into a true gamer. In the Yankees' American League Championship Series against Baltimore, he hit three homers in two games, a record he tied with Seattle's Jay Buhner. He also set a series record of slugging percentage in a five-game series (1.167).

He had dodged a suicidal bullet days before during the American League Divisional Series with Texas. With Saints manager Marty Scott as his guest at Yankee Stadium, things hadn't started so sweetly for Darryl that October week. He went oh for five in the first two games, with one contest's action limited to one failed at-bat.

Yankees manager Joe Torre responded by not playing Strawberry at all in the next two games. It felt to Darryl like a sick replay of last season, when former Yankees manager Buck Showalter had refused to play Strawberry in the postseason. This led to a string of events in Darryl's life and attitude that had him cast as a major league pariah who was worthy only of playing for an independent minor league team like the St. Paul Saints.

After the fourth game of the Texas series, Charysse Strawberry ran into Marty Scott coming into the Yankee's clubhouse to say hi to Darryl. She told him that Darryl wanted Marty's opinion: Should he speak up to his manager Joe Torre and ask for more playing time? It would have been a classic Darryl move from the old days, questioning his manager's authority. "I told them both," Scott later said, " 'Don't say anything to Joe. Things change in baseball. Not just in a season, but in a night. In a few days, you could be a hero of this thing.' "

Darryl agreed to keep quiet, left tickets for Marty in Texas, and played the final two games, hitting three home runs and leading his team into the World Series against the heavily favored Atlanta Braves. In the Series, he kindled or kept several rallies going and fielded the outfield not like a man with a broken toe, but like a player who had finally learned what a mitt was for.

In Game 5, he banged into the wall to snare a bomb that saved the Yankees' 1–0 lead; in Game 6, he opened the game with a belly-sliding catch to start off the Yankees' clinch of the World Series. Afterward, when the team had won the game 3–2 and the Series four games to two, Strawberry joyful and sober, led the team's victory lap around the sides of Yankee Stadium. Not far away on the field with the celebrating team was co-owner Marv Goldklang of the Saints, the man who'd convinced George Steinbrenner to give the Straw one final chance. It had worked: Strawberry had come full circle from the cranky, selfish, speed freak who'd help make the 1986 New York Mets one of the meanest world champion teams in recent memory.

As the Yankee locker room filled up with players spraying each other and guzzling champagne, Strawberry quietly sipped a juice. The party would last in the clubhouse until the wee hours, but Strawberry, still tested for drugs, kept away from the mass.

Every reporter who came his way wanted to know about Darryl's curious and quick redemption from baseball Hades, so Strawberry talked over and over about St. Paul. In *The New York Times,* baseball writer Claire Smith recounted how Strawberry, not so long before in "desperate straits," eventually "found himself in an independent Northern League, playing for St. Paul, light-years away from the major leagues."

Once he got to New York, Smith wrote, "Strawberry still retained his penchant for impeccable timing, especially in the postseason. Then there was his leadership, something the Mets, Dodgers, and Giants never were able to tap into."

Smith continued: "Perhaps the latter quality could only be found once Strawberry hit bottom, in a forgiving hamlet on the edge of oblivion. 'I'll never forget St. Paul,' Strawberry said."

In St. Paul, "a forgiving hamlet," Strawberry's victory in New York was viewed as its own. "It all happened just like I predicted in the middle of the season, when everybody said Darryl wasn't going anywhere," Mike Veeck said. "I knew he'd go up and that every time Darryl Strawberry hit a home run or started a rally for the New York Yankees, he was doing it for all of us who have screwed up our lives and tried to get it all back one more time."

After the season, Darryl went, as promised, to Dallas to visit Marty Scott, stay at his house, and attend a Cowboys game with his former

Saints manager. "He was a father figure to me," Strawberry said later, and not just because of the lecture Scott had given him his first day of practice in St. Paul about how he would be expected to behave with the Saints.

"Now I'm forty-two and he's thirty-six, so I tell him that I'm his older brother," Scott says. Meantime, Strawberry demanded that even though he had just won a World Series ring, he still wanted his ring for being a part of the Northern League champs.

Another Saint to keep in touch with Darryl was Dave Stevens, the three-foot-two-inch legless ESPN producer and second baseman who'd played in St. Paul during training camp and the exhibition season, becoming during that time Strawberry's best friend on the squad. "It was more than just the fact that I helped keep the media away from him by focusing them on me," said Stevens. "We just both understood what it meant when everyone says you're a freak, and all you want to do is play ball."

The national press, meantime, remained focused on the St. Paul connection that got Strawberry on the straight, magical road back to the World Series. "If playing in St. Paul was the cost," wrote *USA Today* sports columnist Deron Snyder, "Strawberry says it was well worth the price. Even when the phone wasn't ringing. 'Sometimes it's good when nobody wants you,' he says."

It had felt just that way to me before, when I'd conducted my very first interview ever with a Saints official, general manager Bill Fanning. It was the morning after I last went out with the woman who would soon be my ex-wife. After she'd signed the appropriate papers at my lawyer's office, we dressed up, went to one of Minneapolis's best restaurants, and I glumly tried to make sense of how I ever thought I could change the ways of the Baddest Girl in the Twin Cities.

In the middle of dinner, just as she was making some remark about which of the wedding presents she wanted to keep, I bit through the bridge that held my front four fake teeth together (a childhood bike accident had left me looking, without a bridge, like a fifties hockey player who'd taken one too many pucks to the mouth).

Sitting at the table, I mistakenly gulped, swallowing my bridge. My front four teeth were gone, my marriage had been destroyed—and tomorrow I had to conduct an interview with Bill Fanning with the smile of a character on "Hee Haw."

As I did that first interview the next morning, I held my hand over my lips as if I was trying to keep myself from telling a secret.

Fanning, who himself had thrown away a promising career in banking in order to run the day-to-day operations of the team, somehow didn't notice, or didn't care, that he was being interviewed by a reporter missing part of his mouth. If he had, according to the baseball credo of always touching raw nerves, he would have made fun of me for it for years. Instead, he told his story, of how making money working in a bank doesn't matter much if what you really want to do is work for a baseball team.

Still, it made sense that Fanning was the money man of the team. "What's good about my job is that I get credit for everybody else in the office's good work," said Mike Veeck after the season ended. "It was the same thing my dad would always say—his staff would come up with all the good ideas, and he'd get the credit, or the blame. Even though I cooked up 'Disco Demolition Night' for him with the White Sox, Dad took the rap."

Fanning would take no rap. Unlike general managers in the big leagues, minor league general managers are not involved directly in player personnel. Instead, they coordinate ad rates and season ticket renewals and oversee all aspects of pre- and postseason ticket sales. He controls budgets and number crunching; other Fanning jobs included counting how many boxes of baseballs the team was using up and giving each player who'd been cut by Marty Scott his final paycheck and a one-way ticket home. In the process, he'd helped the Saints become one of the most profitable minor league teams in the country.

"Does it ever feel weird to be the Mr. Bad Guy who tells them their career is over?" I asked Fanning this year.

"Somebody has to give the bad news in baseball, and I guess it's my job," he said. "But I don't feel like Mr. Bad Guy, and I don't like thinking of myself that way."

In any case, he had his own distractions and problems. Fanning had six kids, including triplets born in the middle of last season. His wife, Donna, who'd moved around the country with Bill so he could chase his dream of working in baseball, took care of a lot of the kid work. Still, she found time to research and begin writing on the history of toilets through the ages. "It keeps me sane," she said, and the pieces she showed me of her tome were really quite good.

Over the hideous St. Paul winter, Fanning would be in charge of the office. In the meantime, Mike was taking off with his wife, Libby, and daughter, Rebecca, for six months to try and rejuvenate the

Charleston River Dogs, a long-pathetic team that Marv Goldklang had bought a few years before.

Working baseball in Charleston had never been easy. In pitcher Jim Brosnan's *The Long Season,* his classic 1960 insider account of being a ballplayer, he remembered his time as a bush leaguer in Charleston. "The mosquitos alone would discourage patrons, not counting the heat, gnats, and segregation."

But Charleston back then had a new positive-thinking owner, Brosnan recounted. "But there is no accounting the mind of a baseball fan, and a minor league owner has to be fanatic," he wrote, "if not about segregation, then why not baseball?"

Times had changed, but the team still stank—and Marv wanted Mike to rejuvenate the still-unloved River Dogs just as he'd given rebirth to the St. Paul Saints.

"Marv and I have been together seven or eight years," Mike said, "and though we don't keep score, he has done a great deal for me. When he asked for help in Charleston, it was the first time I heard him cast about a little."

He also wanted to be back near Maryland, where he'd grown up with his beloved parents and eight siblings. He'd never gone back, but his youngest brother, Chris, had died the year before, and, as they say in recovery-happy Minnesota, he now wanted to do some "family of origin work." Mike, never one to join any club that would have him as a member, said he simply needed to search out his roots.

"Chris had lost a daughter shortly before he died," Veeck said, "and I've never gotten over it. I'm still deeply troubled by it."

Mike wouldn't abandon St. Paul, however, promising to be back in time for Opening Day at Midway Stadium to rip tickets and talk baseball with the fans. The Saints, after all, were still the flagship of the Murray–Goldklang–Schley–Veeck minor league empire.

Already, Mike had ideas for next year's Saints team. Aware that he couldn't repeat the miracle of Darryl Strawberry, he instead began thinking about something his father Bill had always wanted but had never been able to do: find a credible woman to become the first nonmale professional roster player. At the moment, his best bet seemed Lefty Schueler, a relief pitcher and the daughter of Chicago White Six general manager Ron Schueler.

But he had to be sure he had the right woman, who could keep up enough with the men of the Northern League so the Saints wouldn't be vilified for pulling the lowest of stunts. Over the winter, Mike would cogitate and see what his informal network of scouts came up with for a credible woman ballplayer, just as his father had done.

By the middle of winter, Saints hitting coach Barry Moss was telling Mike of a young woman pitcher name Ila Borders, the first female to receive a college scholarship to play on a men's team. She could throw the ball, Moss reported, a respectable eighty miles per hour. Veeck cogitated some more.

He also decided that next year the team would broadcast its radio games via the team of Jim Lucas and Don Wardlow. Wardlow, the only blind color baseball announcer in history, had gotten his first job from Mike in 1990, when nobody else in baseball responded to the 176 letters he and Lucas sent out to teams. Lucas, of course, would take care of the play-by-play.

And Wardlow, missing one sense, could beautifully describe the smell, sounds, and atmosphere of a game. He had even called an inning and a half of a major league game in 1993. Working on-air with Braille cards filled with statistics and trivia, led around by a Seeing Eye dog named Gizmo to do his incisive interviews with players, Wardlow would definitely not be looked upon as a stunt.

For the next six months, meantime, Mike put Fanning in charge of the St. Paul office. Fanning, along with Twig, would take up some of the two hundred speeches Mike did while promoting the Saints around Minnesota every year. Veeck would keep his splendiferous house overlooking St. Paul's Irving Park. There, only a few feet inside, hung the large oil painting of his father in his prime that for decades had hung in Miller's Pub in Chicago, site of some of Bill Veeck's longest, most happy bull sessions with local sportswriters, baseball fans, and anybody who wanted to come by to see the ashtray built into his wooden leg. "Mike truly communes with that picture," says his wife, Libby, of the painting.

The picture would stay right there until Mike and Libby got back from Charleston in the spring, but like his father, Veeck has an incurable case of wanderlust. After winning the world championship with the Cleveland Indians in 1948, Bill Veeck sold the team in 1949, not to emerge until a couple of years later as the owner of the St. Louis Browns, the worst team in the majors, where Mike literally grew up in an apartment situated under Sportsman's Park in St. Louis. "Mike always keeps a bag packed and in the car so he can just pick up and go in a second," says Libby. "But we'll be back. St. Paul is our own little fairy tale."

Mike was running errands the day I stopped by his house to visit with Libby. She was famous at Midway Stadium for her colorful collection of funky hats; she'd also gotten the team involved in the local culture scene by joining the board of St. Paul's Minnesota Art Museum.

Life hadn't always been so easy. She'd met Mike soon after he'd hit bottom in Florida. In fact, he had just been given his first baseball job in years by Marv Goldklang. The Miami Miracle was far from popular, yet Libby tuned in the games each day for a respite from her own troubles. She too, she says now, was near bottom. "I'd been renting my house," she remembers, "and the renters had trashed it and not paid rent. I was going to lose my house, and coming from your typical dysfunctional family, I figured I'd just be one of those struggling people all my life."

And then she heard Mike come on the radio in the middle of a Miracle game and she was entranced by his voice and sense of humor. "I started going over to the ballpark," Libby remembers, "where the games became a kind of healing thing for me too. I finally met Mike at the ballpark, and I'd sit there with him. It was fascinating to talk to a man who believed that work could be fun. He was very charming, and he taught me both baseball and how it can *change* people."

Still, there were problems with the team. The Miracle, averaging only forty fans a game, were forced to move to Pompano Beach, where Veeck's promotions got the average up to a still-paltry seven hundred. "Five years ago, we couldn't pay our bills," Libby says, "and Mike was very sad. He'd done a good job of trying to destroy himself because he felt shut out of baseball, because no one for all those years would return his calls or letters. He had a lot of pain and confusion when he started in Miami, because he couldn't sell anything there. He was scared to death, even when we moved up to Pompano."

Personally, though, things were looking up. "We dated for four months," Libby recalls, "and then, six months later, we decided to have a child. It was all pretty bohemian, and we both loved it. We got married not long after." By then, she goes on, she'd "realized I'd married a man who was not only so loyal to Marv Goldklang, Bill Murray, and the memory of Bill Veeck, but to me. He is the most loyal man I've ever met."

Was there a side of Mike people didn't know? "He's loaded with insecurity, like a comedian," says Libby. "He's that way with me, and he gets nervous every time he gives one of his hundreds of speeches. Maybe that's why he's always asking, 'what would my father do in this situation?' "

And then came St. Paul and Mike's big chance: a sweat equity stake in his own team. "No one had any idea if the Saints would work," Libby says, "but if the magic hadn't happened the way it did, Mike would have figured something to make it happen. But it was a wonderful dream here from the beginning. I didn't know baseball or who Bill Veeck was until I met Mike, but it wasn't until St. Paul that I truly understood how it could heal more than people, but entire towns. Baseball can change people, and I love how the team gave St. Paul some hope because before the Saints, the town really had nothing it felt proud about. Mike helped give the city back to itself, just like he's trying to do in Butte, Montana, or now, Charleston, South Carolina."

His hope, however, remains the major leagues. "Mike's dream is really to run the New York Yankees. He's not kidding," she said. "Here's a man who nobody in baseball would talk to for years—and then this spring the Florida Marlins asked him to come work for them. He was very torn because of his dream to make it back to the big leagues. But it wasn't quite right, and he felt his job wasn't yet done in St. Paul. He also knew I was panicked about having to become a corporate baseball wife."

And so he stayed.

Some of the Saints' losses over the off-season, however, would be permanent. Annie Huidekoper, who'd been in charge of promotions and community relations since the Saints' first season, was finally ready to quit the best job she'd ever had. She'd sat at a desk next to Mike for years, controlling the dysfunctional Saints family, her mellow yin complementing his sometimes fiery yang. Now, after too many summers of twenty hour days, Annie was finally fried. She resigned.

She had been brilliant at getting them into the tent with such promotions as "the Minitron" (a nineteen-inch TV on top of an outfield wall showing replays to the couple of people in Midway Stadium who could see it). She'd come up with the "rally train" atop the Saints' dugout; threw "Mary Tyler Moore Night," where fans all tossed their caps in the air in honor of the Minnesota icon; oversaw the sumo contests; and even looked after the Amazing Jeffo, a blind, not completely untalented magician who Mike had hired to perform at a few games because . . . why not? Was Houdini any good when he started—and he could see!

More than that, however, Annie was the heart, both public and private, of the team. She did everything from booking the singers who warbled "The Star-Spangled Banner" before the game to breaking up fistfights in the stands between smokers and nonsmokers, to arranging speaking engagements for Twig. After Mike, she was Bill Murray's closest friend on the team, and they rewarded her diligence with a slice of the Butte Copper Kings, the minor league team the gang had purchased the previous year. Her dreams had been about being in baseball ever since she'd served as an eleven-year-old bat girl for her father's local Little League team, and she'd made it farther, and better, than even she could ever have imagined. Now, making a 180° turn in her life, she took a job with a St. Paul holistic health center called Holly House.

Tom Whaley, however, the team's operations manager and attorney, would stay, helping Fanning to keep the wheels moving until Mike got back in the spring. "Annie and I were the chief misfits when we both got into this," Whaley remembered. "We weren't conventional by minor league standards, but Mike always stuck with us."

Indeed, looking at Whaley ripping tickets at the turnstiles before each game that year, it was impossible to believe by looking at the thirty-three-year-old that he was anything but an escapee from the state prison or a member of an outlaw motorcycle gang. With a Fu Manchu mustache, a case of perma-stubble, and wraparound omnipresent shades, he looked more like a desperado than the legal man in the Saints' organization, as well as the man who helped Fanning keep a close eye on the bottom line and negotiate deals.

Whaley had started with the Saints from the beginning, throwing away his own private law practice to help run the carny. True, he also played guitar in the popular local rock band Tarwater and could talk for hours about Kurt Cobain or Bob Dylan or the future of rock & roll. But he was also a master of disguise who could go from scruffy-looking ticket ripper to a shaven, suit-and-tied lawyer with horn-rim glasses, a wife, and two small children within minutes. Like all the Saints employees, he was supposed to do everything: that year the team attorney had even been charged at the last second with the important task of finding the St. Bernard that Bill Murray would ride onto the field while doing his imitation of the loathsome Marge Schott. Whaley found one, just in time.

"Like I said, we were all misfits," Whaley said during the off-season. "I was dying to get out of my regular litigation practice, so when I heard St. Paul was getting a minor league baseball team, I wrote Mike a letter out of the blue. He also purchased a piece of lutefisk, the disgusting-tasting salted fish that is one of the symbols of Scandinavian Minnesota.

"I got some frozen lutefisk," Whaley recalls, "wrote my résumé on the back of it, and sent it off to Mike with a letter saying, 'This is what people in Minnesota eat.' I knew it was risky and absurd, but I had to take the chance. My dad had a stroke at fifty-four; he was a successful lawyer and, *boom*, he went down. That killed me and was the reason I wanted to work here. I realized there was no tomorrow, and if you wait around to chase your dream, it ain't going to happen. Do it now or hold your peace."

Magically, Mike wrote Whaley back. "I hate attorneys," Mike wrote, "but you seem like a Renaissance attorney, which intrigues me. We've got a thing going in the Northern League, so call me and I can show you how to ruin your life."

Whaley called, got the legal job and the massive pay cut, and set up shop in the Saints' original office, which was composed entirely of two phones and some card table chairs. Now he too is part owner of the Butte Copper Kings and has come to know both Mike and Murray up close.

"They barely talk to each other, but they really respect what the other is doing," Whaley says. "Mike is fascinated by the bedlam that happens when Bill Murray just walks around in public. And I think a lot of people out there think that Bill's seeming attitude of 'I don't give a fuck about Hollywood' is bitterness. But it's not. He worked for his freedom from that showbiz bull, and he loves the fact that ordinary people come up to him here and say hi. When he's in town, he'll come into the Saints' office in the morning, sit down, and just read the paper like a regular guy. But the pressure can't always be easy for him. That's why I tell Mike that if you have a choice between being rich and being famous, take rich."

And the team that's grown under him? "The Saints aren't the major leagues," he says, "but we're not quite the minor leagues either. It's this nirvana place, an otherworldly home for guys nobody wants. Like Dave." Whaley laughs as he points out a man in his early forties scurrying around the office like his pants are on fire. "He was the biggest misfit of all."

Dave Wright
Courtesy of Bonnie Butler

 Dave Wright, the past season's Saints radio announcer and forever most teased staffer, lets me into his "Northern League car" and we begin driving. We're headed to a restaurant in Stillwater, Minnesota, a bucolic town on the St. Croix River that is the current home to the Minnesota state prison, Jessica Lange, and Sam Shepard. The point of the long drive is so that Dave can play me parts of his massive collection of tapes of radio announcers that he studies for inspiration while driving.

"Growing up in Detroit, I wanted to be a baseball player," he says, "but I was terrible, so I decided my dream was to become a baseball announcer. My hero was Ernie Harwell, the voice of the Tigers, who I used to listen to on a radio under my pillow at the military school I had to go to when my mother could no longer take care of all us four boys. I'm sure it must have broken her heart to send us away."

It sounds like a hellacious childhood, but Dave isn't whining. His father, a chronic alcoholic, was institutionalized when Dave was small. "I guess now they'd put him in treatment, but back then they just locked alcoholics away," he says. "So I moved in with my Aunt Ida, and at age six went to a military boarding school with a little barracks bed. Most of that time I've buried; I'm sure those are my demons."

Dave pauses, looking for the right tapes. "My only regret the first night I broadcast a game for the Saints was that my mom, Aunt Ida, and Uncle Cletus would have been proud. I think of them often."

There are more current heartbreaks in Dave's life. A lifelong bachelor, Dave had shocked the Saints earlier in the year by suddenly getting married, wisely, to a woman who cared nothing about baseball. But his marriage had fallen apart as fast as mine, and I now imagined myself growing old and alone, an old-style bachelor like Dave or Mike Augustin, the beloved Saints' beat reporter who'd hit his fifties without a wife, but with plenty of time to attend small college football games. I shivered as Dave mentioned his estranged wife and matters of the heart, especially when he said, "As I'm sure you'll understand."

Dave tosses in a recording made by the Tigers' longtime Hall of Fame announcer Ernie Harwell about the meaning of baseball called *The Game for All Seasons*. A reverent speech also enshrined in the Hall, Harwell expressed the kind of sentiments that would have gagged me the previous summer when I hated baseball and its hagiographers, be they George Will, Ernie Harwell, or French historian Jacques "Whoever wants to know the heart and mind of America had better learn baseball" Barzun.

Now, however, Harwell's words seemed oddly soothing:

Baseball is a ballet without music. Drama without words. A carnival without kewpie dolls. Baseball is continuity. Pitch to pitch. Inning to inning. Season to season.

"A lot of people tell me I have a radio voice," Dave says, annotating Harwell's commentary like an opera buff pointing out solos and notes of distinction as the work plays on in the background. "But I'm a product of my environment, so I have to be careful not to imitate Ernie."

Dave then played through some classics; the New York Giants' announcer Russ Hodges calling Bobby Thomson's "Shot Heard Round the World," then a rare recording of the Brooklyn Dodgers' announcer Red Barber calling the same play.

He then tossed in a tape of Waite Hoyt, the great Yankee pitcher who played with Babe Ruth and later became the voice of the Cincinnati Reds. "There was a rain delay one day in the fifties," Dave said, "and Hoyt, to kill time, just started telling old baseball stories he'd seen and heard over his half-century in baseball. He was so good that someone made an album of that broadcast. I've managed to get a copy of it on tape."

And then, as a treat for me, Dave threw in a recording of another of his favorites, Dodgers' announcer Vin Scully calling a perfect game thrown by Sandy Koufax in 1965 against the Chicago Cubs. "Scully always mentions the time, which I like," Dave said as he fast-forwarded to the last inning of the perfect game.

Unrehearsed, Scully seemed to be making literature as he described that last half inning:

Three times in his sensational career has Sandy Koufax walked out to the mound to pitch a fateful ninth when he turned in a no-hitter. But tonight, September 9, 1965, he made the toughest walk of his career, I'm sure, because through eight innings he has pitched a perfect game. He has struck out eleven, has retired twenty-four consecutive batters.

And the first man he will look at is Chris Krug—big right-handed hitter—flied to center, grounded to short. . . . And you can almost taste the pressure now. Koufax lifted his cap, ran his fingers through his black hair, and pulled the cap back down, fussing at the bill. Krug must feel it too, as he backs out, puts it back on, and steps back up to the plate. . . . There are twenty-nine thousand people in the ballpark and a million butterflies. . . . A lot of people in the ballpark now are starting to see the pitches with their hearts.

Two and two the count to Chris Krug . . . Sandy reading signs. Into his windup, fastball got him swinging! Sandy Koufax has struck out twelve. He is two outs away from a perfect game. Here is Joe Amalfitano to pinch-hit for Don Kessinger. . . . I would think that the mound at Dodger Stadium right now is the loneliest place in the world. . . . The strike-two pitch to Joe: fastball, swung on and missed, strike three.

He is one out away from the promised land, and [pinch hitter] Harvey Kuenn is coming up. . . . Into his windup, and the two and one pitch to Kuenn: swung on and missed, strike two. It is 9:46 P.M. Two and two to Harvey Kuenn—one strike away. Sandy into his windup. Here's the pitch: *swung on and missed, a perfect game!* [Long wait as crowd noise takes over]

On the scoreboard in right field it is 9:46 P.M. in the City of the Angels, Los Angeles, California, and a crowd of 29,139 just sitting in to see the only pitcher in baseball history to hurl four no-hit, no-run games. He has done it four straight years, and now he capped it: on his fourth no-hitter, he made it a perfect game.

And Sandy Koufax, whose name will always remind you of strikeouts, did it with a flourish. He struck out the last six consecutive batters. So, when he wrote his name in capital letters in the record book, the "K" stands out even more than the "o-u-f-a-x."

I was almost moved to tears by Scully's extemporaneous artistry. "I try to be as precise on the air as Scully," Dave says, "saying to the radio audience where the outfielders are, whether they're standing four or five steps to the left, or whatever. Even if they're blind, listeners will know where they are."

Unfortunately for Dave, a blind man will be one of the two people replacing him in the broadcast booth next year. "Mike said he'd give me two years as the announcer, and then I'd have to go back full-time to being the Saints' PR guy," he says sadly. "Mike tells me my voice is too high, and I said, 'Al Michaels's voice is high.' Then he tells me to take voice lessons, which I did and still do. He also said that Marv Goldklang didn't like my voice."

Maybe, just maybe, Mike would give Dave a second chance at Charleston with the River Dogs. In the meantime, we drive on to Stillwater, listening to old tapes of forgotten announcers, two old-style bachelors, not saying a word to each other about baseball, or brief-lived marriages to women named Francine or Sasha.

I thought 1996 would be all. Spiking my own story, I should have been done. But in the days and months following the Saints' championship, I realized my real reason for crossing the Mississippi to St. Paul wasn't over. I'd discovered the team to be my Lourdes, yet I wasn't wholly healed; somehow I remained damaged goods. I needed to stay around another season, and the Saints executives said okay. For them, the baseball season never ends, and it's amazing how much access a reporter can get when he brings muffins and coffee every morning.

"Baseball's time is seamless and invisible," the *New Yorker's* Roger Angell once wrote, and "since baseball time is measured only in outs, all you have to do is succeed utterly; keep hitting, keep the rally alive, and you have defeated time. You remain forever young." He was writing about the players, but the Saints 1996 Northern

League champs had scattered forever, back to school, work, their parents' basements, or in the case of Darryl Strawberry the World Series. So I took Angell's words to include the lay fan, i.e. me.

So I had rallied—I was over *her,* and I laughed and kept telling my "Peggy Lee marriage" joke whenever men in Minneapolis and St. Paul whose aortas she'd previously ripped out came up, turning from cool cats to sheep, offering their amazement at how I'd tamed the Baddest Girl in the Twin Cities. There were other perverse congratulations, as if I were a rodeo cowboy who'd gone the longest with the most dangerous bronco before getting tossed.

But I had been tossed, and though I was over *her,* I wasn't over *it.* I was never going to let anyone get so close again, no matter how much the 1996 Saints and the Northern League had heartened me with their comebacks, personalities and championships.

And, during the off-season, things were picking up all over. I got hired for good money for honest projects, paid off my credit cards, and now sent in my rent with a check, not the contents of my couch. I replaced the foul-ball shattered windshield of my rust and already battered 1991 "Northern League Car," and subscribed to *Consumer Reports* for their recommendations of new, full size, don't-fuck-with-me automobiles. I knew I could never be Christy Mathewson, but if he were alive, I'm sure he'd buy a Jeep Cherokee. Sold, to the putz headed to Oz looking for a Scarecrow's heart!

But something was still wrong. In the off-season I re-read Bill Veeck's two amazing autobiographies, which I'd long before turned into Nostradamus-like texts of prophecy, an interpretation as crazy as sending a midget to bat for the St. Louis Browns. Now, I went through them again.

Bill Veeck liked to say that his first wife, the circus performer, enjoyed more than anything in life riding side-saddle through rings of fire. I'd known someone like that. Bill Veeck's divorce came through in 1948, he detailed, shortly before his Cleveland Indians won the World Championship. Then, after he rode in the lead convertible in Cleveland's ticker-tape parade in honor of what he'd done, Bill Veeck went home alone.

"Do you know what the saddest thing in the world is?" he wrote. "To go home to an empty apartment in a moment of triumph. Triumph has no flavor unless it can be shared. I thought of my lost marriage. I had never been more lonely in my life."

Me too. As ballplayers would put it, lonely "as fuck all."

Haunted, I saw a vision of me sitting alone in a nicotine-stained smoking jacket, drinking vodka from the bottle, listening on the kind of stereo equipment *Playboy* recommends, to long ago tapes of Vin Scully and Ernie Harwell that had been sent to me for Christmas by Dave Wright, his wife, children and grandchildren. No. This can't be.

I needed to comeback. And besides, there would be a whole new group of players, including rumors of the arrival to the Saints of the first woman, supposedly a legitimate player, ever to pitch in a men's professional baseball league. And besides, I had to hear what a blind baseball announcer sounded like.

So as long as I kept the doughnuts coming into the Midway Stadium office, and even if I didn't, I could hang around all season and try to find the answer to this, a more critical problem than the one I solved last year inside the minor league carnival.

Also, just in case I was invaded by the body snatchers, I could always still butcher Bill Murray for *Rolling Stone*. If I quit dicking around and came through from my end, I was assured by the magazine, there was still the entire next season to run it.

PART TWO

The Season of First Chances

14

1997: First and Only Chances

A toiber hot gehert, vi a shtumer hot dertsailt, az a blinder hot gezen, vi a krumer iz gelofen.
A deaf man heard how a mute told that a blind man saw a cripple run.
—Anonymous folk tale

Winter, 1996–97

And with the sweet light of a new season as reigning league champions came ill news to the Saints, that of the untimely death of its beloved icon, Tobias. This pig was more than just pork, more than just the Saints' mascot who brought baseballs to the Northern League umpires, more than just the mammal Bill Murray talked playoffs with. Tobias was also the very symbol of the Saints' inspired looniness, the healing power of laughter, and a sign of pride for St. Paul.

It was December and cold when Tobias—mighty Tobias—dropped dead on the farm of his owner, trainer and handler Dennis Hauth. Hauth was disconsolate over the loss of his by then thousand-pound pig that Saints fans had watched grow up; it had been announced over the PA last season that when the inevitable day came for Tobias to retire, Hauth had already promised not to sell the beloved porker for bacon, but would instead ship him to Israel, where the laws of Kosher would hopefully keep him safe. "I mean it," Hauth teased me last year. "You got any relatives over there can take care of a big pig?"

And now he was dead. "I don't think Tobias felt any pain," said Hauth, still suffering as the new season began. That pig had style, I

agreed; even though he weighed half a ton, he was a sharp dresser. Tobias, whether running to an umpire in a tuxedo cut for a pig or a ballerina's tutu topped by a queen's tiara, was the king. But as Karl Wallenda said after three of his family were killed falling off a high wire, "We bury the dead, and then the show would go on."

Dennis, luckily, long worried about succession, had been grooming a piglet as the king's heir apparent. The tiny new ball pig was named Hamlet, and he would be prematurely pressed into service as soon as the season started. Hamlet, making his first rounds of the stadium, impressed the Saints' employees who'd gathered to check out the new mascot.

To be honest, some secretly said that sainted Tobias had been getting too disgusting and obese; Hauth frequently had to hose him off on the field between innings. Hamlet, on the other hand, was small and cuddly and, as S. J. Perelman would have written, "button-cute."

Hamlet's debut would signal a year of other unexpected beginnings on the Saints and for me. If last year saw an army of last chancers, 1997 would see a season of unprecedented introductions. If 1996 was about the past, this would be the summer of the future. Besides the untested pig, Mike would hire a blind game announcer, the first in baseball history. Also along for the ride would be the first woman to ever make the roster of a men's professional team. And making his pro debut would be one of the best young players in America, who had just turned down millions of dollars from the Philadelphia Phillies, preferring to play for bupkes with the Saints until the Phillies threw in several million more.

Mike wanted that theme for the 1997 Saints; like his father, Mike also enjoyed giving players their first-and-only shots as much as he did their last-and-final ones. "People thought Dad was crazy when he signed old Satchel Paige at the age of forty-two (most thought him years older) to pitch in the majors in 1948. Paige then helped Dad's team win the world championship," Mike said during the off-season. "He gave Satchel his one and only chance at his dream of striking out major league stars. You still have dreams, whether you're at the end of the line or the beginning of it. This year there are going to be more new beginnings."

In any case, he knew he couldn't repeat last year's magic, when ancient Darryl Strawberry and Jack Morris had turned from wax memories into winners. Still, for several weeks, Mike seriously toyed with the idea of giving another notorious ex-major leaguer one last chance in 1997. Over the winter, he'd negotiated with Steve Howe, the relief pitcher late of the New York Yankees. Howe was a gifted left-hander who'd been an All-American at Michigan, who had won the Rookie of the Year Award in 1980 with the Los Angeles Dodgers, and who also won and saved a game for the Dodgers in the 1981 World Series. But despite such a promising start, his career read more like a police blotter than a sheet of baseball statistics. He'd been suspended seven times from baseball for cocaine- or alcohol-related abuse and had at various times been arrested for drug and weapons violations. Now thirty-nine, his number had run out last year soon after he was cut by the New York Yankees, for whom he had been an erratic relief pitcher, when he tried to board a plane with a loaded handgun.

I gasped when I read in the paper that the Saints were in serious negotiations with Howe. Twelve years before, in between his early suspensions, I'd followed the then-personable, manic Howe for *Rolling Stone* when he played for the San Jose Bees, an "outlaw" team made up largely of drug addicts and head cases thrown out of the major leagues. I, new to the magazine and eager to please Jann Wenner with a wild story, caricatured Howe and the Bees' team owner Harry Steve like I'd done no other before or since. I'd felt guilty for years about that, but was also fearful of ever running into the volatile Howe again. Friendly and funny with me and other reporters a dozen years ago, he'd since been burned in print so often

that he sullenly refused to speak to any writers during his final years
with the Yankees.

Mike and Marty Scott kept talking to Howe, and finally Mike
decided to pass. Howe was too risky, even for the man who'd given
Darryl Strawberry his last chance. Instead, Howe ended up signing
with the Sioux Falls Canaries. I gasped again, because the Canaries'
owner was none other then Harry Stavrenos, the same man I'd ridiculed when his name was Harry Steve and he owned the San Jose
Bees. As the 1997 season neared, I was determined to stay away from
Howe and Stavrenos, both of whom, I figured, had good reason to
dismember me in person for what I had done to them in print.

Lucky for me, Howe wouldn't have fit into the 1997 Saints. Anyway, this was a year of designated beginnings, not endings, although
really every year in the Northern League was about beginnings. Each
season starts over, last year's players replaced by a new group of
faces unwilling to take off their jerseys, give it up, and go home
forever. Mike loved that challenge of trying to build a dynasty, even
though he gave Marty almost all player personnel decisions.

And last year's championship team? Just as Mike had predicted,
Steve Solomon had had the best chance to catch on with a major
league organization. Solomon had been inches from signing with the
expansion Arizona Diamondbacks organization, when the general
manager of that team questioned him about the St. Paul Saints.

Solomon apparently dissed Mike and the team, went the rumors;
sadly the general manager of the Diamondbacks was Roland Hemond, Mike's old friend (and Bill Veeck's former general manager
with the Chicago White Sox), whose recommendation had helped
Mike get back into baseball.

Oops. Hemond apparently called Mike, and Solomon was not
signed after all. And so, at twenty-six, the Stanford graduate finally
cashed it in and became a stockbroker. You *putz*, Solomon. You
could have been a Jewish center fielder, but instead the player who
read *The Wall Street Journal* on the team bus hadn't learned enough
to keep his mouth shut.

No one else on the Saints was signed either, though the Northern
League as a whole placed several players after the season in major
league organizations. Still, for proof that the Northern League
worked, St. Paul could point to several Saints playing in the majors
in 1996. In the coming season, the new Saints would continue chanting the mantra, exactly like the St. Paul team before them, of those
who'd made the Show after playing in St. Paul. Besides Strawberry

with the Yankees, there was still the Gumby-like shortstop Rey Ordoñez of the Mets, Dan Peltier of the San Francisco Giants, who made
the majors after batting .366 for the Saints in 1995. Also still counted
were former Saint Doug Dascenzo, who made the Show with the
San Diego Padres in time for the 1997 stretch run, and pitcher Mike
Mimbs, who continued to be embarrassed about his time in St. Paul
and doesn't like to talk about them. By 1998, Kevin Millar, Saints
class of '93, would make his major league debut with the Florida
Marlins.

Despite the Saints' championship, reliever Romeo Paul Ramanoli
was the only St. Paul player to make the Northern League postseason
All-Star team. Bill Fanning won General Manager of the Year, but
Mike remained steamed at the beginning of the new season because
Fargo's Doug Simunic, not his own Marty Scott, had won Manager
of the Year. "What Marty did with this team [in 1996]," Veeck said,
"was a remarkable piece of managing."

For Marty, this year would be an even bigger pain in the ass, as
he suddenly had to deal with players who, unlike Strawberry or
Morris, sometimes loomed smaller than life. Still, nothing seemed
unusual to the casual Saints fan looking forward to the beginning of
the 1997 season. Besides Mike's carnival to get 'em in the tent, they
would see on the field dozens of new faces looking for their one and
only chance—always an appealing drama.

So the only players invited back to the Saints from the year before
were the eternally injured pitcher Ernie Peterman and Chris Evans,
the undrafted prospect who Marty Scott had uncovered during that
long-ago tryout camp in Orlando in the spring of 1996. Marty had
taken back the right fielder, who'd whined incessantly when Darryl
Strawberry took his position. But even after trading the hotheaded
Evans last year to the Sioux Falls Canaries, Scott still saw something
he liked in the fireplug outfielder.

For Marty Scott, the expected off-season offers from organized
baseball had not come. Marty seemed unconcerned that he hadn't
yet returned to his previous high status in the majors because managing the Saints had changed Marty himself. The change may have
made him undesirable for the straight-arrow jobs of major league
baseball, now largely populated by men who look like corporate
Ken dolls.

Marty, you see, had grown a beard and now looked like a star in
one of Sam Peckinpah's "shoot 'em-ups." Marty's beard, in ways a
powerful statement of individuality, was a "fuck you" to the powers

that be, coming from a decade-long organization man who'd been stripped of his office, options, and parking space. And corporate baseball seemed to understand this. It was a new Marty from last year, and it looked good.

Marty didn't seem to mind the change at all. He was proud of what he'd done with the Saints: he'd led the Saints to five straight Northern League half-pennants and two championships. He was still a professional and continued to take pride in donning a uniform.

He'd had a nice winter with his wife and three kids in Dallas, he reported. And Darryl Strawberry hadn't "big-leagued" him in the off-season and was true to his word to the Saints' manager. After the Yankees won the World Series, Darryl flew to Texas, where Marty, as promised, took him to a Cowboys game. Straw still called Marty "Dad" and continued to ring him up, albeit collect on the manager's phone card. Marty, who could deal just as easily with the mighty as with the meek, would definitely be a good man for the Saints to have around next season.

St. Paul, itself fueled by the national publicity garnered by the Saints, was meantime getting what felt like its own first chance at the publicity, glory, and growth long hogged by its cocky cousin across the river. Written off as the dead Twin City, it began a Renaissance not seen since it was founded in 1848 by Pete "Pig's Eye" Parrant, a daft, one-eyed, rogue fur trapper and moonshiner who once went to war against the federal army when he'd been caught distilling white lightning for much of the Midwest. The federal army pushed Parrant back to some uninhabited land on the Mississippi, where he founded Pig's Eye—a name that wasn't changed to St. Paul until years later.

Now, in the late 1990s, artists, musicians, and literary types were fleeing across the river from Minneapolis, drawn by St. Paul's cheap rents and retro chic. Downtown St. Paul, long a black hole of nothingness, was starting to light up again at night with restaurants and tenants. And the city's beautiful Mississippi waterfront was at last being slowly, and tastefully, developed.

Not only was St. Paul now considered cooler than Minneapolis by those who cared, its proximity to Hazelden, the world's most famous rehab center in the world, had turned it into an internationally known synonym for recovery and healing. "I heard a whisper in my ear," William Moyers, Bill Moyers's son, told the The New York Times in 1998, "and it said, 'St. Paul.'"

Moyers Jr., a recovered addict and CNN reporter, had gone on a crack binge in 1994 and headed into Hazelden. Quitting his job and schlepping his family to St. Paul, Moyers eventually emerged as the clinic's director of public policy, while his father prepared a documentary series about addiction and healing called "Close to Home." St. Paul, it seemed, was acknowledged as the Lourdes of recovery.

No, it didn't hurt that St. Paul was the nearest big city in Hazelden, a place that catered to a clientele whose alumni included Eric Clapton, Calvin Klein, Liza Minnelli, and the twenty- or thirty-something children of many wealthy parents from both coasts. Now a minicommunity of self-exiled, sober, and hip scenesters lived in St. Paul, sipping coffee at places with names like the Day by Day Café.

Dollars came into St. Paul too. The National Hockey League placed a major league expansion team for the year 2000 in St. Paul, the city's first leap ever into the bigs. And when *The New York Times* had a certain intrepid reporter write about the Twin Cities as a winter destination, the article proved to be a wet kiss to St. Paul, with little mention of Minneapolis. St. Paul's mayor Norm Coleman, a Brooklyn-born Jew and former hippie anti-Vietnam protest organizer, was now a Republican who pollsters were showing might very well win the governor's race in 1998, beating out Democratic sons with surnames like Humphrey and Mondale.

There had always been high society in St. Paul, of course, families of ancient grain and train fortunes who still considered the aristocracy of Minneapolis as nouveau riche. These aristocrats still live in the mansions of stately Summit Avenue; the best was built in 1891 by robber baron James J. Hill, owner of the Great Northern Railroad. F. Scott Fitzgerald was born only tantalizing blocks away from Summit Avenue; when he sold *This Side of Paradise,* he ran up and down Summit telling the burghers of St. Paul that he was finally a success.

Much more numerous than the Richie Riches, St. Paul also boasted working-class neighborhoods that had stayed remarkably intact and vibrant over the generations, while Minneapolis had been busy razing and rerazing everything between itself and a possible highway site. St. Paulities are famously nicer than their Minneapolis cousins: despite its cliques of Italian and Polish neighborhoods, the city has welcomed more Hmong refugees from Cambodia than virtually any city in America.

Traditionally, St. Paulities have also felt themselves to be tougher than those in that city across the river. The proof has always been the St. Paul Winter Carnival, a 112-year-old outdoor jamboree in the dead of the region's brutal five-month winter. The carnival, the nation's oldest winter festival, is also St. Paul's civic event of the year—in windchills that sometimes reach sixty below. Windchill that, Minneapolis.

Even at the carnival, St. Paul's whimsy shines through. The most popular event begins with ice sculptors working from 9 A.M. to noon in single- and multiple-block carving contests. Rice Park, the site of the contests, is turned into a gallery of frozen art as competitors—using chainsaws, chisels, and household irons—create visions in ice of everything from the Flintstones in Bedrock to angels in heaven.

There is even a likable whiff of ancient notoriety in certain parts of St. Paul. In the 1930s, St. Paul became notorious as the leading cooling-off spot for gangsters on the lam. Among those who took advantage of the police force's hands-off policy were John Dillinger, Alvin "Creepy" Karpis, Baby Face Nelson, and Ma Barker.

The gangsters are gone, but the present is played out in the same style as the old days. Smoke-filled rooms still exist in St. Paul; it is said that more deals are cut in the Best Western Kelly Inn, a favorite spot for visiting lobbyists and politicos, than in the nearby capital.

In the staid pages of the *The Economist,* meanwhile, the warring Twin Cities were brought up in the context of both cities' 1997 local elections. "They are called the Twin Cities," began the respected European news magazine, "and siblings can really resent each other. For years, St. Paul has felt like the small kid brother of bigger Minneapolis, which sits to the west across the Mississippi." The article ended, however, "In short, St. Paul's star is rising, but Minneapolis is approaching its mayoral election in an apathetic and bitter mood. [The Minneapolis Republican candidate] slogan says it all: 'It's not about being nice.' Especially not about being nice to that uppity little place [St. Paul] across the river."

St. Paul, meantime, acted unaware of Minneapolis's disrespect or growing jealousy. Its charming provinciality came out not only in old-time neighborhoods, but in the way it held grudges.

Mike himself has taken the curse off of Morley Safer, the "60 Minutes" cohost who allegedly called St. Paul "the most boring city in the country." "Years later, their show did a piece on the Saints," Mike remembers, "and Morley had the courage to stand out here with me at the turnstiles and let people from St. Paul tell him what they thought of his comments about their city. St. Paulities admire that kind of courage, so I think Morley is off the hook."

Darryl Strawberry, an outsider in a town that actually invites out-

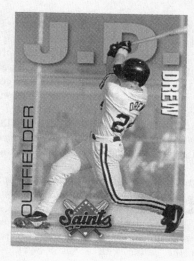

siders (just mind your manners), remained a civic hero. But the city of Minneapolis itself, that beacon of hipness that had given the world Prince, Bob Dylan, and Hubert Horatio Humphrey, would continue only to be referred to in St. Paul as "that town across the river," or booed if you were at Midway.

Mike, with the help of Bill Fanning, was busy plotting the Saints' 1997 season from his winter headquarters in Charleston, South Carolina, where he was trying to revive the woeful River Dogs for his pal Marv Goldklang. His heart, he said, was still in St. Paul; he liked the idea that the Saints themselves stood for healing through laughter.

He wanted his independent Saints to continue to be a kind of Elba for people who, like he used to be, were working out their own personal gripes with organized baseball. When the commissioner of baseball said that the great Japanese pitcher Hideki Irabu would have to play for San Diego and not the New York Yankees, *The New York Times* guessed that while the mess was being sorted out, Irabu might well end up keeping warm by pitching for the St. Paul Saints.

This time, in 1997, Mike would provide a different kind of oasis for the young and untried. The best talent by far was J. D. Drew, perhaps the most sought after amateur player in all of baseball. As a junior at Florida State in 1996, Drew hit 31 homers, stole 32 bases, drove in 67 runs, and batted .455 in 67 games. Chosen College Baseball Player of the Year by *Baseball America,* the bible of minor league ball, Drew was duly drafted by the Philadelphia Phillies.

Drew, as the number-two draft choice overall, wanted a contract for $10 million. The Phillies, on a well-publicized cost-cutting budget, said no and offered many millions less. Whereupon Drew announced he would sit out a year, sue to become a free agent next season, then sign with the highest bidder. Or could he? Organized baseball labor law remained murky, but Drew's agent, Scott Boras, the agent most loathed by baseball clubs, was willing to fight it out in the courts as a test case.

In the meantime, Drew sure as hell wasn't going to report to the Phillies. While he waited for his millions, Drew signed with the St. Paul Saints for $700 a month and a chance to get some at-bats. Despite the fact that one twisted ankle turning a base in Thunder Bay could turn him from a paper millionaire into a pauper overnight, Drew played for the Saints with a gusto belying his position as baseball's prodigal prince.

Even the Saints' tailgaters had kept in shape and good spirits over the winter by practicing for the summer. In the Saints' parking lot in mid-February, two dozen fans led by Vince Jeannette gathered on a snowing subzero day for a tailgate and barbecue party. Wearing snowmobile suits, they all danced to the boom boxes and ate themselves silly. In the corner, wrapped in a heavy shawl, Sister Rosalind Gefre sat in this tundra on a beach chair and sipped a beer.

The sister's own winter had been as eventful as she'd prayed. She had indeed made her pilgrimage to Calcutta, accompanied by local news anchor Kalley King, who'd earlier written a letter to Mother Teresa. Mother Teresa had said c'mon down, and they had. Mother Teresa, frail and in a wheelchair, was able to briefly bless them. "You can't explain it," Sister Roz said in her North Dakota Lawrence Welk twang. "It was beyond anything I'd ever felt before."

"Come here," she said, making me lean closer and feeling my neck.

"You're getting better," the sister said. "You see the sky. You see the beauty of the ball game. Now you have to fall in love again."

What the sister had said after pummeling my spine was right: I was happier, indeed almost normal. I had changed. Over the winter, I'd called *Rolling Stone* to officially cancel my Bill Murray piece, the first and only time in my career that I'd killed one of my own stories.

I could have written it now; *Rolling Stone* was still up for a Murray vivisection to run during the baseball season in the spring or early summer of 1997. My decision to bail, I knew, meant I would never write again for the magazine. "Are you sure?" said my editor. "We could still do it with the right stuff."

By way of an answer, I put in for my expense check, and my "kill fee," which was 75 percent less than the $7,500 I'd contracted for the story. Jann Wenner, just as he'd been in Bill Murray's *Where the Buffalo Roam,* was once again pathologically cheap with my money. Even though he still owes me $114.54, I decided it let it pass. I cared, but I didn't really care.

This year, I knew, I would be spending a little less time with the Saints. I'd figured enough out, taken enough bus rides, and gotten enough of my own shit together to jump off the merry-go-round from time to time and begin my life anew outside Professor Veeck's carnival of healing and laughter. I still went to games and took an occasional road trip, but now I also had the voice of Don Wardlow keeping me up-to-date.

Last year it had been Dave Stevens, the second baseman with no legs. In 1997, it would be Wardlow, a blind fellow working as the color man on the Saints' radio broadcasts.

Wardlow was a revelation, a man who somehow over the radio was able to exactly describe Twig excitedly waving a batter around to second or the smell of the grass on a warm St. Paul night. What made Wardlow's gift even more surreal was that he broadcast games on the low-watt Christian station that broadcast Saints games between radio sermons about the surety of hell. ("Being on that station means we can't make references to alcohol, drugs, or tobacco," Wardlow said, "and we can't tell listeners that the starting pitcher lost all his money the night before playing blackjack.")

Wardlow worked with two partners—play-by-play man Jim Lucas and Gizmo, Don's black Labrador Seeing Eye dog. Still, Wardlow could talk about the grass as if he'd gone out to the field a couple of hours before and felt it. Which he had.

For half an hour before each game, Wardlow would walk the field with Gizmo and just *feel* the field. He'd touch the soil of the infield, test the outfield warning track, and whisk his hand across the length of the grass. Synthetic grass like AstroTurf, he said, was "unforgiving."

Wardlow, armed with 120 Braille cards he'd typed up on his personal Brailler, each card for each game bearing every possible statistic of the Northern League, had a greater command of factoids and baseball trivia than virtually any announcer I'd heard. He also had miles of recorded interviews with Saints and opposing players who were only too happy to talk to this blind man wandering up the foul lines with his dog, feeling the grass for texture as he fiddled with his interview tape recorder.

Further, you could *hear* his heart as he spoke of the game he loved, though he'd never seen it. Twice, I'd sat in the Saints' parking lot while a game was going on, a ticket in my hand, listening to Don Wardlow's call of the game on the radio. In the Saints' program/ yearbook, meantime, Wardlow and Tom Whaley had come up with a full page in Braille to tell the blind fans where to get a bratwurst or pee.

Mike had given Wardlow, Lucas, and Gizmo their first chance in 1990, right after his own blackball had been lifted and he was running the Miami Miracle. "They'd lose ten out of twelve and had a woeful ballclub," Wardlow remembers. "Mike needed something to generate interest. It may have been a freak show when we started, but no longer."

Lucas and Wardlow, who had broadcast games together in college, had just sent a bulk mailing to all 176 professional baseball teams then in the minor leagues. Inside the package was a tape of the duo announcing their blind-and-seeing game and a letter begging for a job or tryout. Only Mike responded, with an offer of a one-game chance to call. "Mike told us it was an opportunity," remembers Wardlow. He would use the pair, the announcer remembers, "for one game for the publicity."

That night Mike became the first person in baseball to put a blind announcer on the air. As a stunt, the experiment was an unqualified success, with national press temporarily focused on Mike's terrible team in the bottom of the minor leagues. But watching Wardlow schmooze with the CNN man before that big 1990 game, Mike realized that Don wasn't tilting at windmills: he was serious about chasing his impossible dream of someday broadcasting in the major leagues.

"Wardlow was holding court on the field with this guy from CNN," Mike remembered, "and then he got real emotional. He got emotional when he talked about 'looking' at the batting cage. He was relating how it felt to reach his dream and how each little experience in the world had moved him up. What he had done was walk up to the batting cage with Gizmo and feel it, grip it tightly. It was symbolic of the fact that he had arrived as an announcer."

In any case, Wardlow now says that being minus one sense only enhances his descriptions of others. "I like to think I can pick up in a special way the crack of the bat, the roar of the crowd, and the sound of the ball popping into the catcher's glove."

In time, Mike watched the Wardlow–Lucas team become professional announcers. "I liked how Don was able to make fun of his blindness sometimes, at the same time he was inspiring people that there was nothing you can't do. He reminds me of my dad and his wooden leg. My father loved it when people came up at the stadium to look at the ashtray he'd built into his wooden leg."

Mike has also learned from his dad the importance of having a fun, offbeat announcer instead of a talking head. The late Harry Caray, who on hot nights would broadcast Chicago White Sox games in his boxer shorts, never planned on leading Comiskey Stadium each seventh inning with a rendition of "Take Me Out to the Ball Game."

Rather, Bill Veeck had one night heard Harry singing the song to the gang in the broadcast booth and, unbeknownst to the announcer, flipped the switch that amplified his horrific singing voice all over the stadium. And so are legends made.

Growing up in New Jersey, Wardlow had no blind role models. Instead, his heroes were Yankees announcer Phil Rizzuto, Howard Cosell of ABC Sports, and Mets broadcaster Bob Murphy. Though he'd been born without eyeballs, Wardlow determined before his tenth birthday that one day he would broadcast a major league game. The New Jersey State Commission for the Blind revoked Wardlow's college scholarship to Glassboro State when he declared his major as "broadcasting."

"They said they were there to provide help for blind kids' futures," Wardlow remembers. "They said they'd be wasting an education by having me major in communications."

Wardlow scraped together his own money, and tried to get a gig announcing Glassboro's baseball games on the college radio station. Seventeen straight staffers said no when he asked them to team up with him. The eighteenth person he asked was Jim Lucas.

Besides broadcasting the college games, Wardlow and Lucas would sit in the bleachers of Yankee Stadium and pretend they were calling a game, eliciting very strange glances, even from fans who were used to seeing very weird things going on in New York's bleachers. "Both my [play-by-play] partner Jim and I love how Red Barber used to call the Brooklyn Dodgers on the radio," Wardlow said. "And Red Barber once said to all aspiring announcers that to properly call a game they should talk as if their microphone is one solitary person—a person who is blind. Jim Lucas doesn't have to pretend because I *am* blind."

And it worked, first for Mike and the Pompano Beach Miracle for two years, then with the late New Britain, Connecticut, Red Sox for four years. In 1993, they even announced an inning and a half of a game between the major league Florida Marlins and the Chicago Cubs on the Marlins flagship station. "Our dream is to go to the majors," Wardlow said. "The only handicap I have in baseball with my blindness is on the team bus when the players are handing around *Playboy* and *Penthouse*. [They] would come and wave those magazines right in front of my face. I'd say to them all, 'Boys, you're making it *sting* now.' "

In any case, Wardlow was affianced and would eventually marry Melanie, a beautiful young woman who walked haltingly with a cane, could barely see, and who would turn you into toast if you showed either her or Don any pity. Yet times can be tough for a blind baseball color announcer.

"The worst was when I was broadcasting from Ontario, and the temperature was three degrees Celsius," Wardlow remembers. "My Braille finger got so cold that I was unable to read my notes right around the twelfth inning of the ball game. I had to wing it by memory; luckily, our team won in the fourteenth."

And sometimes you just have to bullshit. One night Jim Lucas came down with a flu so bad that he couldn't go on the air to call the play-by-play. "We had to get the game back to our fans in Connecticut," Wardlow says, "so I sat right next to the wall where the hometown broadcaster was calling the game. I could hear what he was saying, and I just repeated his play-by-play account on my station, adding my own commentary along the way. Thank God that hasn't happened since."

Someday they think that Mike, their original benefactor, will be running a major league baseball team. When that happens, Wardlow hopes he will bring him and Lucas along. If not, he is sure they'll make it by some other route. "Beyond baseball, I'm here to say to people, 'You can do it, even when people tell you to your face that you're crazy for dreaming it.' "

Dave Wright was not happy that he'd been kicked out of the radio booth for the 1997 season and would return to his role as the Saints' founding publicity director. Still, he carried on like a good soldier, bitching only a little that he was being replaced by a blind man and a dog named Gizmo. In the office, Dave continued to toss out bonbons of weird sports facts that cracked up the employees when they weren't busy teasing him for his utter unhipness. "So what if I don't know the band Canned Heat," Dave said, mentioning a band that had played the original Woodstock, but who he thought was as current as Semisonic.

Still, Dave had his marvelous stories. "Do you remember John X. Congdon, the Madison Square Garden boxing ring announcer?" he asked one day. "In the 1950s, he's introducing a match with heavy-weight champion Ezzard Charles and says, live on the air, right before the fight, 'And now singing the national anthem, that star of stage and screen, Miss Julie London.' And then someone in the crowd yells so everyone can hear on the air, 'Ah, she's nothing but a whore!' At which point, Congdon says, 'Nevertheless . . .'"

Mike wasn't feeling too guilty that Dave would be kicked out of the radio box by Wardlow. "He promised me a chance," Dave said, "and he gave it to me." No one else ever had given him a chance to chase his dream before, and now he didn't know if he'd ever get one again.

Mike, meantime, was about to give the ultimate first chance. It would be his biggest innovation ever, one planned by his father but never done. He was going to find, if possible, a woman whose competence on the field would allow her to play baseball among men. While he waited for the right candidate to surface, his coaches and loose coalition of scouts scoured the land for someone to make history by becoming the first female to play against professional men ballplayers.

During his lifetime, Mike's father had tried in vain to find a woman who could credibly pitch against professional baseball play-ers. It was the next step in both society and promotions, Bill Veeck thought, but he never quite found the woman who he thought could both consistently get men out and take the abuse that was bound to be heaped on her by the public and media of that era.

So it was a big day when the president and co-owner of the St. Paul Saints got a call in early 1997 from Barry Moss, the St. Paul coach who lived in Southern California. "There's this pitcher," Moss reported, "named Ila Borders. And she might be the one."

Moss had clocked Borders's fastball at eighty miles per hour, about fifteen less than an overpowering flamethrower, but perhaps okay

Saints' manager Marty Scott welcomes back Barry Moss to the fold for the 1997 season. The Californian worked with St. Paul in 1995 as a hitting and outfield coach. He returns to that role again this year. Moss played in the Cincinnati and Toronto farm systems as an infielder-outfielder from 1974-81. He later worked for the Reds as a minor league hitting instructor. In 1987, he moved to independent Salt Lake City where he served as a coach for the team that set the modern professional baseball record when they won 29 straight games. He managed the Trappers in 1988-89 and also piloted Erie (NY-Penn League) in 1991 for an overall managing mark of 111-106. He has also worked in the San Diego and Cubs' farm systems. Last year, he was the batting coach for the Cubs' Southern League affiliate at Orlando.

for the low minors because she also had a dazzling assortment of off-speed pitches that served as a perfect setup for her fast-enough fastball.

Mike pondered. If Borders failed, the attempt would be seen as a publicity stunt, like the time his father sent a midget up to bat for the St. Louis Browns. But if it worked, it would be social history. He decided to invite Ila Borders to the Saints' spring training camp. "We gave her no guarantees she'd make the team," Mike said. Paying her own way, she would only be given an opportunity. "The final decision," the team president said, "would be made by manager Marty Scott based on what he saw on the field."

For the next two weeks in May, Borders battled to make the twenty-two man Saints roster and pounded her experiences into her diary.

After my first practice (May 14, 1997):
God, I am scared to death right now. I don't know what to expect. Why did I get myself into this? I love it so much, but then the pressure is so great that I wonder sometimes if it's worth it. Every time I pitch, I feel I lose a part of my soul to someone out there, maybe a fan. Why do I feel this way? Why can't I just be an asshole? It would be a lot easier.

To my surprise, no one gave me shit [at the first practice]. This is really different from college. During practice today, we took pitchers' fielding practice, shagged, hit fungos, and threw.

I did pretty well, but it is so cool here I can't get warm. Because of this, I am afraid I pulled a back muscle. Shit, that is all I need, a pulled back muscle before the season. God, I can't believe I chose this path.

Exhibition games came quickly as the Saints held their abbreviated spring training again in chilly May at Midway Stadium. A few names appeared on the new GON' FISHIN' wall, but Ila stayed on, impressing Scott more with her grit than her fastball. The manager watched her closely and saw she was throwing strikes as well as his own paltry collection of left-handed men relievers. Yes, he decided, he might give Ila her first chance in the upcoming May 22 practice home game against the Duluth-Superior Dukes. Sensing what was about to happen, Ila contemplated the stakes.

Today will be the moment of truth. In all my twenty-two years I have worked toward my dream, and it will come down to this day and one more in one week. No pressure at all. Yeah, right, I've already thrown up twice. It's so funny because I appear so strong to people but inside I'm not.

Sitting in the Saints' dugout before the start of the contest, Ila put on her toughest game face of all and had little and/or nothing to say to the reporters who clustered about her as usual. Asked how she was doing, Ila merely gave the thumbs-up sign, speaking not a word. At the end of the game, she went back to her hotel room and recorded what happened the first time a woman pitched in a minor league game, albeit an exhibition. She had come in at the start of the seventh inning and had lasted through the eighth.

After exhibition game:
Oh my God, I can't believe this. It was a sellout and everyone got on their feet and clapped and chanted my name. I could not get over 6,329 people chanting my name. Never before have I ever experienced such an awesome sensation. I had chicken skin the whole time. I ended up doing great in the first inning [the seventh]. I struck out the first batter, Jeff Jensen [swinging, on a two and two changeup]. I tried to appear calm and cool, but inside it was like I shit my pants. I am still in my uniform. I don't want to take it off. I have worked my whole life, and all I want is to savor the moment,

Ila was the first female to earn a college scholarship and win a game. Ila was selected the Most Valuable Player at Whittier Christian High School in her senior year. She received a scholarship to Southern California College and played there for three years before transferring to Whittier. She posted a 4-5 won-loss record with a 5.22 ERA in 81 innings of work at Whittier in 1997.

because I don't know how long it will last. I will never tell anyone this because they will think I am a weirdo.

"She painted the outside corner and came back with a good changeup," Jensen told John Millea of the *Minneapolis Star Tribune*. "[I] tip my hat to her." She got out of the inning with a walk and two groundouts. The next inning was bad; Chris Evans misplayed an easy catch into a double, and a Saints error sent Dukes scrambling over the plate. Ila had lost the game, but seemed somehow to have won the world.

On the last day of camp, old-time baseball man Marty Scott called her into his office with Barry Moss and the Saints' pitching coach. "You are facing the firing squad," Scott said.

"I don't know if I want to sit down," Borders replied.

Seconds later, she emerged from the office smiling. "I heard the words I've been waiting to hear since I was ten," she said. Scott, knowing he was now in the line of fire too, was gruff when he emerged from the office. "I told Ila if she doesn't do the job, she'll be gone. I told her that her velocity is short, but her work ethic is as good as anyone I have been around."

That night Ila sat alone next to the railroad tracks running directly behind the Saints' Midway Stadium and blasted songs over her boom box by her new and old favorites: Prince, Madonna, Sarah McLachlan, and Melissa Etheridge. "I have fallen in love with train tracks," she would tell her diary. So while the rest of the men who'd survived the Saints' final cut were out partying, she then returned to her room and diary.

Last practice:

I FUCKING MADE THE TEAM! I FUCKING MADE THE TEAM! DREAMS COME TRUE! DREAMS COME TRUE! I cannot fucking believe this. I am so excited I can't even speak. I think I just grew an inch taller. I've done the impossible. I sucked today in practice because I knew this was either the beginning or the end of my dream of twelve years. I laid out in the outfield, wondering about my fate. I wanted to cry, but instead I was strong as usual on the outside. All of a sudden, Barry Moss came out to the outfield and said, 'Ila, come here. We need to talk to you.' I didn't want to go, but I did of course. I had my guard up. They ended up telling me, 'Yeah, you sucked today, but we saw that you were preoccupied. You made the team—you earned the spot. Good luck. You are going to be on the ride of your life.' I wanted to scream and go bonkers, but I had to show everyone I expected this and that I was cool. I raced home (hotel). For at least ten minutes, I was jumping on the bed, screaming.

It all began, Ila recalled with a laugh, with a baseball thrown hard and mean at her head. She was ten years old, the only girl in Orange County's La Hambra, California, Little League. Dug into the batter's box, the first pitch to Ila from the league's fastest pitcher was a beanball that plunked her right in the batting helmet. Her next time up, the same twelve-year-old pitcher hit her in the head again.

"I got the point," Ila said. "I wasn't wanted. Now there are tons of girls in Little League, but back then I was the only one in ours."

But then, on her next at-bat against Mr. Hot Stuff, she hit a triple off the outfield wall. "He was the star pitcher of that league, and from them on I gained the respect of everybody. They saw I could hit and, later, pitch. It was easier than I'd like to admit because the girls that age are bigger than the boys."

Still, she loved playing, especially since she was so good. She led her Little League in home runs with five her first year. She just kept hitting and pitching better than anyone, and she eventually enrolled in Whittier Christian Junior High, because the coach there wanted her on his boys' team.

Then came the firestorm. Other junior high coaches in the league said they wouldn't play against a woman, and even the private school's regents voted against her. But Borders's coach, Ron Enslinger, eventually took the case to court for her right to play. She won.

But in the hallways at school she was treated like a freak. Dressed like a punk rocker during the day, she would listen to Prince, Siouxsie and the Banshees, and Depeche Mode on her Walkman and try to forget the fact, as she put it, "that I had absolutely no friends. It didn't matter that I was doing well on the ball field."

But there were no other options. Borders, a lifelong resident of Orange County, knew she had no chance to play at La Hambra High, her local public high school. "The coach there just said, 'I don't care who you are. We're not taking you,'" Borders remembered.

Instead of going to court again and causing another spectacle of her quest, Borders enrolled in ninth grade at Whittier Christian High School. "The coach there said, 'Yeah, we'll give you a shot,'" she remembered. "And they did, which is all I wanted. And I ended up with a very successful career in high school. I played varsity four straight years and was named Team Most Valuable Player my senior year."

By now, Borders was pitching exclusively. Her high school senior statistics were indeed impressive: she was 5–2, striking out 52 men in 42 innings, with an excellent 2.42 earned run average.

Her personal teenage scorecard, however, remained a shutout. Borders, now a Metallica fan who dressed all in black, then alchemized after school into Xena of the baseball team, was, to put it mildly, not popular among the student body of Whittier Christian. "I already knew I wanted to play professional baseball," Borders said, "and I always knew there would be things I would lose in my life because of that. The girls were all fixing their hair, and I didn't have a boyfriend in high school because they all thought I was a freak. What guy would want to go out with a woman whose dream is to be on the road all year, traveling with two dozen male athletes?"

Colleges across the country, however, had been apprised of this woman out in California with an eighty-mile-per-hour fastball and a dizzying array of pitches. Ultimately, ten colleges said they were interested in having Ila pitch for them. Borders narrowed her choices down to three: "Northwestern," she said, "someplace in Iowa or Tennessee, and Southern California College."

She chose Southern California College, preferring to remain near her parents and three siblings who would be close enough to cheer her on every game from the stands. With that, she became the first woman to be granted a scholarship to a men's baseball team. It also marked the only time that Borders dated a ballplayer.

"We were the best two starters on the team, and it put a little stress on the relationship, to say the least," she said with a laugh. "After that I said, 'No more ballplayers—*ever.*' "

The rest of the team wasn't too keen on Borders from the beginning; half of them didn't even show up when she made her nearby appearance on "The Tonight Show with Jay Leno." "It was tough," Borders remembered, "and what got me through was my family in the stands. One time in San Diego, I struck a guy out, and his girlfriend in the stands literally came on the field with a knife and tried to hurt me! I'm like, 'Man, this is baseball. What the heck is going on here?' My family all had to be escorted back to our car. And that became the kind of nuts I had to face day in and day out at SCC."

Finally she'd had enough. Sick of the death threats, tired of returning to her car after every game to find her tires slashed and side mirror broken off, she transferred in 1997 to Whittier College, best known in history as the place where Richard Nixon ran for student body president on the platform of allowing dancing on campus.

Ila pitched well and was treated much better at Whittier; she ended the season with a 4–5 record in 81 innings. Then, soon after the season was over, she got a call from someone named Veeck.

15

1997: Marty Frets, Twig Pets, and Ila Has Left the Building

There are only two kinds of women: wives and whores.
—Ancient baseball axiom
(This has been repeated by 94 percent of the ballplayers I've ever met.)

June, 1997

The 1997 season started, and it was soon obvious that something was wrong with the Saints. Though every ticket to every game had been sold and the fans were as happy as ever, the chemistry and drama of the championship year before was gone. Though the team battled all year for first place and won the opening-half pennant, they never got their shit together enough to win another championship.

"These aren't nice guys," said Jill Muellner, the night bar manager at Gabe's, as she poured beers she would never allow herself to drink. "The guys from last year were just better people."

Even I could tell there was something missing from this new edition of the Saints. While the drama of last year's season made each visit to the locker room a kind of theater, this time it felt like schizophrenia. Sometimes I'd come in and the Saints would be as giddy as schoolgirls; other times I'd enter and there would be a funeral pall hanging over the clubhouse that no one had a name for.

"What's the deal?" Marty Scott asked in late June, when the Saints gave up thirty runs in three games to the visiting Winnipeg Goldeyes. He closed the locker room after the last game of the series, lost by the Saints 13–8, and went on one of his rare tirades. "Why, in such a favorable setting, are we so dead?" he asked. "I've got a high fever, and it's a pretty sad thing when the sick, fat manager has more life than his team."

Despite my vow to back off a bit, I still kept close tabs on the team, attending every home game and making occasional road trips, always with a radio and earplug so as to catch Don Wardlow call color for the game. They were still my Saints, after all, more healing to the heart and soul than a visit to the *mikva*. And besides, there were still some sights I wanted to see on the road, including the remnants of the biblical flood that since last season had all but destroyed the Red River Valley, including Fargo and Grand Forks, home of the Varmints of the Prairie League.

Fargo native William Gass, who'd fled the Midwest to become an acclaimed novelist, had once written in a short story entitled "In the Heart of the Heart of the Country" that "I want to rise so high that when I shit I won't miss anybody." Getting even, he later admitted in *The Paris Review,* was his motivation. But seeing the destruction, one couldn't help but ache for the good, goofy, large-assed, and generally uncool people of the Midwest who'd long ago sent Gass, and to a much lesser extent me, fleeing for a *sophisticated* coast.

Things weren't much better than Fargo in Iowa, home of the Sioux City Explorers. "I'm afraid we're heading back into the early 1980s, when I buried three [farmer] friends who committed suicide," said Gary Lamb, chairman of the Iowa Farm Service Agency. But there was still baseball for these suffering folks, and I cheered not a peep when I occasionally drove my crunched "Northern League car" to see the Saints play away.

I finally saw the "Corn Palace" of Mitchell, South Dakota, an auditorium for thousands whose façade is made up of thirteen large murals, each containing 275,000 ears of split corn. The sculptures, nailed together to form things like golfers, spacemen, and birds, change yearly.

And there were the ghosts. Once, driving north from Minneapolis on an old back road highway for an away series between the Saints and Duluth, I kept shaking off the mirage of a half-century old team bus headed the opposite direction. Was it the fated original Duluth Dukes, who in 1948 were a team in the low minors affiliated with the St. Louis Cardinals? That year, headed through the Twin Cities on this very road, the Dukes bus collided with a truck; five members of the team were killed and 18 seriously injured. I drove back to the main freeway, shaken by the specter. Nowhere, not in the deepest recesses of anything-goes Hollywood or New York, had I ever seen anything so weird as I did traveling the Northern League circuit.

On the field, there was much more to see than doom, destruction, and benign weirdness. One of my favorite players was veteran Dwight Smith, who'd played nine solid years in the Show, most recently in 1996 with the Atlanta Braves. Always ready with a quote or joke for a pressing rookie or a journalist on deadline, he was as mellow as Strawberry had been intense.

J. D. Drew was also a nice guy with a brain—he'd talk to everybody about anything, except the millions of dollars he was foregoing to play for the Saints. But my favorite Saint, like virtually every other fan in the Northern League, was Ila Borders.

"That *thing*," muttered Singin' Ed Nottle, the tobacco-spitting manager of the Sioux City Explorers.

I had come to love Ed Nottle, the king of Sioux City, had drunk beer with him until we were both loopy the season before, had driven around the local golf course with him before meeting and greeting the fine burghers of their fine town. He had played his record of standards for me, the album that he'd lost his house for, and I'd had to admit he did sound like Frank Sinatra on "Theme from New York, New York."

Aw, Ed, why'd you have to go and call Ila Borders "that *thing*"?

He did so during a postgame interview during the first couple of days of June in 1997 with a Sioux City radio reporter. The Saints were making their first trip through town, and in a postgame interview Ed Nottle had no problem calling Ila a "thing" on the record, in essence a freak, a joke, a stunt for headlines. But I had become intrigued by Borders during her short time in St. Paul and had tried to break through the game face she wore, it seemed, at all times.

Neither Nottle nor her own teammates knew that Borders had already turned down appearances on the "Late Show with David Letterman," the "Today" show, and CBS News and had kept her mouth shut in a story about her in *The New York Times*. "I don't want to show up my teammates and give them any more reason to resent me," explained Borders, twisting the ponytail flowing out from behind her adjustable Saints cap before a game.

Her strategy had worked; the next morning several Saints made sure she read the article where Nottle's remarks were written and vowed revenge for the five-foot-ten, 150-pound pitcher.

"I'll get my revenge myself, with my pitching," she told her teammates. "Truthfully," she went on later, "I'm glad Ed Nottle said that. At least he was honest about how he felt. Anyway, it was what a lot of the old-time baseball guys were already saying about me around the league anyway."

Other old-timers in the Northern League were also publicly telling Ila to go to the Coors Silver Bullets, an all-women's baseball team that traveled the country playing men's teams, sort of a variation of the Harlem Globetrotters novelty act. One of her *coaches* even suggested that Ila go play with the Coors Silver Bullets. An opposing pitching coach told Ila that she would make much more money with the Silver Bullets.

"I respect the Silver Bullets," Borders said matter-of-factly, "but I want to make the major leagues. And the Silver Bullets are still new and getting organized, and sometimes have games against semi-pro teams or guys over thirty who just play on weekends. To make the major leagues, like I've wanted to since I was ten, the best route is by playing in the men's professional minor leagues, like I'm doing."

I'd seen Ila at every game, surrounded by men and women, young and old, shrieking her name and filming her every move. While she played for St. Paul, she later told me, she never let her guard down because she felt friendless, left behind, and alone in the dank facilities that had been provided for her in every stadium. She'd heard just about everything evil that could be said about a woman pitching in a men's professional league, but she was as squishy inside as she was tough and straight-arrowed on the league and in her solitary cage.

Still, even people of intellect wanted to know two things first.

Q: Is Ila straight?
A: Yes.

Question two, sexist and crass, always came as soon as I mentioned how Ila was progressing in her first season as a professional pitcher.

Q: Do you want, paraphrasing David Mamet in *Speed-the-Plow*, to play Hide the Afikomon with Ila?
A: Hell no. Besides it being journalistically indefensible, methinks me not Ila's type.

Maybe I focused on her because Ila was one of the very few ballplayers I'd ever met who'd read books—*real* books. She also wrote, a fact that marked her as more of a freak among her ballplayer peers than the fact that she was a woman.

Maybe I concentrated on her more than the other players because she looked so lonely. As she said in her diary of the season:

I can't tell anyone, so I tell my best friend (paper).

But until she got used to my face, I mostly just stayed away. Ila, pitching for the St. Paul Saints, had more than enough on her hands without being pestered by another of the hundreds of press people who'd shown up to chart her progress.

In time, Ila not only warmed, she proved she was warm. But even with her attitude of wanting to play with the boys, Borders said, she had angered some sporting feminists whose credo is for women to concentrate on competing against other women. In any case, she said, she did her part for the cause, mostly by touching the spirits of the little girls who chanted her name in every Northern League ballpark. "After taking so much crap for so many years, it feels so good to have people at the ballpark tell me, 'Thank you, you're an inspiration,'" Borders said. "That's cool," the twenty-two-year-old continued. "It's nice that others think I actually stand for something."

To win over the Saints players who hadn't made up their minds about having the first woman on *their* club, she performed another baseball ritual: don't show up your teammates. She learned the hard way.

"I was on 'The Tonight Show with Jay Leno' when I became the first woman to get a scholarship and pitch for a men's college team, and I thought that was cool," Borders remembers. "It was also neat when the Baseball Hall of Fame asked for my jersey."

At the same time, she was looked upon suspiciously by the wives and girlfriends of many of her Saints teammates. She wrote in her dairy after pitching in her first exhibition game for the team:

To my surprise, I am making friends with the guys. They are all so wonderful except one, but oh well. They invite me to dinner and golf, but I can't go because I would be hounded the whole time, and I could not just relax and enjoy their company. Another thing is: I don't want to get their wives jealous.

I've seen many jealous girlfriends in baseball. I'm not here to get guys. I am here to set out and live a dream. I wish these wives knew me, so they wouldn't have to worry. They should be worried about their husband with groupies, not me. One wife asked me how her husband acts on the road. Because of this, I stand clear of everyone on the team.

Still, so far, pro ball had been a cakewalk by comparison, even if rival managers here called her a "thing" to reporters. To Borders, the main point was that the Saints were a real time in a real league team with some kind of pipeline to the major leagues.

Meantime, among enlightened fans and the young (if not the old-time managers), Ila Borders, a woman who could actually *pitch,* had become a 1997 Midwest phenomenon in every city of the Northern League she visited. In return for the groundswell of affection for her by the fans, Borders stayed for hours after every game, signing autographs (mostly for girls) and getting her ponytail pulled (mostly by boys, who *then* asked for her autograph). In Thunder Bay, Fargo, and every place Mike's team traveled on the Northern League circuit, she was the Queen of the Ballpark.

"You definitely sometimes run into an attitude in the league about a woman playing," she said, "but it's only in the minors that I've heard 6,329 people chanting my name and cheering for me when I take the mound. I hate to say it, but after being hassled for so long, it gives me chicken skin to hear the PA in every city play Roy Orbison's 'Pretty Woman' or the Doors' 'Love Her Madly' every time I run out of the bullpen to pitch."

But there was a massive downside. Despite the game face she would wear all season, Ila remained palpably lonely. The situation was not helped by the fact that she had to get into uniform in a hallway a cinderblock wall away from the rest of the team's locker room. Since the men had rights to the team's locker room bathroom, Ila was forced before games to use the public lavatory used by fans behind the concession stands. In her diary, she recalled what happened shortly before a Saints game while she was in uniform:

I lost it today in the bathroom. I had to go and pee and I couldn't go into the locker room because a guy was in there. I ended up going to the bathroom in the stadium [women's bathroom behind the concession stand]. A nuts lady takes a picture of me while I was peeing. I lost it. Weird shit.

Since the Saints' showers also belonged to the men, Ila showered at the nearby house where she rented a room. On the road, she waited until she was back at the motel, where she roomed alone.

Before a game started, she usually sat by herself and consumed one of the six biographies of Jackie Robinson she read that season. When she tired of reading, but it wasn't game time yet, she wrote in her diary, stowing it in her bag of baseball gear when the sign came that it was okay to go through the Saints' locker room, into the dugout, and onto the field.

And then, on May 30, playing on the road against the Sioux Falls Canaries, Borders made baseball history when she pitched in her first regular season game for the Saints. The Hall of Fame called again for her jersey; unfortunately, her debut had been a disaster in baseball teams of *Hindenburg* proportions.

Called in by Marty, who'd made the final decision during the team's spring training to keep Borders, she took the pitcher's mound midway through the sixth inning.

The opposing Sioux Falls fans gave her a standing ovation, whereupon Borders uncorked a wild first warm-up pitch that bounced off the Saints' catcher's glove. On her real, first, historic pitch, she hit Canary batter Paul Cruz in the back. She then balked a runner home, gave up a single off her mitt that scored another run, made a throwing error, and gave up another single.

Listening to Don Wardlow on the radio, I felt helpless and inert, like a gang of big bullies were holding me back as they slapped around my sister. "Marty," I yelled alone at home, "get her out of there!"

I don't know if vibes travel, but Marty Scott hustled out of the dugout and pulled Borders from the game. Ila hadn't registered a single out and now had an earned run average of infinity. "She will have to respond," her manager tersely told reporters after the game. "Not too many of these will be tolerated."

Afterward in her hotel room, Borders finally let it all out in her diary.

First game:
   Okay, I want to die. I really do. I can't hide and people are really pissing me off. I go out and suck because I let my emotions overtake my body. And then about twenty reporters come and flash pictures in my face in the dugout. I wanted to fucking kill one right there, but something held me back. I guess I was too embarrassed and humiliated to do anything.

I thought there was nothing that would happen to hurt my soul so bad, but this did it. A sellout crowd and newspaper reporters from across the world [were here to see me]. I think this is the worst moment of my life. I bet the women's lib and Silver Bullets will be calling me soon to rub it in. **AH FUCK EVERYONE.** The person I should be pissed off at right now is me, but I feel so shitty it wouldn't do any good. I can't wait to see this tomorrow in the papers. I guess I will probably be shipped out tomorrow—fuck it. It could have been good. Anyone out there—please kill me and take me out of my misery. At least all the guys didn't give me shit. Then after I had to sign 1,000 autographs. Ah—I can't hide anywhere. **I SUCKED TODAY.**

The very next game Marty sent Ila right back to the mound and into the line of fire. If she bombed again, both he and Ila knew, she would be cut. Now the manager's ass was on the line, and everybody knew that too. Marty was in deep, and he hadn't yet given up on Ila's dedication, the reason he'd kept her on the team in the first place. "If you fall off a bike, you just get right back on it," he told Borders as he sent her out to pitch the eighth inning of the game against Sioux Falls.

"I was pitching for my life," Borders remembered. She gave up a single to the first batter—and then struck out the side. Listening on the radio to Don Wardlow's excited voice, I whooped for joy and danced around my apartment in that *Footloose* way one does when nobody is watching.

Borders too was overjoyed. There was now magic to the playing, she wrote in her hotel room in St. Paul days later, as it became clear that the Saints would continue to pitch her in the late innings against left-handed batters. In baseball parlance, she was a "setup man": her job was to get one or two hitters out in the eighth or ninth innings. In Borders's mind, she was a member of the team. Standing on the pitcher's mound one night, she pointed out in her diary:

Second game (May 31):
    Okay, I am redeemed. I didn't read any newspaper, thank God. From this day on, that is what I am going to do. I can't believe how helpful that is. I ended up striking out the side (3). Another goal met, but most of all a reason to give the manager to let me stay. Credit has to go to Barry Moss, the batting coach

St. Paul Saints — @ SIOUX FALLS — Date 5/31/97

#	St. Paul Saints	Pos	#	Sioux Falls	Pos
1	D. SMITH	CF	1	DUMAS	2B
2	ROGERS	2B	2	TSOUKALIS	3B
3	DATTOLA	LF	3	CASTILLO	RF
4	KENNEDY	1B	4	LANTIGUA	DH
5	BRYANT	RF	5	VOGEL	1B
6	EVANS	DH	6	REID	CF
7	ROBBINS	SS	7	KIMBLER	SS
8	DIONNE	C	8	TANIGUCHI	C
9	MCINNES	3B	9	CRUZ	LF

PITCHERS

St. Paul		Sioux Falls	
~~QUITAJIS~~	P	~~HIDE~~	P
~~LAPHA~~	~~BONDERS~~	~~AARON~~	HOWE
~~PETERMAN~~	MILLER	~~WAGNER~~	SOLLECITO

EXTRA MEN

LH	RH	LH	RH
	ALMONTE		GUZMAN
	DELANEY		ERVIN
	R. SMITH		

SWITCH HITTERS

PITCHERS

LH	RH	LH	RH
~~BONDERS~~	~~LAPHA~~	~~HOWE~~	~~AARON~~
~~MTELLE~~	~~PETERMAN~~		~~WAGNER~~
KENADY			SOLLECITO
SCHMITT			

Marty Scott's dugout scorecard of Ila's first game

who scouted me. He came up to me before the game and told me I already made history and now I can calm down and relax. I wasn't going anywhere, and I would have another shot tonight to redeem myself. No coach has ever done that for me or ever will [again]. This dream is not only for me anymore. It's for Mike Veeck, who took the chance; it's for Barry Moss; and it's for all the other people who I want to show that hard work does make unrealistic dreams come true. I pitched my guts out there tonight. Again I lost a piece of soul, but it's all worth it. Maybe I touched someone out there. God, I am so unstable right now it's funny.

In Sioux Falls, Steve Howe made a special point to go over to Ila and tell her he was rooting for her. He too knew what it was like to be thought of by organized baseball as a one-person freak show, he told her. Good luck. Back home in St. Paul, she continued to get enough men out in the late innings to validate all the chanting. Something magical was happening again, and even Ila, tortured and alone, could feel it.

There is a train that runs behind the St. Paul Saints' field. The engineer driving the train waves to me [and I can see he's saying], "Hi, Ila. Good luck." On the train was a sign that said GO, ILA. This has made my day. This definitely made me feel awesome. All the guys [on the team] were laughing and said, "Yep, you made it, big time." Little do they know though. I can't stop here and don't want to. I want more; I just don't know how much more.

And yet there was still the shit to deal with. In the very next sentence of her diary, she continued:

There is only one guy [Saints player] that I have come into contact with that is an idiot, but God *is* he. He will not leave me alone. He does everything in his power to be right next me. It pisses me off because I can't say anything. Then I'll look like the bad one, the girl that caused trouble. I think he already broke my finger by throwing me his fastball from fifty feet and not telling me he was. Fucking prick. I hope he gets back to him what he has dealt to other people.

And then there was the press, which at times seemed almost to be conspiring against her. The barbs thrown by Patrick Reusse could mostly be ignored. The fat Minneapolis *Star Tribune* columnist, who was beginning to assume the physical contours of Sidney Greenstreet in *The Maltese Falcon,* had, after all, even made fun of Dave Stevens. Reusse might show Ila a little consideration, thought the reporters in the Saints' press box, but such was not the case. On July 19, the columnist with more chins than the Hong Kong phone book wrote a satirical piece about a make-believe movie called *Chasing Ila.*

Spewing sour grapes, Reusse wrote in a mock review:

The mastermind [Mike Veeck] behind a low-budget, semiprofessional baseball team called the St. Paul Veecks [sic] signs a woman named Ila Borders to pitch. This is followed by so many fawning stories and television reports on the soft-throwing lefty that the mastermind announces: "This has worked out so well that we're in heavy pursuit of Scott Aldred [a terrible Twins pitcher]. He has the fastball for it. All he needs is a ponytail."

Even the Associated Press made an Ila-related mistake with ramifications in sports pages across the country. Pitching in Sioux Falls, Ila had had a nice night on June 3 against Sioux City, throwing to seven men, scattering two hits, walking no one, and striking out one. Unfortunately, the AP's man at the game made an error in toting up his statistics at the end of the game, misreading a column labeled BF (batters faced) as BB (bases on ball.)

Presswise, Ila was fucked by the story. Though she'd face seven batters with good results, hundreds of newspapers across the country, including the Minneapolis *Star Tribune,* wrongly headlined stories that she'd given up seven walks in one appearance.

Ila shook it off, telling me she didn't care about the bad pub. But by now I could tell that the silent Ila was seething. Meantime, most of the players, she said, had been nice—or nice enough. She had made it clear that she wouldn't go out with any ballplayers, despite the fact that two handsome Duluth-Superior Dukes had already asked her out and male and female would-be groupies for the talented and attractive woman pitcher lined the route to the team bus after every game. Ila would scribble autographs for them all, then quickly board the bus, grab a seat, and open another book. Her rules, by necessity, kept Ila by herself.

"Going out with a ballplayer during the season would just confirm what a lot of people are thinking," she said, "that I'm out here because I like looking at naked men, when, in fact, what I want to do is make the majors. And besides, my last boyfriend couldn't take the fact that I was a *baseball* player."

With the ground rules clear, Ila had been given one sign of acceptance early in the season by becoming the target of practical jokes that are standard for all first-year players. "I get razzed by my teammates a lot because I'm a rookie," Ila said, "but that's to be expected. It's a ritual. So I didn't mind when they gave me a hotfoot in the bullpen. I expected the pine-tar-under-the-brim-of-my-cap joke. I laughed when they threw a shaving cream pie in my face. I would have been mad if they *hadn't* razzed me like everybody else. I'm a *rookie.*"

When Ila sat in the bullpen in foul territory with the other relief pitchers during games, she would even be passed the tiny binoculars the notoriously wolfish players used to check out prospects in the stands. "They'd say, 'Ila, check her out. Is she right for me?' or 'Ila, that guy over there likes you,'" she said, laughing. "They'd say, 'Ila, get that woman's boyfriend away from her for a while, so I can see if she's checking me out.'"

Borders then paused. She recalled something else, frowned, and expressed the fear that she was sounding whiny. In 1997, Ila mostly took the abuse. Already offered two professional contracts by men's minor league teams for 1998, she was convinced that with her repertoire of pitches she could, within a few years, make the major leagues. This, her rookie year, she said, would be her next step up in history.

Meantime, as her teammates went out after games and partied on the road, she stayed in her motel room, looking for clues to survival in the life and career of Jackie Robinson, her most inspirational "first." And as the players realized that Borders actually could be an effective relief pitcher who wanted no special treatment, there continued to be new signs of acceptance among the Saints.

It also helped that she'd gained the respect of Dwight Smith, the veteran former major leaguer whose easy style and encouraging words to all naturally made him the Saints' team leader. To Ila, gaining Smith's respect wasn't playing team politics; it was more like when Jackie was accepted by his esteemed Brooklyn Dodger teammate Pee Wee Reese during his first year, when other players wouldn't shake the black man's hand.

The rest of the players saw Smith's sign that Borders was a part of the team and were further impressed when she ran out on the field to protect her teammates during a bench-clearing brawl against Madison. And when word leaked out in the St. Paul paper that the "Late Show with David Letterman" was still trying to book her, she told inquiring teammates that the reason she wasn't going on was because she didn't want to fly to New York and miss a game. And when it came out that the "Today" show had also called for Ila, she told her teammates that she said no because she was like all baseball players—she slept until noon.

Instead, she would speak on the field. Later that summer, Borders took the mound against the Sioux City Explorers and her nemesis, Ed Nottle, who'd earlier in the year called her "that *thing*." Borders struck out the first batter she faced, and the second popped up. The next batter walked. Now coming to the plate was none other than embittered ex-Saint Kevin Garner, always one of the league leaders in home runs. At thirty-one, he hadn't retired, as he'd promised to do the year before, but he still hated Marty Scott for trading him from the bright lights of St. Paul to the more pastoral pleasures of Sioux City.

"I couldn't expect to overpower Kevin Garner," Borders said afterward. "But I can outfinesse him. It was David and Goliath."

Garner pounded his chest like a simian, his ritual before every at-bat, as he approached the plate. Ila wound up, threw a lollipop, and Garner lifted a lazy popup that was easily caught in the infield. Garner, a good sport, gave Ila a big grin as he trudged back to his dugout.

While Ila ran off the mound, she didn't look at Nottle. "We passed each other once in the season and *grrrrrrd* at each other," said Ila, laughing. In fact, she went on, "I kind of like old Ed. And what Ed said about me was nothing compared to what I've had to go through to get here. Sometimes I'll say to myself, 'Why are you doing this? Why didn't you take up golf or tennis?' And then I remember. I just love playing baseball."

After making the team and some nice appearances in games, Ila still felt the pressure from the press, which for a couple of months virtually set up camp at the St. Paul ballpark. Ila needed work and couldn't get in an inning without the eyes of the world on her. The *Saint Paul Pioneer Press* published a daily "Borders Watch," while the national press—from *Sports Illustrated* to Fox

News—kept showing up for stories and interviews, which Ila rarely gave—especially if her teammates were around.

She was doing well enough for a rookie; overlooking her first appearance, Ila had a 3.00 earned run average, far below the league average. But the Saints' relief corps, which at one time looked iffy, was too seasoned for her to ever get many innings. Marty, despite his outlaw's beard, still played the game by the book. And in that mystical book, you don't use your rookies, male or female, when you're fighting for first place.

Which, despite the lack of on-field chemistry, the Saints were somehow doing. Battling to stay above .500, the team still found itself in contention in late June for the first-half pennant in the weak Eastern Division. And now that the lethargic Saints were in a race of the mediocre, Marty said he was damned if he was going to trust *any* rookie on the mound.

Hence, although he was proud of signing Ila, Scott was now leery of pitching her (or any other greenhorn) in a pennant race. Marty had given her a spot on the team, but he needed a veteran left-handed closer right now more than a media phenomenon who, if she messed up, would make him look like the manager of a sideshow, not a baseball team in contention.

"What am I going to do with her?" Marty asked me in his windowless office shortly before a game. "What can I do with her?"

"Keep her, Marty," I begged. I'd never before been asked my opinion by a real baseball man. "Keep throwing your fastball pitchers, then bring her in for two batters in the eighth inning. Then they won't be able to time her."

Marty looked up at me like I was the biggest idiot in the world and politely waved me out of his office. Something, I knew, was up—Marty, it turned out, had kindly cooked up a trade where Borders could get away from the media glare and also receive a lot more pitching time.

On June 25, it was announced that Ila had been traded to Duluth, who at 4–16 had the worst record in the league, as well as the second-worst team earned run average (6.11). Marty, who'd told Ila shortly before that night's home game against Thunder Bay that she was a goner, put it simply.

"I told her, 'This is a chance to pitch more often and in a less pressured environment,'" Scott said after the game to a gaggle of reporters. "She wasn't getting a lot of work here," he continued. "She'll get that chance in Duluth, because the fact is that we have four left-handed relievers and that's too many." Though he sounded like a manager, Marty looked like a worried, paternalistic father who'd just sent his daughter for a senior year abroad in satyr-filled Paris.

Ila, stunned, took off her uniform in her segregated runway before the game against the Thunder Bay Whiskey Jacks and then shook hands good-bye with all the Saints. She went outside Midway Stadium and sat shotgun in a pickup truck as she waited for general manager Bill Fanning to give her a one-way ticket to Duluth.

"Thanks," Ila told Fanning as she took the plane ticket through a crack in the window. Fanning looked surprised; most players feel that being traded, no matter the reason, is akin to being dumped by a lover.

"The more pitching the better," she told the general manager. She had appeared in only seven regular season games for the Saints and left with a record of 0–0, six innings pitched, and five strikeouts.

Mike Veeck, however, felt mixed emotions. "This has been a tough day, but Ila won't have the label of being just another Saints promotion in Duluth and she won't have as much pressure there. I believe that she'll pitch better because it's just human nature to be more relaxed when you're not under the microscope. We did everything we could here [for her]. She didn't make appearances, she didn't do Leno or Letterman, she didn't do all the literally hundreds of requests she got. She just tried to pitch. But she didn't get the innings here that she's going to get in Duluth."

It all made sense. The trade had been approved by the Duluth-Superior Dukes' owner, Jim Wadley, a businessman from San Diego. His daughter had been the first girl to play for a boys' Little League team in San Diego County, and she had competed with boys' teams through junior and senior high school.

Mike, however, still was worried. "I'm the most hated man in St. Paul right now," he said. "My three-year-old daughter, Rebecca, loved Ila more than any other player, and she cried when I told her she'd been traded."

Nor was Keith English, the Duluth Duke infielder who'd been traded for Borders, feeling any better. "I got traded for a girl," he told the Duluth newspaper. "It can't get any worse than that. I will probably be the most hated person in St. Paul," English, twenty-two, said. "They're losing their Ila."

Ila felt a little sick as she waited for her plane at the Minneapolis–St. Paul International Airport.

Traded (airport):
God, I feel like I am in a tailspin. What is up and what is down? How could this be? Am I done? I feel like shit. They didn't want me anymore, but I guess someone else did. What's in store for me? God, I don't even know myself. All I know is when I get out there on the mound for the Dukes, they will experience something weird. It's weird how I change. When I am out on the mound, nothing gets in my way. I am in a state of rage, but focusing too. I am afraid of nothing, have confidence, and nothing is going to get in my way. I wish I could be one or the other. (God, who is going to pick me up at the [Duluth] airport? Where can I hide?)

Come early July, perhaps in penance, Mike decided to sign one of the most lusted-after ballplayers in the country for the Saints. Not only would J. D. Drew keep the minds of Midway Stadium fans off Ila, it was also a unique way to simultaneously tweak the nose of organized baseball—and see a player at the beginning of his career whose homers went as far, high, and hard as Darryl Strawberry's.

J. D. Drew was the most remarkable Saint athlete to watch in 1997. At six-foot-one and 195 pounds, the twenty-one-year-old looked like some hero straight out of a Bernard Malamud novel or off a Wheaties box, a center fielder whose multiples of home runs *sounded* different than everybody else's dingers down here in the Northern League. It was the sound of the major leagues, and you didn't have to be Don Wardlow to sense the meaning of that crack of ball against Drew's bat.

He hit a game-winning homer on the first swing of his second at-bat in his first game for the Saints in early July, and playing forty-four games for the Saints, Drew hit 18 homers, drove in 50 runs, and had a club-record slugging percentage of .706. He was, needless to say, voted the Northern League's Rookie of the Year.

Like Strawberry before him, Drew was unexpectedly transformed by the Saints' "Fun Is Good" slogan that Veeck had insisted be the motto and philosophy of his team. But unlike just about everyone else on the team, Drew was going up to the Show, and the Saints weren't his last stop before Palookaville. He'd come to St. Paul just to keep his bat warm and stay in shape. Drew said, but he was enjoying baseball in a way he hadn't in the many years since he'd known he would, barring injuries, be a multimillionaire major leaguer.

"St. Paul is more fun that I can put in words," Drew said after a couple of weeks with the team. "And Marty is a great manager to break in with in pro ball."

"But what about getting hurt?" I asked him. "Wouldn't you rather have a couple million dollars in your hand than several more perhaps waiting for you in a bush?"

Drew laughed. "I'll talk baseball as much as you want," he said, "but if you want to talk finances, you'll have to talk to my agent."

No thank you. Agent Scott Boras was one of the more renowned pricks in baseball. Drew was more fun to talk to and hang around, a fact that shocked the rest of the Saints' players, who were expecting a prima donna who'd already learned to "big-league" the lesser lights of his team, which was everybody.

Drew was having fun, but already he had learned the trick of double-talk-say-nothing that ruled among major league ballplayers. Other Saints would also get a shot at other big league organizations during the off-season, mostly because of the need for the majors' two new expansion teams in Arizona and Tampa Bay to stock their brand-new farm systems. But nobody seemed like he was already there but Drew.

For the Saints' fans, Drew was the new Strawberry. Everybody seemed happy up in the stands. Vince Jeannette's tailgate barbecue in the parking lot continued to draw over 100 people a game, while inside, the 1997 promotions came off with the beauty of the absurd that only Mike Veeck could dream up. For "Inventors Night," the Saints paid tribute to Ron Popiel, the inventor and TV pitchman of the famous Veg-O-Matic, Pocket Fisherman, and the Clapper. "Chia Pet Night" was also a good one, as was the traditional "Bat Day" (Bill Veeck, naturally, had one).

There was also "K-Tel Night," when the Saints honored the nearby record company that over the last twenty years had become the leading purveyors of disco and schlock rock compilation records. "Green Eggs and Spam Night" celebrated the fact that all of the world's supply of the infamous Spam was made in nearby Austin, Minnesota. Every game was turned into Pirandello for the regular Joe.

My favorite was "Jerry Garcia Night," held in honor of the late Grateful Dead leader who had been one of Mike's favorite rock & roll heroes. The Saints took the field in the first inning dressed in tie-dyed uniforms; when Eric Webster, the 1997 PA announcer, introduced the lineups, he sounded as if he'd just swallowed a tab of Owsley's best acid. He used that voice, dripping hallucinogenics for the rest of the game, eerily echoing Chip Monck, the stage announcer at Woodstock. "Stay away from the brown LSD," Webster told the conservative citizenry of St. Paul, "and don't freak out when the same players start showing up again to bat in the third or fourth inning. You aren't," he boomed over the PA, "experiencing a flashback."

Webster too reveled in the absurd. When a visiting player hit a home run, all he'd mumble into his microphone was "Whatever." If an opposing player legged out a double, he might add, "Your ability to move your feet in rapid succession is of no interest to us."

My favorite moment on the field came in the eighth inning on August 10, when Bill Murray took the third base coach's box with the score tied. Murray's presence had been rare in 1997 at Midway Stadium; word in St. Paul was that he'd just gotten married and was tied up in family and film career.

But still he came, now and again. He put on a uniform that day and borrowed Marty's spot in the third base coach's box. The Saints had been losing 9–2 in the bottom of the second inning that August night before they began pecking away at the Canaries. Then, with the score tied 9–9 in the eighth, Murray waved Saints second baseman Lamarr Rogers home as he rounded third base. Rogers beat the throw by microns, and the Saints won 10–9. It was the greatest comeback in Saints history.

Still, the Minneapolis *Star Tribune* couldn't quite get it right. On Father's Day in June, under the "Corrections" section of the newspaper, it was reported that "A column on Page B2 last Sunday incorrectly said the St. Paul Saints baseball team is giving away a vasectomy today."

The misunderstanding had occurred because Mike had mentioned to a reporter that he was thinking of giving away a vasectomy during a Father's Day game for his Charleston River Dogs. Mike had called off the promotion when Charleston's archdiose complained, he said, that he was "belittling fatherhood."

Other than that, all seemed cool off the field. But on the field and inside Marty Scott's baseball head, the world was maddening.

The team was in first place with a 15–16 record by July 4, two games ahead of both Madison and Thunder Bay, but playing, to put it charitably, erratically. The Winnipeg Goldeyes struck out sixteen Saints and won 6–4 on July 9. The next afternoon the Saints clinched a tie for the first-half Eastern title by beating Fargo 8–3 and upping their record to 19–18.

Marty was not especially impressed. The previous week the Saints evened their record by beating Fargo 11–10 in eleven innings. "It was a typical Northern League game; we just couldn't put them away," he said after the game. "It was one of those nights where you have a headache after the game."

Marty was even beginning to question his own judgment, once even publicly accusing himself of overmanaging. It happened in Winnipeg with its short-porch outfield, when he yanked reliever Brian McRoberts in the ninth inning of a Saints 7–5 win near the end of the season's first half. "We've lost five games in the bottom of the ninth," Scott said. "I let the ballpark intimidate me. I almost outguessed myself."

On July 5, the Saints beat Fargo and clinched the Eastern Division half-pennant with a mediocre record of 18–18, but Marty wasn't feeling any better.

Owner Jim Wadley himself picked Ila up from the local airport the night the Saints traded her, got her a meal, and delivered her to the Dukes' ballpark in time for the seventh inning. Now she'd be away from the high-media Twin Cities and could work on her pitching.

Meantime, George Mitterwald, Duluth's manager, didn't know what to make of Borders for her first two weeks with the new team and didn't pitch her at all. Mitterwald, a former major league catcher with the Minnesota Twins, was, to put it mildly, of the baseball old school. So was Mike Cuellar, the Dukes' pitching coach and the 1969 Cy Young Award winner with the Baltimore Orioles.

And so Ila sat on her ass while her two on-field bosses tried to decide what to do with her. They had been to the majors and had that "I've been in the Show" attitude that somehow made it impossible for them to put a woman on the mound against men professionals. Maybe, Cuellar suggested, Ila should reconsider the Silver Bullets.

No way. Less than a month before the Silver Bullets had gotten into a bench-clearing melee with the Americus Travelers, the state champions in the Georgia Recreation and Parks eighteen-and-under league. Though Ila would participate in a bench-clearing brawl herself that season, it would be with a men's team. She knew she would never get to the bigs by playing the Georgia under-eighteen state baseball champions. And still she languished in the bullpen, watching the swirl.

Well, I am getting pretty pissed off. I haven't pitched in almost two weeks. How in the hell am I supposed to stay sharp? This is insane.

What else is weird is the groupies. At St. Paul, there were only two guys that had tons of groupies, here there are tons. These girls just line up for the guys. Girls and guys are now trying to get with me. Funny how I am a nerd.

I am not going to fuck up my dream because of sex. I've seen too many people fuck up themselves because of this. Plus could you see that in the papers the next day? I would lose everything in a second. Because of this, I am first on the bus and sit in the back. Well, I better go, something was just slipped under my door. I pray to God it's not another threat.

And then, with no warning, Ila's Duluth purgatory ended. It was the eighth inning, and the Dukes were trailing the Madison BlackWolf 6–3, when Cuellar ordered her to warm up. She received a standing ovation when she ran from the bullpen to start the ninth in place of Jeremy McGarity, the Dukes' starter. The echoes of the handclaps could still be heard as the first batter Ila faced, Kevin Walton, slammed a curveball into center for a single.

Lino Connell came up next, and he lunged at one of Borders's changeups. The ball tinkled to the Dukes' second baseman, who started an easy double play. Next up was the dangerous Nate Vopata, who had already hit a triple, double, and single in the game. A homer would give the BlackWolf shortstop the cycle—and he had already hit a home run off Ila and her fastball earlier in the year when she was still pitching for the Saints.

Ila began with another fastball, which Vopata fouled off. Then came a curve, which Vopata ground harmlessly to Duke second baseman Ryan Rodriguez. Though the Dukes lost, everyone seemed to leave Wade Stadium with a smile.

First game with the Dukes:
I finally got in and to my surprise did well. I was so nervous,

because I knew this was my test to management and coworkers. Everyone warmed up to me after the game. I finally feel like I fit in. Sometimes I have to watch my ass. They all treat me with respect and actually like me, but I kind of have to stand back so I won't look like I am after anything else than baseball. It was so cold today that Jamison Nuttle and I built a fire in the bullpen. My face was totally smudged black because I was so close to the fire. Nuttle almost burnt all the pitchers in the bullpen because he was igniting the fire with bug repellant with alcohol in it. We burned a bat, towel, and a bunch of napkins. It's weird, I'm having a blast every day.

Because they could, the Saints meantime folded in the second half like Murphy beds. While Marty pulled at his beard over players with their thumbs up their asses, Duluth came out of nowhere and into the second-half pennant race. If they were going to win the championship, Mitterwald would *have* to pitch Borders—his team didn't have enough arms. Indeed, he sometimes left Ila in the most difficult situations, almost as if he wanted her to fail miserably.

Her worst outing all year came in Duluth against the Saints, who pounded her for three hits and four runs in one inning while the Duluth manager refused to lift her in a 16–3 loss. Saints radio announcer Don Wardlow openly rooted for her on the air, but Ila felt humiliated by her failure. And after several weeks, the boys on the bus weren't helping much either.

Well, the guys are going nuts again. Everyone is drinking beer on the bus except two, including me. There are two girls in front of the bus that are BA [bare-assing] the bus and giving the guys frontal and boob shows. Now some guys are BA and giving a frontal view. God, most of them are drunk. Oh shit, the window just broke in the front of the bus because someone's ass was pushed on it too hard. This is what you call buns of steel. This is funny.

There is this guy next to me watching pornos on his laptop. How uncomfortable this is. Is he doing this to test me? He must be lonely and missing someone because he is going off. Now everyone is on it. At least turn the volume down, eh? I don't think they are testing me now. They are just horny.

With Ila's help, the Dukes beat the listless Saints to the division's second-half pennant. On August 20, Duluth beat the Saints 5–3, and St. Paul landed in last place. "The players think they can turn it on and off and still be ready for the playoffs," Marty Scott said after the game, in which the Saints made five errors. "I've got news for them. It doesn't work that way. These guys finished the first half strong, and it seems like it went to their heads."

Indeed. Duluth barely won the second half with a record of 22–20, one game ahead of St. Paul. The Dukes then dispatched the Saints, three games to two, in the first round of the league playoffs. In Duluth, the Saints watched forlornly from their dugout on September 8 as the Dukes, including Ila, hoisted pitcher Jeremy McGarity on their shoulders in honor of his complete game 3–2 win.

Ila's turn for glory would come in a few days, on September 9 during the eighth inning of Game 6 in the league championship against Winnipeg. Mitterwald, his team facing the heart of Winnipeg's batting order, sent in Borders to pitch to the Goldeyes' best hitters.

This is the happiest point in my life. God, am I lucky and blessed. All the pain, pressure, and shit was worth it for just this one moment in time. I pitched one inning in the playoffs against Winnipeg. Plus, I had to face number-two, number-three, and number-four hitters. Every scout was in the stands, so were the presidents of [every] team, president of the league, and others. I got number-two hitter to pop up to shortstop and walked number-three hitter. I got number-four to pop up to the shortstop. I had two outs and a person at first—one more to go. I faced number-five batter, who was in AAA [the highest minor leagues] last year. I ended up striking him out on a fastball on the outside corner of the plate. It was so awesome, because everyone gave me crap about my fastball, but that's what got by him.

Against all odds, the Duluth Dukes had won the Northern League championship, and Ila had survived the entire year to earn the ring each member of a professional championship baseball team is given. "I feel," she says, "like I contributed."

Over the coming winter, Borders prepared for 1998 by spending all of her time either training or working in her mother's day-care center in Orange County, California. I went to visit her there, where I found a young woman determined to add five miles an hour to her fastball in the off-season by throwing 100 pitches a day and lifting weights, "a little, for strength, not bulk." Off-season, she had dropped a few pounds; she'll add ten, she said, by next season by "eating six meals a day."

Her training philosophy, she said, is the same as it was when she was the only girl in the La Hambra Little League. "If the guys run four miles a day, then I'll run five," she said. "If they run three miles in fifteen minutes, I'll do it in fourteen."

And even as an Ila industry had begun popping up, Borders herself was concentrating the winter after her rookie season on improving her pitching and trying to decide where to sign next season: Duluth or Winnipeg. Meantime, her book and movie rights have been purchased by a film production company, and Paramount's Michael Pillar, director of the next *Star Trek* feature film, is already writing the screenplay.

She is familiar, she said, with the word from the baseball *cognoscenti*, who say she will never reach the Show. "I really don't pay attention to that," Borders said as she threw ball after ball into the net. "What I want," she continued, "is to make the major leagues. Every stop along the way I've been told that I can't do it. I was told that I can't play Little League, or high school, or college baseball. And I did. And now I'm playing professionally, and nobody said it was possible. So why should I all of a sudden start believing the people who are telling me that there is no way I'm going to make the majors?"

So maybe it had been worth it, all the hassles up the next rung to the Northern League. When in doubt, she had only to look back at her diary of the season.

A great thing happened to me today on my off day. I went to go sign autographs for the elderly and handicapped. This one guy held my hand and wore a Dukes hat that I signed. He said it was his number-one cherished item. Just when I think I want to change people's lives, they change mine.

It was a disappointing year for the Saints, especially for Marty Scott. Marty, a master psychologist, had gotten along with every team he'd ever managed. As a decade-long major league executive, he'd gained a reputation for tell-it-like-it-is honesty. But the 1997 Saints seemed beyond the reach of even Scott.

"I have never had a problem lighting a fire under a team," Marty said sadly after the season. "But at times I couldn't get through to this team. On a given day, we could beat a Class-AAA team. The next day we would have trouble against a Rookie League club."

Fungo: The act of hitting a fly ball to a player during practice. It is usually thrown up in the air by the batter or fungoer and hit as it descends through the strike zone. The primary purpose of this is to give fielders practice catching fly balls. The batter is often a coach. First printed use: "Then him and Carey was together in left field, catchin' fungoes . . ." (Ring Lardner, Round Up, 1929).
—*The Dickson Baseball Dictionary*

I felt terrible for Marty; that season I was drawn, like Bill Murray, to the old-timers on the team, to "the adults" (as the comedian put it). So for the flip side of the 1997 Saints Job-like manager, I turned to their aged first base coach Twig. For him, the first-chance 1997 season had been as rewarding as the last-chance championship season of 1996.

"Each spring still feels like the first one or I'd quit," Twig told me when I was finally able to pin him down long enough for an interview. At seventy-one, he still liked to scurry around at all times: throwing batting practice, hitting fungoes, picking up lost baseballs, or giving pointers to guys who were never going to play beyond the Northern League.

"Why would you want to interview me?" Twig asked me for over a year. "I'm happy to help you out, but I'm really not that interesting."

Like hell.

"Tell me more of the Twig saga," I asked him as he loaded batting practice balls into a bucket during the Saints' 1997 season.

He shrugged and said, "You know, I didn't have much of a career."

Wayne "Twig" Terwilliger, at age seventy-two, would be back in 1997 for his forty-ninth season inside a baseball uniform. By 1998, he would be one of only four men in baseball history to wear a professional uniform for fifty years. "The one year in the last forty-eight I was out of baseball was 1968, and I was miserable," remembered Twig. "I opened a bar, and the bar was struggling, and I said to my wife, 'Let's get out of here.'"

After Twig stowed all the batting practice balls he'd thrown that day, we moved to the Midway Stadium bleachers. Except for Twig, still in his uniform, the stadium was empty except for head groundskeeper Connie Rudolph—baseball's first woman groundskeeper. As her tractor rounded the infield, Twig waved and smiled at Connie, looked into the sun, and laughed. "So I'm running this bar, and I get a call from the Senators saying, 'You wanna get back in baseball?' And I said, 'In a minute.' So I got back in again. That year off—no good."

"But Twig," I said, "you're seventy-two, you have grandchildren you love, and you have two World Series rings that you earned coaching the Twins and raising superstars. Don't you want to stop taking wee-hour bus rides to Thunder Bay?"

"Every year I'm still alive, I ask myself, 'Well, how do you feel?' " Twig said. "And if I feel good, I say, 'I should stay in baseball because I know I can still contribute.' It's good just to be around the guys and let them know they made a good play or a good move. I know how much that means. I didn't get much of that when I was a player. You wouldn't think of it, looking at me, but I needed that pat on the back. I think doing that for the Saints is my biggest contribution."

Not quite. Beyond giving strokes, coaching first base, and pitching batting practice, Twig continued in 1997 in his role as one of baseball's fungo *maestros*. He was modest about his skill at the peculiar and difficult art. "Oh no," he said. "Now Nellie Fox could *really* hit a fungo."

I pointed out to Twig that Nellie took his secrets to the grave. Nellie Fox had died fifteen years before, with a chaw in his mouth and, later, a plaque in the Hall of Fame. Twig nodded and smiled at the mention of Fox—another of his legendary contemporaries who no one he now coaches for the Saints has probably ever heard of. "That's okay," said Twig, "they're nice kids."

Back to fungoes. "And is it true what they say about Jimmy Reese?" I asked. "That he could place a fungo within a foot of an outfielder?"

"Oh, Jimmy Reese," Twig said, nodding his head. "He was still hitting fungoes in the outfield with the California Angels until he was ninety. He was the best. He really was." Twig nodded.

Suddenly Twig seemed taken aback at hearing the name of Reese, famous among coaches but few else, who died at ninety-two in 1994. A legend among the already anonymous, Reese, it was said, could in practice place a fungo from home plate to a spot on the warning track one foot from the glove of an outfielder running full speed for it. He wielded his fungo bats—specially made sticks longer and narrower than ordinary bats—like Stradavari and guarded them as such.

Twig also guarded his two fungo bats, holding them himself rather than handing them to any bus driver or leaving them in the dugout. They disappear. Fungo bats, shaped so as to guarantee perfect placement from a coach working out his players, were looked on by some as sort of talismans. And these were Twig's fungo bats.

As he was the only living fungo king, one would think the makers of Louisville Slugger would make special fungo bats for Twig, as they do every other coach in the majors, but no. "You should have seen the fungo bats I used to get in the majors. Here [in the Northern League] I have to keep taping them together whenever my fungo bats crack," Twig said. "But that's okay. A fungo bat is a fungo bat."

And they can be used for many purposes. For a coach who wants to let his players rest and lollygag, he can fungo lazy pop flies that no one is forced to move to catch. If his team is bad at fielding in the outfield, a good fungo hitter can hit with his weird bat the exact kind of balls that cause them trouble. And if he is in the mood to punish a player, a good fungo hitter can make his target run after just-barely-uncatchable fly balls all afternoon. In the infield, the fungo hitter can be a prince, or someone who is able to hit bad hops all day to his whiskey-handed ballplayers. It all depends on the day. Or the result of last night's game. Or how much of a prick the coach is.

Twig, on the other hand, is beloved by the players. They gather around his locker to hear his stories, which he usually refuses to tell. Yes, he played fourteen years of professional ball and over a ten-year period played with almost a third of the major league teams. And, yes, his best year hitting was .312, the year he'd been sent down by the Brooklyn Dodgers to the AAA St. Paul Saints. "I was back in the Show in a jiff," Twig tells his Saints. "You can come back. I did."

But Twig's career as a player is not the reason he is one of the four to stay in uniform for fifty years—it's because he is the master of the fungo. The late Jimmy Reese, the king of kings, is another whose fungo-hitting got him half a century in uniform (the others are Connie Mack and Don Zimmer). "Yeah, Jimmy Reese with his fungo bats," Twig says, "he really could hit 'em where they're't. Or were. Depending on the day."

The only reason I knew Jimmy Reese, nee Jimmy Solomon, is that before coaching he had briefly been a Jewish teammate and scrubeenie on some of Babe Ruth's greatest Yankee teams. Yet even with Reese's death, even as he holds his two skinny fungo bats like rare Ming dynasty sculpture, Twig refuses the title of fungo champ.

To me, Twig's habit of quietly refusing to take credit for anything seemed almost Zen-like. And it just ain't over fungoes. When asked about being eighteen years old and in the Marines' first assault wave on to Iwo Jima, Twig just shrugged. Yes, he witnessed the famous raising of the flag on Iwo, he was lucky to be alive, and damn right he felt grateful to be still sitting here talking on a sunny day in the bleachers.

I could have gotten more information from the first sentence on the back of his 1952 Topps baseball card that showed him with the Brooklyn Dodgers:

Wayne had a truly impressive war record, having served with the Fightin' Marines at Saipan, Tinian and Iwo Jima.

Twig sighed and looked up at me. "At Iwo, the Japanese didn't fire until after our second assault wave," he said. "They just let our first wave in before they opened up on us with fire. I was very fortunate to have come out."

He didn't want to talk about it. So we returned to baseball. "The game really hasn't changed at all in half a century," he said. "I mean, forget the money, the artificial turf, and that players are bigger and stronger than ever. You still have to hit the ball. You still have to catch the ball. You still need the right instincts while playing. Baseball has stayed exactly the same."

Twig paused, then thought of one other thing. "Batting helmets," he said. "When I played, no one wore batting helmets. There is no way you're going to tell me it's not an advantage to go up to the plate with that thing sitting on top of your head. I got beaned in the old days before batting helmets, but it never dawned on me then to wear anything but my cap to the plate."

The result was almost surreal, as are many of Twig's stories, all of which check out as true. Indeed, having a fastball plunk him right in the head gave Twig his weirdest, as well as his first, professional RBI. Playing his rookie year in Des Moines, the team was in Denver when Twig came to bat with the bases loaded. The count moved to three and two, and Twig then fouled off several pitches in a row.

"Finally the pitcher beaned me. I got hit right in the head. I was looking curveball, and he threw me a fastball," Twig continued. "So

I got an RBI, but it was a painful one. I somehow wandered down to first base, and the next guy, his name was Bob Orkowski, hit a triple. And I managed to stagger around the bases and finally score. I don't remember too much after that."

Well, when pushed to beef a little, there is one other little change that bugs the ever-cheerful Twig. "Back then we did not get high-fives for hitting a dribbler to second base that moved someone to third," he said. "I don't remember us getting high-fives for that. Now you get a high-five for everything. High-fives are definitely overdone."

It is the older arts of baseball that Twig excels at, like the science of the 100 fungoes he hits each day to the Saints during practice. "The fungo bat," he said, holding his skinny pieces of lumber, "is designed so you don't have to use much effort to hit a good fungo. But I swing a fungo bat like a regular bat. I don't just throw the ball up and *tunk* it, I take a full swing like a baseball bat. If I have a good day and I hit it solid, I hit the good fungoes. You have your good days and bad days of hitting fungoes."

But when the fungoes are popping, sometimes Twig has trouble controlling himself and falls into a fungo high. "Sometimes I get so carried away with infield practice if it's going good. I want to keep it going fast, and then I hurry and get my bat too out in front of the ball," he said.

And sometimes wickedly hit fungoes can be a form of punishment for lollygagging Saints. "Oh yeah," explained Twig, "by really ripping one, it jumps on them. The ball just takes off."

But usually they are meant to teach—subtly. "I say if a player out there is doing well fielding, then don't change anything, no matter how he's doing it. It's when you notice a guy is having a little trouble that you might say, 'Hey, try this, and if that doesn't work, we'll try something else.' Winnipeg is the only park in the league with artificial turf, so we might take some extra balls there just to get used to the hop."

He had hit hundreds of thousands of fungoes and yet never wondered where the word came from. According to William Safire, a dictionary editor named Joan H. Hall had written *The New York Times* columnist with an etymological theory based on the Scottish verb "fung"—which means "to pitch, toss, fling." Ms. Hall had traced the word back to Aberdeen in 1804, and the stanzas "Ye witches, warlocks, fairies, fien's! Daft fungin' fiery pears an' stanes." Baseball's connection, she wrote Safire, is that the fungo is thrown in the air; the *o* was added as in other games like keno, bingo, and bunco.

Twig, hearing me spout the theory, looked at me as if I were a Venusian. He then politely changed the subject. "Like I said, I hit my fungoes differently than you're supposed too. Now Jimmy Reese was an artist—he could place a ball within an inch of anywhere."

Twig's strong, humble pride was set in stone, and all the players treated him as a respected wise man. Not after his life. After the war, Twig said, he played major league ball for the Chicago Cubs before being traded to the Brooklyn Dodgers in 1951. "I was going from a last-place club to a club that was thirteen games in front at the time," Twig went on, laughing. "The rest is history, you know."

Yes. The New York Giants somehow caught the Dodgers in 1951, then beat them in a playoff for the National League pennant with a game-ending home run by Bobby Thomson. Dubbed the "Shot Heard Round the World," marked by Giants announcer Russ Hodges screaming, "The Giants win the pennant! The Giants win the pennant!", it was an epochal event that was most recently and artfully captured in the first chapter of Don DeLillo's *Underworld*.

"Now I realize it was a big deal," Twig went on. "I saw them replay it last night on ESPN with commentary from my old teammate Pee Wee Reese. But at the time all I thought it meant was that I would miss out on the World Series for the first time. I also figured I'd lose about five thousand dollars, which was about what you got back then for being in the Series. That was the exact amount the Dodgers were paying me for the entire year."

So he played with Jackie Robinson, but in a couple seasons, the Brooklyn Dodgers optioned Twig to the St. Paul Saints. "I was like a lot of guys here on the team now," he says. "I was just trying to get someone to notice me down there and give me a chance again."

It worked. He batted .312 for the Saints in 1952 and was picked up by the Washington Senators, a team so historically woeful that it is beyond jokes. But he played against Mickey Mantle, and it was with the Senators that Twig got his most memorable hit. His team may have sucked, but he had his key single memorialized by *The Washington Post*'s Shirley Povich, perhaps baseball's finest beat writer ever and immortal for his lead to Don Larsen's 1956 World Series perfect game. "The million-to-one shot came in. Hell froze over. A month of Sundays hit the calendar."

"I got a bloop hit against the great Satchel Paige to win an extra-inning game," Twig said, "and Povich wrote the article. I don't really collect stuff, but I've still got *The Washington Post* with the headline 'Terwilliger Beats Paige with Single in Tenth.' That's probably the biggest highlight of my entire career."

After that, Twig went over to play for the New York Giants, where manager Leo Durocher kept the locker room filled with more celebrities than anybody until Tommy Lasorda forced the likes of Frank Sinatra and Don Rickles to watch his Los Angeles Dodgers undress. Durocher's wife then was the glamorous film actress Laraine Day, who would host a Giants television show after every game. "Laraine Day was really something else," Twig says, a man who I never once heard talk about any woman but his wife.

"I got to go on her show and sit on her couch twice, for fifty bucks each time," Twig remembered. "The 1950s were an exciting time to be in New York—I lived downtown in Manhattan at 52nd Street and took the subway right out to the Polo Grounds every day." He played with Willie Mays. He dined at Toots Shors. It was a good time.

Like all true Zen masters, Twig refuses the honorific, and has the proper sense of the absurd. In 1955, for example, he was optioned by the New York Giants to their AAA farm team, the Minneapolis Millers. Snow was still on the ground on Opening Day, Twig remembered, and in the second inning someone hit a ball into the drift in right field. "We had a right fielder named George Wilson," Twig said, "and since I'm playing second base, I run out to get the cut off. Well, George, instead of a baseball, throws in a snowball that exploded six feet in front of me."

No.

"Yeah, really," Twig says. "No one believes me, but that happened. True story."

Retired from active play at thirty-five, Twig began managing the New York Yankees' farm team in Greensboro, North Carolina. Over the years, he went on to manage in Burlington, North Carolina; Wisconsin Rapids, Wisconsin; Columbus, Georgia; Pensacola, Florida; and Geneva, New York. Twice he made it within a heartbeat of a major league manager's job when he skippered in AAA, the highest minors, for Hawaii and Buffalo. All told, he compiled a 1,062–969 record as a bush league skipper.

"It was a big thrill for me to manage young people and be successful," Twig said. "I had a good minor league record, but I never got a shot at managing in the big leagues." Twig shook his head, silently expressing the only regret I'd ever seen come from him. But then he returned to his sunniness. "But I came out as a coach, so that made up for it."

And then Ted Williams called for his help with the 1969 Washington Senators. "He said, 'You're my third base coach,' " Twig recalled. "Williams [said to me], 'You know about this part of the game, the hit and run, the bunt, and all that. You go ahead and do your thing at third base and I'll do what I know—the game between the pitcher and hitter.' "

From there, Twig went as a third base coach to the major league Texas Rangers, followed by a long gig as the first base coach for the Minnesota Twins. With them, in 1987 and 1991, Twig won two World Series rings. Then the Twins summarily fired him, with nary a good-bye. "I was a little bit upset," Twig said. "But then I thought about it and realized they had a young guy who was very competent, so agewise it made sense." He paused. "What's great about working with the Saints is that older people now come up to me and say, 'It's terrific that you're still in the game. It's good for we older people. You keep showing 'em we can do it.' "

He paused, then continued. "I didn't really leave the Twins," he said. And then he laughed. "They kind of left me. It was logical that I, as the older guy, should go."

But Mike Veeck picked up the phone as soon as he learned Twig had lost his major league position. And now, said Twig, as long as he could continue both helping out and putting up with the bus rides to Thunder Bay, he'd hang on. There was a hint of redemption and pride that he'd found a place to start over after getting canned by the Twins.

"I was uncomfortable going back [for the belated "Twig Night" at the Twins Metrodome last year]," he said simply. "I knew that event was meant to patch up a bit what had happened, and that was all right. I was glad it was over with."

Twig then shakes his head when asked if he'd been back once between leaving the Twins and "Twig Night." Would he go back now?

"I'm going back for 'Kirby Puckett Day,' " he said of one of his favorite pupils, who was prematurely retiring in 1997 after an eye injury. "But you know that's the only reason I'm going back." But even with that, Twig doesn't sound bitter, but like a proud ex-Marine who'd been shoved out the door by a bunch of suits.

"You're as young as you feel," Twig finished. "Last season I went parasailing in Wisconsin before a game with the BlackWolf, and it was great. I felt twenty-one, and this was my first chance."

I too felt twenty-one again, for different reasons. Bill Murray understood and gave his blessing in August. Two nights before, he'd seen his pal Mike promote his dream concert, starring the living embodiment of antidisco. Duluth's Bob Dylan had heard from St. Paul relatives about how special the Saints were and had turned down $10,000 more from a Minneapolis venue in order to play a live concert from the outfield of Midway Stadium.

The Saints were back in town the next night, and Murray, wearing a golf visor that blinked DYLAN, stood at his usual spot in the owners' box, razzing the Thunder Bay Whiskey Jacks, who the Saints eventually beat 12–4. After the game was over and the happy fans had filed out, Mike kept the stadium lights on for an impromptu game of baseball.

The players were members of the Saints' staff, Bill Murray and family, and any other straggler who wanted to play under the lights. It was an eventful game. Annie Huidekoper broke her nose in left field when a long fly missed her glove and hit her in the face.

Later, Murray, pitching, stood on the mound while Dave Wright approached the dish with a bat. Dave was not smiling. He'd been pissed at Murray since 1995, when the comedian had kicked beat reporter Mike Augustin out of a team-only party. Dave, as the Saints' PR director and Augie's good friend, had never forgiven him. He'd complained to Mike, but since he figured he was one of the little people, Dave assumed the star didn't even know what he'd done.

Dave, always a lousy ballplayer, stepped into the batter's box anticipating to strike out humiliatingly via one of the tricky fastballs and curves Murray had been throwing so far. Instead, in came a slow lollipop pitch right down the middle, and Dave smacked it hard into the outfield for a hit, probably his first since he was seven. Standing on first, Murray looked at him and smiled. In baseball, that pitch was as close as anybody gets to an "I'm sorry."

The next night, as the Saints again battled the Whiskey Jacks, I approached the comedian and finally told Murray some of the terrible things I was going to write about him. He grinned. "I *knew* you were after me," he said. "I just knew it. All *Rolling Stone* does is write bad reviews of my movies six months after they come out."

I approached the very nice woman with Murray and told her what a nice guy the comedian was for giving me hours and hours of interviews that he'd correctly surmised would be used to hang him in print. "You know, Bill has a dark side," she said, laughing mock conspiratorially.

The woman, as cool and un-Hollywood as one would expect of Bill Murray's mate, said she was only the "mother" of three of Murray's children, though others called her his "wife."

Murray then looked at the shy woman standing with me who was wearing a blue-colored Saints cap. An ardent anti-star-fucker, she began dissolving from the scenery by edging slightly behind me, then aiming for Tobias, the ball pig, and her favorite Saint, who was nearby resting between innings as his side-saddles were re-stocked with fresh wares for the home plate umpire.

"And who is this?" Murray said, still smiling, interrupting the woman's getaway, his improv actor's eye catching a character exiting the stage too soon. He waved her back.

"This is Shira," I said, "and I'm in love with her. It took awhile, but the Saints' fixed my karma to fall in love again. I haven't been in love in a very long time."

"I told you last year that that's what the Saints are about," Murray said.

"No you didn't," I replied.

"I just said you had to figure it out for yourself, that I couldn't tell you what this team means or can do."

Damn, he was right. I turned back to Shira, who seemed to have taken a vow of silence, and then at Murray. "She's so smart," I said. "She's so talented. She's so beautiful."

"I see," Murray mumbled, looking us both over and scratching his chin like some hepcat Sherlock Holmes.

Shira, an Iowa Jew from this land where Jews are tougher, wordlessly responded to me for completely embarrassing her in front of a movie star. A pacifist, she ground the heel of her brandless, consciously unfunky sneakers into my designer "Dr. J" tennis insert shoes, a model quickly discontinued by Converse because virtually everyone who bought too-expensive sneakers were so young that they had never *heard* of Julius "Dr. J." Erving, the basketball court's Picasso during the years surrounding "Disco Demolition Night."

"I used to be an old, heartless, schmuck, but I'm not one anymore," I told Murray, paraphrasing one of his final lines in "Scrooged," a slick, big budget Hollywood movie he made in the 1980s. Though she could quote from the original, Shira wasn't familiar with "Scrooged," an overblown update on Dicken's Christmas tale where Murray easily outclassed the picture in his role as a shamelessly exploitative head of a television network.

Shira, meantime, didn't even have or want a television. T.V. pop culture was an anathema to her, and though she could kick the world's ass in Scrabble, she knew neither who Lou Gehrig was, nor how he said good-bye.

This was good. Things were going well.

"I see, you're in love," Murray went on to me, nodding his head in preliminary approval. He then paused, and pursed his lips. "But will this love last?" he asked with a mock-passion resembling the "confessional" speech he gave as a rookie on "Saturday Night Live" two decades before that had made him famous. "Are you two together fool's good, or real gold? Are you the mother lode? There is one obvious way to tell if this is lasting love."

And Murray moved in closer to Shira and I.

It had clicked by mistake that summer, with a barely speaking acquaintance outside Midway Stadium ninety minutes before a Saints night game. Shira, a better photographer then I am an author, had been hired by some slick Eastern magazine empire that needed a quick head shot of me looking properly writerly for an upcoming contributor's page.

We agreed over the phone to meet at Midway Stadium, my home not just away from home, but the one place where I felt *better* than at home. Shira, who had never heard of Midway Stadium but thought she might have once been told of the St. Paul Saints, agreed reluctantly to cross the river from her Minneapolis photo lab, to subsidize her art by nabbing some quick New York commercial rates.

Shira wasn't just crossing the invisible divide between the Twin Cities, she couldn't understand why any writer with pretensions of being *real* would want their picture taken at a *ballpark*. "C'mon," I said when I finished posing ridiculously as if I were Saul Bellow, "stick around for the game. It's only an hour away."

She looked doubtful, until I quoted the-now 1954 cliché said by French deep thinker Jacques Barzun. "Whoever wants to know the heart and mind of America," he wrote in *God's Country and Mine*, "had better learn baseball."

"I *know* baseball," Shira said. "I grew up in Iowa playing third base. A softball broke my pinky finger as a kid." But that had been a long time ago. Now, to be a good sport for at least a few minutes, she went up to Mike Veeck at his turn-style. Ticketless she flashed him her Annie Leibovitz-I'm-a-pro-telephoto lens. Veeck waved her on through, Shira becoming one of the 100 people he'd let in to his sold out tent each night if they had a good enough act or vibe.

Inside, we first went to the souvenir stand, where I told Saints merchandise manager Bill Fisher that I needed to buy a cap. "Adjustable?" he asked, mentioning the one-size-fits-all Saints hat with plastic clasps on the back, "or fitted?"

Fitted, I said, and made Shira try on enough caps until she found one that fit just right. I then threw some bills at Fisher. "Who are you, Daddy Warbucks, mack?" she asked as she adjusted the brim.

"Don't call me mack, honey."

"Don't call me honey, mack."

We took seats where we could find them, and Shira took a deep breath of the fresh baseball diamond only a few yards away. "That grass smells good," she said, settling back, having only now decided to stay a few innings, "no, that grass smells great." She pushed up the Saints cap on her head. "I'm going to get a hot dog," she said, getting up and taking my order too. "I haven't had a hot dog in years."

While she was down at the concession stand, a train ran right behind the outfield fence, its engineer's head stuck out the locomotive's window. The crowd yelled "Train! Train! Train!," and the broadly smiling railroad man waved and blared his horn three times. I could have sworn he was looking directly at me. Something good had just happened inside my chest. Shira soon returned with her hot dog and my requested cheese curds (another Midwest delicacy as terrifying as lutefisk.)

"Did I miss anything?"

"I'm not sure," I said.

Two months later, Bill Murray is staring from a foot-and-a-half away at Shira and I. "Is this love?" he said. "Let's see something."

The film star then bent around Shira's shoulder so he could see the back of the gray Saints away cap which I'd given her—it was the same color Saints cap he always wore.

"Only one way to tell," he continued. "Let's see, is it adjustable or fitted?" Murray asked. And then he stood back. "It's going to work," he said to her. "He loves you. He got you a fitted cap."

She smiled, she fucking smiled.

Confessing to Murray had so lightened my soul that I decided to seek out the Canaries' Steve Howe the next day. I'd been avoiding him all year, but the Saints had taught me the importance of being a stand-up guy. I had to square accounts for what I'd done to him a dozen years before in the pages of *Rolling Stone*. I took a deep breath and went into the visitors' locker room before a game to say hi.

For days I had literally lived and slept in the same room with the Bees, smoked dope with the team, and weaseled out every confidence I could get from every player I could. I also followed around Howe, one of the most personable, outgoing men I'd ever done a story on, as well as the focus of the piece on baseball's biggest madman.

We'd grown friendly enough over the two weeks I trailed him that even though I didn't catch him doing drugs—my mission— Howe did give me the sweat-stained San Jose Bees hat that proved one of his many tickets back to the major leagues.

The searing piece had stuck with Howe; he mentions the *Rolling Stone* reporter who followed him around and named the team "the Bad Nose Bees" in his autobiography, *Between the Lines*. "Do what you did in the Bees article," *Rolling Stone* editors told me when they felt I wasn't being hard enough on Bill Murray in 1996.

Now I had to say . . . I'm sorry?

Howe, I knew, was considered insane by several sportswriters, but I had to let him know, even at the cost of a pummeling, that I felt regret for what I'd done so long ago. When I saw him in the locker room, holding court ten feet away, Howe appeared as if he'd aged three decades, despite the "Kurt Cobain in happier days" goatee he wore.

Smoking a cigarette while he juggled three baseballs, Howe noticed me as he began telling a story to his gathered-around teammates. He stopped juggling and his eyes narrowed. He remembered, which no ballplayer ever does.

"*Rolling Stone!?*" he yelled. And then he shook my hand. "Boys," he said to the rest of the Canaries, "let me introduce you to the man who once upon a time made me notorious in the pages of the *Rolling Stone*. Nice to see you again," he said as he resumed juggling his three baseballs.

I then showed Howe the baseball hat he'd given me a dozen years before, and Howe marveled how the team owner back then had been so broke that he'd outfitted his team with caps held together by cheapo adjustable plastic clasps. Even *girlfriends* of ballplayers were given caps individually fitted in wool. "Harry, Harry, Harry," Howe said, laughing, of the only man willing to give him a chance—then as Harry Steve and now as Harry Stavrenos with the Sioux Falls Canaries.

I then asked Howe for an interview that I could perhaps sell back to somebody in New York, an interview that would give his side of the handgun story that had been so notorious that David Letterman had given Howe his own Top Ten list. And what a story: the tale of a man who was playing for the Sioux Falls Canaries only moments after playing for twelve years in the Show with a 3.03 lifetime earned run average.

He refused with a smile. "I'm not talking to any reporters anymore on the record," he said nicely, flicking his cigarette and putting the balls back in the air. "C'mon down to Sioux Falls this summer, though, and I'll show you some fun. I've got a Harley."

I nodded yes and started walking back out of the locker room so the players could put on their game faces in peace. "Hey," Steve Howe yelled, waving me back. "You can say to New York that I realize that I can't look back. I am at peace now. This isn't the big leagues. But I come to the park every night, and wind is blowing, and the grills are grilling, and I'm with a bunch of ballplayers who are trying to win ball games. That's a great life."

Damn straight.

16

Veeck Goes Fishin' ?

And the loser now
will be later to win
—Bob Dylan, "The Times They Are A-Changin' "

Mike Veeck, like Richard Nixon, sometimes seemed to enjoy letting people think he was not quite from this planet. For example, he named his local cable television show about the Saints "Out of Left Field," an oblique reference to the fact that Chicago's mad were once housed outside the stadium where played the Cubbies, the team that the Veecks have always thought of as their lost Holy Grail.

The Saints' bottom line, however, showed that Mike was as sane as John D. Rockefeller. Rumor in the Saints' office had it that the four owners were splitting a profit of $2 million a year, and over the winter of 1998 Mike refused to put down his team's performance in the previous season.

As the leader of a self-proclaimed "merry band of misfits," he was psychologically prepared for losing. But in six years, the Saints had helped redeem him with three championships and several minor league attendance records, making his ballclub the envy of every other team in the Northern League.

Top dog wasn't a position he was used to, and it made him feel a little weird. At first, he spoke like a typical baseball owner, spouting sports clichés. "I learned [in the 1997 season] that winning is never overrated. You always want one more championship. But this was a good year because it was a tough year. The field was torn up during two concerts, but no one complained. We lost four games to rain, the most ever, but no fans complained. I can't be unhappy when we sell out every time we open the gates."

Mike paused. Baseball had always been about much more than dollars with him, or he would have accepted the executive position he'd been offered by the Florida Marlins shortly before their 1996 championship year. That offer took the "blackballed" label off him in the big leagues, but he wanted to come back on his own terms, and it had nothing to do with salary. Above all else, he wanted to run a team in the Show so he could show baseball what it needed to do to drag the game into the twenty-first century.

It was a topic he was becoming a nationally known expert on. He talked about what baseball needed with Morley Safer on "60 Minutes" and showed up on a "Nightline" panel in 1997, playing the devil's advocate to a bunch of baseball fuddy-duddies who didn't understand the fact that the national pastime was in critical condition. He'd also appeared on "Late Night with Conan O'Brien"; instead of talking baseball, Mike launched into an Andy Kaufman-like absurdist parody of a talk show guest. The always composed O'Brien seemed temporarily flustered, but at the end of the interview, Mike then took out a Saints' standard ballplayer contract and Conan eagerly signed it.

After all, Mujibur Rahman, the owner of a tiny Broadway eatery, had become a regular on "Late Show with David Letterman" and then adopted by the Sioux City Explorers. In 1994, Mujibur even once threw a pitch in the middle of a Sioux City game, then, as planned, walked off the mound, shaking his arm with a faux injury.

So why not Conan? For several weeks, it looked like the talk show host might actually play a game in Midway Stadium; his advance scouts began investigating what would be necessary to nationally televise Conan's debut in pro baseball. (As with so many things in show business, the project died of enthusiasm—everyone wanted to do it, but no one figured out how.)

Despite the national acceptance, Mike was still uncomfortable in his rebel's heart with his newfound status and acceptance into polite society. Take the double message he sent when the Saints relinquished their championship to the heretofore lousy Duluth Dukes in 1997. "The rest of the league, I know, is ecstatic [that we lost]," he said. "The juggernaut has fallen. I was always uncomfortable with that label . . . like suddenly we got legit."

Not since his grandfather William ran the Chicago Cubs had a Veeck cared if organized baseball considered them members of the fraternity. Now Mike sounded in his confusion over his own success like his old man, who sold the Cleveland Indians in 1949, one year after they had won the World Series and set a major league attendance record of their own.

Mike was now silent. Something was cooking, though nothing as dramatic as his father officially burying the 1948 pennant under the Indians' 1949 outfield. "Here, look at this," Mike said in his office, changing the subject. "Isn't this cool?" He then handed over what appeared to be an early hardcover edition of *Veeck as in Wreck,* his father's fantastic first autobiography whose original dustcover showed a typical Bill Veeck pose: smoking a billowing cigarette and watching an unseen ball game with a wry smile.

Closer inspection, however, showed that somebody had computer-generated Mike's head onto his father's dust-jacket body, and the author of *Veeck as in Wreck* was listed on the cover as Mike. Inside was a thick blank book, which Saints fans had secretly passed around during the season, thanking Mike for his ballclub and for saving St. Paul. "Yeah, I like that," Mike said, quickly taking the book back and putting it in a drawer. He'd tied his dad.

Mike, who frequently invoked his beloved father's name and had made Bill Veeck's ghost part of Midway Stadium and the Saints experience, had at last equaled his dad—a bitch of a job when your father is truly larger than life. But something was still bugging Mike. Even though he was a bona-fide St. Paul civic hero, he quickly split soon after the season ended with his family to Charleston, South Carolina, where he'd continue to try and resuscitate the Charleston River Dogs.

As he had last winter, Mike entrusted the office and matters of dough to general manager Bill Fanning, who himself had tossed away a nine-to-five executive's life in order to chase his own cuckoo dream of running a professional baseball team across the country. Also given expanded duties were Tom Whaley, the Saints lawyer-of-a-thousand-faces who, in a matter of hours could go from looking like the team's courtroom litigator (which he was) to a bad ass carney hiding silently behind shades as he ripped tickets at the turnstyles (which he does.) Whaley's rock band Tarwater continued to tear up the Twin Cities, and he agreed to play lead guitar in my own punk rock band *Shiksa Goddess.*

But that's another story.

Meantime, back in the office that off-season, Bill Fanning expressed delight that personable team leader Dwight Smith had already signed with the Arizona Wranglers farm system. Before the 1998 season began, he also guessed, 1997 Saints Scott Bryant, Sean Delaney, David Kennedy, Jake Kenady, Andy Paul, and Jose Prado would catch on with a major league organization.

In South Carolina, Mike continued to stew. He'd remade himself in St. Paul, and now he wanted to remake himself again. He wanted—no, *needed*—to wrap his "Fun Is Good" philosophy around a major league team. Already, some Show leaders were beginning to see the light he'd shone when just about everybody in baseball thought he was daft. In Arizona, the Diamondbacks' general managing partner, Jerry Colangelo, pointed out to *Sports Illustrated* that he'd put a swimming pool behind the team's outfield fence.

"I got the swimming pool idea from Bill Veeck," Colangelo was quoted as saying by none other than Pat Jordan. "[Veeck] had a shower in Comiskey Park for guys who drank too much beer," Colangelo continued. "I was thinking of having the *Sports Illustrated* swimsuit models there for our first game and handing out binoculars to the fans. But I'm not going to do it."

That was smart. Mike could have told Colangelo from his own experience at Midway Stadium that ballpark pools were for the people, men and women, no matter how unsightly their humongous Midwestern butts might look in Speedo bathing suits.

And so, aching for the bigs as much as his Saints players, Mike moved quickly. Flying back to St. Paul in the winter of 1998, he announced without warning that he'd decided to sell his quarter share of sweat equity of the St. Paul Saints. He was also buying for a pittance the Sioux Falls Canaries, for years the worst team in the entire Northern League—and in the process of the sales clear a little cash. Again, there were echoes of his father; after selling his championship team, Bill Veeck next bought the St. Louis Browns, one of the worst ballclubs ever.

Wrote purple-prosed Grantland Rice:

> *Hunters have tackled the elephant*
> *never a job for clowns*
> *The world is full of daring deeds*
> *but Veeck has purchased the Browns.*

Bill Veeck had taught Mike to never be afraid of daring deeds. The son agreed, even when they'd landed him in jail or blackballed him from baseball. So the St. Paul Saints were put up for sale for

$10 million; Mike had been broke when he came to St. Paul in 1993 and he hoped that his quarter-share of a sale would at least give him the ante for putting together a partnership the next time a major league baseball team became available. The price tag seemed fair, now that the minor leagues had become big business. Even crappy teams were selling for millions, and the Saints had become one of the best-known bush league clubs in existence.

Back on Opening Day in 1996, Mike had boasted that his father had died happy and broke, having lived life right down to the nubbin of his peg leg. Now, if the Saints sold, Mike would have a grubstake for the first time in his life.

But could Mike just leave the Saints, *St. Paul*'s Saints, his own baby? How could he abandon his windowless cubicle in the basement of Midway Stadium and take away the Folgers can that held his father's ashes?

"No!" shrieked St. Paul collectively at the news of Veeck's planned departure. The city itself went into shock when the news appeared on the front page of the *Saint Paul Pioneer Press* like a cop murder or deadly fire. Columnist Doug Grow, one of the few writers for the Minneapolis *Star Tribune* who understood the Saints' magic, waxed alarm over Mike's imminent departure. "What if the Saints lose their fizz?" Grow asked. Noting that Sister Roz had been hired in the off-season to ply her massages for the Minneapolis-based NBA Timberwolves, Grow got the sister, who understands neither the rules of baseball nor basketball, to speak about why she preferred the game Mike had brought to St. Paul. "There's a totally different spirit [at Saints games]," she said. "I can't put my finger on what it is yet— maybe it has something to do with the freedom."

Meantime, Minneapolis *Star Tribune* reporter Curt Brown found a despondent-sounding St. Paul mayor Norm Coleman. "Mike Veeck showed us that baseball—and St. Paul—can indeed be fun." The news was so alarming that even St. Paul-based Minnesota Public Radio, the home of Garrison Keillor, Bach, and hourlong reports from Senegal, interviewed Mike on the air about the civic tragedy.

Minneapolis columnist Patrick Reusse wrote nothing.

So, reporters asked why, all of a sudden, Mike was selling his portion of the Saints. Because with a little cash, he told them, and considering major league baseball's pathetic, somnolent current state, he might be let back into the bigs and implement his ideas. With 1998 major league tickets costing an average of $13.60, fans were no longer guaranteed much more than a place to take an expensive nap; Mike would make sure they stayed awake to watch the entire ball game.

On Minnesota Public Radio, Mike expounded further. "You have to have more fun [at the ballpark]. The Twins' approach the last few years has been more staid. Make things fun. I think that people have decided if they are going to pay major league prices, they would like to have major league entertainment. I'm betting that it still holds true about giving people bread and circuses, like they found out some time ago in Rome.

"On a localized level," he continued, "you need to bring laughter back into the [big league] ballparks. When I was growing up, ballparks were joyous places of dreams and hopes. They've simply gotten a little too corporate, and the business of baseball has gotten a little grim and gray. I think a few gags along the way, no matter what the purists say, wouldn't hurt."

Mike even crossed over to Minneapolis to explain his impending self-imposed exile from the Twin Cities on WCCO-AM, the 50,000-watt radio station that broadcast every Minnesota Twins game and billed itself as "the Good Neighbor to the Northwest."

Host Tim Russell expressed sadness that Mike was leaving and wondered what he thought he'd ultimately done for St. Paul and its fans. "I hope my legacy will be joy," he said. "It's not the end of anything. The team still has wonderful people like Bill Fanning, Tom Whaley, and its fans [running the Saints]."

And did Mike actually think he could own a big league ballclub? "I couldn't be more serious," he said. And would he be joined by his Saints partners? Yes, he said, Bill Murray, Van Schley, and Marv Goldklang would in all likelihood also walk away from the Saints. "Probably at some point we'll all go together," he continued. "That's how we work; I don't know if it's [going to be] when I leave. My guess is that you leave the dance with them that brung ya. We'll probably all go out marching arm in arm."

Like his father's tiny cash stake in his own teams, Mike thought his little on-paper nest egg from selling the Saints might convince other Show owners that he wasn't some foolhardy beatnik and pauper out to mock baseball. "I don't have the coin [to buy a team]," Mike said, but he hoped his reception by other big league owners, "would be a little warmer if I could show the wherewithal to at least make a contribution [to the purchase], no matter how paltry."

But why, Mike. Why? Say it ain't so! "I want to still try and realize another dream I have," he said, sounding just like so many other Saints—players and management—over the years.

The somnambulent Minnesota Twins were Mike's first major league target, the same Twins who were putting people to sleep across the river in ever-dwindling numbers inside the Metrodome, universally declaimed as the worst ballpark in the bigs, complete with a huge indoor Hefty bag representing the right field fence. Local octogenarian Carl Pohlad, the Twins' owner, was threatening to sell the team to out-of-town interests if the billionaire banker didn't get a new stadium with a retractable roof. At the same time, Pohlad didn't want to move the Twins and go down in history as Minnesota's Walter O'Malley.

Mike's main partners in saving the Twins for the state would be Clark Griffith, the son and grandson of the former owners of the Washington Senators and the Minnesota Twins; Bill Murray; and a rich cousin. For a reported $86 million, the group would take control of the team with Mike in charge.

But cranky Pohlad didn't like Clark, so Griffith was out. Next, Mike offered $40 million from his group for 40 percent of the Twins, again with himself running the team. Nope, said Pohlad, who seemed like a mannequin next to Mike's exuberance. For a year, Mike had tried to little avail to make peace with the Twins, who'd long derided and/or ignored his team and league. He'd even allowed the Twins to preempt the Saints and throw a day in honor of Larry Doby's fiftieth anniversary as the first black man to play in the American League—never mind that Mike's dad was the guy who brought Doby into the majors, that Doby had stayed close with the Veeck family for years, and that Midway Stadium was the logical place for such a celebration.

But Mike made nice that day and stood smiling, tieless, on the field of the clinically depressed Metrodome as Doby was introduced. Boy, what he could do with a run-down team like the Twins, the Sioux Falls Canaries of the American League.

He's birthed a major success with St. Paul. Maybe, like his father, he just needed to wander away from his winnings and start over at the bottom. Mike pooh-poohed such armchair Freudianism and looked at me as if I'd gotten my degree from a coupon inside a matchbook. "Sioux Falls is a way to stay in independent ball," he said. But then he paused. "I love the Northern League. In a lot of

ways, I *need* the Northern League. Here's where I proved to organized baseball that I wasn't Bill Veeck's crazy son."

He was no different from Darryl Strawberry, Dave Stevens, or
the hundreds of mostly anonymous ballplayers who'd come to
Midway Stadium for one last or only chance over the past four
years. He was no different in his dream than Don Wardlow, the
blind announcer; Ila Borders, the female relief pitcher; or the
fatherless Dave Wright, the Tigers' play-by-play man who he'd
listened to as a boy, under the covers after lights out at the military boarding school where he'd been sent. And then there were
Tom Whaley and Bill Fanning, who'd thrown away their own
lucrative law and banking practices to have a go at running a
baseball carnival.

Mike, meantime, calmed St. Paul's populace immediately after he
announced that he wanted to sell the Saints. Fanning and Whaley
would now run the Saints, he detailed, and the sumo wrestling and
ball pig would continue. Quietly, he put his house in St. Paul on
the market.

Unfortunately, Mike couldn't find a buyer for the Saints—or at
least the *right* buyer. What he wanted most of all was for manager
Marty Scott to raise the $10 million from investors, move from the
dugout to the front office, and run the team as its chief executive
with a chunk of sweat equity. For a while, Marty thought he had
money to invest from Nolan Ryan, who he'd known since his days
with the Rangers, but Ryan ultimately decided to buy a minor league
closer to his home in Texas.

While Marty tried to raise the dough, Mike moved during the
summer of 1998 to Sioux Falls. It felt freaky, he admitted, to own
two teams in the same league, but hey, this was the Northern League.
"It's a weird space to be in," he said, "too weird for me to really
be around."

Vowing not to show up at games between the two teams, Mike
did, however, appear at the Saints' home opener against Sioux Falls.
"As long as I own both teams, I won't know who I should cheer
for," he said. "I'll pull against the Saints when I don't own part of
them anymore, but right now it'd be like yelling at myself."

Fanning seemed unconcerned about the changing of the guard
and said that Veeck might be increasingly invisible at Midway Stadium, but his presence would be felt. "He's still the guy we call and
ask questions to and get some ideas from, but we do less of that

than we have in the past," the general manager said. "Mike is the final sounding board on things we want to do if there's a sticking point. We give him a ring, but normally we just try and muddle through it. We hope we've proven that we know a little bit about what we're doing."

True. But Mike's leaving the Saints had left me feeling as abandoned as I was that night that star reliever Paul "Roma" Romanoli had left me alone in a Winnipeg country and western bar with four Amazonian women with the big hair of old-time astronauts' wives and the accents of Bob and Doug McKenzie (of SCTV fame). "Do you write Roma's pickup lines, eh?" asked one of the friends of the relievers' conquest. "Cuz if you do, they stink, eh?"

But Roma was long gone. Now, with Mike on his way out too, it was another kind of end. I didn't know then if Mike's brand of cheap, gentle, surreal theatrics, which amused the St. Paul Saints' fans for years, would survive. As Mike disappeared into Sioux Falls for the summer of 1998, I looked again at Grantland Rice, and his famous 1948 sports page poem penned in the moments after Babe Ruth's death. It wasn't quite Dylan Thomas, but it indicates St. Paul's feelings after Mike's sudden disappearance.

> Game called by darkness—let the curtain fall,
> No more remembered thunder sweeps the field.
> No more the ancient echoes hear the call.
> To one who wore so well both sword and shield,
> The Big Guy's left us with the night to face,
> And there is no one who can take his place.
> —Grantland Rice, "Game Called"

Bullshit. When the 1998 season began, I knew I could take off my mourning veil. The Saints were still the Saints, and I couldn't stop laughing at the show that most definitely was not the Show.

On the one night when Mike went to see his Sioux Falls team play against his St. Paul team, he admitted he might retry some of his old tricks in South Dakota. Like Gatsby's green light, he was incessantly drawn to one stunt that had failed miserably in St. Paul. "Despite how badly it was received, I'm tempted to try the mime instant replay again," he said, recalling the white-faced actors he'd once hired from the Minneapolis College of Art and Design who were pelted with hot dog buns as they reenacted in foul territory the outcome of the previous play the way Marcel Marceau might have seen it. Mike, who like his father was really from nowhere and always kept a suitcase packed, remained perplexed by the promotions' failure. "I *still* just don't understand," he said, "what Midwesterners have got against mimes."

I wasn't sure either. All I knew was that a baseball team—a bush league baseball team, for God's sakes!—had once again me whole enough to remember how to appreciate the smell of a freshly mowed infield, a finely executed double play, and—hello, Hallmark Cards—love.

Only a couple of seasons after wanting to kill myself, I felt as young as, well, Twig. It was no grand discovery: as Roger Angell, the best baseball writer ever, put it:

> Since baseball time is measured only in outs, all you have to do is succeed utterly; keep hitting, keep the rally alive, and you have defeated time. You remain forever young.

Right on, Roger. Jann Wenner was a million miles away, while on a glorious July night I was in Midway Stadium on "Fargo Night," when the 1998 St. Paul team ran out in garish orange uniforms to mock the supposed bad taste of the city represented by their most-hated opponents, the league-leading Fargo-Moorhead RedHawks. That evening stadium announcer Mike Webster spoke only in the "Yah sure, ya sonuvagun" voice of Marge Gunderson from the film *Fargo* whenever the RedHawks came to bat. Putative Fargoisms, such as "hot dish," "yer darn tootin'," and "you betcha," ran continuously on the scoreboard, while hideous polka music blared at odd intervals to remind the 180th sellout in a row that the Saints were playing Mayberry, and St. Paul, for the night, was really Paris.

The Saints lost that game 5–2, and as the victorious Fargo team left the field, Midway Stadium became hip again with the PA insulting the winners with Tom Petty singing how sometimes the lucky are really losers. Heading back to his dugout, Marty Scott looked as if he needed a case of Rolaids.

Meantime, that same night in Duluth, Ila Borders became the first woman to ever win a professional men's baseball game, pitching six shutout innings and scattering three hits against the Sioux Falls Canaries, a club owned by the only man in baseball willing to give her a chance.

It turned out to be
One of the most beautiful days
I had no idea.
—Phil Rizzuto, "Dream Day"
  (May 26, 1992, New York Yankees
  against the Minnesota Twins)

Epilogue

Mike Veeck—After announcing that the Saints were for sale, Veeck was rebuffed by Minnesota Twins owner Carl Pohlad in his attempt to buy the major league team. In September 1998, however, almost two decades after he'd been banished from the majors, Veeck finally made it back to the Show. Named Senior Vice President for Marketing and Promotion by the Tampa Bay Devil Rays, Veeck and his investors were also allowed to buy a piece of the team that has been estimated as high as twenty percent. Putting his St. Paul house on the market, Veeck slipped silently out of town like the Lone Ranger or Bill Veeck, his mission accomplished in one more city. Saints General Manager Bill Fanning moved into Mike's office, and with Operations Director Tom Whaley ran the team.

Darryl Strawberry's progress with the New York Yankees was watched in St. Paul with the kind of interest reserved for home-grown ballplayers. His 1997 season was horrible; he injured his foot early in the season and found action in only eleven games. "The Yankees are merely asking Strawberry [to stay] healthy enough to give them at-bats and a left-handed threat when needed," wrote Claire Smith in *The New York Times*. Back in shape for 1998, Straw led the Yankees in home runs for much of the season, and ended with 24 jacks in only 296 at-bats. Not once since he'd left the St. Paul Saints had he been accused of any felonies or a failed drug test, and he still went to dinner with Saints manager Marty Scott every time the Yankees passed through the Twin Cities to play the Twins. In New York, Strawberry emerged as the kind of quiet, respected team leader he'd been in St. Paul.

Then, on October 1, 1998, Strawberry was diagnosed with colon cancer in the middle of the Yankees' American League Division Series against Texas. While Strawberry prepared for surgery, his stunned teammates wore his number "39" stitched on to the back of their caps. He left the hospital the day before the Yankees began the World Series against San Diego, where his teammates, manager Joe Torre and owner George Steinbrenner vowed to win it all for Straw and did with a sweep. All of them expressed their love for Straw and gratitude for his inspiration in their post-game interviews.

Bill Murray continued to be lauded as perhaps the finest comic genius of his generation. Although *The Man Who Knew Too Much*, the movie he had to rush off to star in after watching the Saints beat Fargo in a 1996 championship game, received tepid reviews, critics singled him out for praise. "Murray carries the film," *The New Yorker* wrote, "instinctively goosing the flat dialogue into comic shape." In 1999, he was the smash of the New York Film Festival for his role in *Rushmore* and was considered an even bet for a Best Supporting Actor Academy Award.

Younger actors, directors, and comics continued to revere him. In the summer of 1998, Ben Stiller, the *auteur* of Generation X, was put on the cover of *Icon*, a glossy new magazine aimed at post-baby boomers. In the article, Stiller was asked if he felt like an icon. "No," he said. "Bill Murray is an icon. He represents a certain type of comedy. I'd love to be worshipped around the world, but I don't think I've earned that."

Murray is still listed in the 1998 Saints yearbook as team "czar" and remains committed to starring in *Veeck as in Wreck*. Production has been delayed by typical Hollywood script rewrites and difficulties coordinating his and costar Sigourney Weaver's schedules. Mike never asks Murray about the movie.

Marty Scott is still trying to round up the money to buy and run the Saints from the front office. "I love Twig," the manager says, "but I don't want to be in uniform and out in the field for fifty years." Meantime, the 1998 Saints were once again driving him to distraction, as Thunder Bay won the first-half championship. "You know how some teams play just good enough to win?" he asked. "Well, we play just good enough to lose."

The 1998 Saints won a club-record nine games in a row and were in contention for the first-half championship until they blew the last series at home against Madison and the Thunder Bay Whiskey Jacks snuck in as the winners. It was the first time since 1994 that the Saints hadn't won the first-half crown of the Eastern Division. They did win the second half to qualify for postseason play, but were smoked by loathsome Fargo in the championship after beating Thunder Bay in the divisional finals.

Ila Borders was converted into a starting pitcher by the Duluth-Superior Dukes on July 9, 1998. On July 24, 1994, she became the first woman to ever win a game in a men's professional baseball game, pitching six shutout innings and scattering three hits as the Dukes beat Mike Veeck's Sioux Falls Canaries 3–1. Before her next start against Fargo–Moorhead, RedHawk manager Doug Simunic threatened to forfeit the game rather than have his team face a woman pitcher. He was bluffing, and Ila stuck his face in it by pitching another six shutout innings. (She didn't, however, get the victory this time.) By the end of the season, though, she'd been profiled on "60 Minutes" and in The *New York Times*.

J. D. Drew lost his bid to sign with whomever he wanted and returned to the Saints in 1998 until his agent, Scott Boras, could come up with a holdout plan B. Playing thirty more games for the Saints, he hit .386, with 9 homers and 33 RBIs. Chosen by St. Louis in the first round of the 1998 draft, Drew finally signed with the Cardinals for a guaranteed $7 million over four years, with options that could bring him another $1.5 million. The most the Phillies had offered him was $3.1 million. Drew immediately left the Saints, who were paid the standard $3,000 for having one of their players signed to a major league organization. "If I had to [hold out] again, I'd play for the Saints," Drew said. "I've had so much fun there while I waited."

Kevin Garner didn't retire as promised at the end of 1996 and spent 1997 with the Sioux City Explorers. In 1998, the 32-year-old former phenom who never made the Show signed with the Thunder Bay Whiskey Jacks, then was traded to Sioux Falls. He still called his faux autobiography *In Pursuit of a Nightmare*.

Marty Neff signed in 1997 with the Bend, Oregon, team in the Western League, one of the new independent leagues that had sprouted with the success of the Northern League. He batted .241, with 6 home runs. In 1998, Ed Nottle invited him back to play with Sioux City, where he once again flourished. By midseason he was batting .350, with 9 homers, was third in the league in RBIs, and made the Northern League All-Star team. Once again, Neff was living in the team clubhouse and sleeping on the trainer's table.

Paul "Roma" Romanoli, left the Saints after 1996 in order to play pro ball in Europe.

Steve Solomon became a stockbroker in Los Angeles.

Daryl Henderson and **Kenishi Kato,** disappeared into Chicago and Japan.

Glenn Davis retired from baseball and returned to his farm in Georgia.

Singin' Ed Nottle deeply regrets calling Ila Borders "that *thing*" and has come to admire her grit, if not her fastball. He is still the king of Sioux City and can he heard singing at supper clubs around the Northern League. His wife finally made him throw out the 20,000 unsold copies of the record he pressed while he was with the Oakland A's, which were taking up too much space in their garage. Though the album cost Ed his house, he has a new one.

Monica Toppen never got the memorial built to Otis Redding in Madison, and disappeared from the Northern League radar. She did, however, find her Christy Mathewson, a promising professional starting pitcher on the East Coast who prefers to remain anonymous. Though Monica doesn't want her exact whereabouts known, she still plans to someday own her own minor league baseball team.

Hillory and **Dakota Sadie** retired after the RedHawks inaugural 1996 season and disappeared back into Fargo. Two new "Scoreboard Girls" are now chosen every year, but it's just not the same.

Dave Wright resigned his position as public relations director of the Saints, a job he'd held since the team's inception in 1993. Hired for the same position with the United Way of St. Paul, Dave still smarted from getting kicked out of the broadcast booth by a blind radio announcer in 1997. He is still in touch with Mike Veeck, however, and might move to South Dakota next year to broadcast Canaries games. Meantime, he continues to listen to old Ernie Harwell tapes while driving his properly rickety "Northern League car." After the 1998 season, he got married to Lynne Larkin. Finally Dave had found a woman who didn't mind that he could recall the exact batting order of the 1968 Detroit Tigers, but couldn't remember what he'd eaten for breakfast that day.

Don Wardlow and **Jim Lucas,** the blind-and-seeing Saints radio team, was rehired for 1998 and have been offered positions with the team in 1999.

Roger Maris—The single season home run record of sixty-one in 1961 held by Fargo's favorite son was broken by St. Louis Cardinal Mark McGwire (who finished with seventy) and Chicago Cub Sammy Sosa (who finished with sixty-six) in 1998. Their race not only reinvigorated the dwindling fan interest in major league baseball, but also refocused attention and a reappraisal of the late slugger who'd suffered so much a generation before while beating Babe Ruth's record.

ESPN ran an hour-long documentary on Maris as a reluctant, quiet North Dakota hero who'd deserved better, and who finally might be elected to the Hall of Fame by the sportswriters he battled for so long. Unlike Roger, McGwire and Sosa were cheered each home run along the way by fans and reporters in each city they played. McGwire especially went out of his way to honor Maris's memory in words and deed as he chased the record. Roger's survivors began attending Cardinals games as he neared the holy mark, and when McGwire hit number sixty-two, the first thing he did after touching home plate was climb into the Cardinal's box seats to hug each member of the Maris family. In death, Maris had finally gained the public and media respect that had eluded him for much of his career. Rest in peace, Roger.

Rupert Murdoch did buy the Los Angeles Dodgers from the heirs of the evil Walter O'Malley, confirming rumors that he'd really launched the FX cable channel to eventually use as a national stage to televise his team, like the Cubs and White Sox on superstation WGN or the Braves on WTBS. "Baseball Minnesota," the exhaustive documentary on the Saints' 1996 season, served as Murdoch's electronic beard, escorting his channel with product until the boss purchased the Dodgers.

Jill Muellner is still sober and the night bar manager at Gabe's. Her nose job, broadcast by FX, turned out well, and she is still considered one of the most beautiful women in St. Paul.

Jody Beaulieu was promoted from running the on-field "dizzy bat spin" and sumo contests to director of community relations. Though she is still teased mercilessly by the Saints' staff about Pat Jordan's crush on her, her boyfriend, who is in medical school, could break him in half.

Annie Huidekoper remains a part owner of the Butte Copper Kings and now works in a Chinese medicine clinic, where she plans promotions for hire.

Eleanor Mondale remains a CBS News correspondent and Minnesota's crown princess. Her name appeared in Kenneth Starr's report on Bill Clinton's affair with Monica Lewinsky. Ms. Lewinsky, it seemed, had thrown a shit fit when stopped at the White House gates because Eleanor was interviewing the President, whom she'd known since her father was the Democratic nominee for the office in 1984.

Little **Hamlet** proved just as stylish a ball pig in Midway Stadium as the still-mourned Tobias. **Dennis Hauth,** maestro of the porcine delivery system, has begun nurturing a future Saints mascot named Hambino in case anything should happen to Hamlet.

The Minneapolis *Star Tribune* sports section continued to ignore the St. Paul Saints in favor of the Minnesota Twins, who by 1998 resembled a pretty good AAA team. While the rest of the paper had by now caught on, the sports section, led by the still-bullying Patrick Reusse, refused to include any Saints in its "Minnesotans in the Minors" column.

Jann Wenner still owes me $114.54.

Kevin Millar became the next ex-Saint to make the majors in 1998. Signed by the Florida Marlins' organization after his 1993 year with the Saints, Millar finally joined the major league club in 1998. In his second game in the Show, appearing on an ESPN nationally televised Sunday night game, Millar broke his wrist while swinging at a pitch and was not expected to return for the season. Figures.

Wayne "Twig" Terwilliger, seventy-three, suited up as first base coach for the 1998 St. Paul Saints. He'd made it to his fiftieth season in a professional baseball uniform, a feat shared by only three other men in baseball history. On August 6, the Saints threw "Twig Night" before a ball game. Arne Carlson, the governor of Minnesota, came on the field and read from a piece of papyrus that today was "Twig Day." St. Paul mayor Norm Coleman then read a proclamation crediting Twig with everything short of inventing the polio vaccine—but mostly it just thanked Twig for helping St. Paul get its pride back.

Even the Minnesota Twins, who'd canned Twig in 1992 because they felt he was simply too old, came across the river to bear homage. On the field, Twin general manager Terry Ryan looked as uncomfortable as an atheist in church. His tight black jacket and neck-cinched tie didn't help any. PA announcer Eric Webster told the crowd that Ryan would have to take off his tie, which he did, though he looked

Mike Veeck, Bill Fanning and Twig, holding his 50th-year uniform in front of the Midway Stadium mural. The uniform is to be sent to the Hall of Fame.
Courtesy of Neal Karlen

just as uncomfortable, remaining the only man on the field to wear a jacket.

Then a Marine in full dress gave a speech about the war heroics of Twig that concluded with an incomprehensible number of sentences ending with the words *"semper fidelis"* ("always faithful").

Twig finally took the microphone, and before another sellout of 6,329 at Midway Stadium, looked around. He began by thanking Mike Veeck for giving him a last chance and the Saints for letting him still hit a 100 fungoes a day. "I'm sorry if I've ever been a pain in the ass to you guys [at practice], because you're great guys," Twig said to the players, who were already on their feet, applauding.

"Fifty years ago I batted .196 for the Des Moines Bruins and led them to the Western League pennant. And I hardly thought that in fifty years I'd still be standing here in uniform. But here I am.

"Is this a great game or what?"

Acknowledgments and Author's Note

This is a work of non-fiction based on three years of interviews. All names are real except for the groupies, and I have changed identifying details about the bar in Winnipeg. The only composite is My Evil Twin, a minor character who is an amalgamation of two people amongst the crowd of New York filmmakers who made visits to St. Paul's Midway Stadium that summer.

First, as ever and always, I want to thank Suzanne Gluck, Uber Agent at International Creative Management in New York. Equal parts friend, protector, *mentsch*, and fairy godmother, Suzanne is responsible for birthing each of my books, especially this one. Without her, there is no way I could live out here in Flyoverland chasing circuses; she has also done me the great favor of always telling me the truth about my dopier ideas for potential books or wives. I owe you so much, Suzanne, that I'll be sending you good karma well into our next reincarnations.

Stephen S. Power, Avon Books Senior Editor, edited the sentences and ideas of this book with the time, care, and smarts supposedly gone from 1990s publishing; if there were any justice, he would be on the cover as co-author, and not just because he literally saved this book when I'd given up by making its case before Lou Aronica, Avon Books Publisher. Thanks Lou, for giving me a Bill and Mike Veeck–like second-shot, and many kudos to Avon editor Bret Witter for taking on all the pains and pressures of closing out the paperback, like Rollie Fingers called in for the 9th inning of the World Series. And much thanks to the Avon copy desk for putting up wth my last second changes.

Karen Gerwin, Suzanne Gluck's assistant at ICM, pep-talked me to the end of this book. Karen's predecessor, Marsinay Smith, ordered me back to the ballpark. Yedida L. Soloff, and later Krista Stroever, Stephen S. Power's assistants, got me through the end-game. Robin Davis-Gomez in Avon's Managing Editorial Department; Mark Hurst, the copyeditor; and Debra Weaver in Avon's legal department, also did superb jobs. Avon's Marie Elena Martinez passionately published this book as if it were *War and Peace*. Thank you all for putting up with my occasional bouts of authorial hysteria.

ICM lawyer Susan Kaufman calmly chased away some sharks so I could work on this labor of love. Without Susan, I'd be working the drive-thru window at Arby's.

Author Peggy Orenstein provided a great sounding board as a baseball fan, famous feminist, normal person, and Grade A friend since junior high school. It's an honor to know such a professional smarty-pants.

Saints co-owners Mike Veeck and Van Schley let me into their heads; Marv Goldklang, who more than anyone got Darryl Strawberry back to the Show, let me spy on him. Manager Marty Scott let me onto the Saints bus. Twig is God. General Manager Bill Fanning humiliated me always, while his wife Donna treated me with unstinting kindness. See Bill, that wasn't a vanity interview. Tom Whaley, the team's Operations Manager, lawyer, and Tarwater's guitarist, revealed how to be a master of disguise. Press relations gurus Dave Wright and Eric Webster did me uncountable pain-in-the-ass favors. Thanks.

So many others past and present in the Saints office deserve kudos that I'm lamely listing you alphabetically rather than detail how you helped. So, l'chaim, Liz Adams, Jody Beaulieu, Dan Craighead, Pat Cunningham, Bill Fisher, Gizmo, Mike Haiduck, Greg Harrington, Dennis Hauth, Amy Hermsdorf, Annie Huidekoper, Kelly Komppa, Jason Lonstein, Jim Lucas, Steve and John Marso, Pete Orme, Bob St. Pierre, Brent Proulx, Connie Rudolph, Rod Teichrow, Tom Tisdale, Don Wardlow, and Sarah Webster.

Out in the parking lot, Vince Jeannette, his girlfriend Rosie, and the rest of their merry band were always willing to feed me or break into my car when I'd locked my keys inside for the umpteenth time. And then there was Gabe's owner Giggles. Sister Rosalind Gefre proved that a 74-year-old nun with the grip of the Crusher could give both an unbelievable massage— and an insight into a Higher Truth. Thanks for sharing it all. Inside the ballpark, Bill Tyler, aka "The Webster" and online publisher of the Northern League Fan's Guide, gave me free his smarts and league map. Terri Klein was a queen. Jenni Soderbeck and Jenny Kotval were princesses. And Crystal Roth, if you ever date a ballplayer, I'm telling your dad, Bob, when he gets out of the beer line.

Bonnie Butler took photographs of it all on the cheap, and let me use her as "bait" to elicit naughty talk from the ballplayers. Thanks a lot—and beware of Boo Boo.

I was treated with great kindness and help in every city in the Northern League. I would especially like to thank Dave McMillan, Jim Wadley and Elizabeth Marsh in Duluth; Bruce Thom, Josh Buchholz, Kyle Richardson, Julie Opgrande, and Dave Wallis of the Fargo Forum in Fargo; Bill Terlecky, Ryan Richeal, and Jennifer Watkins in Madison; Ed Nottle and Todd Jamison in Sioux City; Shelly Poitras in Thunder Bay; Ripper and Amy Hatch in Sioux Falls; and Sam Katz and Jonathan Green in Winnipeg.

I also owe my gratitude to several fine reporters and writers whose brains

I picked and/or whose work I used for research. They include the late, great Mike Augistin of the *St. Paul Pioneer Press*, Tom Dyja, Jack El-Hai of *Minnesota Monthly*, Dana Kiecker and Anthony LaPanta of *Media One*; Tom Keegan of the *New York Post*, John Millea, Doug Grow, Sid Hartman, and Dan Barreiro of the *Minneapolis Star Tribune*, *GQ*'s Peter Richmond, and Mel Antonen and Walter Shapiro of *U.S.A. Today*. David Jackson, most recently of the *Minneapolis Star Tribune* also proved a valuable, professional resource and has a great future as a reporter. David Gates unknowingly convinced me this was the book to write over a cup of coffee, and Jonathan Alter provided expert social commentary on Disco Demolition Night from someone who was actually in Chicago that 1979 summer. Brian Tunkel was never less than illuminating. So was Bob Plapinger of Plapinger's Baseball Books. And Bob Klapisch wrote an excellent book on Darryl Strawberry's rise and fall in *High and Tight;* he also co-authored with John Harper *Champions*, the chronicle of the 1996 Yankees. Steve Perlstein's *Rebel Baseball* and Stefan Fatsis's *Wild and Outside* are excellent accounts of the Northern League's history and spirit. Gerald Eskenazi's *Bill Veeck: A Baseball Legend* was an invaluable resource and a damn good read. John Helyar's *Lords of the Realm* told baseball as it is. WCCO-TV's late Dave Moore always knew wat up wit' dat, as does his wife, Shirley! Dave, come back.

I also received important help from Scot Mondore, Senior Researcher at the Hall of Fame in Cooperstown. Back home, Kari Anderson and Mary Laing were ace researchers and tape transcribers, while Max Levine always saved me from computer hell. Many FX people were a joy and utmost professionals: thanks Ellen Cooper, Tony George, Isabella Ironside, Dina Ligorski and the entire Minnesota crew, especially Tom Forlitti, Brad Jacobsen, Eric Johannes, Nate Payton, Kristina Schatz, and Catherine Whyte.

Essay king Phillip Lopate gave me the *batzim* to put myself in, while editors who kept me solvent with assignments include Beth Arky, Jan Benzel, Tim Campbell, Susan Chumsky, Lucy Danziger, Stephen Dubner, Robert Friedman (with an assist from David Hirshey), Trip Gabriel, Melody Gilbert, Barbara Graustark, John Habich, Alex Heard, Susie Hopper, Jon Klein, Ruth Koscielak, Linda Lee, David Mahoney, Kate Meyers, Adam Moss, Tim Moss, Jill Rachlin, Susan Reed, Fletcher Roberts, Nancy Roberts, Constance Rosenblum, Graydon Royce, Amy Spindler, Laura Swift, Al Tims, Nancy Walker, Doreen Weisenhaus, and Dana White. And Chuck Rikess always provided Pynchon-like inspiration.

Abbie Kane, still the queen of Minneapolis rock and roll, let me live on her ground floor when I shattered my leg and needed a place to finish this book without climbing stairs. Dr. Kathleen S. Peter is a swell surgeon, physical therapist Karen Johanson made sure I wouldn't walk like Ratso in "Midnight Cowboy," and Olivia Walling brought me uncountable dinners when I was typing flat on my back. So did Anne Fredrickson—as Ralph Kramden would have said it, baby, you're the greatest. And Jeanne Hoene,

ACKNOWLEDGMENTS AND AUTHOR'S NOTE   355

as always, was right there, like a Rockne. And Julie Anderson explained it all to me.

To properly list the contributions of the following friends would take up another twenty. The best I can do is list them in alphabetical order: Richard Abowitz, Jody Abramson, Tim Appelo, Beth Arky, Rebecca Bachman, Jane Barrash, Dawn Bass, Bill Bates, Roberto Benabib, Susan Bender, Barbara Berger, Dan Bergner, Laura Billings, Hillery Borton, Carolyn and Dr. Stuart Bloom, David Brauer, Jessy Danel, Change Inc.'s Richard Mammen and Rev. Jim Nelson, Richard and Etta Saunders, Richard, Jr. and Charles Day, Deb and Will Durst, Jimmy Erickson, Elaine Gale, Neal Gillett, Ron Givens, Ann Distelhorst, Mona, Emily Goldberg, Tom Goldstein, publisher of *Elysian Fields Quarterly*, Traci Hirtenstein, Tricia Hummel, Katherine Lanpher, Carole Katz and Jonathan, Devra, and Noah Levy, Jim Leinfelder, Michael Macrone, Malka Margolies, Jenny McCarthy, Andrea Michaels, Michael Moore, Jody Nelson, Marcey and Norman Mastbaum, Dr. Kari Nelson, Nancy Northup, Steven Okazaki, Mike O'Neil, Geoff and Sharon Pollock, Janet Ray, Abe Schwartz, Karen Schneider, David Stagner, Kate Staples, Chuck, Soraya and Jake Strouse, Nancy Traver, Brian Tunkel, Laurel Ulland, and Jennifer Waters.

Bruce, Bonnie, Charlotte and Dr. Markle Karlen never gave me grief about missing every clan event so I could travel to Thunder Bay. And finally there are my two young god children. To Hannah Pollock I would warn only never to date ballplayers (we've already talked about musicians.) To Zeke Simon, I would repeat the batting advice and life lesson his late grandfather Stan Simon taught me:

Keep your eye on the ball and don't turn your head. You might miss something.

Index

NEAL KARLEN is a veteran freelance writer whose work now most often appears in the *New York Times*. He was also a staff scribe at *Newsweek* (which was cool) and a contributing editor at *Rolling Stone* (which, surprisingly, was not). The author of *Babes in Toyland: The Making and Selling of a Rock and Roll Band*, he is no stranger to traveling with his subjects for years on end in order to write about them. Mr. Karlen lives in his hometown of Minneapolis, Minnesota, but his spirit resides in St. Paul.